LIFE

OF

OLIVER P. MORTON

VOLUME I

AMS PRESS
NEW YORK

O. P. Morton

LIFE

OF

OLIVER P. MORTON

INCLUDING HIS IMPORTANT SPEECHES

BY

WILLIAM DUDLEY FOULKE

VOLUME I

INDIANAPOLIS—KANSAS CITY
THE BOWEN-MERRILL COMPANY
1899

Library of Congress Cataloging in Publication Data

Foulke, William Dudley, 1848–1935.
  Life of Oliver P. Morton, including his important speeches.

  1. Morton, Oliver Perry, 1823–1877. I. Morton, Oliver Perry, 1823–1877 II: Title.
  E506.M87 1974   328.73′092′4 [B]   77-168129
  ISBN 0-404-04592-8

Reprinted from an original copy in the collections
of the Wilbur L. Cross Library, University of Connecticut

From the edition of 1899, Indianapolis
First AMS edition published in 1974
Manufactured in the United States of America

International Standard Book Number:
Complete Set: 0-404-04592-8
Volume I: 0-404-04593-6

AMS PRESS INC.
NEW YORK, N.Y. 10003

" The people saw him as he lifted high
  His arm of iron.   In his warlike face
Was seen the fire of conflict, and his eye
Shone with a quenchless light, while from his place
He thundered forth his challenge ; and the race
That served the times, and doubted, and sat still,
While men were bleeding and the black disgrace
Still wrapt its coils about us, felt the thrill
And rose, and stood, and went to battle at his will."

JOHN CLARK RIDPATH.
Dedication Morton Monument.

TABLE OF CONTENTS[1]

VOLUME I

CHAPTER I

EARLY LIFE

CHAPTER II

MORTON AT THE BAR

[1] The contents of *speeches*, *letters*, *etc.*, in this table are printed in italics.

(v)

CHAPTER III

EARLY POLITICAL LIFE

CHAPTER IV

MORTON LEAVES THE DEMOCRATIC PARTY

CHAPTER V

MORTON AND WILLARD

CHAPTER VI

FROM 1856 TO 1860

CHAPTER VII

THE CAMPAIGN OF 1860

CHAPTER VIII

MORTON'S WAR SPEECH IN THE COURT-HOUSE

CHAPTER IX

MORTON BECOMES GOVERNOR

CHAPTER X

THE CALL TO ARMS

CHAPTER XI

KENTUCKY NEUTRALITY

CHAPTER XII

MILITARY APPOINTMENTS

CHAPTER XIII

THE SOLDIERS' FRIEND

CHAPTER XIV

ROCKVILLE SPEECH—WAR TAX—ARSENAL—MILITARY AS-
PIRATIONS

CHAPTER XV

THE KIRBY SMITH CAMPAIGN

CHAPTER XVI

KILLING OF NELSON—REMOVAL OF BUELL—THE DRAFT

CHAPTER XVII

THE POLITICAL CAMPAIGN OF 1862

CHAPTER XVIII

PEACE LEGISLATURE—MORTON'S MESSAGE—HENDRICKS AND TURPIE ELECTED SENATORS

CHAPTER XIX

ATTACKS ON MORTON'S FINANCIAL ADMINISTRATION— POLITICAL ARRESTS

CHAPTER XX

CRITICISMS OF THE WAR—SOLDIERS' RESOLUTIONS—THE MILITARY BILL

CHAPTER XXI

SPEAKS AT PIKE'S OPERA HOUSE AND AT CAMBRIDGE— VALLANDIGHAM CAMPAIGN

CHAPTER XXII

"I AM THE STATE"

CHAPTER XXIII

BATTLE OF POGUE'S RUN—MORGAN'S RAID

CHAPTER XXIV

FILLING QUOTAS—RECEPTIONS OF VETERANS—THE HUNDRED-DAY TROOPS—MORTON RE-NOMINATED—CAMPAIGN OF 1864

CHAPTER XXVI

OTHER DEBATES WITH M'DONALD—THE SOLDIERS' VOTE —ELECTIONS OF 1864

CHAPTER XXVII

KNIGHTS OF THE GOLDEN CIRCLE

CHAPTER XXVIII

ORDER OF AMERICAN KNIGHTS AND SONS OF LIBERTY

CHAPTER XXIX

THE NORTHWESTERN CONSPIRACY

CHAPTER XXX

THE TREASON TRIALS

CHAPTER XXXI

THE LEGISLATURE OF 1865—CLOSE OF THE WAR—DEATH
OF LINCOLN—SPEECH AT TIPPECANOE

CHAPTER XXXII

WELCOMING THE VETERANS HOME—MORTON ON RECON-
STRUCTION—HIS RICHMOND SPEECH

CHAPTER XXXIII

PARALYSIS—MESSAGE TO THE SPECIAL SESSION—JOURNEY
TO EUROPE

CHAPTER XXXIV

FIRST STEPS IN RECONSTRUCTION—MASONIC HALL SPEECH

CHAPTER XXXV

CAMPAIGN OF 1866—MORTON ELECTED SENATOR

TABLE OF CONTENTS

VOLUME II

CHAPTER I

FIRST DEBATES IN THE SENATE

CHAPTER II

MORTON'S GREAT SPEECH ON RECONSTRUCTION

CHAPTER III

INDIANA POLITICS—ADMISSION OF SOUTHERN STATES— SEYMOUR AND BLAIR CAMPAIGN

Greenback sentiment among Indiana Republicans—County convention January 12, 1868—State convention February 20—Greenback platform.. 45

CHAPTER IV

FINANCIAL VIEWS AND MEASURES—RESUMPTION

CHAPTER V

THE FIFTEENTH AMENDMENT

CHAPTER VI

TENURE-OF-OFFICE LAW—GETTYSBURG SPEECH— RECON-
STRUCTION OF MISSISSIPPI AND GEORGIA—
ENGLISH MISSION

CHAPTER VIII

DEPOSITION OF SUMNER FROM THE COMMITTEE ON FOREIGN RELATIONS—THE WASHINGTON TREATY—SAN DOMINGO AGAIN

CHAPTER IX

KU-KLUX INVESTIGATION

CHAPTER X

LECTURE UPON "THE NATIONAL IDEA"—PATRONAGE—CIVIL SERVICE REFORM—AMNESTY

CHAPTER XI

THE FRENCH ARMS DEBATE

CHAPTER XII

THE CAMPAIGN OF 1872—MORTON RE-ELECTED TO THE SENATE—SPEECH ON PRESIDENTIAL ELECTIONS

CHAPTER XIII

LOUISIANA ELECTIONS—PINCHBACK

CHAPTER XIV

CALDWELL BRIBERY CASE—"BACK PAY"—OHIO CAMPAIGN OF 1873

CHAPTER XV

PANIC OF 1873—CURRENCY BILL AND VETO——RESUMPTION

CHAPTER XVI

THE CHIEF-JUSTICESHIP—INTERSTATE COMMERCE—WOMAN SUFFRAGE—CAMPAIGN OF 1874

CHAPTER XVII

CONTROVERSY WITH HENDRICKS—OHIO CAMPAIGN OF 1875

CHAPTER XVIII

THE MISSISSIPPI ELECTION—TRIBUTE TO ANDREW JOHN-
SON—CONTROVERSY WITH SENATOR GORDON

CHAPTER XIX

THE CINCINNATI CONVENTION

CHAPTER XX

THE HAYES-TILDEN CAMPAIGN

CHAPTER XXI

CHINESE IMMIGRATION—DISPUTE OVER THE ELECTION

CHAPTER XXII

THE ELECTORAL BILL

CHAPTER XXIII

THE ELECTORAL COMMISSION—THE FLORIDA, LOUISIANA, OREGON AND SOUTH CAROLINA CASES

CHAPTER XXIV

KELLOGG CASE—HAYES' SOUTHERN POLICY

CHAPTER XXV

JOURNEY TO OREGON—FINAL ILLNESS—DEATH

CHAPTER XXVI

MORTON'S CHARACTERISTICS

VOLUME I

MORTON THE GOVERNOR

CHAPTER I

EARLY LIFE

On the eastern edge of Indiana, a little south of the middle of the state, lies the county of Wayne, rich, fertile and well peopled. The landscape is of more than common agricultural beauty. The trees of the native forest which still remain are strong, stately and vigorous. The land is undulating. The two main branches of the Whitewater river flow southward about fifteen miles apart. Cambridge City lies upon the west branch and near the western border of the county, while Richmond, now the county seat, a thriving manufacturing city, lies at a point four miles from the Ohio line, where three small streams unite to form the east or main branch of this little river.

Every part of the county is now intersected by excellent turnpike roads. The most important of these is the so-called National road, constructed many years ago by the general government from Cumberland, Md., to Springfield, Ill. The river at Richmond, and for some distance south, flows through a narrow gorge of no great depth, with limestone cliffs on either side. From the top of the cliff on the west bank the land rises gradually for two or three miles. This is now a fine farming district dotted with comfortable houses; and there is little to show that its present condition is the outgrowth of a civilization not much older than the tale of years allotted to a single life. Near the highest part of the rising land, upon an unfrequented by-way which leads south from the National road, is a small frame house, and near it an

(1)

older building two stories high, used as a barn, although the window frames opening through its decaying weatherboards show that it was, in earlier times, a dwelling. In a field west of the house a clump of trees marks the site of an abandoned well, some distance east is a brick dwelling, also deserted, and just back of it, an old log cabin, turned into an outhouse and falling to decay. Hard by is a small ravine filled with forest trees, while away to the east and southeast stretches a slope of farm land down to the Whitewater.

A stranger standing upon this place would find it hard to believe that he was on the site of Salisbury, at one time the county seat of Wayne county, a town which rose and disappeared during the first part of the present century.

In early days the surroundings were very different. The survivors of those times tell us of a single path winding through the forest and leading to a hamlet of thirty or forty dwellings, mostly log cabins, built on each side of the road; of a log court-house in an open square, and, at no great distance, a small log jail. They tell us, too, of a block-house, with portholes, built by the first settlers, to which they might betake themselves when threatened by an attack from Indians.

Salisbury, once established, began to grow. Thither flocked the men of the county, upon all great occasions, to the trials and to the musters where General Noble, with his cocked hat, is still remembered as a striking figure. They brought with them their own food in their wagons or saddlebags, and sought the shelter of the court-house or of the great trees near by. The men were clad in deerskin trousers, moccasins and blue hunting shirts, with a belt to which a knife was fastened and from which hung a tobacco pouch of pole-cat skin. The women wore gowns of homespun cotton with calico or gingham bonnets. The country folk came to town on horseback, the woman sitting behind the man on the same horse.

Their life was as plain as their appearance. Their dwellings were cabins of one room, built with the help of neighbors who came to the house-raising. These cabins were constructed of logs of equal size, notched and saddled, and were roofed with oaken clapboards held in place by "weight-poles." The chimney was built outside the wall, sometimes of rough stones, but oftener of sticks and clay. The fire-place was large enough for a huge back-log. The small windows let in the light through greased paper or deer-hide. A bed made of posts and boards fixed to the floor, a crane for the fire-place, a shelf for odds and ends, wooden hooks over the door for gun and powder-horn, a clock, a few cooking utensils and dishes, a spinning-wheel, a table and some splint-bottomed chairs made up the household fittings.

Their food was just as simple; corn bread, hominy, pork, honey, beans and game were the commonest articles of diet; wheaten bread, fruit, tea and coffee were luxuries seldom enjoyed. Money was so scarce that nearly all their dealings were carried on by barter.

The prosperity of Salisbury was short-lived. Soon after the completion of the court-house, a treaty was made with the Indians by which a strip of land twelve miles wide was thrown open for settlement on the west, and when the state of Indiana was organized, Centreville, a little hamlet just built, four miles away, succeeded in wresting the seat of justice from the older town. Salisbury began to decline; the buildings were taken down; some of them were moved to Richmond, and in 1826 the abandoned county seat contained only ten families. It was in this little hamlet in its declining days that the great Senator and War Governor of Indiana was born.

Oliver Hazard Perry Throck Morton (for thus the name stands in the family register) was the fourth child of James Throck Morton and Sarah T., his second wife, and was born on the 4th day of August, 1823, in the two-story frame house in Salisbury then kept by his father as a tavern.

The name Throckmorton was that of an old English family,

one branch of which had come to Rhode Island when that colony was first settled.

In February, 1631, there appeared in the harbor of Boston the ship "Lion," Captain William Pierce. Among her passengers were Roger Williams and his friend, John Throckmorton. The coming of the ship had been eagerly looked for. Sickness and famine were in the colony, and a special day of fasting and prayer had been appointed. But before the day came, the "Lion" was reported between Boston and Nantasket. She was well laden with all that was needful, and the day of fasting was turned into a day of thanksgiving.

John Throckmorton first established himself at Salem, but upon the settlement of Providence Plantations by Roger Williams he moved thither, and on "4th month, 10th, 1637," he is named with Williams in a land grant as "neighbor Throckmorton" and in a deed dated 1638, as "my loving friend and neighbor, John Throckmorton." He was among the fifty-four persons to whom were allotted the first house lots in Providence. But he did not remain there long. Filled with a spirit of adventure, he obtained, on October 2, 1642, from the Dutch authorities of New Amsterdam, a license to make a settlement at a place in Westchester county, N. Y., which was called after him, Throg's-Neck. He went thither with thirty-five associates. In October, 1643, there was a massacre by Indians in which members of his family were killed, and after some years he went back to Rhode Island, where he is named as a freeman in 1655, and as a deputy in the colonial legislature in 1664–73. Meanwhile New Amsterdam had passed into the hands of the English and had become New York, and in 1665 Governor Nicolls made a grant of certain land in Monmouth county, N. J., to twelve men on condition that one hundred families should establish themselves there within five years. This grant was known as the "Monmouth Patent." The grantees at once began to sell shares of land, and John Throckmorton was one of the buyers.

He did not himself move to New Jersey. He continued to live in Providence in the house next to Roger Williams, but his sons, John Throckmorton, Jr., and Job Throckmorton, went to Monmouth county, and their names are recorded among its earliest settlers. From them came numerous descendants, many of whom still live in the neighborhood, while others have moved to eastern Pennsylvania, to Virginia and other parts of the South and West.

Among these descendants was James Throckmorton, who was born in New Jersey, May 4, 1782. This man, in the settlement of his father's estate, believed that he had been over-reached by his brothers, and was so embittered by the thought that he was unwilling to bear longer the name of those who had wronged him. From that time on he called himself James Throck Morton, or, more commonly, James T. Morton. He moved, early in life, to Ohio, where he married his first wife. He was one of those engaged in building the Hamilton and Cincinnati Canal, but he was unfortunate in his contracts and lost much of his property. He was afterwards an inn-keeper, and then a shoemaker, a trade which he carried on, first at Salisbury and afterwards at Centreville. His circumstances were, however, considered good at that time, for the community in which he lived.

His first wife bore him three children—Maria, William S. T. and James. James died in infancy. Maria married Edward K. Hart and moved to Keokuk, Iowa. William lived at Centreville, and amassed quite a fortune.

On February 14, 1815, James T. Morton married at Springdale, Ohio, his second wife, Sarah Miller (daughter of John and Hannah Miller), the mother of Senator Morton. Sarah Miller was born at Elizabeth, New Jersey, February 12, 1788. The few surviving neighbors who knew her (she died in 1826) speak of seeing her often on horseback. She was a large, robust, fine-looking woman of strong character, good sense, remarkable memory and excellent conversational powers. While Senator Morton, no doubt, inherited something of Puritan sturdiness and patriotic spirit from his father's family, yet his splendid physique, his energy and indomitable will came mostly from the mother's side.

The name given to the boy was that of Commodore Perry. It is said that Oliver's father had served in the war of 1812, and had conceived an intense admiration for the hero of the battle of Lake Erie. But Oliver Hazard Perry Throck Morton was too much of a name for practical use. In early life all his initials appeared in his signature. His name was written O. H. P. T. Morton. But even this was inconvenient, and when he began the practice of the law, his preceptor, John Newman, called his attention to the formidable appearance of a professional sign with so many initials and to the drawback it might be in a community of primitive prejudices. So two-fifths of this obstacle to prosperity were quietly dropped and the subject of the present biography is known to history as Oliver P. Morton.

There is not much to tell of Morton's childhood. His mother died July 11, 1826, after giving birth to her fifth child. All these children, except Oliver, had died before her. He was only three years old at the time of her death.

There was no one to care for the child at Salisbury. But John Miller, Oliver's maternal grandfather, owned a farm at Springfield (now Springdale), Ohio, where he lived with his wife, Hannah, and his two daughters, Polly and Hannah Whittaker, both widows.

It was determined then that Oliver should go to Springfield to be brought up by his two aunts, Polly and Hannah. Here he lived until he was fifteen years old, in a careful and thrifty family of old-fashioned Scotch Presbyterians. The minister would come and examine them in the catechism, and at these times, as Oliver remembered, they always had wine and cake upon the sideboard.

Oliver studied his catechism at home. He had read the Bible entirely through at a very early age, and afterwards was required to read it all once every year. On Sundays, when the family went to church, they took their lunch with them and stayed all day. The boy would sit on the hard benches, by his aunt's side through the long service, until he became utterly weary. This gave him so great a distaste for religious exercises that he was known, in his later life, as a "non-professor." Yet this early training left its marks upon his character, and the force and simplicity of his diction show unmistakable traces of his intimate knowledge of the Bible.

In most things, Morton was much indulged by his aunts. The two sisters were bred in the old belief that it was the duty of the woman to wait upon the man, and they were very fond of the boy. Barring his religious obligations, they let him do much as he pleased. Hannah taught school in the neighborhood, and "Perry," as the boy was called, was one of her pupils.

One taste developed early. Morton was a voracious reader. Isaac Burbank, the father of his future wife, was a merchant at Centreville, Ind., from which place he frequently went to Cincinnati to buy goods. It was a two days' journey, and it was his habit to stop at the Millers' over night. The boy would give to Burbank the little money he had saved, to buy books for him at Cincinnati. He was especially fond of works of history and biography. On one occasion Burbank brought him the "Life of Marion." Young Morton sat up all night to read the book and finished it by morning.

Yet Morton was not generally noticed as a boy of extraordinary parts. He was quiet and undemonstrative, showing outwardly few characteristics different from those of the ordinary boy raised in the country. He was large and sturdy, and fond of athletic sports, excelling most of his companions

in running, leaping and swimming. He used to relate an effort
he made to ride standing upon a bareback horse, an attempt
naturally followed by most unhappy results.

Morton's father moved to Centreville when Salisbury fell
into decay. The shoemaker's shop had been transferred
thither on wheels. When, in 1837, Samuel K. Hoshour
opened a school known as the "Wayne County Seminary,"
which gained some local celebrity, it was determined to send
Oliver thither for his education.

Mr. Hoshour had come from Maryland. He afterwards
became well known in Indiana for his learning and piety. He
was a man of classical education, and was thought to be a
profound scholar. He was a "plain-spoken" man, sometimes caustic, but kind of heart, pedantic, honest, a man of
deep religious convictions and a preacher in the Christian
church. He was at one time president of the Northwestern
Christian University at Indianapolis.

In his autobiography Mr. Hoshour says: "I had not only
the youth of the immediate community but many from
abroad, representatives of the best families of the state of Indiana and other states, such as Governor Wallace's two sons,
sons and daughters of professional men, even the son of an
Indian chief, stalwart in form, submissive in temper, but tar-
dy in intellect. In this school were embryo judges, governors, and a United States Senator, O. P. Morton.

"As I have always been committed to the Solomonian philosophy, which is couched in these words, 'He that spareth
his rod hateth his son (or pupil), but he that loveth him
chasteneth him betimes,' I had occasionally to apply that
philosophy to some wayward and defiant natures. Did it
seldom but effectively. This phase of my administration
awoke at one time the poetic spirit of a Tennesseean, who
several times endangered his back to write a doggerel on the
school, the last stanza of which was:

> " 'O Lord preserve us every hour
> From the birch of S. K. Hoshour.' "

In this school the boy Morton remained a year. One of his fellow pupils thus speaks of him: "Ol, as we called him, was a good-natured, big-souled boy. He was kind to his school-mates, and we all liked him. He was so slow in recitations that he sometimes had the appearance of 'making it up' as he went along. In our debates we always liked to have him on our side."

When Morton was fifteen years of age, the entire family at Springdale moved to Centreville, and a short time afterwards, (on October 12, 1838) the grandfather, John Miller, died.

Morton could not devote any great amount of time to general education. No one could be idle in that busy little community. It was discreditable for a boy not to work. He must either learn a trade, serve as a farm hand or go into a store. So young Morton entered the office of Dr. Swain, who kept drugs for sale. He became an apothecary's clerk and his ultimate object was the study of medicine. But his appetite for books was too strong. A difficulty soon occurred between him and the doctor, because the boy gave to his books much of the time which the doctor thought ought to be given to his duties. The doctor came into the store one day and found Oliver reading. He struck the boy. The blow was returned and they parted company. A family council sat in judgment upon Morton's reprehensible conduct and decided that he should be "bound out" for four years to his brother William as an apprentice to learn the hatter's trade. Morton did not relish this, but there was no help for it. His brother was thrifty, energetic and exacting and got from Oliver all the work possible. Many of the Senator's friends in later life remember him first as a "cub hatter" with a block of wood and a skin from which he was plucking out the long hairs by the roots with a shoemaker's knife ("pulling musk-rat," as it was called), or blackened with dye, working at a copper tank set in masonry with a fire burning below it. There were two or three other apprentices in the same shop.

Morton at last could make a hat without assistance. The hats made then were very heavy and large; many of them had wide brims. Some of them are kept to-day and shown as relics in the little town.

Morton, up to this time, had given few signs of his ability. He was an overgrown boy, big, shy, awkward, industrious, steady in his habits. '' He was the most backward beau I ever saw,'' said a young woman whom he sometimes visited. But he was not much given to visiting young women. He did not go into society. He was, however, fond of music. He belonged to the village band[1] and played on the cornet, clarionet and flute. Accounts differ much as to the character of the music. But his one consuming passion was his thirst for books. All the leisure time that he could get he gave to reading. He devoured every book he could borrow; even old newspapers were food for his insatiable appetite.

Morton was not made for a hatter. He found the work so irksome that he resolved to quit it. He had inherited some hundreds of dollars from his grandfather's estate, and he determined to use a part of this in getting a better education. His term as an apprentice was nearly ended, but his brother would not release him. Usually, the apprentice received a small outfit at the end of his term, but Morton agreed to forego this, in order to be free that he might go to Oxford, Ohio, and pursue his studies. So in 1843, six months before his apprenticeship expired, he entered the little college which bore the pretentious name of '' Miami University.'' Of this institution it has been said: '' It was a sort of short cut to learning, fostering energy, self-dependence and practical common sense.'' Here he spent two years. He did not take the whole course and did not graduate. He confined his studies to those things which he thought would be most use-

---

[1] Senator Ingalls says : '' Morton once told me that the proudest moment of his life, before he became of age, was when he marched into his native town of Centreville at the head of the band playing the key bugle.''

ful to him. The classics were included but mathematics and the English branches received the most attention. He was rated in the college register as an "irregular," but this did not hinder him from winning that front rank among his fellows to which his talents and force of character showed that he was entitled. Although quite a plain boy, he was considered "a good fellow." His splendid physique and his sociable disposition drew to him the regard of that little community. He was a leader in athletic games, and those who saw him in later life, broken down by paralysis, remembered with a pang the days of youthful vigor when he kicked the foot-ball clear over the dormitories at Oxford.

Isaiah Mansur, his room mate, tells of him that a band was organized in the college and that Morton joined it and tried to play on the bugle, but made such a din that the neighboring students threatened to lynch him. This did not stop him, nor did anything else until Mansur broke his horn and threatened to drive him out of the room if he ever blew anything there bigger than a French harp.

"An irregular" could not aspire to college honors, yet even without this stimulus Morton stood high in his classes. His time was short and he must learn all he could. There were others who outranked him in languages. In mathematics he had no superior.

In the "Erodelphian," one of the college literary societies, his ability was conspicuous. Here the competitive friction of mind with mind struck fire from the flint. This society was divided into four sections, and the members of each were required, once every four weeks, to read essays. Morton and three colleagues, one from each of the other sections, presented their essays in the form of a manuscript journal called the "Erodelphian." The editorial staff of this unprinted paper was considered strong, and Morton stood easily at its head. His style was remarkable for simplicity, clearness and strength.

But his chief delight was in extemporaneous debate. Caring nothing for literary display, his aim was to make his thought clear, impressive and forcible. When he left Oxford he had the reputation of being the best debater in the little college.

At Miami University his orthodoxy was seriously shaken. Among the subjects in the college curriculum was the "Evidences of Christianity." Paley's work was used, and Morton got the book to study with the class. But he wanted to find out for himself what was in it, and in four nights he read it entirely through. He then asked to be excused from that subject, saying, "The book will confirm me in unbelief. I have read it through and the evidences are not satisfactory." He was accordingly released from attendance.

CHAPTER II

MORTON AT THE BAR

MORTON had been careful and economical at college. During part of the time he had prepared his meals in his own room and he had saved in every way he could. But time was of the greatest value to him. He must hasten with his preparation for the bar, for this was the calling he had made up his mind to follow. Two years were all that he could afford to spend in general education. Another voice, too, called him away. Before going to Oxford he had become acquainted with Lucinda M. Burbank, a young woman of Centreville, the daughter of that same Isaac Burbank who, in Morton's boyhood at Springdale, had brought books to him from Cincinnati.

Morton's friendship with Miss Burbank began at Oxford. She had a brother who was also a student there and a close friend of Morton's. At the end of the first year, she went, with a party of young women, to attend commencement. Morton fell desperately in love with her, and followed up his suit with the same determination with which, later in life, he pursued the objects of his public career. At last he won her hand. His love affair had made him restless, so he left Oxford in the spring of 1845, without taking a degree, and immediately began the study of the law.

His means were slender and he had not yet become established in business, but his heart was strong, his love was ardent and he could not and would not wait. On the 15th of May, 1845, he was married. The marriage was a happy

(13)

one. Mrs. Morton was a woman of quiet, retiring manners, practical, affectionate, entirely devoted to him and to their children. During a life of great political activity, he left all home matters, and in many cases, money matters, exclusively to her, and it was greatly due to her prudent administration that Morton, who became very careless of his personal affairs, remained throughout his life in reasonably comfortable circumstances. He repaid her devotion with tender affection. Her presence and care were a necessity for him.

Five children were born to them at their home in Centreville, of whom three still survive.[1]

It was just before his marriage that Morton, then twenty-two years of age, entered the office of John S. Newman, at Centreville, as a law student. Newman was then the leader of the Wayne county bar. He was a careful lawyer, a skillful pleader, a "safe" counselor, a man of excellent judgment. Morton's two years at college, while they had not given him a finished education, had taught him how to study, and he grappled with the law like one who intended to master it.

Newman said of him that he was "laborious in his studies, strictly temperate in his habits, and genial in his manners. He was a very thorough reader, and possessed in a remarkable degree the power of thinking at all times and in every place."

There were then a number of law students at Centreville. They entered upon a race in the study of Blackstone, and all read it very rapidly. After they were through, Morton examined himself to see how much he knew of it. He found that he could remember very little, so he began over again, studying

---

[1] John Miller Morton, born April 16, 1846.

Mary Elizabeth Morton, born December 10, 1848, died October 24, 1849.

Sarah Lilias Morton, born August 10, 1850, died January 2, 1852.

Walter Scott Morton, born December 2, 1856.

Oliver Throck Morton, born May 23, 1860.

everything with great care. He afterwards attributed much of his success at the bar to the thorough groundwork of legal principles, which he acquired in this second perusal of the great commentator.

In the fall of the same year, after only a few months' preparation, the young man purchased two hundred dollars' worth of books from Newman's library, and went into partnership with his preceptor. The library of a practicing lawyer at Centreville at that time was very meager. Six volumes of Blackford were all the Indiana reports then published, and with Wendell, Johnson, Hill, Cowen, the Massachusetts series and Pickering, they constituted nearly the entire stock of law reports, while Blackstone, Kent, Story's Equity, Cooper's Equity Pleading, Tidd's Practice, Chitty, and Toller on Executors, made up the bulk of the treatises. There was not much citation of authorities. Instead of looking up cases, the lawyer would take a walk in the woods and think out the logic of the situation. But the decisions of that period were quite as sound as the more elaborate opinions of to-day. There was not so much law learning, but the very absence of this helped the development of native ability and intellect.

Centreville was no easy place for a young lawyer beginning practice. The best legal talent in the state was collected in this little town. Besides Mr. Newman, George W. Julian (afterwards distinguished as an anti-slavery leader in Congress), Nimrod H. Johnson, James Raridan, Charles H. Test, Joshua H. Mellett, names that have been eminent in Indiana, were engaged in regular practice, while Caleb B. Smith, afterwards Secretary of the Interior under Lincoln, and Samuel W. Parker, a well-known advocate from the neighboring county of Fayette, frequently attended court. The town contained a sort of aristocracy of political and professional eminence. In such a place a young man had to struggle hard for a foothold.

Morton remained in partnership with Newman something

over a year.   In the spring of 1847 we find him associated
with Charles H. Test.   His new partner was a man of genial
disposition, fond of a good story, which he could tell better
than any man in Centreville, and much given to poking fun
at everybody within reach.   Innumerable are the traditions of
the Wayne county bar, with which his name is associated as
chief actor in some madcap prank.   He afterwards became
judge, and died at a ripe age.   With this associate, Morton
remained about two years.

In the summer of 1848, while he was in partnership with
Test, he made a canvass as candidate for prosecuting attorney.   There were six or seven counties then in the circuit,
with a very large Whig majority, and Morton, who was a
Democrat, stood no chance of election.   But for a young
lawyer, even a hopeless candidacy was of advantage.   It
brought him to the notice of the people, and an added client-
age was often the result.

Newman and Test were greatly Morton's seniors, and while
he was with them, the burden of the business naturally rested
upon the shoulders of the older partners.   The papers still on
file are mostly in their handwriting.   The younger partner
had to go through the usual apprenticeship of small cases
before the country justices.   Henry Jarboe, a well-to-do
farmer, was Morton's client in one of these early cases, and
thus tells the circumstances: ''When I bought my farm in
1846 there was a mortgage upon it to the school fund, and
the man I bought it of did not tell me about this, but he said
the title was clear.   When my first note for the purchase-
money fell due, I wanted to deduct this mortgage from the
four hundred dollars which I was to pay, but the man who
held my note would not let me do it.   The case was tried
at Jacksonburgh (a small village a few miles west of Centreville) before 'Squire Beard.   Morton hired a horse to come
to the trial.   The horse fell with him on the road, and when
he came to the 'Squire's he was covered with mud.   We tried

the case and he won it and saved my money. When I went
to Centreville afterwards, I asked Oliver what he was going
to charge me. He said 'You have got some good winter
apples in your orchard; bring me six or eight bushels.' This
was in the fall of 1847.''

In the spring term of 1849 we find Morton practicing law
alone. The papers on file are now in his own handwriting.
He was accurate and lawyer-like, considering his experience
and opportunities. His practice had not yet become extensive.

But it was only a short time that Morton remained alone.
In the fall term of 1850, we find him associated with Nimrod H. Johnson, a lawyer younger than himself, under the
firm name of Morton & Johnson. The new partner was a
man of brilliant parts and fine literary tastes, eloquent, im-
provident, erratic, impulsive. During this partnership Johnson became prosecuting attorney.[1]

The business of the new firm grew rapidly. We find the
name appearing more and more frequently upon the docket,
until it became second to none except that of Newman &
Siddall, a firm in which the reputation of Morton's old preceptor still retained the most important business in the
county.

Morton remained in partnership with Johnson until he was
elected judge in 1852.

While there was a large Whig majority in Morton's county
and circuit, the General Assembly of Indiana was Democratic.
Vacancies on the circuit bench were at that time filled by the
legislature, and when, in 1852, a vacancy occurred in the
sixth circuit, which embraced Wayne county, Morton was, on
February 23 of that year, elected judge by that body without opposition. He received his commission from Governor

---

[1] Shortly afterwards, he was elected judge of the court of common pleas,
a position which he filled with ability.

2—MOR.

Wright, and entered upon the duties of his office on March 1. He was very young, his education had been defective, his practice was of quite recent growth, yet he is spoken of in high terms as a judge.   While serving in this capacity, he first became known to the people of Indianapolis.   During the summer of 1852, he exchanged circuits with Judge Wick, of Marion county, and B. R. Sulgrove, an attorney who appeared before Morton at this time, thus described him: " He was only twenty-nine years old, but his manner and a certain weight of language gave the impression of greater age. He had no cases of any considerable consequence to deal with, but in such as he decided, his characteristic disregard of non-essentials showed as conspicuously as later.   His first words laid hold of the 'nub' of the case, and all that followed peeled off the husk, and he was done.   He was not fluent in his judicial utterances, nor yet hesitating nor uncertain, but he spoke slowly, as if he were studying the effect of every word as he went on.   He gave the impression rather of solidity of judgment, than readiness of apprehension."

Morton served as judge less than eight months.   Judicial duties were not wholly to his taste.   He was born for combat, and preferred the struggle of the bar to the calm of the bench.   The new constitution of Indiana went into effect on the 1st of November, 1851, before Morton's election.   Under this constitution the circuit judges were to be chosen by the people of the respective circuits.   The first popular election was to be held in October, 1852.   There was a strong Whig majority in Morton's circuit, and his term expired with the election of his successor.

Now occurred a remarkable episode in his history.   He felt his shortcomings in the lack of a thorough legal training. His only professional education, before he commenced to practice, had been a few months' study in the law office of Mr. Newman.   This was not enough.

He was about thirty years of age.   He had been married

more than seven years. He had been engaged in active practice for a considerable time, and had served as circuit judge, yet he determined to go to the Cincinnati law school before resuming his practice at the bar. It required some courage to do this, yet he knew that he needed the training, and that was enough. He remained at Cincinnati during the winter term of six months. While in that city he shared an apartment in a boarding-house with Murat Halstead, afterwards editor of the Cincinnati *Commercial*.

Morton was intensely studious. He wanted to learn all the law he could in the shortest possible time. Halstead says of him that he wore the biggest hat and boots in the house, and that he was a somnambulist, possibly the result of overstudy. On one occasion he walked out of the window to the roof of an adjoining building. ''He was not talkative. He had remarkable power. His smile was winning and his ways persuasive. He had the amiabilities that become a strong man.''

When his term at the law school was over, he returned to Centreville and resumed the practice of law. Among his early associates in that town was John F. Kibbey. They were both Democrats in a Whig community, they had worked for a short time at the hatter's trade together. Kibbey had been studying law in Morton's office before Morton became judge. In the spring of 1851, Morton had been employed to visit the counties bordering the Ohio river to select and buy desirable tracts of land. He took Kibbey with him. They found the country so unpromising that no purchases were made. During this trip, however, Morton, who had formed a favorable estimate of Kibbey's ability, offered to take him into partnership. So in 1853, after Morton's return from the law school, the firm of Morton & Kibbey was formed. It continued for more than seven years, and until the senior partner became Governor of Indiana. The selection was a wise one. Both at the bar and in private life Morton was

happy in choosing associates.   Kibbey was a careful student,
painstaking and diligent in searching authorities and drawing
pleadings, but very timid before court and jury.   Morton,
on the other hand, disliked office work, but was extremely
efficient in the conduct of a trial.   The team thus matched
was a strong one, and Morton now became easily the leader
of the Wayne county bar.

The methods of practice in the little town of Centreville
were quite different from those of our large cities.   Court was
in session only a small part of the time.   In the circuit there
were two terms each year, and three in the court of common
pleas.   Each term would last about three weeks.   Every
morning the bar of the county would assemble at half past
eight o'clock to "make up issues" and attend to matters of
practice preliminary to trial.   As soon as these were disposed of, the trials would begin, and the lawyers not engaged
in them would congregate in a room adjoining the court-
house, or under the trees in the green, or in some attorney's
office across the street, and discuss the topics of the day.
The lawyers were in each other's company much of the time.
There was little business during vacations and they visited
each others' offices a great deal.   The office of Morton &
Kibbey consisted of two large rooms on the second floor of a
building near the court-house.   A small circulating library
called the "Mechanics' Library" had been established in
Centreville in 1852, from a bequest known as the McClure
fund.   Kibbey was librarian, and the books were kept in the
office of the firm, which became a sort of rendezvous, not only
for the bar of the county, but for others of a literary turn, who
would come for books and sit and talk half the morning.

Morton found this library very useful.   The way he absorbed its contents was peculiar.   He read very rapidly and
would "skip" whatever seemed unimportant.   What he
wanted was to get at the kernel of a book as soon as he
could.   If he did not find it, his verdict on the work was

soon given. "There is nothing in it." As soon as he finished a book he liked to talked about it and discuss its contents with his friends. He was exceedingly fond of Scott's
novels, especially of "Old Mortality." "David Copperfield"
was also a favorite, and he enjoyed the humor of Artemus
Ward. "Trumps," by Geo.Wm. Curtis, "The Vicar of Wake-
field" and Macaulay's Essays pleased him. His favorite
poem was "Gray's Elegy." He was much interested in
Lamartine's "History of the Girondists" and the characters
of Vergniaud and Dumouriez impressed him, particularly the
latter. Some of the traits of Dumouriez were not unlike
those which he exhibited himself, later in life.

The office of Morton & Kibbey was always open. No one
ever thought of locking the door. Here the younger members of the bar would congregate and indulge in pranks and
jokes at the expense of any one within reach. Morton found
a good deal of fault with his junior partner and some of his
associates because they turned everything to ridicule, and
would never talk seriously. Chess was a favorite amusement
with the lawyers of Centreville, and they played a great deal
during the long vacations. Morton was fond of the game
and would sit for hours at it humming a tune, or whistling the
"Soldiers' Chorus," from Faust, wholly absorbed and often
quite forgetful of dinner or supper. At last he had to give
this up. It engrossed too much of his attention.

When Morton, after his term at the law school, came back
to the bar, affairs at Centreville were greatly changed. While
he had been in partnership with Johnson, Jehu T. Elliott was
upon the bench. Elliott was an able and affable judge who
came down from New Castle every term and stopped at Lash-
ley's tavern while holding court. He was a clear-headed lawyer, portly and judicial in appearance, somewhat indolent—he
would rather spend his evenings chatting with the lawyers than
poring over papers and authorities—very kind to the young
attorneys whom he often invited to his room for a quiet talk—

a man who was entirely in his place on the bench, always master of the situation, and for whom the bar entertained the highest respect. Elliott presided and two lay judges nodded assent to all that he said and did. There was a certain plain dignity about the court. At the time Morton was raised to the bench, the associate judges were dispensed with. When he returned from Cincinnati and recommenced practice with Kibbey, a very different man presided. A political accident had led to the election of one Joseph Anthony, a paralytic, an ignorant tavern-keeper of Muncie, who was unable to decide the plainest propositions of law. When puzzled over some simple question, he would helplessly ask the attorneys why they could not settle the matter themselves. In the adjoining county of Henry, the bar determined to try no cases at all before such a judge, but continued everything from term to term hoping to force Anthony to resign. That complacent judge, however, seemed quite well satisfied with such an arrangement, and had not the slightest intention of relinquishing an office where the duties were light and paid him much better than keeping tavern. The circuit under his administration became a laughing stock. Under the constitution of Indiana, Anthony could not be removed during his term of office except by impeachment. After a time, however, an act was passed creating a new circuit and confining the activities of this worthy jurist to the county of Delaware from which he came.

Anthony had been elected by a fusion of various parties against Jacob Julian, the Whig candidate, a man who was then unpopular with the Wayne county bar. Morton and Kibbey were Democrats and not friendly to Julian. They had supported Anthony, and it was soon found that the new judge had great respect for Morton's opinions upon questions of law, especially in matters where Julian took a different view of the case. Under these circumstances the difficulties of the situation were not insurmountable. Nimrod H. Johnson,

Morton's former partner, was upon the bench of the Common Pleas.

Morton spent but little time in office work. He seldom drew a pleading. An inspection of the docket of "Morton & Johnson" and "Morton & Kibbey" reveals very few entries in Morton's handwriting. He spent much of his time out of doors, talking with his fellow-townsmen. "Ob" Morton, as he was called, was sociable in his disposition, after he had overcome the backwardness of his boyhood, and was very popular with the townsfolk. He liked a discussion as well as a joke, and his strong bass voice, so effective before the jury, could often be heard ringing in contagious laughter in the street. His partner attended to the office work and kept the briefs of the cases. Morton rarely looked at these until an issue of law or fact was to be presented, but after the trial commenced, he was industry itself. He would walk the floor all night, if necessary, dictating his argument, and Kibbey would take down the notes. He afterwards prepared many of his political speeches in the same way. Before a jury he was irresistible. He discarded all the rubbish in the case, seized the main point and dealt sledge-hammer blows.

An associate says of him: "I found he could present his case in the clearest possible way in a few words. I had to put the matter in several aspects, to go around the subject and look at it from different points of view. Morton never did this. One statement was conclusive."

In his speeches there was no rhetoric, little ornament, and very seldom any wit. In presence, voice and action he was strong, deliberate, magnetic and impressive. He would hold the attention of all who heard him and compel them to follow every link in the chain of his logic. Of gestures he used but few, and those principally with his right hand. He was not graceful, but such was his power in speaking that no one noticed whether he was graceful or not. He carried his cases by main strength. The impression he produced on those

who heard him is shown by the following story, told by one
present at the McCorkle trial, an important criminal case in
which Morton took a leading part. '' It was a beautiful October day. There was a picnic north of town, and many of
our party went to the court-house to hear the speeches. The
room was crowded. At that time the defendant had the
right to make the closing argument. Caleb B. Smith was
leading in the defense. He was assisted by George W. and
Jacob B. Julian, while Morton and Kibbey, with John Yar-
yan, were associated with the prosecuting attorney in behalf
of the State. The defendant had been stealing money from
Burke's Bank. Cale Smith was sitting against the wall, reading some of the papers in the case and waiting for his turn.
Morton was talking to the jury. He had on a pair of light
trousers, a white Marseilles vest, a big gold buckle on his
watch fob, and a swallow-tailed coat. These coats were then
worn pretty generally by professional men. He had a mous-
tache and short chin beard. He was a large, noble-looking
man. I remember particularly that he had a fine leg and a
large, soft hand, quite white and with a good deal of hair on
the back of it. Morton spoke for half a day. It was a jury
of farmers. I remember the effect the speech had on me. I
never heard anything like it. I have heard Morton often,
but I believe now that it was the greatest speech he ever
made. From that moment I made up my mind I would be
a lawyer.''

One incident of Morton's law practice would be an interesting subject for psychological investigation. A case was
pending in which his success depended upon his being able to
find a certain authority bearing directly upon the question at
issue. He had seen this case and mentioned it in his
argument, but had lost the reference and could not tell
where to find it. He thought about it all one evening, but went
to bed as much in the dark as ever. While asleep, he dreamed
of the place where it was to be found, and upon waking he

went to his library, took out the book, turned to the page, and found it.

A masterly speech, delivered in defense of Jacob Thompson, who was indicted for the murder of his child, spread far and wide the fame of Morton as an advocate. The body of the child, horribly mangled, had been found near a railway station, and suspicion was directed to the parents. Both were arrested, and the mother, broken-hearted, died in jail before the trial. The affair had aroused great interest, and the evidence, as well as the sentiment of the community, was against the accused. With the gallows · staring him in the face, Thompson sent for Morton, to whom he denied his guilt, and attempted to explain the incriminating facts. But his manner was so marked with embarrassment, and his story was so confused, that Morton could not believe it. In looking into the facts, however, Morton discovered that some time previously his client had tried to put his child into the care of Shakers living in that vicinity, but that they had refused to take it, believing that the father was insane. Insanity, therefore, became the defense. Morton prepared the case with much care, and after the evidence was in, he spoke for four hours to the jury. The speech is still remembered by those who heard it as a marvelous demonstration of the conquering power of argument and reason. He believed that his client was not guilty of intentional murder, and ten jurymen were converted by him to the same belief. There were two, however, who remained obstinate in favor of conviction, and on a second trial, a compromise verdict of manslaughter was returned and Thompson escaped with six years' imprisonment.

One who met Morton at the bar said: ''In the four years before he was called into the service of the State he literally annihilated everybody connected with the bar of Wayne county, and walked rough-shod over all the other lawyers of his circuit.'' His practice soon became so large that he was on one side or the other of all the important cases in the county. Sometimes there was an earnest rivalry to secure his services. One night two adversaries started at the same time for the same purpose—one from Cambridge City, the other from Richmond. The Richmond man reached Centreville first, and Morton appeared in his behalf.

Morton's aid was invoked in railroad litigation, and large fees began to pour in. It is among the traditions of the bar that he received a fee of ten thousand dollars in a single suit, a thing quite unheard of, up to that time, in Wayne county.

He was also called to neighboring counties, particularly to Randolph and Henry, and sometimes he went to Indianapolis to take part in important litigation. Jos. E. McDonald remembers that he was associated with Morton in a suit to foreclose a mortgage on the New Castle, Logansport and Chicago Railroad and to set aside a lease of the property. Morton made the principal argument for the bondholders, which resulted in a decree setting aside the lease. This was in 1859. From that time he was in the front rank of the bar, not only of his county and district but of the entire state. Sometimes he was called to Ohio, and later in life, he spoke with satisfaction of the encouragement given to him by Tom Corwin on one of these occasions. He said, "I made a speech in the court-house in Lebanon. I went there to defend a man who was on trial for murder. I was very much interested in the man and had prepared my case with great care. I was pretty well posted in it. Mr. Corwin was in the court-house and I did not know it. He stayed through the argument, and when I was done, came forward through the crowd and congratulated me. I was very much flattered and invited him to come and see me. He came to my room after supper, and we sat and talked until morning. He was the most brilliant man in conversation I ever knew. There was a freshness in his humor and something genial in his nature of which one never tired."

In the Indiana Supreme Court, Morton was not as successful as in the trials below. The reason is plain. Cases in that court were presented upon written briefs. Oral arguments were almost unknown. Success depended largely upon the diligence with which the attorney prepared and arranged the authorities. Writing briefs for the Supreme Court was not at all to Morton's taste. He would postpone this part of his work until the last minute, and sometimes it was neglected altogether, or left to his partner, Kibbey. For Morton, the stimulus of actual, visible combat was necessary. In the Supreme Court his transcendent powers as an advocate were of no avail. About eighty cases, extending from May, 1851, until May, 1862, are reported, in which Morton appears as counsel.

Some odd cases appear in the list. Among others was the suit of Culbertson v. Whitson, upon a contract for the sale of twenty-five head of fat hogs. Whitson tendered slaughtered hogs and Culbertson refused them. The circuit court held that the tender was bad. Julian, for the appellant, contended that he had the right to elect to deliver them, dead or alive. Morton, with Newman and Siddall, appeared for Culbertson and filed a printed brief, containing, among other things, the following humorous argument:

"The issue submits, for the consideration of the court, the very grave and mooted question, what is a hog? No tribunal can approach such a question without a deep sense of its importance, and of the awful responsibility involved in its decision. . . . According to Noah Webster, a hog has no existence without the faculties of breathing and squealing— take these away, and he is transformed into pork. . . . The appellant, in his brief, insists 'that a hog is a hog, dead or alive, and that it is hard to make anything else but a hog out of a hog.' We think the reverse of this proposition would be nearer the truth, and that the appellant would be compelled to exert his capacity to its utmost tension before he would succeed in making a hog out of a hog; but he would find no

difficulty in converting a hog into pork, lard, bacon, carcass
or almost anything else but a hog.''

Unfortunately the court was not convinced by this luminous
demonstration, but in its efforts to grapple with the great problem involved, it seems to have sought light outside the record,
for in the opinion it is gravely written: ''We understand that
among hog dealers, two kinds are recognized and well
understood, to wit, gross hogs and net hogs; the gross hog is
the live hog, and the net, the dead hog.''[1]

It was while Morton was practicing law at Centreville that
he became associated with the order of Odd Fellows. In
July, 1854, he was elected Grand Master of the Grand Lodge
of Indiana. He esteemed highly his fellowship in this organization, but later in life the pressure of his public duties was
such that he had little time to devote to the fraternity.

During the last years of his practice, Morton accumulated
enough money to buy a few acres of land and to build a neat
brick dwelling a little west of Centreville, on the brow of a
knoll overlooking the quiet valley of Noland's Fork. He was
so much attached to this home in after life that he never
came back to Centreville without going to see it. Often he
stopped his carriage on the brow of the hill, and walked to
the front of the house, to sit for an hour looking out on the
valley.

He was once asked what he was thinking. ''I do not
think at all, I rest,'' was his weary answer.

---

[1] Morton generally disliked to say anything funny in his professional or
public life. This was not because he did not possess the faculty of humor,
but because he saw the pitfall into which it led. " There have been many
young men," he said, " who have wrecked themselves by being witty. A
politician who goes into wit must expect to sacrifice everything else to it.
He will gain no reputation as a sound man. His judgment will be suspected."

CHAPTER III

EARLY POLITICAL LIFE

In 1844, on the day of the Presidential election, a young man of large frame, with high forehead, dark eyes and straight hair, rather overgrown in appearance and with clothes that fitted him none too well, rode into Centreville upon a gray horse bespattered with mud. It was "Ob" Morton, then a student at "Miami University," who had come home from Oxford, twenty-eight miles away, to cast his first ballot. He dismounted, went to the polls and voted for James K. Polk, the candidate of the Democratic party.

Political feeling was running high. "Harry of the West," as Clay was called, was the idol of the Whigs. The people of Wayne county knew him well. It was only two years before, at Richmond, that he had delivered his crushing rejoinder to Mendenhall, the Quaker Abolitionist, who had presented to him a petition asking him to free his slaves. But this triumph had been a Pyrrhic victory, the consequences of which had come to plague him.

Most of the Wayne county people were Whigs. But to the Democrats of Centreville, the zeal of the young college boy, who had unexpectedly appeared among them, was very gratifying, and from that time Morton was much esteemed among the men of his party in the little town.

Morton's political principles were inherited. His father had been a Democrat and so was he. The name of Jackson had a power as magical as that of Clay. Polk was the fig-

(29)

ure-head, "The Old Man at the Hermitage" was always the
leader and the hero.

The Whigs favored a liberal construction of Federal authority, a national currency and a protective tariff, and they supported a system of internal improvements to be made by the
general government.

The Democrats contended that the Federal government
was of limited powers, that the constitution was to be strictly
construed, and that it did not authorize such improvements,
nor the chartering of a United States bank, nor the fostering
of "one branch of industry to the detriment of another."
" Polk, Dallas and the Tariff of '42 " was their war-cry.
Their platform favored "the re-occupation of Oregon and the
annexation of Texas." Upon these propositions the Whig
convention had been entirely silent, and the Democrats had
the advantage of an aggressive position in respect to that
most tempting of all political issues—territorial expansion.

The slavery question was not brought to the front. Oregon was to be a fair offset to Texas. Morton was a friend of
territorial aggrandizement, and was in favor of extending our
boundaries in both directions. He was a strong believer in
our "manifest destiny." He had not yet become aroused to
a sense of the wickedness of slavery.

For many years he continued to be an orthodox member
of the Democratic party. In 1847 he favored the acquisition
of the additional territory from Mexico. He supported Cass
in the campaign of 1848. He was against the Wilmot Proviso, not that he liked slavery, but because he believed that
the Missouri Compromise kept it out of all the territory north
of 36° 30', and that the territories west of Texas and south
of that line would be unsuitable to that institution. The law
of Mexico having excluded it, it could not be introduced, he
thought, except by positive statute, and such an enactment
would not be acceptable to the people. There was no need,
therefore, for the Wilmot Proviso, and it was a "disturbing

element" in the party, likely to injure it. Slavery agitation was undesirable.

One of the most important agencies in the development of Morton's political views, as well as of his intellectual powers, was the "Dark Lyceum," a debating society of Centreville. It had been organized by George W. Julian, Neil McCullough and a few others. The "Lyceum" met in the second story of the old seminary building, where Morton had gone to school. Its sessions were held in the dark, so that members might speak and gesticulate with greater freedom. In 1850 it was reorganized, and the number of members was increased to sixteen. They were all young lawyers or law students. A room was fitted up and a small library was bought for the society. It was a secret organization, but there was no initiation. Its pretensions were great. It was a very "ancient society." Records of indisputable authenticity had been preserved in a cave through many centuries. Appelles of Cos had belonged to it, and, indeed, the most distinguished men of all ages and all countries had joined it. At one time it was supposed that Demosthenes was its founder, but subsequent investigation showed that he had merely resuscitated a society much more ancient. It had its beginnings among the early Chaldean astronomers. It had been connected in some occult manner with the Areopagus. While passing through the Roman period it had gathered in such members as Cicero and Cæsar. Indeed few men of great distinction had ever escaped.

A premier was chosen every evening to preside. Each premier appointed his successor. Every member, in turn, as his evening came round, was to introduce some proposition and open the debate. The subject was not announced beforehand. There was a prelate who took care of the library and of the morals of the members. The library was small, so most of his energy was devoted to the ethical branch of his duties. He reported any misconduct. On one occasion, he submitted a serious charge against a member, that of dyeing his whiskers. The culprit pleaded that the dye was iodine prescribed by a doctor for a pain in the jaw. After much forensic oratory, the accused was exonerated. Another practice of the Lyceum was known as "word discussions." Some member would propose a single English word, and the etymology of the word, its history, its various meanings and its uses, with illustrations drawn from reading or from memory, would be discussed. Other subjects engaged attention—the Monroe Doctrine, the temperance question, Kossuth and Hungary, and invisible oratory waxed warm and fierce as great problems of state were disposed of. Occasionally a member would propose something metaphysical or sentimental. "Worship is Transcendent Wonder" is remembered as the theme of one of the debates. It is safe to guess that this subject was not suggested by Morton. A question debated in the old Lyceum as well as after the re-organization was the "Wilmot Proviso," and more than one member became identified with the Republican party as a result of these discussions. It was the opinion then formed, more than anything else, that opened Morton's eyes to the iniquity of slavery, led him to oppose the Kansas-Nebraska bill, and brought about his final rupture with the Democratic party.

The compromise of 1850, although introduced by Clay, was not a mere Whig measure. Anti-slavery Whigs, like Seward, opposed it, and it received much support from Democrats. Morton, and some of his fellow-partisans of Wayne county, thought that it should be accepted as a "finality." About this time, the Democrats of Morton's district held a meeting at Milton, a little town in the southwestern part of Wayne county, at which the question was discussed whether they should nominate a candidate of their own for Congress. In this convention Morton favored a separate nomination, but he was out-voted. The greater part of the Democracy supported

George W. Julian, the Free-soil candidate, but some refused to do so, and among them was Morton.   Julian was defeated by about seven hundred majority.

The compromise of 1850 was one of the causes of the Democratic victory of 1852. Morton took an active part in the campaign, making speeches in favor of Franklin Pierce, to whom Indiana gave a majority of not far from twenty thousand.

3—Mor.

CHAPTER IV

MORTON LEAVES THE DEMOCRATIC PARTY

A REMARKABLE feature of Morton's character was the slowness and steadiness of its growth. He did not quickly reach the full maturity of his mental powers. His political views underwent several radical changes during his eventful career, but these were not so much the somersaults of caprice as the evidences of a healthy intellectual development.

Morton's early political life had been the result of inheritance and surroundings. He had drifted with the stream. Now he began to breast it.

One of the most important events in his career was his separation from the Democracy in 1854. Up to that time he had voted with his party through thick and thin. He had not been aroused to the iniquities of slavery; he had believed in the narcotics of compromise and silence.

The feelings of the people of Indiana were not unfriendly to the South nor to her "peculiar institution." The state was considered one of the "outlying provinces of the empire of slavery."

In 1851 a new constitution had been submitted to the people, forbidding negroes from coming into the state and punishing those who employed them. It had been ratified by a popular majority of nearly ninety thousand. Morton had voted for it. Moreover he had always been opposed to "abolitionists."

This then was his attitude when a new issue arose, the question of the repeal of the Missouri Compromise. What was he to do?   Hitherto he had been tolerant of slavery for two reasons; first, because its evils had not come close enough to his doors to impress themselves upon his convictions, and, in the second place, because, like many statesmen of the generation just passing away, like Clay and Benton, Jackson and Webster, he considered that the concord of the people and the preservation of the Union were of such paramount importance that he would do all he could to discourage the "agitation" which might imperil them.   The maintenance of the Union was indeed at all times the cardinal object of his political life.

So he believed with his party in the efficacy of the Missouri Compromise and in the " finality " of the measures of 1850. But now it was the slave power itself which had broken faith and stirred again the embers which he thought were dying upon the hearth.   The very reason by which he had justified his Democracy was now the reason why he could no longer uphold it.   But perhaps something might be done to keep his party from following the perilous lead.   He would not break with his old associations if he could help it.   He loved his party dearly.   He was in good standing and extremely popular.   The Democracy was still dominant in Indiana. His chances of preferment were good.   After the Pierce campaign he had been named in the *Sentinel*, the state organ of the Democracy, as a probable candidate for United States Senator.   The people of his district were now talking of nominating him for Congress.   He knew the obloquy which attached to the party renegade.   Perhaps the Democracy might be held back from taking the fatal step, a step which was not only wrong, but meant party disintegration and defeat.   He would do what he could to stay the movement.

As soon as it was found that the Kansas-Nebraska bill was likely to become a law, Morton began an agitation against it in his own district.   The bill passed the Senate on the 3d of March, and in the same month, just after the opening of the spring term of court, Morton, with other Democrats of Wayne county, prepared remonstrances against it. These were circulated through the county by jurors, witnesses and parties attending court, and were universally signed. They were forwarded to the House of Representatives where the bill was pending.

A state convention of the Democracy had been called for the 2d of May. On the 15th of April the Democrats of Wayne county met, and Morton headed the delegation which was selected to represent them in the state organization. A resolution was unanimously adopted in favor of Morton as the next Democratic candidate for Congress. As the time drew near for the holding of the state convention, the Kansas-Nebraska bill passed its various stages in the House of Representatives. The measure was forced through by the weight of the strong Democratic majority in both branches of Congress. Still there were many who resisted the party lash, and the feeling against the bill was very bitter. In the March election in New Hampshire, the Democratic majority had been swept away. In April, Connecticut had registered her opposition. These were but the preludes to the election in 1854, which wiped out the Democratic majority in Congress.

Morton hoped that his party in Indiana might still be kept from an explicit endorsement of the bill. The Democracy in one of its previous state conventions had declared against the further extension of slavery in the territories.[1] But as the time for the present convention drew near, the outlook grew darker, and Morton made up his mind that he would be true to his principles even if he had to leave his party. He was much troubled over the matter. He went to Indianapo-

---

[1] A resolution of the Indiana Democratic Convention of 1849 declared "that the institution of slavery ought not to be introduced into any territory where it does not now exist; that inasmuch as California and New Mexico are in fact and in law free territories, it is the duty of Congress to prevent the introduction of slavery into their limits."

lis a day or two before the convention was to meet, saw many
of the delegates, and tried to persuade them not to endorse
this fatal bill.   He went personally to Jesse D. Bright and
urged him not to force the party to the adoption of so dangerous a resolution.   In reply to Bright's answer, that the
Indiana Democracy was strong enough to carry any measure,
Morton remarked, "Yes, anything that is right, but not such
a measure as that."   He met Joseph E. McDonald.   They had
a long talk together, walking up and down Washington street
until late at night.   Morton urged McDonald to oppose in
convention any resolution endorsing the Kansas-Nebraska bill.
But McDonald did not see his way clear to do this.   The
prospect was that the bill would be approved by the convention, and Morton said if such were the case he would not be
bound by the action of that body.   Indeed, he made it generally known that if the Democracy assumed the responsibility of this measure he would no longer act with the party.
Othniel Beeson, an upright and influential farmer of Wayne
county, one of Morton's fellow-delegates to the convention,
thus relates what happened:

"I well remember the circumstances that surrounded
Governor Morton when he walked out of the Democratic
party. He and myself were two of the nine delegates appointed
by the Democrats of Wayne county to attend the convention
held at Indianapolis in May, 1854.   We met, and Jim Hughes
was made president. A resolution was offered that votes cast in
the convention on all subjects should be by counties, and that
the vote should be a unit.   Morton raised a point of order
and argued it at length, claiming that each delegate had the
right to cast his vote as he pleased on all subjects before the
convention, and the president sustained the point of order.
The great question then was upon the Nebraska bill which repealed the Missouri Compromise of 1820.   Morton, Judge
Test and myself, and one of the other delegates from our
county, were determined never to indorse this bill.   The

other five delegates were ready to accept it. After the first vote taken had developed a large majority in favor of the Nebraska bill, Ben Edmonson, of Dubois county, offered a resolution to expel all the Anti-Nebraska delegates from the convention. A vote was taken and the resolution was carried. Morton and I walked out amid hisses and taunts, ' Your heads are getting kinkey,' ' Go and equalize yourselves with niggers.' As we walked down the aisle I suggested to Morton that we stop and give them a few blue damns, but his answer was, ' No, let us not show them that much respect.' But by the time we reached the door I was too full to go out without giving vent to my feelings. I stopped, turned my face to them and made the following speech : ' Hell dawns upon the Democratic party from this day onward.' ''

Thus Morton was driven from the convention of the party in whose faith he had been born and bred, to whose principles he had steadfastly clung until these had become inconsistent with its own past traditions and with all human progress. Thus did the Democracy expel the man whose voice and acts were to be so potent in keeping it for more than a quarter of a century from power.

From this time Morton was drawn more and more closely to men of other organizations who thought with him upon the all-absorbing question—to Whigs, Free-soilers and whatever else came from the winds of heaven in opposition to the Kansas-Nebraska bill. But he had not yet entirely broken his connection with the Democracy. He was still upon the county committee. His county had recommended him for Congress. If the convention in his own district should repudiate the bill, he could still, without inconsistency, accept the nomination and run as an Anti-Nebraska Democrat. In the "Old Burnt District" there was a very strong sentiment opposed to the repeal of the Missouri Compromise. The war of the two factions was hot and bitter. On the 26th of May the district convention was held at Cambridge City, a

town in the western part of Wayne county. A number of
Morton's friends met at his room in the Capital House in
that city, the evening before the convention, among them
Schuyler Colfax, Dr. Sexton, W. K. Edwards, and John
F. Kibbey. To them he read a letter which he had prepared, giving his views upon the "Missouri Compromise"
and his reasons for opposing the Kansas-Nebraska bill. He
said that if the convention indorsed this bill he could not be
a candidate, nor could he act longer with the party. Morton
was not present at the convention. He was Master of the
Grand Lodge of Odd Fellows, and was attending the session
of that body in Indianapolis. But his letter was read. There
was a vigorous fight upon the resolution indorsing the bill,
but the "Nebraska men" at last carried the day by a small
majority, and from that hour Morton ceased to be a Democrat.

At this time all was uncertainty as to his political future.
With what party should he now co-operate? Was it to be
with his old adversaries, the Whigs? Was it be with the
Free-soilers, the "Abolitionists," men whom Morton himself
had regarded as political Pariahs, men who had been endeavoring, as he thought, to imperil the Union by senseless agitation? Should it be with the Know-nothings, a secret,
oath-bound organization, formed only a short time before,
whose narrow policy would proscribe Catholics and exclude
foreigners from citizenship until they had lived in the country
twenty-one years? Another movement began at this time
and absorbed great attention. The Maine-Law agitation had
traveled westward. "Prohibition," with the search, seizure
and confiscation of intoxicating liquors, was the demand of the
temperance men. On January 12 a hundred delegates met
in a temperance convention at Indianapolis and issued an address to the people. The agitation was strong in Centreville.
Morton took quite a warm interest in this movement. On
one occasion he defended in court some "crusaders," enthusi-

astic women, who had taken the law into their own hands and had destroyed the stock of a saloon-keeper. Many members of the county bar had signed a pledge not to undertake the defense of a man whom they believed guilty of selling liquor, a rather inconsequent resolution, which might well lead to the conviction of the innocent, but which the *Journal*, the leading paper in the state, called "a noble stand and one which will reflect great honor upon those who have signed the contract." The next legislature passed a prohibitory law, but it was declared unconstitutional by the supreme court. Was Morton to join the ranks of the temperance agitators?

History developed rapidly during the next few months. The Democratic party became sectional with its stronghold at the South. The Southern Whigs joined it in a body and gradually the Whig party melted away. The fragments of every movement in the North coalesced upon the Anti-Nebraska issue, and many of the Northern Democrats wheeled into line in opposition to the Kansas-Nebraska bill. The *Journal* notices the defections under the title "More Abolitionists." In the next House of Representatives the Democratic majority had disappeared.

Many and various were the names adopted by the new party of opposition. At Ripon, in Wisconsin, a coalition meeting of March 20 suggested the name "Republican," which was adopted at the state convention of Whigs and Free-soilers on the 6th of July "under the oaks." In Indiana the combination became known as the "People's Party."

The "Free Democracy," as they were then called, had met in state convention on May 25, and declared the Kansas-Nebraska bill "a violation of faith, a conspiracy against humanity, a link in the chain of the supremacy of slavery," and had recommended the calling of a state convention to combine all elements in opposition to it.

On the 6th of July the opponents of this bill in Morton's congressional district, met at Cambridge City and nominated

D. P. Holloway for Congress. Efforts were made by the
Know-nothings to nominate Morton, but he was not willing to
connect himself with that organization.

On July 13th a state convention was held. Something had
to be conceded to each of the factions, so the platform contained a temperance plank, a modified demand for the restric-
tion of the foreign vote and a thorough-going Anti-Nebraska
resolution. Nominations were made for the minor state
offices. The new party was called by the Democrats in derision, "the Abolition, Free-soil, Maine-Law, Native American, anti-Catholic, anti-Nebraska party of Indiana." Nevertheless the "People's Party" performed valuable service. It
was the preliminary organization of the Republican party in
the state. Morton became one of its most active and valuable members.

With his former partner, Judge Test, he started out on
the campaign. On the 6th of September, Douglas, Bright
and Pugh spoke in the court-house square at Indianapolis,
and on the 11th it was announced that Test and Morton, both
former Democrats, would speak on the other side upon the
following Saturday. They addressed a crowd which filled the
court-house, and Morton spoke for nearly two hours. He began
by showing that the Missouri Compromise was the action of
the South, forced upon the North, like its repeal, with the aid
of the votes of a few Northern men. He spoke of the universal acquiescence in it, and the frequent assertion of its sanctity
by those who now declared it void. He next spoke of the
"preposterous humbug" of popular sovereignty as declared
by the Nebraska bill, which left the settlers free to regulate
their domestic institutions "subject only to the constitution."
The South held that the constitution carried slavery into all
the territories, and the Nebraska bill, as the South construed
it, established slavery in all. The hypocrisy of the Douglas
men in hoping that slavery would not go into the territories,
after doing all in their power to enable it to go there, reminded

him of the story of the Quaker sailor who, when a British man-of-war closed with an American vessel, pushed back each Englishmen who clambered over the bulwarks and let him drop into the water, saying: "I do not want to drown thee, I hope thee can swim."

The October elections came on and not only was the new party successful in Morton's county and district, but it carried the state by eleven thousand majority. Nor did the political excitement stop when the victory was won. In the latter part of October, a meeting was held in Washington Hall at Indianapolis, at which Morton, in an elaborate argument, exposed the fallacies of the Kansas-Nebraska bill.

On the first of November he spoke at a "People's Jubilee," as it was called, held in the State-House Grove.

Meanwhile, in Kansas events crowded upon each other thick and fast, to justify Morton and those who withdrew with him from the Democratic party. The bars had been let down and freedom and slavery started together upon a mad scramble for supremacy.

Civil war between the settlers and the border ruffians kept alive the agitation throughout the country. The feeling against the extension of slavery grew deeper and more earnest. The "People's Party" of Indiana again assembled in convention, and Morton spoke. He urged the importance of union and co-operation in resisting the extension of slavery. He made an argument against the provision in the state constitution allowing aliens to vote. He commended the prohibitory law.

Morton continued his activity in other parts of the state. On July 28, he addressed a convention at Crawfordsville in a speech two hours in length, and we hear of him at Lafayette a little later.

It is easy to see from the speeches of Morton the influence which the Know-nothings had in the formation of the fusion organization known as the "People's Party." Morton would not join the Know-nothings. The Anti-Nebraska men would not concur either in their secret measures, their opposition to the Catholic church or in their exclusion of foreigners from the suffrage for twenty-one years. But they were ready to go with them as far as seemed reasonable. The constitution of Indiana permitted aliens to vote if they resided within the state for a single year. They could not become naturalized citizens of the United States for five years, and the fusionists insisted, with much reason, that the restrictions of the Federal government were moderate and wise, and that aliens should not participate in this ultimate right of citizenship until they had had a fair opportunity to become acquainted with our institutions. In after years, however, the matter was not found to be important enough in Indiana to justify continued agitation.

The Presidential campaign was now approaching. All eyes were riveted on Kansas. The supporters of the Free-soil movement, who in most of the Northern states now bore the name of Republicans, had as yet no national organization. One must be made. After much correspondence and many calls from state committees, a preliminary convention was announced to meet at Pittsburgh on the 22d of February, 1856. The appointment of delegates was of course informal. They were in part self-constituted, in part sent by various self-appointed meetings and conventions of Republicans in the different states. Wayne county took an active part in the movement, and a meeting of the citizens was held at Richmond on February 18, at which resolutions were unanimously adopted that the exclusion of slavery from territory now free was the paramount issue, and the common ground on which all could unite. The resolutions appointed Oliver P. Morton. Rev. Thomas A. Goodwin and William Grose delegates to the convention.

So Morton was present at the birth of the Republican party. The Pittsburgh convention was well attended, and was earnest and even radical in its spirit. It provided for the holding of a national convention in Philadelphia on the 17th of June, for the nomination of candidates, and it put forth a stirring address to the country. The resolutions demanded the overthrow of the administration, and the admission of Kansas as a free state, and urged every constitutional form of resistance to the bringing of slavery into the territories.

When Morton returned to Indiana, political feeling was running high in his own county. On March 1 a Republican mass meeting was held at Milton. His old friend Othniel Beeson presided. At the request of the meeting, Morton addressed the audience in a two hours' speech, insisting that the present sectional strife and the discord and murders in Kansas were the legitimate fruits of the repeal of the time-honored compact of 1820. He appealed to moderate men and patriots of all parties to make common cause in restoring to liberty the territories which, by a solemn compact of the fathers, had been pledged to it forever.

CHAPTER V

MORTON had been coming rapidly to the front in the new party of freedom. He was now one of its leaders, and it was not strange that his friends in the eastern part of the state should cast their eyes upon him as the best man to carry their standard in the coming campaign. As early as the fall of 1855 he was spoken of as the candidate for Governor. The Brookville *American*, a paper published in a little town some twenty-five miles south of Centreville, set forth his qualifications in no stinted phrase. In his own county he soon found an advocate in the "Richmond *Palladium.*" He appears to have been much talked of, but for some reason he did not at first want the nomination, and we find in the Indianapolis *Journal* of January 30, 1856, a statement authorized by him that he would not be a candidate under any circumstances. But this did not end the matter. At the meeting of Republicans in Richmond, on February 18, when he was sent as a delegate to the Pittsburgh convention, it was unanimously resolved to support him as a candidate for Governor at the People's convention in May.

Meanwhile the Democrats had met at Indianapolis on the historic "8th of January" and adopted a platform approving the Kansas-Nebraska bill, condemning "secret political orders," opposing all prohibitory legislation and favoring that policy which would soonest assimilate naturalized citizens with the mass of our people.

Ashbel P. Willard was nominated for Governor. Willard

was born October 31, 1820, in Oneida county, New York, and educated at Hamilton college; he studied law, and settled in Indiana about 1844. In 1850 he was elected to the legislature, where he became chairman of the Committee of Ways and Means and leader of the House. His manner and address were captivating, and so popular was he in his party that in 1852, when Joseph A. Wright was nominated for Governor, Willard became candidate for Lieutenant-governor and was elected. As president of the Senate he was courteous, prompt, a warm partisan, not over-scrupulous.

The "People's Party" met in convention on the 1st of May. Morton's candidacy had not been discussed until a day or two before the meeting. Indeed it was not until that time that he had decided to take the nomination. It was believed that he was the man demanded by the necessities of the occasion. He was able, conservative, popular, and had been a Democrat. It would not do to nominate a man who was too radical in his anti-slavery views. Such a candidate would drive away many to whom the name of "abolitionist" was full of terrors. There would not be much trouble, it was thought, in securing the adhesion of Whigs, Free-soilers and Americans. These had nowhere else to go. The main point was to get as many Democratic votes as possible, for, in spite of the election of 1854, Indiana was still a Democratic state. And who could do this better than one who had been a lifelong Democrat, and who, seeing the iniquity of the present course of his party on the slavery question, would persuade others by the same arguments that had satisfied himself? Among such men Morton was easily the chief.

When the convention met, there were no other candidates. Immediately after the permanent organization had been formed and the convention had listened to a speech from the president, Henry S. Lane, it was moved that Morton be nominated for Governor by acclamation. The motion was received with long-continued cheers. When they subsided calls for Morton were made, but it was suggested that the question had not been put. The president declared that the "ayes had a majority by what had been said," and it was carried by general consent. In the afternoon session, Morton was called upon, and spoke of the necessity for the immediate and unconditional admission of Kansas as a free state. He would not interfere with slavery where it was, but would resist its extension into free territory.

Scarcely had the nominations been made, when Willard, who had great confidence in his own powers as an extemporaneous speaker, sought to force a joint discussion. On the very day of the convention, bringing a witness with him, he gave Morton a written invitation to a conference to make arrangements for such joint debate. Morton answered that he could not begin his canvass regularly until about the first of July, that he would then make the arrangements that Willard desired, and that whatever time he could spare before that, he would use in visiting places were Willard had already spoken. But on May 15, long before the time named, Willard, who had an engagement to speak at Centreville, after his arrival in that town, asked Morton to speak with him at the meeting. Morton accepted the invitation. This was the first of the series of meetings which they held together. The description given at this time of Willard and his oratory from the two standpoints of Republicanism and Democracy are such that no one could recognize the portrait as the same. With the Democrats he was the "young man eloquent," "the Clay of Indiana," while to the Republicans he was the type of bombastic assertion and empty declamation—"the greatest roarer of the age."[1]

---

[1] McDonald says of him, "He was the best stump speaker I ever knew," while in Republican papers he was described as "A sort of pioneer beau, arrogant and impudent, ignorant and garrulous, eloquent and the pride of his party."

The *Western Democratic Review* had called him "the best popular

The descriptions of Morton were just as varied as those of Willard. The *Sentinel* declares him to be "dull and of limited ability." Democratic speakers, when they showed that Willard's record was "fair, unequivocal, consistent and natural" declared that "that of his Black Republican opponent Morton was as begrimed as Othello's visage." In what particulars this was the case does not appear.

The fact is, both these candidates were remarkable men, and of decided ability, though of a different kind. They were both very young to be aspirants to the Governorship. Willard was not yet thirty-six, and Morton was not thirty-three. Both had been poor boys, yet each had succeeded in acquiring something of a college education; both had studied law; they had both grown up in the Democracy of Jefferson and Jackson; they had both supported Polk and Cass and Pierce, and believed in the compromises of 1850; they were both zealous partisans, popular and of inspiring presence.

But here the resemblance ends. In other matters they were wide apart. Willard was an eastern man, a political adventurer. Morton was a son of the soil. Willard was convivial, and many are the stories of his prowess at drinking bouts. Morton, while not a total abstainer, was extremely temperate. Willard was the Democratic politician, right or wrong, Morton became a Republican because his convictions had made him one. Willard appealed to passion, imagination and prejudice, Morton, to the intellect and conscience. Willard was the stump speaker, Morton the logician. Willard could talk with equal fluency on any subject, anywhere and at any moment, Morton could not talk at all unless he had something to say, and when he had, few men could speak more to the purpose. Willard loaded his speeches with gro-

---

orator in the United States," while B. R. Sulgrove says, "Willard was to Morton about like a fluff of goose-down to a storm of sleet, it might smother for a moment, but it couldn't cut or hurt, he was a perennial spring of words, *vox et praeterea nihil.*"

tesque ornamentation, Morton used none. Willard indulged much in ridicule, invective and personality, Morton abstained from these. Willard was rapid, fluent, diffuse, discursive; Morton was measured, strong, compact, and he talked always to the point. Willard was impetuous and violent, Morton was slower, always self-contained, and had greater reserve power. Willard had more forensic experience, Morton had to depend solely upon his native ability. In appearance, voice and gesture they differed as much as in their mental qualities. Willard had a head and face cast in a fine mould, florid, with blue eyes, auburn hair and open countenance. Morton was pale, huge, massive, more reserved, with a lofty forehead, dark eyes and black hair. Willard's voice was loud, high and clear, Morton's was strong, full and deep. Willard's gesticulation was like his speech, energetic, sometimes violent, Morton's gestures were few, not graceful, but earnest and impressive. Willard's manner was triumphant and often arrogant. He could utter trifles in such a way as to persuade his hearers that he had won a victory. Morton relied more upon the thought and matter of his speech than upon the mere incidents of language, voice and gesture. "His speeches were rather a quarry than a building."

Willard was not unacquainted with Wayne county. He had visited Centreville in 1852 when he had been a candidate for Lieutenant-governor. The people had not forgotten how vigorously he had harangued them, how he had thrown off his coat and disclosed through his open shirt front a shaggy breast. The audience which now gathered at his meeting was not very large, not so large as it would have been had it been known that Morton and Willard were to meet in joint discussion. Willard seems to have prepared for the occasion. He had on hand a number of questions to propound to Morton. Morton learned of the debate for the first time after Willard's arrival. Willard had both the opening and the close. Yet Morton was on his own ground, in his own community, among

his friends, and he seems to have more than held his own.
" Jasper," the correspondent of the *Palladium* (Republican),
tells us that Willard insisted that the Free State movement in
Kansas was rebellion against the government—yet that
in almost the same breath he argued that the people of Kansas should be allowed to make their own laws without interference by Congress.   Among the questions propounded by
Willard to Morton, there was one asking whether he regarded
the Fugitive Slave Law as unconstitutional, and, if elected,
whether he would execute it?   Morton answered that to him
the law was odious; that if the question were a new one, he
would be inclined to adopt the opinion of Webster, that
the power to enact such a law belonged to the states and not
to the general government—but that the long practice of the
government and the decisions of the courts had settled the
question in favor of its constitutionality.   Morton, in his
answer to Willard, was calm and dispassionate.   He said that
the present canvass was to decide whether the people of Indiana were in favor of the extension of slavery.   For himself
he agreed with the prevailing sentiment throughout the North
and took strong ground against consigning any free territory
to the system of African bondage.

As the campaign went on, the civil war in Kansas, the sack
and burning of Lawrence by Missouri free-booters, the brutal
attack of Brooks upon Sumner in the Senate chamber, had
aroused the indignation of the North.   Early in June, Buchanan
became the Democratic candidate upon a platform sustaining
the Kansas-Nebraska bill.   On the 17th of that month, Fremont was nominated by the Republican convention.   The
resolutions declared it the duty of Congress to prohibit slavery
and polygamy in the territories, and demanded the admission
of Kansas as a free state.

Morton and Willard met a second time at Newcastle on the
12th of June, where, as the Republicans claimed, "Willard
was completely unhorsed and discomfited."   Just before they

entered upon this discussion, Morton asked Willard to make
some joint appointments for July. Willard declined to do
this, but said that in August it could be arranged. Morton answered that he had several appointments made, that he
must review his engagements to avoid a conflict, and he understood Willard to say distinctly that he was in a like situation. After the discussion, Willard left the town, and, two
days later, an editorial appeared in the *Sentinel*, purporting to
give an account of the meeting at Newcastle, declaring that
Morton was no match for Willard, and had refused to canvass
the state with him. Morton believed that Willard had inspired
this statement.

Morton continued his canvass through the southern part of
the state, speaking nearly every day. On his return home,
near the end of June, he found letters informing him that
Willard had declared at Gosport and other places that Morton
had refused to make a joint canvass. So he addressed to
Willard a note proposing appointments for joint discussion,
and the bearer of the note (Mr. Defrees) was authorized to
arrange times and places. A speedy answer was requested.
Willard did not send an answer, but informed Defrees that he
had appointments out until the 9th of August, and that he
could not hold any joint discussions before that time. Further
engagements were then made for Morton, terminating at
Bloomington on August 7.

On the 16th of July Morton met Willard and Defrees at
Indianapolis, and the subject of appointments was again discussed. It was agreed that Willard and Defrees should meet
and arrange times and places, but Willard left the city without seeing Defrees. Some fourteen days passed. The Republican committee proceeded to make another list of appointments for Morton. Willard, on learning of this, published a card giving the impression that Morton had declined
to meet him, yet professing to believe that these last appointments had been made for both, and complaining that they

had been made without consulting him.   He then announced
meetings for himself at the same times and places.   Morton,
on August 9, answered by a card in the *Journal*, giving a suc-
cinct statement as to the appointments, and adding, ''Why
they were made without consulting him no one knows so well
as himself, and that they were not made for him is clear from
the fact that the persons making them had no authority whatever to act for him.''

A card from Defrees corroborated Morton's account.   But
Willard determined to follow up Morton's appointments and
make him all the trouble possible.

Willard first went to Bloomington, where Morton had an
appointment on August 7, and he caused hand-bills to be
posted as follows: ''Both Parties Present.   Hon. Ashbel
P. Willard, Democratic candidate for Governor; Hon. James
Hughes, Democratic candidate for Congress, will be present
at the appointment of Messrs. Morton and Hendricks, in
Bloomington, August 7, and participate in the discussion, if
agreeable to Messrs. Morton and Hendricks.   Turn out and
hear both sides.''   And on the day of the appointment Willard wrote Morton the following letter:

DEAR SIR—I desire to address my fellow-citizens, who will assemble
here to-day, and to discuss with you the questions submitted to their decision. As to the time you shall occupy, I am satisfied with the arrangement made at Newcastle. An early answer is requested.

A. P. WILLARD.

To which Morton replied:

DEAR SIR—Your note is received and its contents noted. An appointment was made several weeks ago for Mr. Hendricks, candidate for Congress, and myself, at this place, to begin at one o'clock this afternoon. I
can not accept your proposition to divide the time without cutting off Mr.
Hendricks' speech, a thing I have no right to do, and against which I
protest. The central committee of this county, in whose hands the arrangement of the meeting has been, remonstrate against your proposition,
regarding it as being, under the circumstances, highly improper.

That I am and have been at all times ready to meet you since I commenced the canvass you are well aware, and I would do so to-day gladly were the matter left to me, or did it concern me only.

O. P. MORTON.

Willard and Hughes, however, were present, and insisted upon participating in the discussion.

After the meeting commenced Hughes repeatedly interrupted Morton with questions during his speech. Morton answered several of these, but, finding they did not stop, he declined to allow further interruption. Hughes thereupon rose and called upon the Democrats to leave the meeting. A number followed him out and gathered at a neighboring corner, where Hughes harangued them, followed by Willard. The *Journal* declared that the purpose of Willard was to annoy the Republicans with the noise, and added: "He succeeded in this, for in the production of noise he has no equal short of a steam whistle or a pig under a gate, and his crowd helped him."

Willard could not, however, destroy the effect of Morton's speech. It made a powerful impression. Mr. John W. Foster,[1] who then heard him for the first time, thus describes him. "He was in the full strength of his young manhood, with a magnificent physique and a mind trained by the study and practice of the law, and he had warmly espoused the cause of the Republican party, which was fighting its first battle. His earnest defense of freedom in the territories against the encroachments of the slave power is still fresh in my memory; and I estimate very highly the influence of his services in that campaign in moulding the sentiments of the young men of the state, who five years later so heartily responded to his call to defend the life of the nation."

On the 15th of August, Morton began, at Corydon, the other series of appointments which had been arranged for

---

[1] Afterwards United States Minister to Mexico, Russia and Spain, mediator between China and Japan, and Secretary of State under President Harrison.

him by the state committee. Corydon had been the old capital of the state in its pioneer days. It was then a rural town near the Ohio, quite remote from railroads, and was the county seat of the conservative and Democratic county of Harrison.

From three to four thousand persons were assembled. A procession was formed in the public square and marched to a grove three-fourths of a mile east of the village. Godlove S. Orth, who was present with Morton, spoke first. After he had been speaking three-quarters of an hour Willard appeared in front of the stand and said that he had come there for the purpose of discussing public questions with his competitor, and desired to know whether he could be heard. Orth told him that that was a question for him and Morton to decide. Morton arose and related his proposition to Willard and the conference with Defrees, and said that, inasmuch as Willard had failed to keep the engagement, he did not feel at liberty to yield farther. Willard replied that he could not discuss the matter of engagements then; that he would present it to the people in his own way. He then turned to the audience and said that as many of them as wished to hear him speak would repair to the court-house. The Old Liners cried out, "To the court-house! To the court-house!" when a small squadron, perhaps a hundred, arose and followed their candidate, and those remaining raised a great cheer for Morton.

Willard was soon accommodated with a joint discussion. At Leavenworth Morton debated with him, and the two candidates now began to hold discussions quite regularly.

We have no complete report of any of these debates. There are many now living, however, who remember the general impression they produced. Alvin P. Hovey, who afterwards became Governor of Indiana, was present at the debate at North Vernon, "down in the Pocket." He was a leading Democrat of that town, and Willard stopped at his house. His sympathies were with Willard, whom he regarded as the better stump-speaker, while he considered Morton the more logical debater. Willard on that occasion compared the Democracy to a full-rigged man-of-war, and contrasted it with the Republican party, a black-hulled piratical brig.

The joint debates continued for some time; we have an account of one at Spencer, in Owen county, as late as September 18. Each of the candidates also had appointments alone. We hear of Morton at a barbecue at Shelbyville, a place which has become the home of the barbecue in Indiana. He was present and spoke at the Republican rally at Indianapolis, on the evening of October 13.

Morton, as the campaign advanced, grew very confident of success. He believed that the bad faith of the Kansas-Nebraska bill, the outrages upon the free-state settlers, the attack upon Sumner in the Senate chamber, and the intemperance of the advocates of slavery, would be too heavy a burden for the Democracy to carry. His son John, then a boy of ten years of age, can remember his father holding him on his lap or trotting him on his knee singing the refrain:

> " Buck and Breck, neck and neck,
>   Go along so slow,
>   A-tugging at the Kansas load,
>   Whoa-ho, whoa-ho, whoa-ho."

Morton, who had not then had much experience in the details of politics, took the statements of the Republican committeemen with less allowance than he should have done, and made estimates that he "would come down to the National road from the North" with a majority which Willard could not counterbalance in the South. After the ballots were counted, and it was found that Willard had been elected by a majority of about six thousand, Morton was much disappointed. He was in Cincinnati, and came to the office of the *Commercial* to learn the result. He was worn out with the campaign, and as the adverse news came in, he sat down in a chair, greatly discouraged, and said to Murat Halstead that he was through with politics and was going back to the law for good. The Democrats naturally did a good deal of crowing, while the Republicans began to find evidence of frauds and illegal voting. Day after day the papers were filled with the details of importations of voters and other evidences of corruption.

It is very certain that such importations of voters took place, but whether they were extensive enough to change the out-come of the election is more than doubtful. The Democratic party was, under ordinary conditions, the stronger in Indiana. Willard was personally popular, and there was no cause for surprise at the result. Yet Morton received more votes than any other candidate of his party. When the presidential election came on in November, Buchanan's plurality in the state was not far from 20,000, showing how much stronger Morton was than the Republican National ticket, and how well he succeeded in keeping the conservative and the "American" vote. In this campaign, indeed, Morton had organized the Republican party in Indiana. Up to this time it had been an inchoate combination of the elements opposed to the pro-slavery Democracy. It was now a compact body, whose purposes were definite, a party well equipped for political warfare.

Nothing came of a contest which the Republican committee promised to make before the legislature. Morton was defeated. But in that future which he could not see, this defeat became a blessing. He was reserved for greater things. Had he been elected in this campaign with Willard, he could not have become the great War Governor. The constitution of Indiana does not permit successive elections to the Governorship. What changes might have happened, not only to the state, but to the fortunes of the Union arms, had Morton in his first campaign obtained the object of his desires!

CHAPTER VI

BUCHANAN was elected, yet the Republicans were as full of spirit as though they had won the victory. Morton's own depression passed away, and we soon find him as active in politics as ever. He reflected the prevailing sentiment when, on the 7th of January, having been called to preside at a meeting of Republicans in the hall of the House of Representatives, he expressed his satisfaction that the party possessed so much vitality, and his hope that Kansas would come into the Union free, followed by other territories. Then the pernicious idea of preserving the balance of power between the free and slave states would be destroyed. While the South agitated that subject, there could be no peace. "Our creed," he said, "is plain. We do not assail slavery where it exists entrenched behind legal enactments, but whenever it sallies forth, we are pledged to meet it as an enemy of mankind."

In 1855 the state Senate had been a tie, and a majority of the House of Representatives had belonged to the People's party. A United States senator was to have been elected, and Joseph G. Marshall was the candidate of the party. By Willard's casting vote the Senate had refused to go into joint session, so no election had been held. There had not been sufficient justification for this arbitrary act.

In 1857 the position of the two parties was reversed. The Democrats controlled the House, and would have a majority on joint ballot, while the Republicans held the Senate. There were two United States senators to be elected. The Republicans contended that one of these was their property, of which they had been defrauded two years before, and they naturally showed a disposition to retaliate. So this Republican meeting of January 7 resolved that the Senate was under no obligation to elect by joint convention. Bright and Fitch had been nominated by the Democratic caucus. But the Republican Senate refused to meet the House. This was the identical way in which Willard had prevented the election of Marshall. But Willard was a better Democrat than logician. The theory was put forth that, inasmuch as there had been a joint convention for another purpose, a majority of the members of the legislature could meet on the day to which that convention had adjourned and elect Bright and Fitch whether the Senate consented or not. Willard declared in a Democratic caucus that if a majority of the legislature met in joint session and elected Bright and Fitch he would commission them, and the Senate of the United States would not refuse to receive one whose commission bore the great seal of Indiana. Amid much enthusiasm this course was adopted. Bright and Fitch received their commissions and held their seats.

Among the Democratic members of the state Senate was Leroy Woods, who had been appointed by Governor Wright " Moral Instructor of the Penitentiary," with a salary of six hundred dollars. He had accepted the office. By this act he had forfeited his senatorship. But he still held his seat and helped the movement for the joint convention. The Republicans wanted him out of the way. The committee on elections, of which John R. Cravens was chairman, had reported against Woods with a resolution declaring his seat vacant, but the Democrats could prevent his removal by breaking up the two-thirds quorum required by the Indiana constitution. This was the state of things when Morton came over from Richmond one day, and Sulgrove, editor of the *Journal*, explained to him the situation. Morton replied: " When the Democratic senators and the president of the

Senate go out to attend their convention in the hall of the House, what is to hinder the Republican majority left behind in the Senate chamber from going on with business? They have not voted an adjournment, and the minority has no right to do so. The Republicans are then the Senate. Suppose, when the Democrats are out they put one of their men in the chair and adopt the resolution declaring Woods' seat vacant by consent, so that no record of yeas and nays will appear, will not Woods be ousted for good and all?'' Sulgrove agreed and spoke of the matter to Senator Cravens, who fell in with the plan. The Democrats went to the joint convention at the appointed time. Lewis Burke, of Wayne, was put in the chair, and Woods was ousted, just as the Democrats came back raging, but too late to save their man.

After Buchanan was inaugurated, and while he was attempting to force the Lecompton constitution upon the people of Kansas, Morton was engaged in an active and lucrative law practice at Centreville. But he still found opportunities to speak on political subjects in various parts of the state.

On March 4 the Republican convention was held for the nomination of state officers. Morton was chosen president. George W. Julian, Morton's fellow-townsman, was strongly opposed to the conservative policy adopted by Indiana Republicans in the organization of the party. Julian was an abolitionist who had done valuable work in the early days of the anti-slavery agitation. He had served one term in Congress, from 1849 to 1851, and was afterwards defeated. He had been a candidate for Vice-President upon the Free-soil ticket in 1852. He was radical, able, eloquent, and uncompromising toward all who differed from his way of thinking. When Morton withdrew from the Democratic party Julian considered him too ''conservative'' for full ''fellowship with the faithful.'' Julian also denounced Know-nothings in the bitterest invective, and did not want them in the Republican party. Even the anti-Nebraska allies were hardly welcome, for they merely ''hated slavery territorially,'' and had been willing to protect it, not only within the states but south of the line drawn by the Missouri Compromise.   Morton, more moderate, more recently awakened to the dangers to be feared from the slave power, more practical in his remedy, would unite and strengthen all opposing elements.   Julian did not like the influence which Morton had acquired in the new party.   Clad in the armor of "principle" and "robust hatred of slavery," he sharply criticised, not the enemy alone, but many of those who were working in the same cause with himself.   He had considered the time of the repeal of the Missouri Compromise as a " season of hopeful chaos, promising new and higher political creations if wise counsels had prevailed," but as it was, " it only furnished valuable lessons for our guidance."   He had been opposed to Morton's candidacy in 1856, and though he had taken the stump for Morton, in the campaign against Willard, he afterwards spoke of the ticket as " a combination of weaknesses, instead of a union of forces."

On July 4, 1857, in a speech at Raysville, he declared that the People's party had been "conceived in mere policy and lust for office, and managed by unbelieving politicians, and that cowardice was stamped upon its features."   He did not regret Morton's defeat in 1856, for he said: "Had the slippery tactics of our leaders received the premium of a victory it would have been far more disastrous in its influence hereafter than merited defeat, which may even bless us as a timely reproof for our unfaithfulness."

Julian had come with his radical friends to this 4th of March convention to reform the party according to their own ideas.   Indiana was still behind many of her eastern sisters in anti-slavery sentiment.   Morton would go as far as all could safely go together, but the party should not be broken up for the sake of advocating advanced views.   He knew the differences which were likely to arise.   On taking the chair he made a speech counseling a spirit of harmony.   "It is idle to expect that what we do will be what everybody wants. Such a convention as that was never held. There are diversities of opinion as to the platform and as to the candidates, but whatever these differences are, I hope that when a candidate is nominated every man in the convention will consider that his own act." He then spoke at length of the changing phases of politics, produced by the gradual aggressions of slavery. One question after another had been swallowed up, until at last there was no other issue before the country. The pro-slavery party had taken every foot of territory from the north. Mr. Buchanan had said that Kansas was as much a slave state as Georgia, and if that were so, then Nebraska and Washington were equally surrendered to slavery, and there was no free territory in the Union.

The convention adopted a rule common in political bodies, that all resolutions, when introduced, should be referred to the platform committee without debate, and this was accordingly done. When the committee reported, Mr. Julian asked for an explicit re-affirmation of the platform of the Fremont convention at Philadelphia, which had denied the power of Congress or of a territorial legislature to legalize slavery in any territory, and had affirmed the duty of Congress to prohibit it. Morton ruled that, as these things had not been referred to the platform committee, Julian's motion was not in order. An appeal was taken from Morton's ruling. A motion was made to lay the appeal upon the table. This cut off debate, and the motion was carried amid considerable confusion. Julian declared that Morton's rulings were an attempt "to gag all opposition to the platform," and, after the appeal was sustained, he attacked the platform and the proceedings with great severity. Morton called one of the vice-presidents to the chair, took the floor and proceeded to reply. He declared that in so far as his conduct had been arraigned by Mr. Julian, he had nothing to say. The convention had made a rule and he was bound to enforce it; he had done nothing more. Objection had been made to the platform because it did not re-affirm the words of the Philadelphia resolutions. If it declared the substance, that was enough. "These men who insist on having a platform express to the very letter all that they believe, and refuse otherwise to support the party, are very much such persons as the clergyman who had to have a prayer exactly fitted to the case or he could not pray at all. He was sent for by the family of a man who had been bitten by a rattlesnake and was dying. He examined his prayer-book, but finding no form appropriate to this calamity the unfortunate victim had to die unaided by his ministrations. Now, the men who met at Philadelphia made their own platform. They were men of sense. They did not hunt for a form in some platform of 1854 or 1852, but they made just such a one as suited their present case, and why should not we do so too?" Morton's speech settled the matter, and the resolutions reported by the committee were adopted "with a great shout."

Morton was, as we have seen, a strong believer in the policy of the extension of territory. After it had become reasonably certain that Kansas would come into the Union as a free state, he was standing one day in his law office at Centreville, looking at a large map of the United States which hung upon the wall. He was examining carefully the Mexican states to the south, and studying their names. "Kibbey," said he to his partner, "if Kansas and Nebraska come in as free states the other territories will be free, too, and the present issue between the Republican and Democratic parties will be over. Now we have a new party and we must have a living issue. The Democratic party has always been the champion of the extension of territory, and I think the Republicans ought to be ahead of them in advocating the acquisition of Mexico." Morton began to prepare a speech upon this question. But the South would not stand idly by and see her supremacy in the territories slip away without a struggle. Her new aggressions and demands kept the old question alive, and pushed aside all other matters. So Morton's speech on Mexican annexation was never delivered.

CHAPTER VII

THE CAMPAIGN OF 1860

As the presidential election drew near, the outlook for the Republican party grew brighter. The feeling in the North was very strong against Buchanan's doctrine that the territories were consigned to slavery by the constitution. The harsh provisions of the fugitive slave law were brought home to the people by circumstances of peculiar atrocity which sometimes attended the enforcement of those provisions. There had been much mismanagement and peculation, and Congress had refused to provide a remedy. Moreover, the quarrels between the two factions of the Democratic party were fruitful of bright hopes for its adversaries.

Although the Douglas wing had the upper-hand in Indiana, the administration had many friends. Foremost among these was Jesse D. Bright, who had been the imperious leader of the Indiana Democracy for a score of years. Douglas had voted against the claim of Bright to a contested seat in the Senate, and Bright, a man who never forgot friend or foe, himself a slaveholder and a friend of the slave-power, took part with the Buchanan wing of the party against Douglas. Governor Willard, too, during the few months of life that were left him (he fell ill in the summer of 1860 and died in October), Dr. Athon, auditor of state, Cyrus L. Dunham, secretary of state, and John L. Robinson, United States marshal for Indiana, were all active in behalf of the administration.

Thomas A. Hendricks, a Douglas man, was nominated for governor, and David Turpie for lieutenant-governor. Hendricks was a man of ability, non-committal, skillful, adroit. Turpie was a young man of brilliant parts, fertile in thought and eloquent in speech.   But although there was a nominal reconciliation of the factions of the Democratic party, and although both supported the state ticket, the spirit of harmony was not there.   After Breckinridge had been nominated for the presidency at Baltimore, Bright organized a separate state convention, which nominated Breckinridge electors. Victory could not follow such divided counsels.

As the time drew near for the Republicans to make their nominations, there were two men toward whom all attention was directed.   Henry S. Lane was the most distinguished man among those who had come from the Old Line Whigs, and Oliver P. Morton, among those who were of Democratic extraction.   Morton having been the candidate for Governor four years before, it was natural that the first thought of the party should be directed toward him.   A number of county conventions had instructed their delegates to vote for him. Morton undoubtedly expected the nomination.   But certain supposed considerations of expediency finally turned the sentiment in favor of Lane.   Friends of both candidates proposed the following arrangement; if the Republicans carried the legislature, Lane should go to the Senate, and Morton would then succeed to the office of Governor.   But this plan was not satisfactory to Morton.   He would rather go to the Senate himself than become Governor, and if he took the lower place on the ticket, ought he not to have the choice? But it was determined otherwise, possibly for the reason once given in homely phrase by one of his Wayne county supporters, a prominent member of the Society of Friends, to whom Morton had stated what he preferred: " Oliver, we can't let thee go to the Senate."   "Why not ? " asked Morton.   " Because thee is a good man for either of these places, and Henry Lane would make a good Senator but he would not make a good Governor.   So he must go to the

Senate and thee must stay and be Governor.'' Morton at last determined to make the sacrifice, for such it then seemed to be. He would be loyal to the party whose cause he had made his own. His claims should not stand in the way of its success.

The state convention assembled. There was a great throng outside the hall, unable to gain admission, and the meeting adjourned to the state-house yard, where an immense audience collected. Mr. Meredith, of Wayne county, moved that the convention nominate by acclamation Colonel Henry S. Lane for Governor. Thomas H. Nelson, of Vigo, moved to amend. There was, he said, one who had championed the Republican movement in its infancy, and of whose ability and manliness all had grateful recollection, whom he desired to nominate for the second place. It was not the place his friends had wished for him, but it was a place where he could serve the cause, and Mr. Nelson believed he would accept the nomination. If he would do so, it would be the most chivalrous act of his career, and would endear him still more to the party that esteemed him so highly. He begged to nominate for Lieutenant-governor Oliver P. Morton. Mr. Meredith accepted the amendment, and the proposal was unanimously adopted.

This nomination to the second place was undoubtedly a disappointment to Morton. Could he have looked into the future and seen the career which it opened to him, he would have valued it more highly than even that senatorship which he was not to have for the very reason that his abilities fitted him for either place.

Morton's acceptance was appreciated by his party, but it exposed him to the satire of the enemy. ''His love of his country,'' said the Rushville *Jacksonian*, '' is so irrepressible that he will serve it in the capacity of town constable.''

Morton soon began his work in the campaign. On March 10, he delivered, at a ratification meeting in Terre Haute, a carefully prepared address. Without any introduction he plunged into the midst of his argument. Popular sovereignty, he said, was the right of the people of a territory to form and regulate their domestic institutions in their own way; it was the right of self-government. If this right existed, it was inherent, not derived from the constitution. If the people of a territory had the right of self-government, they had the right to choose their form of government and to organize and inaugurate it. They had the right to elect their legislature, Governor, judges and all officers of state; and Congress had no power to provide for them a form of government through the medium of the Nebraska bill or otherwise. Thus the territories, instead of being mere dependencies of the general government, in a state of pupilage and preparation for admission to the Union, would be absolute and independent sovereignties, having rights and powers greatly exceeding those of the states.

But if the other view of the constitution were adopted— that view which had received the sanction of all parties, congresses, legislatures and courts, for more than fifty years— these difficulties were swept away. That view regarded the territories as dependencies, to be governed, trained and prepared for admission into the Union as states.

To the charge of "sectionalism" made against the Republican party, he answered that a sectional party was a party which sought to promote the interest of one section regardless of all others. The residence of the members of a party had little to do in determining its character. The religion of our Savior could not be termed sectional, even while its professors were limited to Jews, for its spirit comprehended humanity everywhere. The great principle of the Republican party was the preservation of the territories to freedom and the protection and elevation of free labor. Surely a purpose so beneficent could not be either selfish or sectional. It comprehended the highest interests of those living in the slave states, as well as of the people of the free states. There was but a small minority of the inhabitants of the slave states who were really interested in the preservation and enlargement of the institution of slavery, an institution which rested as a crushing incubus upon the prosperity of these states. Our country was one and our people were one, and any damage suffered by one portion was an injury inflicted upon the body of the nation. Tried by this test, the Democratic party was even less than sectional, for its purpose was the promotion of the special interests of the minority in one section, to the manifest injury of the majority in the same section. The number of slave-holders would not exceed one-twelfth of the free white population of the slave states, yet by their wealth, their intelligence and their monopoly of capital, they were enabled to govern the majority of non-slave-holders by whom they were surrounded, to direct the policy of the Democratic party and aspire to the government of the United States. The fact that the Republican party was not permitted to organize, that Republican presses were not permitted to publish, nor Republican speakers to speak, in many Southern states, proved nothing but the existence of a despotic power wielded by the minority. As well might the sectional character of the Christian religion be proved by the persecution and expulsion of the primitive Christians from Rome, as the sectional character of the Republican party, by the absence of that party from the South.

Morton maintained that the Republican party, and not the Democratic party, was true to the early traditions of the nation. "In politics," he said, "conservatism is an adherence to old opinions, doctrines and expositions of policy or constitutional law; it is opposed to innovations, novel doctrines and new fangled theories; it prefers the known to the unknown, the tried to the untried, and chooses rather to walk by the light of experience than to pursue the chimeras of speculation. If it can be shown that the Republican policy of oppo-

sition to the general diffusion of slavery, of the preservation of the territories to freedom, and of the protection and
elevation of free labor, is coeval with and antecedent to the
adoption of our constitution, that it was the recognized policy
of the government for more than half a century, that it was
the faith of Washington and religion of Jefferson, that it was
woven into judicial action and legislation, and was the common creed and property of all parties until within a few years
past—then its claim to conservatism is fully established.
Measured by this standard, the Democratic party will be
found to be radical, revolutionary and subversive. Departing from its own creed, revolutionizing a long course of
judicial decisions and subverting the practice of the government, it has erected into an article of faith the new, dangerous and portentous dogma, that the constitution, by its own
inherent power, establishes slavery in all the territories, and
that there is no power in Congress nor in the people of the
territories, or, to use the language of Mr. Buchanan, in his
late message, that there is no 'human power' that can exclude it therefrom; that the many acts of Congress, beginning in 1789 and continuing until 1848 prohibiting slavery
in the territories, were unconstitutional and void; and the
many judicial decisions of the state and federal courts recognizing the power of Congress to provide such legislation
sprang from gross and ill-considered views of the Federal constitution. Especially is this new dogma dangerous and portentous when we reflect that it drags after it as an inevitable
consequence, just as the locomotive draws the train, that other
dogma, that the constitution also carries slavery into all the
states, and that no 'human power' can exclude it therefrom,
and that it looks to the fulfillment of the prophecy made by
Senator Toombs, that he would live to see the time when he
could call the roll of his slaves beneath the shadow of the
monument of Bunker Hill.''

Morton maintained that the agitation of the slavery question was traceable to the deliberate breach of a time-honored compromise which had had its origin in a critical period of our political history, and which had given peace to the Union.

"The President, in his late message," continued Morton, "congratulates the country on the final settlement of the slavery question by the decision of the Supreme Court of the United States in the Dred Scott case. He forgets that the Democratic party has taught the country that constitutional questions are never settled. The Dred Scott decision has simply unsettled what had been regarded as settled for more than fifty years. The Missouri Compromise was thought to be settled for more than thirty years, but it was repealed by the Nebraska bill. It is now idle to talk about the settlement of anything until it shall be done on correct principles. Five slave-holders sitting on the bench of the Supreme Court can not settle forever vital questions of freedom against eighteen millions of people in the free states. In the course of a few years, these judges will have passed away, to stand at the bar of another tribunal, whose decisions are final, and their places will be filled by new men, who will have the same right to review their opinions that they had to trample upon the opinions of all who had gone before them. . . .

"It is a matter of proud congratulation that there is not one disunionist within the pale of the Republican party. There is no part of the Republican platform upon which a disunionist can stand. While the disunion fanatics of the North are bitter foes and denouncers of the Republican party, the disunion fanatics of the South are members of the Democratic party, and not only so, but they are members in good standing, occupying its highest places of honor, directing its councils and manufacturing its platforms. Some of these already declare that the Union is a forlorn hope; others, that it can only be preserved upon the contingencies which are not likely to happen, and many, that the election of a Republican President by a majority of the people of the

United States, in the mode prescribed by the constitution, would be just cause for the dissolution of the Union. We do not say that the Union may be preserved upon certain conditions; we do not measure our fidelity to it by our success, but we say, 'It must and shall be preserved,' whatever party may be in the ascendant. We do not say the Republican party first and the Union afterward, but we say the Union first, last and all the time, and that we will wage uncompromising warfare upon all parties that contemplate its destruction.''

To the charge of being an abolitionist he thus replied:

. . . . ''I am opposed to the diffusion of slavery. I am in favor of preserving the territories to freedom, of encouraging, elevating and protecting free labor, at the same time conscientiously believing that with slavery in the several states we have nothing to do, and no right to interfere. If this makes me an abolitionist then I am one, and my political enemies may make the most of it.''

Of the homestead law he said: ''The actual settlers, the hardy pioneers, braving the dangers and submitting to the hardships of the wilderness, are they who erect new states and enlarge the boundaries of our national wealth and power. They are public benefactors, and should not be required to pay tribute for their benefactions. Their homes should be given to them by the nation, upon condition that they improve them and thus add to the aggregate of our national prosperity. It is not important that we have very rich men in this country, but it is important that all have homes and a competence, and be made feel that their country is a nursing mother, whose devotion to their interest and protection of their rights can only be requited by a life of patriotism.''

Here was a political speech, devoid of ornament and meager in illustration, with no introduction, no peroration, with little attempt at arrangement—a naked presentation of the Republican gospel of that day, stating for the

most part things which had been told before. And yet none
the less was it a remarkable speech. Behind every sentence
there was something more than the mere words expressed,
there was the evidence of the speaker's power, of the simple,
massive quality of his mind.

No presidential nominations had yet been made. But it
was not long until the delegates of the parties came together
in their repective national conventions. The Democrats met
first. At Charleston, where pro-slavery feeling was most
extreme, they began their turbulent sessions. The Southern
wing demanded an explicit declaration that neither Congress
nor a territorial legislature could abolish slavery in the territories. The Douglas men were willing to pledge themselves
to carry out the determination of the Supreme Court. That
was as far as they would go. Under the lead of Yancey, the
Southern delegates withdrew and organized a separate body.

The original convention adjourned to meet in Baltimore on
the 18th of June, the seceders to meet at Richmond, Va., on
June 11.

"The Constitutional Union" party held its convention in
Baltimore, and nominated Bell and Everett. It determined to
pursue the impossible course of ignoring the slavery question
and recognizing no other political principles than the constitution, the Union and the enforcement of the laws.

On the 16th of May, the Republican convention met in Chicago. Its proceedings were marked by the most earnest enthusiasm. It was essentially a convention of the free states.
There were delegates from the border, and an imperfect representation from Texas, but none from the body of the cotton
states. No one would risk his life by attending.

There was little difficulty with the platform. The resolutions reported expressed the views of all. "We hold in abhorrence all schemes of disunion." "We denounce the lawless invasion . . . of any state or territory." "The new dogma
that the constitution, by its own force, carries slavery into any

and all of the territories . . . is a dangerous political heresy.'' ''The normal condition of all the territory of the United States is that of freedom.'' ''We deny the authority of Congress, of a territorial legislature, or of any individuals, to give legal existence to slavery in any territory.'' ''We brand the recent reopening of the African slave trade as a crime against humanity.'' Kansas, said the resolutions, should be admitted free. A protective tariff, a homestead law, river and harbor appropriations and Federal aid for a Pacific railroad, were all favored and demanded.

The real contest of the convention was in the nomination of the candidates. Seward was the leader of the party. New York and the greater part of New England were for him. But by many he was thought to be too radical. He had talked of a ''higher law'' than the constitution, of an ''irrepressible conflict'' between slavery and freedom. In the doubtful states, New Jersey, Pennsylvania, Indiana and Illinois, where ''abolitionism'' was still proscribed, it would be dangerous to fight the battle under such leadership. Morton and Lane both united in declaring that Seward's nomination meant a Democratic victory in Indiana. Curtin said the same of Pennsylvania. Gradually the elements opposed to Seward united upon Lincoln. The contest in the North must be against the Douglas wing of the Democracy, and who so able to cope with Douglas as his old opponent in Illinois? So Lincoln was nominated, and a campaign of great enthusiasm was inaugurated in behalf of a candidate whose pure character, kind heart, strong convictions and shrewd good-sense inspired the confidence and won the affection of all. But no one then knew how great a man he would prove to be in the terrible emergency which was approaching.

The Richmond convention adjourned to Baltimore to bring about '' a reconciliation of differences on the basis of principle,'' and the delegates applied for readmission to the Douglas convention. On the fifth day a second crisis came, the convention again divided, and most of the delegates from the slave states went out. Those who remained nominated Douglas, while the seceders chose Breckenridge. Subsequent union became impossible, and the fate of the Democracy was sealed.

It was on June 19, during these dissensions at Baltimore, that Morton began, at Martinsville, Indiana, his series of joint debates with David Turpie, his competitor for the office of Lieutenant-governor. Turpie said, in his opening speech, that the doctrine of popular sovereignty was drawn from the principle that government must be founded upon the consent of the governed. The people of the territories had never consented to be governed by Congress in respect to slavery. The Democratic party had built its political creed upon the doctrine of non-intervention by Congress in the rights of the people, a doctrine ignored in 1820, but re-established in 1850, in the organization of New Mexico and Utah, and subsequently embodied in the Kansas-Nebraska bill. Morton and his political associates had conspired to rob the white man in Kansas and Nebraska of his rights and to confer them upon the negro of Massachusetts. The Democracy said to the fanatics North and South, who demanded congressional action concerning slavery, that they should not be gratified. It rebuked alike the abolitionist and the fire-eater. . . . "Morton," said Turpie, "carried away by the whirlwind of abolition agitation, cries loudly, ' I was once a Democrat,' just as Satan walks the burning marl below and says, ' I once abode in heaven.' "

Morton began his reply by discussing the subject which Turpie had just called the "whirlwind of abolition agitation." He asked: "Who brought it about? Did we not have peace until, with ruthless hands, you laid hold of the compromise of the fathers, and has not the bloodiest page in our history followed as a legitimate result?" Douglas, he said, had offered to slavery the fair plains of the West, without any more right to them than Satan had to the kingdom of the world. The definition which the Democratic party gave of popular sovereignty was illustrated in Nebraska and Kansas, where the people in their territorial legislatures had prohibited slavery, and Democratic governors had vetoed the prohibition.

"Will Mr. Turpie, who has such faith in the consent of the governed, inform us whether the people of the territories have the right to exclude slavery? If the slave-holder has the right to go there and hold his slaves he is entitled to protection in the enjoyment of his property. I deny the right. If the right exists, fair dealing requires that it be protected. The territories belong to the Union and not to any class. They are to be governed for the common good of the whole nation. If the Federal constitution takes slavery into them, and authorizes the holding of slaves there, while they remain territories, will it not equally authorize slavery after they have become states?"

On the following day Morton and Turpie spoke at Nashville, in Brown county, a Democratic stronghold, in a primitive neighborhood far removed from railroad communications. Here Morton had the opening and close. He read letters written some years before by Joseph E. McDonald and other prominent Democrats, showing that the Democratic party had then been in favor of the Wilmot Proviso, excluding slavery from the territory purchased of Mexico.

On the third day they met again at Bloomington, and Morton read the following resolutions which had been adopted by a state Democratic convention at Indianapolis some years previous:

"*Resolved*, That the institution of slavery ought not to be introduced into any territory where it does not now exist.

"*Resolved*, That inasmuch as New Mexico and California are, in fact and in law, free territories, it is the duty of Congress to prevent the introduction of slavery within their limits."

'Here,'' said Morton, "I can find the Republican doctrine in its purity.''

It is easy to see from these debates how engrossing was the subject of slavery. In this discussion, as in most of those between Morton and Turpie, that subject was the only one spoken of, and a critic, who was present, thought it strange that candidates for an important state office should ignore the very existence of the state and not give it even the cold respect of a passing notice. But the instinct which led to this neglect was a true one. The event proved that even in the office to which this election opened the door; the great national issue was to swallow up and absorb all questions of state administration.

Morton, at this time, was in the prime of life, thirty-seven years old, in perfect health, full of energy and vigor, with a sound mind and a sound body, the very picture of well-developed manhood. He had the prestige of leadership in his party and the experience in joint debate upon the stump which he had acquired in the campaign of 1856, in competition with so brilliant an antagonist as Willard. Turpie was then little more than thirty years of age. He was born in Ohio in 1829, he graduated at Kenyon, studied law, practiced at Logansport, had been twice elected a member of the legislature (in 1852 and in 1858) and had served upon the bench both of the common pleas and of the circuit court. He afterwards became United States senator. He had scholarly tastes and a ready and brilliant flow of thought and language. But in this canvass it is no discredit to him to say that he was overmatched.

After Morton's engagements with Turpie were concluded, he continued his canvass alone. At a later period in this campaign he delivered, at Fort Wayne, a speech which embodied in maturer form his conclusions upon the slavery question. Although delivered without notes, it bears evidence of careful preparation, and it is an admirable presentation of the

creed of the Republican party at this period.   In regard to
the extension of slavery into the territories, he said:

"Slavery is local and municipal; it can only exist by
virtue of positive law.   Before it can exist in any state, territory or community, there must be a law enacted authorizing
and creating it.   In other words, there is no general principle
of law enabling one man to hold another as a slave.   The
law of nations, which recognizes the right of men, everywhere, to hold property in lands, in horses and cattle, in
gold and silver, and in every species of inanimate goods,
does not recognize the right of man to hold property in his
fel'ow-man.   The common law which our fathers brought
with them to this country, and which forms the basis of the
law of every state in the Union, save one, recognizes the
right of men to hold property in all these things, but does
not admit the right of man to hold property in man.

"There being, then, no general principle of law by which a
slave can be held as property, it follows that the territories
are free because of the absence in them of any law authorizing slavery, and hence, before you can hold a slave in a territory, there must be a law made for that purpose.   Another
consequence flowing from this doctrine is, that slavery in the
states is entirely and absolutely within the control of the
states in which it exists; that the people of the free states
have no power to interfere with it in any respect whatsoever;
but that its regulation, preservation or destruction, belongs
exclusively to the people of the state in which it is established.   It was the recognition of this principle that led to
the insertion of the clause in the constitution for the recovery
of fugitive slaves, for, according to this doctrine, if a slave
went beyond the jurisdiction of the state in which he was
held, into a free state, even by an escape, he was a free man,
and could not be recovered and sent back to slavery, because
of the absence of any general law recognizing the relation of
master and slave.   Hence, in framing the constitution, the

slave states insisted upon the insertion of a clause which would give them the right to recapture their fugitives from slavery. There is no clause for the recovery of any other species of property, and the reason is this, that all other property is recognized and recovered by general principles of law. The question then is, what power or tribunal can legislate for the territories upon the subject of slavery? The territories are the property of the general government, and the right to acquire them will not be disputed. If the government can acquire, can it not govern that which it acquires? Would the right to acquire, without the power to govern the thing acquired, be of any value? The right to govern is, therefore, an incident to the right to acquire. The territories belong to all the people of the United States, and not to any particular part of them. They belong to them in their corporate, national and governmental capacity. This being the case, how shall the people of the nation express themselves, or make manifest their wishes respecting their property—these territories—except through Congress? Have they any other voice or medium of expression? A territorial government would represent but a very small fragment of the entire nation.

"But we are not limited to this principle from which to derive the power of Congress to govern the territories. It is plainly and explicitly declared in the constitution, that 'Congress shall have power to make all needful rules and regulations for the government of the territory and other property belonging to the United States.' The gentlemen who drafted this provision understood that it conferred upon Congress plenary power to legislate upon the subject of slavery, and upon all other subjects appertaining to the territories, and it was so understood by men of all parties, North and South, East and West, for more than fifty years. This construction has only been called in question within a few years past, by the Democratic party under the pressure of new and extravagant demands made by the South.

"The present government began its life in 1789, by re-enacting the Ordinance of 1787, which declared that slavery or involuntary servitude should never exist in the Northwestern territory, except as a punishment for crime, whereof the party had been duly convicted. The new government thus set out in its journey of national life by a legislative declaration against slavery, and from time to time that declaration has been renewed, up to and including the administration of Millard Fillmore. The doctrine of the power and duty of Congress to exclude slavery from the territories has been the faith of every party. It was the doctrine of the old Federal party, of the old Republican party, of the Whig party and of the Democratic party throughout its honest and honorable days. Upon this time-honored doctrine we stand, and by it we will fall, if fall we must. We want no new views of the constitution. Its construction was settled by the first Congress and by every department of government for more than half a century. That construction is in harmony with the plain reading of the instrument. It regards the territories as the children of the republic, to be trained in the nurture and admonition of free and benign institutions, so that when they have arrived at the age of majority they will be qualified to take their places in the family of states, and be admitted to all the privileges and advantages of the Union; and as these territories are to become our future partners in the Union, and in the administration of the government, we have a deep interest in the formation of their characters and habits. Our destinies are to be placed in their hands, as well as theirs in ours, and we are deeply interested that they shall contract no habit and establish no institution that shall mar their permanent usefulness, power or prosperity as members of the Union. We are, therefore, interested in seeing to it that they do not contract the bad habit of slavery, polygamy or other great national and social vice. As our children are to the family and society, so are our territories to the Union and our great society of states. We believe that slavery is a moral, social and political evil, that is a curse to any people, a foe to progress, an enemy of education and intelligence, and an element of social and political weakness. For these reasons we are opposed to its further extension.

"But there are other considerations of a more personal and selfish character. If we do not exclude slavery from the territories, it will exclude us. Free labor will not go to any considerable extent where slave labor exists, because it is degraded and dishonored by the association. Hence, while there are thousands that come to Indiana, Ohio and other free states from Kentucky, Virginia and other slave states, there is hardly one for a thousand who goes hence to the slave states. The introduction of slavery into a territory prevents you and your children from going there as effectually as would a legislative act. It erects a barrier to your emigration which you will never surmount. If you would, therefore, reserve these territories as an inheritance to you and your children, to which you and they may retire when your own state becomes too crowded, or the pressure of circumstances makes a removal necessary, you must preserve them free. Free labor and slave labor will not flourish in the same bed. You can not graft the one upon the stalk of the other. Where slave labor strikes its roots deep into the soil of a territory, free labor will not grow, but perish. We are all personally interested in this question, not indirectly and remotely, as in a mere political abstraction, but directly, pecuniarily and selfishly. How can you, my Democratic friends, labor for or even consent to the building up of an institution in the territories which turns you and your children out? If you do not care for yourselves, at least you should care for your children. You owe to them a duty quite as high and sacred as

6—Mor.

that which you owe to your party. But it is said that the
slaveholder has just as good right to take his slaves to the
territories as you have to take your horses there from the
state of Indiana, and that if he be prohibited from so doing
it creates inequality. Let us consider this proposition a moment. Can not the slaveholder go from Kentucky to Kansas
and take with him every species of property which you can
take from Indiana? And may he not pursue, when he ar-
rives there, every vocation that you could, going from Indiana? If so, then you and he are on a perfect equality. But
if he takes slaves he takes what you can not, and this creates
inequality. Not only so; he takes what particularly excludes
you from the territory, and thus creates the grossest inequality. The truth is there is no equality where there is not
freedom, and slavery engenders inequality, both socially and
politically. . . .

" It has been the boast of the Democracy that it was pro-
gressive. I love that progress which implies a growth in
grace, an accession of wisdom, and the trimming of our
lamps by the light of experience; but the progress of the
Democracy has been from good to evil principles, from light
to darkness—beginning with the prohibition of slavery in
the territories and its confinement to existing limits, and end-
ing with efforts for its universal empire—seeking to unbar the
gates which our fathers erected to shut out the horrid commerce in human beings which comes across the seas. And
so great has been its progress that it is now encamped upon
ground that our fathers regarded as accursed. . . ."

Speaking of the doctrine of " Non-intervention by Congress with slavery in the territories," Morton continued:

" They say Douglas is the author. Not so. It was first
asserted by Cain, when he denied to the Lord that he was
his brother's keeper. It was afterwards affirmed by the Levite,
when he walked by on the other side and left the man who
had fallen among thieves weltering in his blood. . . .

In his speech on the Lecompton constitution, speaking of slavery in Kansas, Mr. Douglas said he did not care whether it were voted up or voted down. . . . Mr. Douglas made this declaration to prove to the South that he had no lingering sentiment in favor of liberty—no remaining partiality for free institutions—but he miscalculated the effect. It shocked the public conscience both North and South. . . .

" Under this declaration the North can not take Mr. Douglas, because he is indifferent to freedom; the South can not take him because he is indifferent to slavery. . . ."

In this speech we find a growth in Morton's sentiments in regard to slavery. He no longer utters a mere protest against the repeal of a " time-honored compromise." He demands affirmative action to prevent the spread of "that greatest of human afflictions."

Still Morton was conservative. It was as a resuscitation of the views of the fathers that he advocated resistance to the spread of slavery. "The doctrine of the power and duty of Congress to exclude slavery from the territories has," he said, "been the faith of every party." Indeed his great hold upon the people of Indiana was due to his conservatism. He was only a little in advance of the sentiment of the masses. Hence they trusted him. Extreme views, even though more correct, according to the standard of abstract principle, would have driven them away.

His experience, popularity and energy combined to make him the Republican leader in this campaign, and, although the post of honor was nominally given to another, he did more work than any one on the ticket, not only in making speeches, but also in the management of the canvass. The fatigues of the campaign proved too much for him. About the first of September he was confined to his bed by an attack of chills and fever, which compelled him to cancel some of his appointments. But as soon as he was able to leave home, he started out again with his usual energy, and kept on until the end. As the October elections approached, the Democrats felt that the current was against them, and when the news of the result came, it was found that Lane had been elected Governor by a majority over Hendricks of 9,757. The notion of the political managers that he was a more "available" candidate than Morton was hardly justified, for Morton had a majority over Turpie of 10,178. All the Republican state officers were elected, and the legislature was Republican in both branches.

Thus did Indiana declare to the country her conviction that slavery ought not to be extended into the territories.

CHAPTER VIII

MORTON'S WAR SPEECH IN THE COURT-HOUSE

INDIANA was an "October" state, but the election of the state ticket did not end the campaign. The great national struggle was to be decided in November and the enthusiasm of the Republicans remained at a white heat. There were mass-meetings everywhere, with processions of "Wide Awakes" and "Rail Maulers." The Democrats too were busy, but they could not stem the torrent, and when the November election came, the Republican vote was greatly increased.

Lincoln was to be the next President, yet he had not a clear popular majority throughout the country and his support had come almost wholly from the North. In the eyes of the people of the South he was a "sectional candidate" elected by a minority. This was the thing to which they had vowed never to submit. Sooner than this, they would break up the Union.

The mutterings of secession which had preceded the election soon become more distinct. South Carolina took the lead. On the 5th of November, the legislature of that state met to cast its electoral vote for Breckinridge. Disunion sentiment was well-nigh unanimous among the members, and a convention was called to meet on the 19th of December and determine the question of secession. A convention, according to Southern dogma, embodied the "sovereignty" of a state, and an "ordinance," a word of mystic import, was thought to express the supreme will of the people in the most solemn form.

South Carolina was about to secede. The other states of the South had not yet spoken. In such a crisis what was the Federal government to do? What ground must be taken by the Republican party and by the new administration? Should "the erring sister" be permitted to "depart in peace" or must she be "coerced" into submission? This question had not yet been seriously considered. The views of the incoming President were little known. Even Buchanan's variegated expositions of the constitution had not yet appeared. Public opinion at the North was chaos. Many of the party leaders favored acquiescence in secession. Horace Greeley counseled it in the New York *Tribune*. The Indianapolis *Journal*, the organ of the Republican party in Indiana, quoted the *Tribune* with approval. "No rational man" it said," can resist the argument against secession as a right, but any rational man may hesitate before deciding that the constitution shall be preserved at the expense of civil war." Yet with a true instinct, the great body of the party revolted at this conclusion. Letters poured in upon the *Journal* protesting against its views. The need of the hour was a leader of clear head and firm convictions, who should embody in luminous argument the logic of the popular demand for the maintenance of the Union. The first distinct utterance came from Morton's lips. He had already, in his campaign speeches, given hints that the Union ought to be preserved by force, if necessary; and now that the issue had passed from the field of conjecture and hypothesis, and the crisis was close at hand, he began to formulate more definitely his ideas upon this subject. Within a few days his matured thought was embodied in one of the ablest and most eventful speeches of his life. A meeting was called at Indianapolis for November 22, by invitation of the "Rail Maulers," to congratulate the Republicans upon the victory recently won. A violent snow storm prevented the contemplated torch-light parade, and the celebration was confined to a meeting in the court-house. The Governor and Lieutenant-governor elect were both present and delivered addresses. Lane spoke first. His speech was full of the spirit of concil- iation. He referred to the strong ties between Indiana and many of the Southern states, to the gallantry of the Kentucky sol- diers, and to the aid they had so frequently rendered the early settlers of Indiana, when these settlers were attacked by Indi- ans. But the general sentiment of his hearers was for war, and Lane's speech was received in silence. Morton followed.

"We hear much said," he began, "against the policy of coercing South Carolina in case she attempts to secede.

" What is coercion but the enforcement of the law? Is anything else intended or required? Secession or nullifica- tion can only be regarded by the general government as indi- vidual action upon individual responsibility. Those con- cerned in it can not intrench themselves behind the forms of the state government so as to give their conduct the sem- blance of legality, and thus devolve the responsibility upon the state government, which of itself is irresponsible.[1]

" The constitution and laws of the United States operate upon individuals, but not upon states, and precisely as if there were no states.

" In this matter the President has no discretion. He has taken a solemn oath to enforce the laws and preserve order, and to this end he has been made commander-in-chief of the army and navy. How can he be absolved from the respon- sibility thus devolved upon him by the constitution and his offi-

---

[1] Lincoln said, in his Inaugural, March 4, 1861 : "It follows, from these views, that no state, upon its own mere motion, can lawfully get out of the Union ; that resolves and ordinances to that effect are legally void ; and that acts of violence, within any state or states against the authority of the United States, are insurrectionary or revolutionary, according to circum- stances. I therefore consider that, in view of the constitution and the laws, the Union is unbroken ; and to the extent of my ability I shall take care, as the constitution itself expressly enjoins upon me, that the laws of the Union be faithfully executed in all the states."

cial oath?[1]   Can it be done by the resolutions of conventions,
by the advice of the newspapers, or even by a decided pre-
ponderance of public opinion?

"There is but one way in which the President can be absolved from his duty to exert all the power reposed in his
hands by the constitution to enforce the laws in South Carolina, and that is, by our acknowledgment of her independence.
The constitution provides that Congress may admit new states
into the Union, but there is no provision for turning one out, or
permitting one to go out.   A state once admitted into the
Union becomes a part of the body of the nation, and severance or secession is not contemplated by the constitution as
permissible or possible.   .   .   .   .

"If Congress possesses the power to acknowledge the
independence of a state, and thus to place it without the
pale of the Union, that power must result from an inexorable
necessity produced by a successful revolution.   While a state
is in the Union, there is no power under the constitution permitting the general and state governments to enter into negotiations with each other.   No government possesses the constitutional power to dismember itself.

"If the right does exist in this government to acknowledge the independence of South Carolina, or of any other state,
that right can only be exercised by an act of Congress.   The
President, of himself, does not possess it, and consequently,
until released from his duty by such acknowledgment, he
must exert his power to enforce the laws.

"If an attempt at secession be made, there is but one of
two courses to be pursued, either to allow the seceding
state peaceably to go and set up for herself an independent

---

[1] Lincoln said, in his Inaugural: "In your hands, my dissatisfied fellow-
countrymen, and not in mine, is the momentous issue of civil war.   The
government will not assail you.   You can have no conflict, without being
yourselves the aggressors.   You have no oath registered in heaven to destroy the government, while I shall have the most solemn one, to preserve,
protect and defend it."

government, or else, by the police or military power of the United States, to compel an observance of the laws and submission to constitutional obligations.

" Let us consider what would be the consequence of adopting the former course. If we allow a state peaceably to secede, we thereby concede the right of secession in the most substantial and solemn manner. It would be sheer nonsense to allow a state, especially a weak one like South Carolina, to secede, and yet deny that other states may retire in the same manner whenever they see fit. We can not, therefore, allow South Carolina to secede without conceding the right, and thereby settling the principle as to the remaining states. The right of secession conceded, the nation is dissolved. Instead of having a nation—one mighty people—we have but a collection and combination of thirty-three independent and petty states, held together by a treaty which has hitherto been called a constitution, of the infraction of which constitution each state is to be the judge, and from which combination any state may withdraw at pleasure.

" It would not be twelve months until a project for a Pacific empire would be set on foot. California and Oregon, being each sovereign and independent, would have a right to withdraw from their present partnership and form a new one, or form two separate nations. In doing so they would act with a far greater show of reason and a far better prospect of success than South Carolina. They are separated from the other states by thousands of miles of barren plains and snow-clad mountains. Their commerce is naturally with the East Indies and the islands of the Pacific Ocean. The tie of commercial interests between them and the other states is weaker than that which binds together any other sections of the republic.

"The right to secede being conceded, and the way to do it having been shown to be safe and easy, the prestige of the republic gone, the national pride extinguished with the national idea, secession would become the remedy for every state or sectional grievance, real or imaginary. And in a few short years we should witness the total dissolution of that mighty republic which has been the hope and the glory of the world.[1] We should then have before us the prospect presented by the history of the petty states of Greece and Italy and the principalities of Germany. Need I stop to argue the political, intellectual, social and commercial death involved in this wreck and ruin?

"We must then cling to the idea that we are a nation, one and indivisible, and that, although subdivided by state lines, for local and domestic purposes, we are one people, the citizens of a common country, having like institutions and manners, and possessing a common interest in that inheritance of glory so richly provided by our fathers. We must, therefore, do no act, we must tolerate no act, we must concede no idea or theory that looks to or involves the dismemberment of the nation.

"And especially must we of the inland states cling to the national idea. If South Carolina may secede peaceably, so may New York, Massachusetts, Maryland and Louisiana, cutting off our commerce and destroying our right of way to the ocean. We should thus be shut up in the interior of a continent, surrounded by independent, perhaps hostile nations, through whose territories we could obtain egress to the seaboard only upon such terms as might be agreed to by treaty. Emigrants from foreign lands could only come to us

---

[1] Lincoln's Inaugural: "If a minority in such case will secede rather than acquiesce, they make a precedent which, in turn, will divide and ruin them; for a minority of their own will secede from them whenever a majority refuses to be controlled by such a minority. For instance, why may not any portion of a new confederacy, a year or two hence, arbitrarily secede again, precisely as portions of the present Union now claim to secede from it? All who cherish disunion sentiments are now being educated to the exact temper of doing this." And again, "The central idea of secession is the essence of anarchy."

by permission of our neighbors, and we could not reach any Atlantic port except by passports duly viséd. In such a condition of affairs the seaboard states would possess immense advantages, which may be illustrated and understood by comparing the wealth, prosperity and power of the seaboard kingdoms of Europe with those shut up in the interior. Can it be possible, then, that Kentucky, Tennessee, Arkansas and Missouri can ever become so infatuated, so utterly demented, as to subscribe to the doctrine that a state has the right to secede, thereby placing the existence of their commerce, their peculiar institution, their everything, within the power of Louisiana, commanding, as she does, the outlet of the Mississippi and the entrance to the Gulf? As the matter now stands, the port of New York is the property of the nation, held for the benefit of all the states, the revenue there collected being disbursed for the benefit of all

"But we are told that if we use force to compel submission to the laws in South Carolina, this act will so exasperate the other slave states as to lead them to make common cause with her. I am not willing to believe that treason is so widely spread, and that sympathy with South Carolina will be stronger than devotion to the Union. Should such be the case, however, it should not, in my judgment, change the course we ought to pursue. If the people of the other Southern states will not permit the enforcement of the laws in South Carolina, it would be evidence that they were intending to follow her example at their own convenience. If they intend to stay in the Union and adhere to its fortunes, they will thrust no obstacles in the way of the general government to prevent its compelling obedience to the laws. Mere caprice and pride will not determine their action in a matter so momentous, involving the destinies of millions for all time. But if they intend to secede we can not know the fact too soon, that we may prepare for the worst. I am not willing to be-

lieve that the bad example of South Carolina will be followed
by any other states—certainly by not more than one or two.

"*If South Carolina gets out of the Union, I trust it will be
at the point of the bayonet, after our best efforts have failed to
compel her submission to the laws. Better concede her independence to force, to revolution, than to right and principle.*
Such a concession can not be drawn into precedent and construed into an admission that we are but a combination of
petty states, any one of which has a right to secede and set up
for herself, whenever it suits her temper, or her views of her
peculiar interest. Such a contest, let it terminate as it may,
would be a declaration to the other states of the only terms
upon which they would be permitted to withdraw from the
Union.

"The lopping off of South Carolina by the sword of revolution would not disturb the unity of the balance of the nation, but would simply be a diminution from its aggregate
power to the extent of her resources and population. Although the American revolution terminated so disastrously
to the British government, after an enormous expenditure
of blood and treasure, accompanied by such humiliation
of the national pride, still the integrity of the remaining portion of the empire was preserved. Had our claims to
independence been at once recognized and conceded by the
mother country, and the thirteen colonies peaceably allowed
to constitute a separate government, and take their place
among the nations of the earth, an example would have been
set and an admission made, of which every colony, island and
dependency of the empire would have speedily claimed the
benefit. The Canadas, the East and West Indies and Aus-
tralia would, in turn, have pointed to this epoch in history as
a palpable and unconditional avowal of the doctrine that they
had the right, under the British constitution, at any time
peaceably to terminate their allegiance to the crown, and
secede from the empire. An admission of the existence of

such a right could only have been retracted at the end of numerous and bloody wars.

"Shall we now surrender the nation without a struggle and let the Union go with merely a few hard words? Shall we encourage faint-hearted traitors to pursue their treason, by advising them in advance that it will be safe and successful? If it was worth a bloody struggle to establish this nation, it is worth one to preserve it; and I trust that we shall not, by surrendering with indecent haste, publish to the world that the inheritance which our fathers purchased with their blood, we have given up to save ours.

"*Seven years is but a day in the life of a nation, and I would rather come out of a struggle at the end of that time, defeated in arms and conceding independence to successful revolution, than purchase present peace by the concession of a principle that must inevitably explode this nation into small and dishonored fragments.*

"But of the result of such a struggle I entertain the utmost hope and confidence. He who compares our glorious war for independence with a war set on foot to propagate human slavery, to crush out liberty of speech and of the press, and to inaugurate and revive, with all its untold and indescribable horrors, the African slave-trade, must have an indifferent idea of the justice of that Providence who holds in his hands the issue of battle. To employ the language of a great statesman, 'Surely the Almighty has no attribute that could take sides with rebels in such a contest.'

"I will not stop to argue the right of secession. The whole question is summed up in this proposition: 'Are we one nation, one people, or thirty-three nations, thirty-three independent and petty states?' The statement of the proposition furnishes the answer. If we are one nation, then no state has a right to secede. Secession can only be the result of successful revolution. I answer the question for you—and I know that my answer will find a response in every true American heart—that we are one people, one nation, undivided and indivisible.''

At the conclusion of Morton's speech a paper was handed to him, of which the following is a copy:

"This is understood to be a meeting of rejoicing over the election of Abraham Lincoln.

''Will the speaker please state to his audience:

''1. Whether or not he and his party rejoice over the universal bankruptcy and ruin now about to fall upon our country, as a consequence of that election?

''2. Whether they rejoice that the free laborers, about which they have told us so much, are on the eve of being turned out and starved as a consequence of that election?

''3. Whether they rejoice at the prospect of fraternal strife and internecine war, which now presents itself in the immediate future as a consequence of that election?

''4. Whether they rejoice in the humiliation of being compelled, by the exigencies of the times, to accept the very principle announced and maintained by Stephen A. Douglas (whom they have denounced and vilified for his steadfast advocacy of it) as the only basis of Union and peace hereafter; or, on the other hand, whether they rejoice in the certainty that the honest adherence to their own principles and doctrines will insure the speedy destruction of their country, and demonstrate the failure of republican governments to the world?   GORDON TANNER.[1]

Morton read the paper and then said

"Since I recognize as a gentleman the person whose name is signed to this paper, I will with pleasure attempt to respond to his interrogatories.

"I answer to the first question, that we rejoice over our victory because it is the triumph of truth and the success of

---

[1] Tanner at this time was Reporter of the Supreme Court. After the attack on Sumter he enlisted, and Morton made him the first major of the Twenty-second Regiment. He was mortally wounded at Perryville.

correct and time-honored principles. Should bankruptcy and ruin fall upon the country, we should deplore it most deeply; but we should not regard it as the consequence of the election of Abraham Lincoln, or feel that any responsibility rested upon us, but in it we should recognize the legitimate results of the means employed by our adversaries to effect our defeat and destruction.

"To the second question I answer, that should free labor lose its reward and free laborers their employment, we would mourn over their calamities, seek to alleviate their sufferings and redress their wrongs, and, as we know the authors of the crime, we would hold them to just accountability in this world, and believe that the Almighty will do so in the next.

"To the third question, I answer, that we do not rejoice 'at the prospect of fraternal strife and internecine war.' From such a prospect we turn away with horror. But should they come, we can rejoice in the conviction that they are not the just consequences of the election of a President according to the forms of the constitution. But we know those who would rejoice. They are those who, for months and years past, have labored to alienate the hearts of this people from each other; who, for political purposes, by all the arts of defamation, have poisoned the Southern mind against the North, and sought to array the sections in deadly hostility against each other; who have broken compromises and kept no faith; who have incited civil war in Kansas and justified the attempted subjugation of a free people; who, for political purposes, have prophesied that calamities would follow Lincoln's election, and are now laboring to fulfill the prophecy, and instead of seeking to allay the troubles in the land are exerting all the means in their power to aggravate the difficulty and widen the breach. They seem exceedingly anxious to be able to tell the people, 'I told you so; see what you have done by voting for the man of your choice.'"

"The fourth question, as you perceive, is quite lengthy, and has a very considerable stump speech injected into the body of it. My friend, Governor Lane, understands parliamentary law, and I ask him whether I may not call for a division of the question and consider it by sections.''

Governor Lane assented.

''To the first branch of the question, I answer that we have not 'vilified' Stephen A. Douglas for his 'steadfast advocacy' of a principle or for any other cause. He has been upon all sides of the vexed question. Within the last twelve months he has undergone more changes than the moon. He has advocated nothing steadfastly but Stephen A. Douglas.

''To the last branch of the question, I answer that we do not rejoice in the certainty that an honest adherence to our principles 'will insure the speedy destruction of our country and demonstrate the failure of republican government to the world.' On the contrary, we believe that our principles are those of the constitution of the fathers, and that peace can only be restored and the safety of our institutions secured by bringing the government to that ancient, just and liberal policy upon which it was founded and administered for many years.''

In the midst of the stirring tumult of great events by which this speech was followed and surrounded, it has been almost forgotten by the world. But to those who fell under the spell of its irresistible logic its influence was unbounded and lasting. It was the speech demanded by the emergency. Its effect was incalculable, not only in the state, but over the entire country. It was like a substance dropped into a solution ready to crystallize. The sentiments which it declared were the principles which afterwards guided the conduct of the administration and the policy of the Republican party. It is related of Lincoln that when he read it he said, ''It covers the whole ground, and declares the necessary policy of the government.'' The British minister at Washington sent a copy to the English foreign office as an indication of the course likely to be pursued by the new administration. The pitiless alternatives of coercion or national ruin were never held up to view more clearly than in the severe and simple diction of these sentences.

In the meantime public opinion ripened rapidly. On December 3, Buchanan sent to Congress his annual message, a remarkable piece of political patchwork. It ascribed the discontent of the South to the anti-slavery agitation. There was no right to secede, he said, and yet the Federal government could not prevent secession. The message recommended an amendment to the constitution which should recognize slave property and protect it in the territories.

A cabinet crisis approached. Cobb resigned, and Thomas of Maryland took his place. Then Cass withdrew, and Attorney-General Black was appointed to succeed him, while Edwin M. Stanton took the place of Black as Attorney-General and infused new life into the councils of the administration.

Meanwhile in Congress, debates and harangues, projects, compromises and resolutions followed each other in bewildering confusion, making vain effort to placate the implacable—Powell's Senate committee of thirteen, Corwin's House committee of thirty-three, Crittenden's compromise, Adams' amendments, Corwin's declaration of Congress, Winter Davis' recommendation to the states—everybody had his nostrum or opiate. Each member sought to outdo the rest in concession and surrender to an adversary who would make no terms.

The South Carolina convention met on the 20th and passed the ordinance of secession. On the 24th, the members from that state retired from Congress. Two days later, Major Anderson withdrew with his little garrison to Sumter. The other forts and government buildings at Charleston were seized by the secessionists. Commissioners from South Car-

7—MOR.

olina to treat with the Federal government arrived in Washington, and demanded the withdrawal of the Federal troops. Under pressure of public sentiment and of a cabinet animated by Stanton, a refusal was returned. Then Floyd resigned. From this time wiser counsels prevailed. Buchanan turned over the government to the Union members of his cabinet. The "Star of the West," sent to the relief of Sumter, was fired upon, and had to return. Jacob Thompson, the most venomous among the plotters of disunion in the bosom of the Federal government, resigned on the 8th of January and was succeeded by John A. Dix. Thomas soon withdrew and thereafter the cabinet was wholly devoted to the Union. The President now sent to Congress a new message breathing a new spirit. It was his duty, he said, to collect the revenues and protect the public property so far as he could under existing laws. Congress must enlarge the provisions of these laws. The right to use military force defensively was clear. Buchanan recommended a compromise line, the North to control the territory above it and the South, below it. "On Congress alone," he said, "rests the responsibility."

Secession ordinances were now passed in rapid succession, and the forts, arms and government property in the seceding states were seized, until little remained except Sumter and the fortifications at Pensacola, Key West and Tortugas.

Public sentiment in Indiana was an epitome of public sentiment in the nation at large. Many panaceas for conciliation were devised. The influence of "slaveholders traveling through the Northern states with their slaves" would go far to restore harmony. The re-adoption of the Missouri Compromise would set everything right. A good many dismal editorials in the *Journal* looked forward to the dissolution of the Union. A meeting of citizens at Cannelton, in Perry county, on the Ohio, resolved that in case of a separation they would never consent that that river should be the boundary. If a line was to be drawn between the sections it must be drawn north of Cannelton.

On the 8th of January, the Democratic party in Indiana, in its state convention, opposed "the coercion of the Southern states." The resolutions declared that if civil war occurred it would be the duty of Indiana to act with other conservative states as a "mediator between the contending factions." "All our actions should be directed towards preserving the Union or reconstructing it, if dissolved, and if Congress effects nothing, it will be the duty of the Indiana legislature to call a convention of the people to declare authoritatively the position of Indiana at the present crisis." This looked like revolution in the bosom of the North. Mr. Hendricks, who had been the Democratic candidate for Governor, supported these resolutions.

"Union meetings" (as they were called) were held everywhere throughout the state, the object being to propose some concession which should bring the South back to the Union.

The legislature which convened on the 10th of January repeated, in its small way, the follies and weaknesses of Congress. There was the inevitable jumble of resolutions introduced "to calm the excited state of the country." Even before the organization of the House of Representatives, Horace Heffren (who afterwards acquired an unenviable notoriety in connection with the Sons of Liberty) offered a resolution that the members would support no person for any office who was not in favor of the perpetuation of the Union upon a compromise of the slavery question. Mr. Stotsenberg offered a resolution calling for a convention of the states "to hear the grievances of South Carolina;" Mr. Lomax, a resolution recommending the repeal of personal liberty bills. Mr. Tarkington introduced the Crittenden compromise bodily. A resolution was adopted that the navigation of the Mississippi must not be interfered with. Another was introduced to give to slaveholders the right of transit for slaves through Indiana.

The message of Governor Hammond (who had succeeded Willard on the death of the latter) told the legislature that the cause of the trouble was "fanatical agitation on the question of slavery," promoted by a "dangerous class of political teachers who belonged to the ministry." The South, he said, should have full and equal rights in the territories. "We of the free states," he continued, "must stop this discussion of the moral issue and look upon slavery only as a political question!"

The Republicans seemed to have a clearer notion of the struggle which was approaching.

Mr. Murray, on January 12, introduced a resolution denouncing as treason the hostile acts of the South, approving the President's assertion of Federal authority and tendering all needful aid in money and men. Mr. Jenkinson moved a request to the Representatives of Indiana in Congress to vote supplies, and Mr. Bundy offered a resolution that the laws must be executed and the Union preserved by force, if necessary.

Such was the condition of affairs when, upon the 14th of January, Henry S. Lane succeeded Governor Hammond in the executive chair, and Oliver P. Morton entered upon his duties as President of the Senate. Governor Lane delivered an inaugural address, but Morton confined himself to a few formal remarks, invoking the kindness of the Senate in aid of his inexperience. He remained president of that body only two days.

CHAPTER IX

MORTON BECOMES GOVERNOR

AFTER the October election had made it certain that the Republicans would have a majority in the General Assembly and would elect to the United States Senate the successor of Senator Fitch, the understanding that Lane was to have the place and that Morton was to be Governor became a matter of general comment. It was severely criticised by the Democratic press, which denounced it as a "bargain," and a great injustice to another prominent Republican, the Hon. Caleb B. Smith.

But on the evening of the 15th of January, Lane was unanimously chosen Senator by the Republican caucus.

After he had been elected and had resigned the governorship, Morton was sworn into office and addressed both branches of the legislature, announcing his determination to maintain an economical administration and to sustain every effort of the general government in enforcing the laws.[1]

He soon had a rare opportunity to array public opinion on the side of the Union. On the 22d of January the legislature adjourned to take part in the ceremony of raising the national flag on the dome of the state-house. A select committee had arranged a program which included remarks by Governors

---

[1] The correspondent of the Chicago *Tribune* thus characterized the new Governor: " He is about thirty-six years of age, of splendid build, having a large Websterian head and noble forehead. He is one of the most intellectual men of the state, and upon the stump or at the bar few men are his equals."

Lane and Hammond and by Messrs. Hendricks and Voorhees, as well as a review of the military by Governor Morton.

This program was apparently prepared to prevent the utterance of any sentiment offensive to the South. In Democratic eyes Governor Lane was the mildest and most harmless of Republicans, not likely to say anything that would hurt, while Hammond, Hendricks and Voorhees were ''safe men.'' Morton was not to speak.

A great multitude assembled. Lane delivered his address and was followed by Hammond, who recommended the Crittenden compromise, and by Hendricks, who spoke of ''state equality,'' a phrase much in vogue with those who claimed that the rights of the South had been invaded by those who denied to its ''peculiar institution'' free access to the territories. But the ''conservatives'' (as they loved to call themselves) had reckoned without their host. The instincts of the people were truer than those of the politicians. Morton was there and the multitude were determined to hear him, for amid such surroundings he was the incarnation of popular patriotism. They called loudly for him. In response to the demand, he came forward, and under the inspiration of the occasion made one of his most eloquent speeches. With characteristic directness he went at once to the heart of the matter:

''I am not here to argue questions of state equality,'' he said, ''but to denounce treason and uphold the cause of the Union. It is proper on this occasion to renew our allegiance to the flag which floats over the dome of the capitol.

''We live at a time when treason is running riot through the land. Certain states of this Union, unmindful of the blessings of liberty, forgetful of the duties they owe to their sister states and to the American people as a nation, are attempting to sever the bonds of the Union, and to pull down in irretrievable ruin our fabric of government, which has been the admiration and wonder of the world. We are lost in astonishment at the enormity of the wickedness and folly of this attempt. Surely it requires no prophetic eye, no second sight to perceive that social and political destruction will speedily overtake the seceding states if they persist in the desperate and criminal enterprise in which they are now engaged. The civilized world looks upon their unholy schemes with horror, and the voice of the nation is raised in solemn rebuke of that treason which is aiming a fatal blow at the liberties of the world. It is a time when the hearts of all men should beat in unison, and every patriot join hands with his neighbor and swear eternal devotion to liberty, the constitution and the Union.

"In view of the solemn crisis in which we stand, all minor, personal and party considerations should be banished from every heart. There should be but one party, and that the party of the constitution and the Union. No man need pause to consider his duty. It is inscribed upon every page of our history, in all our institutions and on everything by which we are surrounded. The path is so plain that the wayfaring man, though he be a fool, can not err therein. It is no time for hesitation; the man who hesitates under circumstances like these, is lost. I would here in all kindness speak a word of warning to the unwary. Let us beware how we encourage them to persist in their mad designs by assurances that we are a divided house, that there are those in our midst who will not permit the enforcement of the laws and the punishment of their crimes. Let us diligently search our hearts and see if there are any partisan prejudices, any party resentments that are, imperceptibly and unknown to ourselves, leading us aside from the path of duty, and if we find them there, pluck them out and hastily return. For myself, I will know no man who will stop and prescribe the conditions upon which he will maintain that flag, who will argue that a single star may be erased, or who will consent that it may be torn, that he may make choice between its dishonored fragments. I will know that man only who vows fidelity to the Union and the constitution, under all circumstances and at all hazards; who declares that he will stand by the constituted authorities of the land, though they be not of his own choosing; who, when he stands in the base presence of treason, forgets the contests and squabbles of the past in the face of the coming danger; who then recognizes but two parties—the party of the Union, and the base faction of its foes. To that man, come from what political organization he may, by whatever name he may have been known, I give my hand as a friend and brother, and between us there shall be no strife.

"When the struggle comes, if come it must; when the appeal to arms is made (which may God in his infinite mercy avert), we must then rely not on a standing army but on the citizens of the land—on those men whose hearts beat high with pulsations of love for the Union, and who will strike for it with their strong arms.'

From the time of the delivery of this speech there was less uncertainty and hesitation, less talk of expedients and more of the duty of sustaining the government. While war was much talked of at this time, there were not many who really believed that it was coming. Morton saw more clearly than the rest, and to his friends he freely avowed his opinion that the outcome of the national difficulty must be war, and that public opinion must be prepared to meet it. But he felt that the border slave states would risk so much by clinging to the South that he doubted whether they would secede. His conclusions were prophetic.

On the 19th of January, the General Assembly of Virginia sent to the different states an invitation to a convention called for the purpose of adjusting the controversies between the North and the South. Virginia appointed five commissioners.

Two days later Governor Morton sent to the legislature this invitation. He had no faith that any good would come of such a convention. Still Virginia had sent the invitation, and a regard for the feelings of the border states would not permit it to be ignored. But if Indiana accepted, Morton would see to it that her representatives did not give encouragement to the enemies of the Union. The Democratic members of the General Assembly knew with whom they had to deal, and they did their best to keep the appointments out of the Governor's hands.[1]

But on January 31 a joint resolution was passed by which he was authorized to select the commissioners.

The convention was to meet February 4. There was no time to spare, and he determined to make no mistake in his men. On February 1 he appointed Caleb B. Smith, Pleasant A. Hackleman, Godlove S. Orth, Thomas C. Slaughter and Erastus W. H. Ellis, all Republicans. Before appointing them he addressed to each the following written interrogatories:

1. Would you favor any proposition of compromise that involves an amendment of the constitution of the United States?

2. Would you be in favor of any proposition by which slavery should be recognized as existing in any of the territories of the United States, present or to be acquired?

3. Would you favor granting to slavery any additional guarantees?

4. Are you in favor of maintaining the constitution of the United States as it is, and of enforcing the laws?

Smith, Hackleman and Orth responded in writing the same day, Ellis on the 2d, and Slaughter on the 3d, all substantially answering the first three questions in the negative and

---

[1] There were several wordy encounters during the debates, one of which led to a "meeting" between two representatives, Heffren and Moody, with bloodless result, the encounter having been interrupted by officers of the law. A resolution was introduced to expel both of the members for duelling, but nothing came of it. Several amusing passages enlivened the session, among them a discussion as to whether the negro was a man, a proposition which Mr. Heffren vigorously denied.

the last one in the affirmative.   The answers were preserved by Morton for use in case the action of the men appointed should not conform to their declarations.[1]

He insisted that the commissioners should write him frequently and tell him how the negotiations progressed.   Their letters show the distracted state of public opinion and the almost irresistible pressure exerted to induce them to make all sorts of concessions for the sake of keeping the border states in the Union.   There was no hope of the states that had seceded.   These would not send commissioners to the convention.

The delegates of these states now met at Montgomery, Alabama, and organized a Southern confederacy.   On February 9, Jefferson Davis was elected President and Alexander H. Stephens, Vice-President.

Meanwhile the " Peace Congress " pursued its deliberations.   A committee, consisting of one member from each of the twenty-one states represented, was appointed to report what it might deem " right, necessary and proper to restore harmony and preserve the Union."   Caleb B. Smith was the representative from Indiana.   On the 15th of February, the committee reported a series of resolutions, which were adopted by the convention and submitted to Congress with the request that they be referred to the states for ratification as amendments to the constitution.   The commissioners from Indiana did not carry out in full the views they had expressed in their letters to Morton.   But nothing came of the proposed amendments, so it was not necessary for him to disclose the change of front on the part of the men he had chosen.

It was on the 11th of February, while the Peace Congress

---

[1] Lincoln said :   " Entertain no proposition for a compromise in regard to the extension of slavery.   The instant you do they have us under again. All our labor is lost and sooner or later has to be done over.   .   .   .   The tug has to come, and better now than later."

was at work in Washington, that Lincoln stopped at Indian-apolis on his way to the inauguration. He was met by the Governor, the members of the legislature, and a great multi-tude of citizens. Lincoln had not spoken at this time of his policy or intentions, and Governor Morton desired, if possi-ble, to draw out some expression of the views of the Presi-dent elect. So he delivered a brief speech of welcome, in which he referred to the Union as "the idol of our hopes, the parent of our prosperity, our shield and protection abroad, and our title to the respect and consideration of the world." He thus continued:

"You are about to enter upon your official duties under circumstances at once novel and full of difficulty, and it will be the duty of all good citizens, without distinction of party, to yield a cordial and earnest support to every measure of your administration calculated to maintain the Union, pro-mote the national prosperity and restore peace to our dis-tracted and unhappy country. Our government, which but yesterday was the theme of every eulogy, and the admiration of the world, is to-day threatening to crumble into ruins, and it remains to be seen whether it possesses a living principle, or whether, in the fullness of time, the hour of its dissolution is at hand. But we are full of confidence that the end is not yet, that the precious inheritance of our fathers will not elude our grasp or be wrested from us without a struggle, that we are but passing through one of those civil commotions that mark the history of every great nation, and that we shall emerge from the present gloom into the bright sunshine of peace and march forward with accelerated speed in the path of prosperity and power."

Lincoln, after returning thanks for the reception given him, answered: "I will only say that to the salvation of this Union there needs but one single thing, the hearts of a peo-ple like yours. Of the people, when they rise in mass in be-half of the Union and the liberties of their country, truly may it be said, 'the gates of hell can not prevail against them.' In all the trying positions in which I shall be placed, and, doubtless, I shall be placed in many such, my reliance will be upon you, the people of the United States, and I wish you to remember, now and forever, that it is your business, and not mine; that if the union of these states and the liberties of this people shall be lost, it is but little to any one man of fifty-two years of age, but a great deal to the 30,-000,000 of people who inhabit these United States, and to their posterity in all coming time. It is your business to rise up and preserve the Union and liberty for yourselves and not for me.

"I am but an accidental instrument, to serve but for a limited time, and I appeal to you again to bear constantly in mind that with you, and not with politicians, not with Presidents, not with office-seekers, but with you is the question, 'Shall the Union, shall the liberties of this country be preserved to the latest generations?'"

When Morton became Governor, the finances of the state were in the utmost disorder. In January, Governor Hammond had borrowed $125,000 to pay the interest on the public debt, and he had given the obligations of the state for repayment in May, out of the revenues for 1860, which would then be collected. Several appropriations made by the last legislature were overdrawn, and there was only $5,000 in the treasury, not enough to pay current expenses. On the 24th of January, Governor Morton reported to the legislature the financial condition of the state and recommended that $50,-000 be borrowed at once from the State Bank or the Sinking Fund (he preferred the former) and that the law be amended so as to provide proper penalties for the refusal of county treasurers to pay over moneys due the state on demand. There were sums in the county treasuries, which, if paid, would relieve the state from embarrassment. The loan to be made should be repaid out of these.

The warden of the state prison at Jeffersonville now declared that he must have $18,000 immediately, or the prisoners must be turned out. This sum had not been included in the Governor's estimate, so the House Committee of Ways and Means reported a bill to borrow $75,000 from the commissioners of the Sinking Fund. The bill was hurried through its three readings, and on the 25th of January transmitted to the Senate. Here it encountered lively opposition. The debate was postponed, amendments were proposed, and the bill was re-committed. Matters became more and more pressing. The state agent would soon draw further funds to pay interest on the state debt, yet no final action was taken by the legislature. It was not until February 20, with the prospect of immediate default staring them in the face, that the minds of certain senators "underwent a change," and the bill was passed

A number of extensive frauds had just been committed upon the state. Prominent among these was one in connection with the building of the prison at Michigan City. The legislature cf 1859 had appropriated $50,000 for this purpose. About $120,000 had been expended and the prison was still far from complete. Rumors of corruption were rife, and a joint committee of thirteen was appointed to investigate. The report of this committee, signed by eleven members, charged that there were shocking frauds and irregularities, and that Governor Willard had been implicated in the irregular practices. The minority report, signed by Horace Heffren and James R. Slack, controverted these allegations. The upshot of the matter was that the building contract was surrendered and a new board of directors was elected.

But the state prison episode was but a trifle by the side of the gigantic frauds which had come to light in connection with the swamp lands of the state. It had been the policy

of Indiana to bring these lands into a tillable condition by
giving them to persons who would drain them. Each individual who took land was to drain every acre he obtained;
but, by a secret understanding between state and county
officials and certain land speculators, during Willard's administration, thousands of acres had been made over to persons
who never drained the tenth part of what they received,
while the officers were constantly making illegal drafts upon
the swamp land fund.

The military condition of the state was even worse than its
financial condition. The state militia, arms, accoutrements,
etc., existed only on paper. In early times the Indiana militia had been in high repute. Thirty years previous to this
the number of men enrolled had been between forty and fifty
thousand, but in 1834 the organization had been given up and
the arms scattered and lost, and when, on the 21st of January, 1861, Mr. Gresham offered a resolution authorizing the
Governor to have the arms in the present arsenal overhauled,
Mr. Heffren contemptuously said: "I understand that there
are thirteen muskets and two rusty horse pistols."

Mr. Gresham introduced a militia bill, but the Democrats
did not intend that it should become a law. They had the
organization of the present non-existing militia in their own
hands, Governor Hammond having appointed the bulk of
the officers just before his term expired.

The bill passed the House, but it could not get through the
Senate. The Democratic members determined to "bolt"
before they would permit the enactment either of this bill or
of the "apportionment bill," to redistrict the state for the election of members of Congress.

A "bolt" is not an uncommon thing in Indiana. The
constitution requires two-thirds of each branch of the General
Assembly to constitute a quorum, so that it is in the power of
a minority of more than one-third to put a veto upon any
specially obnoxious measure by running away, and thus stop-

ping all legislation. Upon such occasions the party in the majority always denounces the "bolt" as "unlawful" and "revolutionary," but that party seldom fails to make use of the same reserved power when it is again in the minority, and the measure proposed is sufficiently offensive.

On the evening of March 5th, the Democratic members of both branches of the General Assembly held a caucus, and pledged themselves to bolt, if necessary, to prevent the passage of the apportionment and military bills. The crisis came next day in the Senate when an effort was made to read the apportionment bill for the third time. The Democrats retired and no quorum remained.[1]

It was now the turn of the Republicans to hold their caucus, which they did on the evening of March 7. Morton was present. Some rasher spirits had made up their minds to keep up the fight till the end. But the appropriation bill had not been passed. The Democrats could stop everything if the apportionment and militia bills were persisted in, and this would result in discrediting the administration of the Republican party. Therefore Morton spoke in behalf of concession and compromise, and the Republicans agreed to postpone these bills until the 8th of March so as to let the legislation required by public interests proceed. The erring brethren were invited back and the obnoxious bills were not pressed, even after the appointed day.

The only measure which passed providing for the public defense was an act authorizing the Governor to take all state

---

[1] After waiting some ten or fifteen minutes the President announced, "I am informed by the doorkeeper that the Democracy has seceded." Upon the call of the Senate, only thirty members (less than a quorum) answered to their names. The doorkeeper was sent after the absentees, and upon his return the following colloquy occurred: The President—"I would ask if the doorkeeper has found the absentees?" The Assistant Doorkeeper (from the doorkeeper's chair at the door)—"I saw them pretty nearly all in a batch, and the answer was: 'Tell them to go to hell.'" Mr. White—"I move we don't do that." The motion was agreed to.

arms and equipments not in possession of military companies and to distribute them among volunteer organizations.

At the outbreak of the rebellion there were, perhaps, less than 500 stand of effective small arms in the state, besides eight pieces of weather-worn and dismantled cannon, and an unknown number of flint locks and altered muskets which Morton collected and found to be useless except for drill and guard duty.

Not only were the financial and military resources of Indiana in the worst possible shape, but the credit and reputation of the state were at a low ebb. Gigantic schemes for internal improvement in 1836–7 had drawn in their train bankruptcy and the repudiation of a former state debt. Indiana did not stand well in the money market. The stream of emigration flowed past her doors into the states beyond. Her military reputation had been tarnished by injurious reports of the conduct of her soldiers at Buena Vista, and there was a certain evil repute which everywhere hung over the name of "Hoosier."

Such was the condition of Indiana, her treasury bankrupt, her credit poor, frauds everywhere, no money, no arms, no ammunition, no militia, except on paper—and even this organization in the hands of officers many of whom were in sympathy with rebellion—a legislature with a formidable minority, reluctant and revolutionary, having the power and the will to stop even the most needful measures of public defense—such was the condition of the state when the most gigantic war in American history broke out, and demanded resources and energy for which prosperous times and undivided patriotism would seem barely sufficient. But the will and intellect of the great war Governor were equal to the emergency.

CHAPTER X

THE CALL TO ARMS

LINCOLN, who had gone to Washington secretly, to avoid a conspiracy in Baltimore against his life, was inaugurated on the 4th of March, and delivered that admirable address, conciliatory, yet firm, which will remain a classic in the literature of American statesmanship. Seward, Chase, Cameron, Welles, Smith, Blair and Bates were chosen for the cabinet.

There was at this time a strange lethargy, vacillation and timidity in public opinion. Men would not believe in the desperate purposes of the South. There was still strong faith that much might be done by conciliation, especially in the border states, which had not yet seceded.

Morton saw more clearly than others the impossibility of compromise. There was danger that in trying to conciliate the South, the North itself might become apathetic. He would go to Washington, see the President, state his convictions and do what he could to strengthen the administration in the determination to enforce the laws. So he visited Mr. Lincoln and told him that if the administration would adopt a vigorous policy, Indiana would support it, that at least six thousand troops should be ready to march in defense of the Union, that the state, although divided in opinion in regard to the antecedents of secession, would be loyal when the time came for action, and that nothing could more discourage the Union men than a lack of decision on the part of the administration. Moreover, Morton wanted arms for the state troops, and although the Federal armories were almost empty, he obtained an order for five thousand muskets.   Events soon took the course which he had urged.   It was determined to send provisions to Sumter, and in case of resistance (not otherwise) to throw re-inforcements into the fort.   Sumter was attacked and soon surrendered, but all over the North spread the flame and fury of patriotic wrath at an unprovoked assault upon the nation and the flag.   Before this there had been parties and factions, now there was but one thought— the rebellion which had lifted its red hand must be put down. The administration, which had been criticised by everybody as neither hot nor cold, was now the object of earnest devotion and loyalty.   Douglas, the leader of the Northern Democrats, announced that ''he was prepared to sustain the President in the exercise of all his constitutional functions to preserve the Union, maintain the government and defend the Federal capital.''   On the 15th of April, the day following the evacuation of Sumter, Lincoln issued his proclamation, calling for seventy-five thousand troops to suppress ''the combinations of men engaged in obstructing the law,'' and to maintain the integrity and existence of the Union.

Nowhere was the fire of patriotism more intense than in Indiana.   It burned away every other feeling.   On Friday, April 12, the word came that Sumter had been bombarded. ''Through the long Saturday that followed, business was at a stand. . . . The streets were black with breathless multitudes awaiting the tidings of the seventy loyal men in an unfurnished fort, bombarded by ten thousand raging rebels. At ten o'clock a dispatch was announced, 'Sumter has fallen.'

''Young men and men in middle life looked at the white faces and wet eyes of old and venerated citizens who stood in the street waiting for tidings, and a great stillness fell upon them.   They turned to separate and creep silently to their homes.   Another dispatch appeared, 'Mr. Lincoln will issue a proclamation to-morrow calling for 75,000 volunteers.' Cheer upon cheer responded."

No one present upon the eventful Sunday which followed will ever forget it. The country's cause was the theme at the churches; it was in the prayers, in the sermons and in the songs. In Indianapolis two immense meetings were held, one at the court-house, which was adjourned to Metropolitan hall, and the other at Masonic hall. Resolutions were passed pledging to the government "the lives, the fortunes and the sacred honor of the people of Indiana, in whatever capacity and at whatever time the country might require them."

The men who had expressed sympathy with the South had to keep very quiet. Proprietors of obnoxious newspapers were required to hoist the flag over their offices and to take an "oath of allegiance," improvised by the patriotism of the multitude. Many of the doubtful were invited to "come out and avow their sentiments," and it was greatly to their interest that these sentiments should be strongly in support of the Union and of the war to maintain it. Only three days before, the Indianapolis *Sentinel* had said that Governor Morton could not make good his promise to the President of 6,000 volunteers; that the people of Indiana did not intend to engage in a crusade against the South.[1]

The sudden explosion of public feeling now made matters unpleasant and even dangerous for the editor of that paper. Threats were made of personal violence and of the destruction of the establishment, and it was not long before Morton was constrained to place an armed guard in the *Sentinel* building to protect it from an apprehended attack. The Cincinnati *Enquirer*, which in February had laughed at Mor-

---

[1] Even while the struggle was going on in Charleston harbor that paper said: "The abolition and disunion administration has attempted the coercion of the Confederate States. Such are the first fruits of Republicanism. . . . If the men of the South had yielded without resistance, they would have stood disgraced before the world."

ton's war sentiments, and said he would command a Quaker regiment under Lincoln—"'His sword is at his side fe fi fo fum,'" was equally impressed with the undesirable character of any attempt to stem this torrent of public opinion.[1]

Morton, the moment he heard of the attack on Sumter, at once set about making preparations to equip and send as many men as possible to the front.[2]

---

[1] Even Mr. Hendricks thought it necessary to avert the suspicion of disloyalty by writing the following letter to the Indianapolis *Journal:*

"Indianapolis, April 24, 1861.

"MR. EDITOR—My attention has been called to an editorial in the *Journal* this morning, in which it is stated that, at a Union meeting held at Shelbyville a few evenings since, a committee was appointed to wait on me with the request that I should speak; that being called upon by the committee, I refused to speak, saying that I had no hand in originating the difficulty and would have nothing to do in extricating the country from its perilous condition.

"The writer has been wholly misinformed. I never heard of the appointment of such a committee, and suppose that none was appointed. No committee waited upon me with such a request. Had I been so honored, I certainly should have responded. I have never withheld my views upon any question of public interest from the people of Shelby county. Upon all occasions when it appeared proper, I have expressed my opinions in relation to our present troubles. Since the war commenced I have uniformly said that the authority of the government of the United States is not questioned in Indiana, and that I regarded it as the duty of the citizens of Indiana to respect and maintain that authority and to give the government an honest and earnest support in the prosecution of the war until, in the providence of God, it may be brought to an honorable conclusion and the blessings of peace restored to our country— postponing until that time all controversy in relation to the causes and responsibilities of the war. No man will feel a deeper solicitude in the welfare and proud bearing of Indiana's soldiery in the conflict of arms to which they are called than myself.

"Allow me to add that, in my judgment, a citizen or newspaper is not serving the country well in the present crisis by attempting to give a partisan aspect to the war, or by seeking to pervert the cause of the country to party ends."

[2] He had been trying to collect arms for some time, but had succeeded only indifferently. The total result of his collections in all parts of the state under the act of March 5 was, " 3,436 small arms of sixteen different kinds but of uniform infirmity." Early in the year, he had drawn

On the morning of April 15, before the news came of Lincoln's proclamation, he sent to the President the following telegram: "On behalf of the state of Indiana, I tender to you for the defense of the nation, and to uphold the authority of the government, ten thousand men."

After the President's proclamation was issued, the quota of Indiana was fixed at 4,683 men, to be enrolled in six regiments, and to serve three months. This was less than half the number tendered. The call was entirely inadequate. Morton knew that more men would be needed. On the 16th he issued a proclamation calling upon the loyal and patriotic men of the state to the number of six regiments to arrange themselves into military companies and forthwith report to the Adjutant-General,[1] to be mustered into service. Indianapolis was named as the place of rendezvous, and the land since occupied by the fair grounds near the city was secured for this purpose and called "Camp Morton."

The answer from every side was immediate and enthusiastic. Public meetings were held everywhere. Recruiting quarters swarmed with men eager to go. The contest in every neighborhood was as to who would be accepted. Old men and boys came into this competition and made false declarations of their ages, that they might have a chance to serve. The day after the proclamation was issued five hundred men were in camp, within three days twenty-four hundred, within a week twelve thousand. Companies came forward without orders in the mere hope that they would be accepted. Men who could not get into companies at home came alone or in squads to the rendezvous and joined in the general clamor to be taken. The quota of Indiana had been filled more than twice over. What was to be done with the surplus?

---

from the war department one six-pounder cannon, and about 500 rifles, the quota of Indiana for 1861. Later on he went to Washington and got the order from the President for 5,000 muskets. But on the 24th of April he was told that only 3,500 could be furnished.

[1] Gen. Lew Wallace was appointed by Morton to this position.

Morton knew well enough that these men would all be needed. He would at once have placed an overwhelming force in active service. He would have made the war "instant and terrible." He tendered to the government six additional regiments *without condition as to the term of service,* and promised that if accepted they would be organized in six days. But communication with Washington by telegraph was cut off and he got no answer. Something must be done to arm and equip these men. Provision must be made by the state for a great and costly war. The legislature had adjourned only a few weeks before, but it must be called together at once. So on the 19th Morton issued his proclamation convening it upon the 24th. On the 23d he sent a special messenger to Washington to tender the six additional regiments, but he did not await the answer. The state must arm and equip these men whether the Federal government would have them or not. They would soon be useful enough. The state might at any time be invaded by armed bands from Kentucky. Morton's determination not to dismiss any was hailed with great satisfaction by the men collected at the capital, as well as by those who were still at home impatiently awaiting the order to come. On the 24th the legislature convened, and the next day the two branches met in joint session in the hall of representatives, when Governor Morton delivered to them a message which has become historic in Indiana. In it he said:

"We have passed from the field of argument to the solemn fact of war, which exists by the act of the seceding states. The issue is forced upon us and must be accepted. Every man must take his position upon the one side or the other. In time of war there is no ground upon which a third party can stand. It is the imperative duty of all men to rally to the support of the government, and to expend in its behalf, if need be, their fortunes and their blood. Upon the preservation of this government depends our prosperity and greatness as a nation, our liberty and happiness as individuals. We should approach the contest, not as politicians, nor as ambitious partisans, but as patriots, who cast aside every selfish consideration when dangers threaten their country. The voice of party should be hushed, and the bitterness that may have sprung out of political contests be at once forgiven and forgotten. Let us rise above these paltry considerations and inaugurate the era when there shall be but one party, and that for our country. The struggle is one into which we enter with the deepest reluctance. We are bound to the people of the seceding states by the dearest ties of blood and institutions. They are our brothers and our fellow-countrymen. But if they regard not these tender relations, how can we? If they wage war upon us and put themselves in the attitude of public enemies, they must assume all the responsibilities incident to that position. But while I deplore deeply the character of the contest in which we are engaged, nevertheless we should meet it as men.

"To our sister state of Kentucky we turn with hope and affection. She has grown rich and prosperous in the republic; could she do more if she were out of it? It would be a sad day that would sever the bond which binds these states together and place us in separate and hostile nations. I appeal to her by the ties of our common kindred and history, by our community of interest, by the sacred obligations that bind us to maintain the constitution inviolate, to adhere to the Union, and stand fast by that flag in defense of which she has so often shed her best blood. I pray her to examine her past history and perceive how the tide of her prosperity has flowed on unbroken and ever-increasing, until her limits are filled with material wealth and her people are respected, elevated and happy; and then to inquire if this is not the result of that Union she is called upon to break, and of that government she is invited to overthrow. To ask Kentucky to secede is to ask her to commit dishonor and suicide. I trust that the good sense and patriotism of her people will not suffer her to be dragged by the current of events, which has been cunningly invented for that purpose, into the vortex of disunion; nor permit her to be artfully inveigled into an armed neutrality between the rebellious states and the Federal government. Such a position would be anomalous and fatal to the peace and perpetuity of the Union. There is no ground in the constitution midway between a rebellious state and the Federal government upon which she can stand, holding both in check and restraining the government from the enforcement of the laws and the exercise of its constituted authority. Such an attitude is at once unconstitutional and hostile. At a time like this, if she is not for the government, aiding and maintaining it by the observance of all her constitutional obligations, she is against it. If the voice of her people can be heard, I fear not the result. Secession can only triumph, as it has triumphed in other states, by the stifling of the voice of the people and by the bold usurpation, by demagogues and traitors, of the powers which rightfully belong to the people alone. And I might here remark that it is quite manifest that the schemes of the authors and managers of the rebellion extend far beyond the dissolution of the Union and embrace the destruction of the democratic principle of government, and the substitution of an aristocracy in its stead. In the seceding states the control of public affairs has been withdrawn substantially from the people, and every proposition to submit to their consideration measures of the most vital importance has been contemptuously overruled; and we are in truth called upon to fight not only for the Union, but for the principle upon which our state and national governments are founded. . . .

"I recommend that one million dollars be appropriated for the purchase of arms and **munitions of war**, and for the organization of such portions of the militia as may be deemed necessary for the emergency, that a militia system be devised

and enacted, looking chiefly to volunteers, which shall ensure
the greatest protection to the state, and the greatest unity
and efficiency of the force to be employed; that a law be enacted defining and punishing treason against the state; that
a law be enacted suspending the collection of debts against
those who may be actually employed in the military service
of the state or United States; that suitable provision be made
by the issue of the bonds of the state, or otherwise, for raising
the money herein recommended to be appropriated; and that
all necessary and proper legislation be had to protect the
business, property and citizens of the state under the circumstances in which they are placed.''

The General Assembly, almost to a man, seemed animated
by the spirit which ran through this message. It responded
with alacrity to the Governor's recommendations. He asked
an appropriation of one million dollars and more than two
millions were appropriated. The bonds were provided for,
the militia system inaugurated, the additional troops taken
care of, treason against the state defined and punishment provided, counties authorized to appropriate money for army
purposes, and other salutary legislation enacted. The law
suspending the collection of debts against soldiers was the
only recommendation neglected, and this was omitted on
account of its doubtful constitutionality, a matter which in the
press of affairs Morton had no doubt overlooked. This was
par excellence a ''star and stripe'' session. The first glow of
the war fever was upon the members of the legislature and their
resolutions and speeches breathed the fervor of enthusiastic
patriotism.

Heffren, who, less than three months before, had declared
that he would leave his native land and ''rather become a
private in the Southern army than commander-in-chief of the
Abolitionists,'' had now experienced so great a change of
heart, that, at the opening of the session, he placed in nomination for speaker the Republican candidate, Cyrus M. Allen,

in a speech advocating "union, harmony and concession and the protection of our homes." Allen was unanimously elected.

Only one voice had sufficient hardihood to reiterate the words of sympathy and toleration for the South, which, in the preceding session, had been the staple oratory of many Democratic members. This was Mr. Polk, of Johnson county, who introduced a resolution "that we respect the sympathies of the border states for the reason that their institutions and interests are kindred with those of the Confederate states and we will recognize a neutral position on their part." He supported these resolutions in a rambling speech, which he read from manuscript.

The "member from Johnson" soon found that he had stirred up a hornets' nest. Mr. Gresham declared the resolutions an insult to the House, and moved that they be rejected. There was great excitement. After some discussion, Mr. Polk expressed his regret that he had created so much feeling, and offered to withdraw the resolutions. But the House would not allow it. Speaker Allen came down from the chair and scored the resolutions and their author most unmercifully. He hoped there would not be a solitary man opposed to their rejection. When the vote was taken, it was in fact unanimous.

Equally emphatic was the expression of the House in regard to the conduct of Jesse D. Bright, who represented Indiana in the United Senates Senate, and who had avowed his sympathy with secession. On May 23 the House requested his resignation, and near the end of the session declared that he was no longer an inhabitant of the state and had forfeited all right to represent it, and the Senate was requested to declare his seat vacant.

Thus the legislature which, only a few weeks before, had been vacillating, turbulent and inefficient, was now animated with new life, and acted with zeal, enthusiasm and unanimity. One who looks into the record of this session and compares it with the winter session will find it hard to believe that the same members were taking part in it, so great was the change wrought by the inspiration of the attack on Sumter. These men had been translated to another sphere of action. They had "passed from the field of argument to the solemn fact of war."

They were controlled, moreover, by a sentiment among the people at large, which would brook no flinching from the great duty of the hour.

There were several occasions, in fact, when the action of the members seemed to lag behind the enthusiasm of their constituents, and especially of the soldiers at Camp Morton. A "vigilance committee" was organized, and part of its duty was to look after the political morals of the legislature and the press, and to see that there was no lack of patriotism. There was some confusion and delay in passing the "Six Regiments" bill, for the organization of the troops which had not yet been taken by the general government, and the members who occasioned the delay became very obnoxious. One afternoon a Mr. Smith, of Bartholomew, read to the House a paper he had received from the vigilance committee, denouncing as traitorous certain sentiments expressed by him and threatening that if the legislature should adjourn without making provision for the support of the volunteers, those who were found to have caused the failure would never leave Central Indiana. There seemed to be a disposition to make light of this letter, but the "Six Regiments" bill was quickly passed. On May 7 an effort was made to investigate the vigilance committee, but the majority had too much sympathy with its purposes to make any effort to suppress it, and the matter was treated as a joke. Every member in danger from vigilance committees was recommended to turn himself into a vigilance committee and take care of himself, and the resolution for inquiry was laid upon the table.

An immense trade was going on at this time between Kentucky and the states lying to the north and south of it, and provisions and equipments were sent South in great quantities down the Ohio and Mississippi rivers, and over the Louisville and Nashville Railroad. The Federal government at first took no steps to prevent this and the initiative was left to individual action. The vigilance committee undertook the task, and in this Morton sustained it. With the aid of detectives he did much to break up the sending of supplies to the Southern army. Upon his suggestion, an agent of the treasury department was formally placed on duty at Indianapolis, with authority to detain contraband articles on their way South. Seizures were often made. Muskets, cartridges, percussion caps, provisions, etc., were turned over to the authorities to be held subject to the order of the government. At Vincennes, Evansville and New Albany several consignments of military goods were captured.[1]

The complete change in public feeling is also shown by the character of the petitions which flowed in upon the legislature. In January and February there was presented every few days a communication from some "Union meeting" in favor of the Crittenden compromise or other accommodation

---

[1] Morton sent word to the Federal authorities that the citizens of Indiana were taking advantage of the brisk demand for their surplus products in the South and that such a commerce was the channel by which the rebel armies would be supplied. He suggested that trade should be cut off with all the states which had refused to furnish volunteers. It was not long before the Federal government found it necessary to take this course, and on the 8th of May the Secretary of War ordered that provisions, as well as munitions of war, should be stopped at Cairo. On April 24 Morton telegraphed to Governor Yates, of Illinois: "I learn by dispatch received to-night that John Grace, of Rising Sun, started South from Madison last Thursday with a flat-boat loaded with bacon for Vicksburg. He was at Louisville on Sunday. Have him stopped at Cairo. It is for Southern troops." On May 10 Morton telegraphed Secretary Chase: "I hope you will not rescind your order in regard to the shipment of provisions over the Louisville and Nashville road. Virginia agents have been supplying themselves that way."

with the South. Now the petitions came from mass meetings at Indianapolis demanding the raising of more regiments, the immediate arming of the people, and the equipment of calvary to protect the southern counties.

The trouble at the outset of the war was not in the supply of men, these came in such abundance that the government would not receive them, but they lacked arms and accoutrements. We have seen the fruitless efforts of Morton to collect the arms of the state.

On the 29th of April the legislature passed an act directing the Governor to procure a supply sufficient for twenty thousand men.

Anticipating this bill, and anxious to be early in the market, Morton, on April 27, directed Calvin Fletcher, of Indianapolis, to proceed to manufactories of arms and make careful examination as to the kinds that could be purchased and the prices.

Mr. Fletcher's mission accomplished but little, though he prosecuted it in all directions. Afterwards his son, Professor Miles J. Fletcher, Superintendent of Public Instruction, was sent upon a similar errand, and with a like result. Several other agents also made ineffectual efforts. In the meantime Morton continued to set forth the needs of the state to the Federal authorities. He wrote a pressing letter to the Secretary of War requesting twenty thousand stand of arms and a supply of artillery. In May he wrote to General McClellan, then commanding the western division of the army, that the condition of Kentucky was alarming, that the people on the border were defenseless, and that batteries and heavy guns should be provided. But the general government was unable to afford the aid demanded. Indiana must rely upon its own resources.

On the 30th of May the Governor appointed Robert Dale Owen agent of the state to procure arms and equipments. Mr. Owen started at once for New York. From that day till he closed his labors, on February 6, 1863, all purchases on behalf of the state were made through him.

A few days after the legislature had convened the three months' regiments were formed into a brigade under General Thomas A. Morris, and sent to West Virginia where they took a leading part in the earliest campaign of the war.[1]

Many are the stories which come down to us of "the three months' picnic," as this campaign was called. Of serious fighting there was very little. The attack upon the camp at Philippi, from which the enemy incontinently departed, leaving his breakfast for the Hoosiers, the fun of catching stray rebels and administering "the oath of allegiance," the skirmish at Rich Mountain under Rosecrans, the capture of the gorges of Laurel Hill, the chase of a foe who would not stand and resist, the surrender of Pegram to McClellan, the extermination of secession influence in West Virginia, the establishment of the "Loyal Covenant" organized by the Wheeling convention—all this was very encouraging. It afterwards led to the appointment of McClellan as Commander-in-Chief of the Union armies. But it was quite misleading as to the character of the stern tragedy in which many of the men were soon to take part, and as to the strength and courage of the enemy by whom they were to be confronted. The awakening came when, on the 22d of July, just after the troops had been ordered

---

[1] Their passage through Cincinnati excited enthusiasm. The Cincinnati *Commercial* said: "The Governor of Indiana has out-generaled the Governor of Ohio. The contrast in the condition of the troops of the respective states proves it. The former has sent four admirably equipped regiments to the battle-field and has two more ready to march at an hour's notice. The Governor of Ohio has not a single regiment in camp or in field properly equipped for service. The Hoosier troops are all armed with rifled muskets, are uniformed, and furnished with their complement of camp equipments." A few days later, in noticing the passage through Cincinnati of other regiments, the *Commercial* said: "The stout and brawny appearance of the Indiana troops was universally remarked. . . . They were armed with the new U. S. muskets of the most approved pattern. No Ohio troops have such arms. Whose fault is it?"

home at the end of their three months' service, the news came of the defeat at Bull Run and the rout of the Union forces, who fled in a confused mob and did not halt until they reached the shelter of the capital. Amid the seething turmoil of confusion, indignation and despair which followed this disaster, the Hoosier troops, who had been placed amid more favorable surroundings and had lost in the campaign only twenty-four men by battle and disease, returned as conquering heroes to their homes.

While they were still engaged in the campaign Morton had dispatched messengers to them with letters urging them to re-enlist, and when they came back, in the latter part of July, arrangements were made to reorganize them. There would have been little trouble in persuading them to enlist for three years had it not been for an unexpected delay in mustering them out, which caused great dissatisfaction. They had not yet become accustomed to arbitrary military restraint. They wanted to go home to their families for a short visit, and could not understand why they were not allowed to do so. Time and again they were assured that on the following day they would be discharged and paid, and each time they were disappointed, until they lost patience and threatened to mutiny and to destroy the government offices and the lives of the men who were deceiving them. But their confidence in Governor Morton was unshaken. Through his expostulations the outbreak was averted and the men persuaded to await their discharge. When they were mustered out, many of them were so exasperated that they declared they would never enter the service again, and it was only through the persuasion of the Governor that the dissatisfied were induced to enlist, until the great body of these troops had returned to the Federal service. These men, with the other three years' troops who enlisted in 1861, were perhaps the most efficient soldiers which Indiana furnished at any time during the war. They were "the bulwark and pride of the army."

Morton was persistent in urging the government to accept troops more freely and to impose fewer restrictions as to the kind of service in which they might engage. Being desperately in earnest himself, he believed that the Union forces ought to be overwhelming, and that no effort should be spared to bring out the last man required. His tender of the six additional regiments was followed, on the 20th of April, by a tender of ten regiments to be ready in six days, but he could not get the government to take them. On April 22 he tendered one or more regiments of cavalry, but Cameron answered that cavalry could not be accepted.[1]

The legislature had acted in accordance with Morton's views, and on May 7 the " Six Regiment Bill " had been passed, authorizing the troops which Morton had collected and organized upon his own responsibility to be called into the service of the state for one year. They were to be subject to the order of the Governor, with power to transfer them to fill any subsequent requisition of the President.

On May 3 Lincoln issued his second call for volunteers for three years. Indiana's share was four regiments, and on May 16 the Secretary of War sent his requisition for that number. The question was submitted to the men in camp whether they would enlist for three years and the regiments which should send the highest number of volunteers for that term were to be chosen. The bulk of the men promptly agreed to go. On May 21 four regiments were turned over to the general government and the rest remained in the state service. But Morton knew that this second call, like the first, would be inadequate. The patriotism of the people at this time would furnish all the troops demanded. Why limit the call

---

[1] The original call for seventy-five thousand men for three months provided that they should be organized into companies of sixty-four each. On the 20th of April the Governor telegraphed the department that in Indiana the companies had organized a hundred strong, and he urged that they be permitted to remain at that number. After a spirited correspondence the department yielded.

to four regiments? He besought Indiana men who were in Washington to urge the acceptance of more troops.

At last his importunities were heeded. Ten other regiments were raised and accepted in advance of the President's July call for five hundred thousand men.[1]

On July 18 Morton procured from the President an order accepting the two regiments remaining in the state service for the unexpired portion of their twelve months' enlistment. An incident attending the tranfer of one of these regiments to the Federal service illustrates Morton's influence over the soldiers.

Only two companies of the 12th regiment had been provided with rifles. There was great dissatisfaction among those who had to retain their smooth-bore muskets, and many of the soldiers refused to be transferred to the Federal service. The colonel and other officers of the regiment used their best efforts to quiet the disturbance, but these efforts were inef-

---

[1] On May 13 Morton telegraphed to Holloway, Commissioner of Patents : " I hope you will press upon the war department the importance of taking six more regiments from Indiana for three years." He several times addressed Caleb B. Smith, Secretary of the Interior, to the same effect. On the 22d he telegraphed to McKee Dunn and David Kilgore, members of Congress, asking them to urge the acceptance of more troops. Cameron returned a short answer : " The quota of Indiana is four regiments and no more." But Morton was not to be put off. He sent to Smith the following : " Can you not aid us in getting the acceptance of six additional regiments for three years ? There is much ill-feeling here from the apprehension that Indiana has nobody in Washington to speak for her. I mention this for your benefit."

Ohio was getting ahead of Indiana and Morton's ire was aroused. On May 24, 1861, he sent the following dispatch to Smith : " Governor Dennison told me to-day the department had accepted twenty-one regiments from Ohio for three years, while they only take four from Indiana. The three-months' men tendered their services for three years and are rejected. What can this mean ? Why this discrimination against Indiana ? McClellan reviewed the troops to-day and expressed his astonishment at their proficiency. Will you not see that justice is done Indiana ? We want the three months' men accepted for three years."

9—MOR.

fectual.   Finally Governor Morton was called in.   The regiment was drawn up in line and he addressed the soldiers, telling them that their government needed their services; that he regretted that they could not be furnished with the best arms, but that these could not then be had; that if they waited until such arms could be obtained another Bull Run might be the result;   that if they would proceed to Washington with the arms they had, they should be provided with rifled muskets at the earliest moment possible.

At the close of the Governor's appeal he asked them if they were satisfied, and every soldier answered "yes."

After the disaster at Bull Run there was no difficulty in getting troops accepted.   New regiments were rapidly organized.   By the 1st of September there were sixteen from Indiana, and by the 6th of January, 1862, that state had contributed to the Federal army forty-eight regiments of infantry, twelve regiments of cavalry and seventeen batteries—in all, 53,035 men.

CHAPTER XI

WHILE Beriah McGoffin sat in the executive chair of Kentucky the Unionists of that state looked to Morton for protection and support. They used to call him "the Governor of Indiana and Kentucky," and their affection for him was unbounded. The circumstances which led to this feeling form an interesting episode in the history of the war.

For two generations, the ties between Kentucky and Indiana had been very strong. Indiana had been wrested from British power by Kentuckians under George Rogers Clarke. In pioneer days Kentuckians had threaded the forests to protect its infant settlements from Indian depredations. In many places they had established themselves upon the land and founded the towns. When Tecumseh's tribes had threatened the destruction of the whites, Kentuckians had crossed the Ohio and taken part in the battle of Tippecanoe, which put an end to the struggle and restored security. As time went on a thriving trade had been established between the two states, and the friendship which followed closer business relations had been strengthened by numerous intermarriages, and had received official recognition at the hands of the respective executives in mutual visits made and hospitalities exchanged between Governor Wright, of Indiana, and Governors Crittenden and Powell, of Kentucky.

The traditions of Kentucky were peculiar. Being a slave state, originally a portion of Virginia, and settled chiefly from the mother commonwealth, she had inherited the characteristics and shared many of the thoughts and feelings of states already in rebellion. But there were points of difference. Her slave population was not large. Her physical conditions were not especially adapted to slave labor. Her geographical situation presented a frontier accessible for several hundreds of miles to an invader coming either from the North or from the South, and if she seceded she would become the battle-ground of the war. But more important still were the political sentiments of her people. While the first generation of her settlers had adopted the state-rights creed, embodied in the famous resolution of 1798, the belief in this disintegrating doctrine had been extinguished by the powerful influence of Henry Clay. Whatever the shortcomings of that eminent statesman, the key-note of his life was an enthusiastic devotion to the Federal Union. His influence over Kentucky was unbounded. "The spell which the great magician cast over his people was like the glamour of mediæval enchantment. It bound them in helpless but delighted acquiescence in the will of the master." He was the advocate of an enlarged construction of the powers of the general government, of a protective tariff, of a United States bank, and of the great compromises for the preservation of the Union and peace between the sections. He owed, as he declared, "a paramount allegiance to the whole Union, a subordinate one to his own state." After Clay died, and the spell of his personal presence was no longer felt, this sentiment of loyalty to the Federal government was weakened, but it could not be entirely obliterated. When the cotton states seceded, opinions in Kentucky were greatly divided. A large majority of the people were undoubtedly for the Union, but only conditionally so. Their sympathies were mostly with the South. It was common to hear among them such declarations as these: "The Northern troops shall not march over our soil to invade the South;" "When it becomes clear that the war is an abolition crusade, waged for the destruction of slavery, Kentucky will arm against the government.'' Nobody advocated the coercion of the South, and secession was denounced largely because it had been undertaken without consulting Kentucky.

At this time the Governor's chair was occupied by Beriah Magoffin, a politician of the most pro-slavery and Southern type. It was his purpose to carry the state out of the Union if he could. In the latter part of January he called the legislature together in special session, and to this body he delivered a message, denouncing the election of Lincoln as resting upon sectional animosity. He declared that his efforts had been used to bring about a convention of the slave-holding states to demand reasonable guarantees, but that the proposition had met with limited favor, and that the time for it had passed; that in a few days eight states would declare their sovereign independence, and to that extent, at least, our Union would have ceased to exist. He recommended a constitutional convention to which should be referred the future Federal relations of the state, and urged the appointment of commissioners to meet representatives from the border states in convention at Baltimore.

All this meant nothing more nor less than secession. He had called the legislature together to provide for a convention and to pass the ordinance just as the Gulf states had done. But the legislature was not ready for the final step. It refused to adopt the Governor's propositions, but recommended the assembling of a national convention to amend the Federal constitution. Yet the sympathies of its members were mostly with the South. In answer to certain resolutions passed by the legislatures of Maine, New York and Massachusetts those bodies were informed, that whenever armed forces should be sent to coerce the states which had seceded ''the people of Kentucky, uniting with their brethren of the South, would resist such invasion.'' When the attack was made on Sumter, and the President issued his call for troops (measures which consolidated the North in support of the Union and the war), public opinion in Kentucky was, if possible, more distracted and divided than before. To the President's call Magoffin answered: "Kentucky will furnish no troops for the wicked purpose of subduing her sister Southern states." The Governor convened the legislature again, which, when it met, approved of his refusal by a vote of eighty-nine to four.

About this time appeared the remarkable doctrine of "armed neutrality," which figured prominently for some months in the politics of Kentucky, and which was referred to in Governor Morton's message. It is not possible to explain nor, indeed, to understand exactly what this doctrine was. At a so-called "Union meeting" in Louisville, held about this time, it is thus expressed:

"We oppose the call of the President for volunteers for the purpose of coercing the seceded states, and we oppose the raising of troops in this state to co-operate with the Southern Confederacy.

"The present duty of Kentucky is to maintain her present independent position, taking sides, not with the administration nor with the seceding states, but with the Union against them both, declaring her soil to be sacred from the hostile tread of either, and, if necessary, to make the declaration good with her strong right arm."

That is to say, Kentucky would stay in the Union, but she would refuse obedience to the Federal government, and would resist its armies if they came within her borders. And in this impossible way she was to remain an "oasis of peace in a desert of war."

If this policy could have been carried out to the end, the Confederacy would have been the gainer, for besides refusing to comply with the demands of the Federal government for troops, Kentucky would have presented an extensive barrier, across which it would have been impossible to pass to reach

the states lying further south.   But a continuance of neutrality was impossible, and as matters turned out the assertion of
this doctrine was of ultimate advantage to the Union cause,
since it delayed secession until a healthier public sentiment
had grown up and the state government had fallen into better hands.

It was on the very day that Morton had delivered to the
legislature the message in which he had spoken of the relations of Indiana to Kentucky that he received from Magoffin
the following telegram :

" Will you co-operate with me in a proposition to the government at Washington for peace, by the border states, as
mediators between the contending parties?

"B. MAGOFFIN."

Morton believed that this invitation was designed as a trap.
If he should accept it, he must abandon his active support of
the government and the raising and arming of troops.   A
mediator could not arm on behalf of one of the parties whose
claims were before him.   Magoffin never thought that Morton would enter into such a scheme.   What he wanted was a
refusal of his invitation, as well as of a similar proposition
which he had just made to Governor Dennison, of Ohio.
Armed with these, he would proclaim to the legislature and
the people of Kentucky that the North was bent on coercion,
and would do nothing for peace, and that the only course open
was to join the South in rebellion.   But Magoffin had not
taken the full measure of the man with whom he had to deal.
Morton responded at once :

" I will unite in any effort for the restoration of the Union
and for peace which shall be constitutional and honorable to
Indiana and to the Federal government, and will, if you so
appoint, meet you to-morrow at Jeffersonville.   Answer.

"O. P. MORTON."[1]

---

[1] Governor Dennison of Ohio did not want to commit himself until he
had found out what Morton intended to do and on the same day he tele-

This was not what Magoffin wanted. Morton had not re-fused to talk of peace, but he had not compromised his posi-tion. The restoration of the Union, of which Magoffin had not spoken, came first in the answer of Morton. The propo-sition for an immediate conference looked like coming to close quarters. Magoffin knew the treachery of his own purposes, and he did not care to have it exposed in a personal inter-view with Morton.

It was only the day before this that Dr. Luke P. Black-burn had made a speech in New Orleans, in which he had de-clared that he had been sent by Magoffin to apply to the Gov-ernors of Mississippi and Louisiana for arms; that Kentucky was in heart, as she would be in a few days in act, shoulder to shoulder with her sister states in the Southern Confederacy.

It is not possible to say now how much of this Morton knew when he answered the telegram, but Magoffin evidently feared that he knew enough to make a personal interview a dangerous matter, so on the following day (April 26) he re-plied:

" I have answered a dispatch from Governor Dennison say-ing that I would meet his representatives, or send commis-sioners, at Spencer House, in Cincinnati, on Tuesday even-ing, four o'clock. Please meet us there or send commission-ers. I can not go to Jeffersonville to-morrow. Answer.

" B. MAGOFFIN."

A dispatch from the Confederate Secretary of War to Ma-

---

graphed : "Governor Magoffin inquires whether I will co-operate with him in a proposition to the government for peace by the border states acting as mediators between the contending parties, and says that he has an understanding with you on the subject. Tell me what that is, or advise me whether the proposition looks merely to preserving peace between the border states or to the adjustment of the controversy between the gen-eral government and the seceding states. Had you not better send me your views at large by a special messenger in addition to telegraph?"

Morton communicated to Dennison his answer to Magoffin, and urged Dennison to join in the interview.

goffin, asking for troops and showing that the Kentucky Governor was engaged in efforts to send them, was now published in the Louisville *Journal*. The Governor of Indiana became all the more eager for the personal interview. Dennison had informed Morton that he could not be present, but Morton was very urgent and sent a number of telegrams insisting that the Governor of Ohio should come. In one of these he asked Dennison to go to Cincinnati the night before the proposed conference, that they might confer together in advance. In another he said of Magoffin: "He can not fail to develop his policy. I regard the meeting as a very important one." Finally, Dennison agreed to be present. On the 28th Morton sent to Magoffin the following answer: "I will meet your Excellency at the Spencer House, Cincinnati, on Tuesday next, at 4 P. M. I expect to meet you in person." This was exactly what Magoffin did not want. He did not dare to submit to the cross-examination which such an interview might involve. Morton was present at the appointed time, and so was Dennison, but Magoffin did not come. He sent instead, Colonel Thomas P. Crittenden with a note stating that the colonel was fully authorized to represent him. Morton and Dennison told Crittenden that they desired the personal presence of Magoffin, and Crittenden sent him word to come. Crittenden also addressed to Morton the following letter: "Dear Sir: I have been instructed by the Hon. B. Magoffin, Governor of the State of Kentucky, to solicit the co-operation of yourself and the Hon. William Dennison, Governor of the State of Ohio, in an effort to bring about a truce between the general government and the seceded states, until the meeting of Congress in extraordinary session, in the hope that the action of that body may point out the way to a peaceful solution of our national troubles." Governor Morton replied next day (May 1): "I hold that Indiana and Kentucky are but integral parts of the nation, and, as such, are subject to the government of the United States, and bound to obey the requisitions of the President, issued in pursuance of his constitutional authority; that it is the duty of every state government to prohibit, by all means in its power, the transportation within its own limits, of arms, military stores and provisions, to any state in open rebellion and hostility to the government of the United States, and to restrain its citizens from all acts giving aid and comfort to the enemy; that there is no ground in the constitution midway between the Federal government and a rebellious state, upon which another state can stand, holding both in check, and that a state must take its stand upon one side or the other, and I invoke the state of Kentucky, by all the sacred ties that bind us together, to take her stand with Indiana, promptly and efficiently, on the side of the Union, the action of the Federal government in the present contest being strictly in accordance with the constitution and laws of the land. Entertaining the views above indicated, I am compelled to decline the cooperation solicited by you. I take this occasion to renew the expression of my earnest desire that Kentucky may remain in the Union, and that the intimate political, social and commercial relations which exist between her and Indiana may never be disturbed, but may be cemented and strengthened through all coming years.'' Magoffin did not answer Crittenden's message asking him to come in person to the conference, but on the following day, May 20, he appeared in Cincinnati. The two other Governors, having no reason to expect him, did not wait. He had been requested by Morton to be there in person, but when he came he excused his delay by the claim that '' he did not know he was expected,'' and in explanation of his neglect to give notice of his coming, he said, that he had '' started off without taking time to reply.''[1]

---

[1]A correspondent of the Cincinnati *Enquirer* thus attempts to explain Magoffin's conduct: "He did arrive in Covington at the appointed time, but could not get across the Ohio river. . . . In place of courte-

Governor Magoffin had doubtless convened the second special session of the Kentucky legislature for the same purpose that he had called the first, to carry the state out of the Union amid the whirl of excitement caused by the outbreak of the war. Tennessee and Virginia, which had hitherto delayed secession, and whose fidelity to the Federal government would make the withdrawal of Kentucky geographically impossible, went out about this time. Magoffin wanted Kentucky to go with them. His message accused the President of usurpation. He declared that the constitution had been violated, the Union broken, and that the state ought to be armed and a convention called. But his second attempt was no more successful than the first. Although the legislature approved of his refusal to furnish troops to the President, they would go no further. "Armed neutrality" was the limit.

Indeed many of the Union men themselves were parties in the work of raising this most illogical barrier against the greater danger which confronted them. By this means they would "educate the people" to more patriotic views. They would first delay and then kill the secession movement. Magoffin had lost credit by his premature efforts to carry the state out of the Union. He now published a letter in the Louisville *Journal*, denying that he had been engaged in a secret effort to send troops to the Southern states. But the terms of this communication were not ingenuous, and its imperfect statements only served to throw further light upon his unwillingness to meet Morton and Dennison.

The Kentucky problem was a great puzzle to the Indiana legislature. The situation was not fully understood, and the

---

ously waiting till morning, Morton and Dennison left in three hours, after first writing Magoffin a disrespectful letter declining to enter into any negotiations to effect the object which all had in view from the beginning. The tone and manner in which Governor Morton, of Indiana, refused to go on with the negotiations were coarse and rude as was the letter he left for our Governor. We hope to get the state of Kentucky armed, when we think we shall be more respected. . . .   A KENTUCKIAN."

secession element south of the Ohio was credited with greater strength than it actually possessed. The legislature was much distracted between the fear of offending Kentucky on the one hand and the fear of obstructing the government on the other. Resolutions were introduced and schemes devised almost as illogical as "armed neutrality." But nothing came of them. The problem of keeping Kentucky in the Union had to be managed more skillfully and quietly than could be done by resolutions of the General Assembly.

Morton believed that any effort by that state to maintain a neutral position would result in as much real harm to the Federal government as if the state seceded; that to refuse free transit to the Union army was itself an act of rebellion. He was determined to do what he could to make Kentucky a loyal state. He realized that the defense of Indiana could be most effectively made south of the Ohio river. He took every opportunity to urge the Union men of Kentucky to place her unconditionally on the side of the national government. He had secret agents in different parts of that state who kept him posted as to the plans of the secessionists. He communicated to the administration the defenseless condition of the Indiana and Ohio border if Kentucky should secede, and pressed upon the war department the importance of fortifications and gunboats on the Ohio, until Secretary Cameron twitted him with being frightened. The subsequent invasion of the state by Morgan indicated that his apprehensions were not without foundation. A meeting of the Governors of Ohio, Indiana and Illinois was called to consider the crisis. It was held at the Bates House, in Indianapolis, on the 21st of May. General McClellan, as military commander of the department, was invited to the consultation. Morton insisted upon energetic measures. A memorandum was signed by the three Governors and forwarded to the President, stating that they concurred in the opinion that the United States should take possession, by force, of prominent points in Kentucky, such as Louisville, Covington, Newport and Columbus, and the railroads leading to the South. If Colonel Anderson and others could raise regiments of Kentuckians to occupy these points it would be advisable to have them thus occupied. If Kentuckians could not be found, United States regulars would be the next best for the purpose, but these places ought to be occupied at an early day, even if it had to be done by volunteers from adjoining states. The Governors believed that this course would save Kentucky to the Union, and that otherwise the secessionists would control her.

The more cautious policy of the President was not willing at that time to adopt any measure which would arouse the antagonism of the people of Kentucky. But he sent to Louisville a young, energetic Kentuckian, Lieutenant Nelson, of the navy, to influence public opinion. Major Anderson, also a Kentuckian, who had been much praised for his valor in the defense of Fort Sumter, was commissioned to receive volunteers from Kentucky and Virginia and was sent to Cincinnati for that purpose. Home guards were organized, and Nelson brought 5,000 muskets to Louisville, which were distributed among them. The Kentucky legislature adjourned on the 24th of May. Among the most prominent of its Union members was Lovell Harrison Rousseau, who now resolved to raise a force of Kentuckians for the Union. He stated his plans to the President, who authorized the undertaking, but in deference to public sentiment it was determined to humor the advocates of ''neutrality''[1] until the result of the approaching congressional election should be known, so these troops were organized outside the state, at ''Camp Joe Holt,'' near Jeffersonville. Morton took an active part in the enterprise. He made Rousseau heartily welcome,

---

[1] On May 20, after it was found that "armed neutrality" was as far as Kentucky was willing to go, Magoffin issued his proclamation notifying the United States, and Confederate States, that he solemnly forbade any movement upon Kentucky soil.

gave permission to Indiana citizens to enlist in his regiments, and allowed companies to be organized in Knox and Dearborn counties. Morton was in frequent consultation with Kentucky Unionists, and busied himself in securing and distributing arms and in urging the government to prompt and energetic action.

At this time "Kentucky neutrality" was given a great deal more respect than its intrinsic merits deserved. General McClellan on one side and General Buckner (who commanded the state guard) on the other, made a sort of treaty providing that the government would allow no troops to enter Kentucky and that the state should remain neutral, although, if the Confederate armies entered on one side the Federal forces might do the same on the other. But it was easy to see that such an arrangement must soon come to nothing. Recruiting had been going on in the state for both armies.

On the 20th of June the congressional election was held. The popular majority for the Union was not far from fifty-five thousand, and nine out of ten of the Congressmen chosen were outspoken Union men. A law passed by the late legislature requiring an oath of allegiance to the United States soon brought about the disorganization of Buckner's state guard. The secessionists went South, the Unionists became bolder. In July Federal camps were established within the state, and at a general election on the 5th of August a legislature was chosen in which the Union members outnumbered the others three to one.

A conspiracy was now set on foot to carry Kentucky out of the Union by force. The leaders met in Scott county on the 17th of August, to mature their plans. Magoffin was to demand the withdrawal of the Federal troops, an agitation in favor of the Confederacy was to be undertaken in the central part of Kentucky, and Confederate troops were to invade the state from the South. And in this manner the attempt was actually made. On August 19 Magoffin wrote to President

Lincoln, demanding the removal of the troops. Lincoln replied that he did not think the Governor's request represented the wish of the people of Kentucky, and regretted that he could find in Magoffin's letter no desire for the preservation of the Union.

Three public demonstrations were announced—a meeting in honor of Vallandigham, in Owen county, on September 5; a "peace" meeting at Frankfort, the capital, on September 10; and a state-rights meeting at Lexington, on the 20th. Meanwhile the Confederates made ready to enter Kentucky from the South.

It looked as if a crisis were approaching. Morton had agents in various parts of the state, who kept him informed of the drift of affairs. On August 29 he telegraphed to the Assistant Secretary of War that civil war in Kentucky was inevitable; that a force should be ready to march to the support of the Union men at a moment's warning, and that arms should be provided for the home guards in the border counties. On September 2 he telegraphed again: "At the risk of being considered troublesome, I will say the conspiracy to precipitate Kentucky into revolution is complete. The blow may be struck at any moment, and the southern border is lined with Tennessee troops, ready to march. If we lose Kentucky now, God help us!" On this occasion his views were reinforced by a dispatch to President Lincoln from J. T. Boyle and James Speed, on behalf of the Union men of that state, declaring that Kentucky desired that Morton be authorized to send to the Ohio river five regiments and two batteries. The President accordingly directed him to send these regiments to such points as General Anderson might approve.

But the efforts to drag Kentucky into secession proved abortive. The demonstration in honor of Vallandigham, the peace meeting at Frankfort, and the other projects for an agitation had failed to produce the uprising which was expected.

On September 4 the Confederate General Polk entered the

state and seized Columbus, an important strategical point near its southwestern corner. There was now a great flurry among the neutrality men, and protests were sent to the Confederate government, but Jefferson Davis telegraphed to Polk that necessity justified his action.[1]

Buckner now issued a proclamation in the most florid style of Southern declamation, declaring that Kentuckians had seen a portion of their own people drawing from beneath a cloak of neutrality the assassin's dagger which was aimed to pierce their hearts. "With the poniard at the breast they expect us to caress the hand of the assassin and to lick the dust from the iron heel of tyranny which is raised to crush us." He urged Kentuckians to follow him. "Let our lone star shine as an emblem of hope from the deep sky-blue of our banner, over brothers who join in the grasp of friendship."

There were a good many who joined. In the early period of the war there were more Kentuckians in the Southern army than in the Federal forces. But the Union feeling of the state was now aroused. The new legislature, which had met on the 2d of September, was notified by Magoffin on the 9th that Polk had seized Columbus. It directed the Governor to issue his proclamation that "Kentucky expects the Confederate troops to be withdrawn unconditionally." The Governor vetoed the resolution upon the ground that the Federal troops were not also included. But Magoffin's power for mischief was now at an end. The legislatiure passed the resolution over his veto and he made the proclamation. Jefferson Davis, as well as Polk, now offered to withdraw if the Union forces would do the same. The legislature declared that this condition was an insult to which Kentucky could not listen without dishonor, and that the invaders must be expelled. A law was passed making enlist-

---

[1] A day or two afterwards General Grant, learning of this seizure, offset it by the occupation of Paducah at the mouth of the Tennessee, a place of equal military importance.

ment in the Confederate army a misdemeanor and the invasion of the state a felony. The enlistment of four thousand volunteers for the Federal service was authorized. "Kentucky neutrality" was at an end. Magoffin, who vetoed several of these measures, now found his vetoes ineffectual. In the following year, unable to accomplish anything for the South, and met at every point by a hostile and distrustful legislature and people, he resigned.

Governors Morton and Dennison had been for a long time ready to assist the Union men of Kentucky whenever an emergency should require it. General Anderson had written to Morton asking for troops to repel the invasion from the South. One of Morton's agents, who was in Frankfort watching the movements of the secessionists, telegraphed the Governor on September 16 that a message had come to Magoffin stating that General Zollicoffer had marched his brigade through Cumberland Gap into Kentucky. On the 18th Buckner, with five thousand troops, took possession of Bowling Green, and sent forward a detachment to occupy Munfordville on the Louisville road. The object of Zollicoffer was thought to be Frankfort, while the forces under Buckner threatened Louisville.

Just before Bowling Green was taken, the Kentucky troops, under Colonel Rousseau, were ordered from Jeffersonville to St. Louis to join Fremont. This would have stripped Louisville and rendered its occupation by Buckner an easy task. When Morton learned the condition of affairs he had the order countermanded. Rousseau's men crossed the Ohio into Kentucky, joined the home guards and were sent out on the Nashville road under command of General Sherman. Morton sent every available man in Indiana to the defense of Louisville. The arms in the Indianapolis arsenal were forwarded to Jeffersonville and distributed from that place. He also called upon the administration for troops, and was far from

10—Mor.

satisfied with the failure of the President to respond to his demands. Lincoln doubtless had his hands full in attempting to supply the needs of other sections of the country.

Indiana had already given more than her quota of the troops demanded by the general government. But in the eyes of her patriotic Governor this was not enough. On October 2 he issued a proclamation setting forth the condition of affairs in Kentucky, the invasion of the state from the South and the impending danger to Louisville. He referred to the old friendship between the two states, and insisted that the best defense of Indiana could be made by repelling the invaders from Kentucky. Indiana, he said, had already done as well as any other loyal state, and better than many. Her troops were in every camp from the Potomac to the Missouri, and wherever their valor had been put to the test, they had been found equal to the occasion. But because other states had not done their whole duty, it would be madness for Indiana to refuse to do even more to crush the rebellion and bring about the speedy restoration of the Union. The sooner this was done the quicker the conflict would be ended. He therefore called upon all men capable of bearing arms to cast aside their ordinary pursuits and enroll themselves in the ranks of the army.

Upon those who remained at home he urged the duty of making provision for the families of the soldiers. All should give freely of their substance for the relief of those whose husbands, fathers and brothers were risking their lives for their country.

The people responded with alacrity. On October 8, General Sherman was appointed to the command of the troops in Kentucky. He was much oppressed by the difficulties of the situation. The recruits from Ohio and Indiana were accumulating, but there were no equipments nor organization, while recruiting for the Federal service in Kentucky was slow and difficult.[1]

About this time, Secretary Cameron stopped at Indianapolis, on his way from St. Louis to Washington, and in company with Senator Chandler, took supper with Morton at the Governor's mansion. He was quite talkative and laughed heartily at Sherman's idea that it would take two hundred thousand men to recover the Mississippi states. He made no secret of his belief that Sherman was crazy, and unfit for any military command. He derided Sherman's notions of the need of cavalry and artillery as old-fashioned and silly, and was boyish in his fun over the " Minie rifle," and over improved arms generally. The old smooth-bore musket, in the hands of well-disciplined infantry, he regarded as the best kind of arms. Morton listened to this talk in silence.

Sherman's forces were, however, sufficient for the immediate occasion. The Confederates were in even greater need of supplies than the Union troops, and no attack was made upon Louisville.[2] The condition of the Union forces kept steadily improving. On the 20th of January, 1862, General Thomas defeated Zollicoffer at Mill Spring. In February Grant won his brilliant victory at Fort Donelson, and Sidney Johnston was compelled to abandon Bowling Green and to fall back two hundred miles along the line of the Memphis and Charleston Railroad. The danger of Confederate supremacy in Kentucky for some time to come had passed away.

Morton's efforts on behalf of the Union men of that state inspired them with warm admiration for him. George B. Prentice, in the Louisville *Journal,* thus expressed the pre-

[1] Sherman had a consultation with Cameron, and told him that sixty thousand men would be needed for the defense of the Ohio Valley, and two hundred thousand men for an offensive campaign.

[2] About this time Morton urged upon the authorities at Washington that a large force should be concentrated at Louisville, and moved thence to Nashville, dislodging the Confederates at Bowling Green.

vailing sentiment: "The call of the patriotic Morton upon the people of his state will endear him still more deeply to the people of Kentucky, who already appreciate the great obligations they are under to him. He has been emphatically Kentucky's guardian spirit from the very commencement of the dangers that darkly threaten her existence."[1]

---

[1] The Lexington *Observer* said: "There is no man in the nation to whom Kentucky owes a larger debt of gratitude than to Morton. . . It has been well that having virtually no Governor of her own, she could find so invaluable a friend in the Governor of a neighboring state."

The following incidents are also in point. Shortly after Kentucky had been cleared of Confederate troops, a lady of Frankfort, the owner of a large number of slaves, visited some friends in Indianapolis, and inquired for Governor Morton. Upon ascertaining that he was absent and would not return for several days, she prolonged her stay, saying she would not leave Indiana until she had seen him, "because he is our Governor, as well as yours, and has been, ever since the beginning of the rebellion."

Colonel Silas F. Miller, of the Galt House, in Louisville, saw a well-known secessionist walking along the street and laughing, on one occasion when Morton was in town. He knocked the man down, and when asked about it, said he did not propose that any damned secessionist should laugh while Morton was there.

CHAPTER XII

MILITARY APPOINTMENTS

ONE of Morton's most perplexing tasks during the early period of the war was the selection of officers for the army. Prior to July 22, 1861, it was his duty to appoint all officers of Indiana troops, and by the act of Congress passed on that day he had the power to commission all regimental and company officers for the volunteers raised in the state. The responsibility for the selection of these men was very great. Morton had no military experience, and there were not many men in Indiana who had such experience. There had been five Indiana regiments in the Mexican war, and there were a few West Point graduates in the state. That was about all. The people had received no military instruction.

Morton had to work in the dark. He was obliged to commission many men whom he did not know, and concerning whose fitness he had to rely wholly upon the opinion of others. Some he knew, but had little means of determining their qualifications for military service. And he had to consider, not only the fitness of the men commissioned, but also the wishes of the volunteers and of the people, and the effect of his appointments upon the *morale* of the troops, the encouragement of recruiting and the consolidation of public sentiment in favor of a vigorous prosecution of the war. He had to settle rival "claims," allay jealousies, and incur the enmity of the disappointed. But in Morton the military as well as the political instinct was very strong, and native ability supplied, in great measure, his lack of experience.

First of all he determined that, as this was a war for the preservation of the Union, all mere party preferences should be laid aside. He would consider nothing but the best interests of the country. He would use all possible means to induce every able-bodied man to enter the army. Democrats must take part in the struggle as well as Republicans, and must receive equally fair treatment, and the list of his appointments at the outbreak of the war contains the names of great numbers of Democrats selected to fill important positions.

He went farther than this, perhaps even too far, in his wish, to strengthen the Union sentiment in the Democratic party. We have seen that in the January session of the legislature, Horace Heffren had become notorious for his bitter attacks upon the administration, and his expressions of sympathy with the secessionists. But Heffren had become "converted," and Morton urged him, as well as John C. Walker, Gordon Tanner, and others of similar feelings, to take part in the work of raising troops. They did so; they enlisted and Morton appointed them to office. On the 25th of May, Heffren announced to the legislature that the Governor, without his solicitation, had tendered him a major's commission in the Thirteenth Regiment, and he asked to be excused from further legislative duties. This appointment aroused a storm of opposition in Morton's own party. Mr. Bingham, a Re publican, introduced a resolution censuring the Governor, and supported it in an energetic harangue.

Heffren answered that it would be better for his accuser to enlist, as he had done, than to introduce this matter of discord.[1]

---

[1] Heffren's subsequent conduct showed that his conversion had not been complete. "His appointment," says Sulgrove, "did not make him loyal, nothing short of omnipotence could do that, but it made him hold his tongue and act like a loyal man for a while."

The legislature recognized the patriotic motives which dictated this appointment, and laid the resolution upon the table by a vote of seventy to nine.

There was another appointment which gave Morton much trouble. Immediately after the first call for troops, he made his old friend, Isaiah Mansur, commissary-general. When Mansur entered upon the work of his office, the difficulties which confronted him were certainly great. Many thousand troops had rushed to Indianapolis, in answer to the President's call. There was no time to organize the department, or learn the duties of the place. Purchases had to be made at once upon a large scale, without system, generally without competition, and the troops to be supplied were not yet accustomed to army rations, but looked for such fare as they were used to at home. Mansur soon brought down upon himself a storm of wrath. The meat was too salt, the dried apples were wormy, the coffee was "effeminate." One man from Hancock county said that "a wild goose could take a grain of coffee in its bill, swim down the Mississippi from St. Paul, and make a better beverage all the way to the gulf than the soldiers got at Camp Morton."

These complaints were general, and the legislature upon investigation found that the rations issued were not in accordance with the commissary's schedule, that there had been favoritism on the part of employes, that the coffee was "basely adulterated" with parched beans, and that fourteen-ounce packages were distributed as one pound, though it did not appear that Mansur had made anything by this. Bad meat, however, had been furnished by the commissary-general out of his own pork-house which he rather naively explained by saying that the commissary's duties were hard and that "if anything was to be made out of the sales he thought he had as good a right to make it as any one." On May 25 the House of Representatives requested Mansur's removal. The Governor accepted his resignation, and appointed Hon.

Asahel Stone as his successor. Stone administered the office with economy and care.

Such appointments as those of Heffren and Mansur were eagerly taken up by all who were displeased with Morton upon other grounds. Thus M. C. Garber, editor of the Madison *Courier*, attacked him viciously in the columns of that paper.[1] "He is willing," said Garber, "to strengthen himself by uniting as far as possible the debris of the Democratic party to his fortunes." No selection could satisfy this editor. Morton appointed too many lawyers "who spent their time in the taverns talking politics." The policy of the Governors of Ohio, Indiana and Illinois was "a succession of blunders." They had been hurrying about with the speed of locomotives attending to details which would have been done better by a "dollar-a-day" clerk.

Morton went to Madison and answered these attacks in a speech to the soldiers and citizens, delivered on Main street in that city in the latter part of July. We have no other record of this speech than the comments of the *Courier*. Mr. Garber "did not wish," he said, to "push the controversy any further." He had prudently staid away from the meeting.[2]

Another appointment made by Morton, and criticised with bitterness, was his choice of Solomon Meredith as colonel of a regiment which the latter had been raising in the eastern part of the state. Meredith was a man inexperienced and

---

[1] When the Governor established camps of instruction at Richmond, Lafayette and Terre Haute, for the six regiments which had not yet been accepted, this was denounced by Garber as an exact parallel to the policy of Secretaries Floyd and Toucey under Buchanan. The border towns on the Ohio, he said, were left exposed and would be cut off from the rest of the state.

[2] Morton became suspicious that some person near him was furnishing the information upon which these attacks were based. The manuscript of one of Garber's editorials was placed in Morton's hands and it was found to be in the handwriting of Mr. Cravens, who was then upon Morton's staff. Morton confronted Cravens with the paper, and dismissed him.

uneducated, but courageous and energetic. Later in the war he earned distinction, and commanded the Iron Brigade at Gettysburg. George W. Julian, in a communication to the Cincinnati *Commercial*, asserted that Meredith had raised his regiment without authority, had imposed upon the President and induced him to write a letter to Morton accepting it, and that Morton had used this letter to justify himself in making an unpopular and improper appointment.

But such criticisms fell for the most part upon inattentive ears. There were not many complaints at that early period of the war. As a general thing, the people of the state were willing to co-operate heartily with an executive who, in the midst of great obstacles, was doing his best to cast the full strength of Indiana on the side of the Union. It is always the unsatisfactory selection which causes comment. The great mass of excellent appointments, like the thousand acts which go to make up good reputation, pass without specific notice. While it would be idle to say that grave mistakes were not made, the officers chosen by Governor Morton were in the main selected with skill and judgment, and their conduct during the war reflected credit upon the state.

The entire number of commissions issued by Morton was 18,884. Of these less than one and sixth-tenths per cent. were dismissed or resigned for the good of the service.

In a speech made many years afterwards, he thus spoke of his experience: "When I first began to make appointments of officers during the war, not understanding the business (it was all new to me), I tried to please everybody and his friends, but I soon found that would not do. I found that out almost immediately, and I then determined that I would follow the dictates of my own judgment without fear or favor—that I would do the best I could. I did not know whether I would come out of the war with a single friend or not, but I had to go to the point where I felt that it would make no difference. I sometimes made mistakes, sometimes

I appointed the wrong man, but I congratulate myself that the officers from Indiana, as a body, compared favorably with the officers of any other state, and that few of them disgraced the state, or dishonored their commissions."[1]

---

[1] Morton resented any interference with his right to make appointments and control the organization of the troops. For instance, in a telegram to Congressman Kilgore at Washington, dated May 22, 1861, he said: "By an agreement gotten up with two or three colonels, Colfax has gone on to tender the six regiments of three months men for three years. This can only be done properly by the Governor. The attempt is to supersede me with the men and officers. He will be there to-morrow morning."

Again, in July, he thus addressed the President: "I learn incidentally that the Indiana delegation has nominated men to be appointed brigadier-generals. I do not know who they are, and have not been consulted. I have had much more to do with the officers than any member of Congress, and have had much more responsibility in connection with the organization than any of them, and believe I should at least have the chance of being heard before any action is taken." The President replied that the appointments had not been made, and asked Morton to telegraph his recommendations.

CHAPTER XIII

THE SOLDIERS' FRIEND

MORTON'S efforts were not confined to raising troops and providing them with officers. He took it upon himself to see that the soldiers of Indiana did not suffer for lack of clothing and other necessary articles. It made no difference to him that this duty belonged to the Federal government. These troops were Indiana men; they had gone to the field in response to his call, and he did not intend that they should suffer. One case illustrates the persistency of his efforts in their behalf. Some Indiana troops had been sent to West Virginia, and were, during the latter part of August, under the command of General Reynolds at Cheat Mountain Pass. Although it was still summer, the men were beginning to suffer during the chilly nights which in that mountainous region betokened the coming of autumn. Morton, on learning that these troops were not provided with overcoats, applied to the United States quartermasters, first at Indianapolis, then at Cincinnati, and finally to Quartermaster-General Meigs, at Washington. Two lots of four thousand each were forwarded, but neither of these reached their destination.

It is interesting to trace the insistent dispatches by which, day after day, Morton sought to follow up these two consignments through the hands of inefficient and dilatory officials.

Some of the overcoats were distributed to other troops; some of them were lost by a flood on the Kanawha river. Morton was emphatic and bitter in his complaints of the negligence and incompetency which confronted him at every point. He sent his private secretary, Holloway, in search of the coats, then his commissary-general, Asahel Stone. It was not until October 7, after nearly six weeks of continuous efforts, that the supplies finally reached the troops in West Virginia.[1]

---

[1] On August 20, Morton, who was then in Washington, telegraphed to his representative in Indianapolis: "Urge Major Montgomery to get over-coats from any good material, and do not wait for a public letting. Do have them made at once. The men are suffering for them, and I am distressed. Perhaps a few thousand can be furnished at once by Captain Dickerson."

In pursuance of this telegram, application was made to Montgomery, who was the United States quartermaster at Indianapolis. He could not furnish overcoats, so Vajen, Morton's quartermaster-general, went to Cincinnati and applied to Captain Dickerson, assistant quartermaster at that place. Dickerson sent four thousand coats to General Rosecrans, who was in command of all the troops in West Virginia. Meanwhile Morton, who was still in Washington, applied to United States Quartermaster-General Meigs, who telegraphed Major Vinton, in New York, to have four thousand overcoats made for the Indiana men. Morton returned to Indianapolis, learned of the consignment forwarded by Dickerson, and on September 2 telegraphed to Meigs as follows: "We have supplied from Cincinnati overcoats for our troops in West Virginia. Will you please direct Major Vinton to send the four thousand overcoats you ordered to the Indiana regiments in Maryland and about Washington? If he will send two thousand more, making six thousand, it will be enough for all the Indiana troops in those places."

In regard to the four thousand sent by Captain Dickerson, Morton telegraphed the fact to General Reynolds at Cheat Mountain Pass, and added, "Will you look after them at once, and see that somebody else does not get them?" To this Reynolds answered (September 3), "The Thirteenth Regiment is well clothed. The Fourteenth and Fifteenth are ragged—all require overcoats. Requisitions were made on the quartermaster's department a month since for the clothing required, and it ought to be here in a few days." Morton then inquired (September 4), "On what quartermaster did you make the requisition?" and Reynolds replied: "On the quartermaster at Beverly." Morton (September 5) then informed Dickerson of this requisition and added: "The men are suffering from cold on the mountains." On September 10, finding that the troops had not been supplied, he telegraphed to General Meigs: "General Reynolds made a requisition for supplies for Indiana troops in West Virginia more than a month ago, and nothing heard from. Four thousand overcoats sent for same troops were stopped and held subject to order of General Rosecrans. The clothing Major Montgomery purchased for same troops is held by Captain Dickerson in Cincinnati. Is there no help for this state of

Morton was determined that the soldiers and the people should know how these delays occurred, so the telegraphic correspondence was given to the press. His efforts to relieve

things? The troops are suffering." On the following day Morton inquired of Captain Leib, the quartermaster at Clarksburg, Va., "Have any overcoats reached you?" And Leib answered (September 12), "The overcoats arrived here yesterday, and will be sent to Webster this morning." Three days later Adjutant-General Wheat informed Morton that the great coats went forward from Clarksburg, on the 12th. But still they did not reach the troops, so Morton telegraphed to General Rosecrans, on September 17: "I am in constant receipt of news from Reynold's brigade that our troops are nearly naked. All I can do will not get them clothes. Will you do me the favor to have Captain Chandler send them some? If I attempt to send them from here Captain Dickerson will inform me that he is attending to that. Orders must come through you. Please oblige me in this." To this dispatch Morton did not receive an answer for some time. Meanwhile he learned from Reynolds on September 19 that only twelve hundred overcoats had arrived, and from Captain Stewart, commanding a cavalry company of Indiana men, he received, the same day, the following:

"I have seen Captain Chandler. He tells me you had better attend to the uniforms for my company, as the government is very slow about these things. My men are actually suffering for want of warm clothing." So Morton again (on September 20) appealed to Meigs: "Of the four thousand overcoats sent to Western Virginia for the Indiana troops, they got twelve hundred. Requisitions made six weeks ago have not been filled, although Captain Dickerson says the articles have all been sent to General Rosecrans' quartermaster. The last dodge was that requisition must be signed by Captain Chandler, who is with Rosecrans, far away from Reynolds, and where the supplies are. Captain Stewart's cavalry are almost naked, and have sent home for supplies. My opinion is that in the quartermaster's department in Western Virginia there is great incapacity or fraud, and that abuses are becoming insufferable. I pray you give it your attention."

On September 25 General Rosecrans telegraphed to Morton: "Your dispatch is received. Ten thousand uniforms have gone down to General Reynolds; none have reached this moving column. I feel even more discouraged than General Reynolds. The necessity of pursuing the enemy prevents attention to clothing the troops. The difficulty now appears in a fair way to be remedied. I have caused inquiries to be made as to those overcoats. I think they will be found on their way from the railroad to Huttonville." But still the ten thousand uniforms did not arrive.

Meanwhile Morton was equally persistent and equally unsuccessful in following up the four thousand overcoats ordered of Colonel Vinton in

the troops met with universal approval. Even the Indianapolis
Sentinel gave him unstinted praise.

New York. In answer to his dispatch of September 2, asking that these
should be sent to the Indiana troops in Maryland and about Washington,
General Meigs telegraphed from Washington: "All overcoats in New
York have been ordered here, and the six Indiana regiments named in
your dispatch will be supplied from this place."

But the troops got no overcoats. Morton learned by a dispatch from
Vinton that they were sent on the 22d of August, and on September 6 he
inquired, "To whom were the four thousand great coats for our troops
sent?" Vinton replied September 7th, "To Captain Craig, at Bellaire,
Ohio." Morton telegraphed Craig, "Did you ever receive them?" And
Craig answered (September 9), "I received four thousand great coats, but
with them no advice as to what troops they are for. The regimental quartermasters of Indiana troops can make a requisition upon me, approved
by General Rosecrans, and I will deliver immediately." Morton at once
notified Reynolds and added, "Send a man after them so as to be sure."
He also telegraphed to Craig, "Keep the coats for Reynolds." Reynolds
answered Morton as follows: "Requisitions have been made in due form
twice. The first time more than a month ago, and in accordance with
orders from department. . . . . Overcoats not yet arrived." And again
Morton notified Meigs. But all this was to little purpose, for when, later
in the month, Morton telegraphed to Craig again, he learned that "There
was nothing in the invoices on the boxes nor in the letter of advice to
show that these overcoats were for any particular troops. Twelve hundred have been issued to Indiana troops at Cheat Mountain Pass and the
rest to parties equally destitute." Morton now found the twelve hundred
overcoats were the entire result of his efforts, and that the troops were
suffering more than ever. So he telegraphed again to General Meigs,
and when Commissary Stone returned to Indianapolis, Morton sent word
to D. C. Branham, an Indiana Congressman in Washington, "General
Kelly, at Grafton, will receive three thousand overcoats to-day from Cincinnati. Will not General Meigs order him to issue two thousand of
them to the Thirteenth and Seventeenth Regiments? They are suffering
dreadfully. The clothing sent to Rosecrans was packed in a warehouse
on the Kanawha, while our men were suffering, and the rise of the river
inundated and ruined it. Our men also want uniforms and shoes. The
roads will soon be impassable. Urge Meigs to take steps to relieve them
immediately." This is communicated by Branham to Meigs, who answered, "I order shoes to Grafton from Philadelphia to-day. Overcoats
go into the field. Some neglect in Western Virginia in distributing the
large supplies sent to that state." But Morton, not content with asking
Meigs' intercession, also telegraphed directly to General Kelly, at Grafton, Va.: "Captain Dickerson informs me that he has sent within a few

As the fall season advanced Morton realized that it would not do to rely wholly upon the general government to look after the comfort of Indiana soldiers. Voluntary contributions would do much to supply their wants, so, on October 10, he issued an appeal "to the patriotic women of Indiana," calling attention to the approach of winter and to the sufferings which the troops must undergo. Many articles, he said, which, to men with houses and warm fires, were hardly more than luxuries, to those with no protection but a tent, no bed but the ground, were absolute necessaries and might save many lives which would be lost without them. These things, it was hoped the patriotic women of Indiana would supply. An additional blanket to every man would preserve hundreds to their country and to their families. Two or three pairs of good, strong socks would be invaluable to men who must often march all day in the snow, and lie down with cold and benumbed feet, on the frozen ground. Good woolen gloves or mittens, while adding greatly to the comfort of the men, would materially increase their efficiency. The sewing societies and benevolent associations, by giving their energies to this work, could speedily provide the necessary supply, and women who had no opportunity to join such associations could emulate each other, and see who should do most for their country and its defenders.

---

days three thousand great coats, five thousand blankets and other supplies. Will you please do me the favor to issue two thousand of these great coats to the Fifteenth and Seventeenth Indiana Regiments under General Reynolds; also four thousand blankets. They are perfectly destitute. I will take this as a personal favor. Their destitution has been a matter of great mortification to me." And Kelly answered "Your request shall receive my personal attention."

Reynolds reported on October 7: "Clothing is coming forward. In a few days we will have a supply for the Thirteenth, Fourteenth and Seventeenth, except shoes, socks and caps, the last not so important. Shoes and socks are much needed. These regiments have suffered greatly, but not a man among them has any fault to find with the Governor of his state. They are all informed of the exertions made in their behalf, and appreciate them, and when opportunity offers, will show their appreciation."

This appeal met with a cordial response, and so liberal were the contributions, that in the latter part of the winter the quartermaster-general issued a circular stating that he had enough. The commissary-general was charged with the duty of distributing these supplies, and agents were sent to various places where the troops were stationed to do the work.

Morton also determined to take into his own hands the matter of supplying Indiana soldiers with overcoats for the coming winter. He purchased ten thousand of these at $7.50 each, and got the Federal government to assume his contract. He procured from Quartermaster-General Meigs an order for ten thousand more, to be forwarded to Indianapolis. He went to New York, and, through Robert Dale Owen, bought nine thousand more. This made twenty-nine thousands in all. For a portion of these last he paid the government price of $7.75, but five thousand of them he was compelled to purchase at $9.25 each. The demand was great and the price had gone up.

An account of these things soon reached Indianapolis, and was published in the home papers. It excited the wrath of Major Montgomery, the quartermaster at Indianapolis, who thought that Morton was interfering with his duties. Montgomery had purchased four thousand great coats through Robert Dale Owen, and imagined that this was part of the purchase referred to. He published the correspondence between Owen and himself, and added: "His Excellency has done so much to merit the thanks of his state that it is not necessary to 'steal thunder' for him and misrepresent the general government."

On October 31, 1861, appeared another card from Montgomery, denouncing the effort to "put wind into the sails of his Excellency."

On November 6 Morton published an answer saying that he regretted that Montgomery had made a statement about a matter of which he knew nothing, but had guessed through the medium of excited feelings. The transactions were entirely different.

Morton also had difficulty with the Indianapolis quartermaster regarding the purchase of the overcoats for $9.25. Montgomery informed him that General Meigs prohibited purchases at more than $7.75. Morton answered that he was sorry that such instructions had been issued as no overcoats could be purchased for that price, adding: "Indiana will not allow her troops to suffer if it is in the power of her officers to prevent it, and if the general government will not purchase supplies at these rates, Indiana will."

Matters had now reached such a point as to demand Montgomery's translation to other fields of usefulness. Morton could not tolerate him, and it was largely through the solicitations of the Governor that he was sent to another jurisdiction, from which, on November 11, he discharged his Parthian arrow in the shape of a card to the *Sentinel*, admitting his error in regard to the Governor's purchase, but saying that Morton had suppressed the fact that the coats were not those prescribed by army regulations, and adding: "The pruriency for fame not earned, discovered by the Governor, will surprise some readers, but will be no less instructive. It will enable them to place a proper estimate upon his pretensions in other matters."[1]

---

[1] The *Sentinel* naturally took Montgomery's side in this controversy. At first it doubted the quality of the overcoats which could be furnished for $7.50. The coats were too cheap. Then it learned of a house willing to make the same coats for $6.60, and the coats were too dear. That contract was "a fat take" for somebody. What was Morton's object in seeking Montgomery's removal? etc. The answer in the columns of the *Journal*, to the editor who made these insinuations, was an *argumentum ad hominem*, pithy and energetic. "It was he who, on at least two occasions, with trembling knees and pallid lips, appealed to Governor Morton for protection against the violence of his neighbors, who were convinced of his disloyalty to the government and determined to punish it. That protection was promptly and generously extended, but when the danger was past the ingrate turned upon his protector with new slander, and has

Toward the end of November, 1861, Morton appointed a number of financial agents to visit the Indiana regiments, receive the funds which soldiers wished to send to their families, and deposit these in the "Branch Bank," at Indianapolis, subject to draft.

The good work accomplished in the distribution of the supplies furnished by "the patriotic women of Indiana" had satisfied Morton that a permanent organization should be created for this purpose, and he decided to establish a "Military Agency." Dr. William Hannaman was made general agent and took charge of the receipt and distribution of supplies.

Morton thus describes the growth of this organization in his message to the legislature of 1863:

" I very early adopted the plan of sending agents to look after the condition, and, as far as possible, to supply the wants of the Indiana troops. These agents had their instructions to follow in the track of our armies; to pick up the disabled, who might have fallen by the wayside; to visit the hospitals, report the names of the sick, wounded and dead, and afford relief wherever it could be afforded; to inform the state authorities what kind of supplies were needed and where; to visit the troops in the field, ascertain their wants and condition, and aid in having their requisitions for supplies promptly filled. These agents have generally performed their duty well, and, I believe, have been the instruments of saving the lives of hundreds of our gallant soldiers, and of relieving a vast amount of suffering and destitution. Many of their reports are descriptive of sufferings, sorrows and death, that would melt the stoutest heart, and show better than can be learned in any other way, the dreadful horrors of war. The labors of these agents were not confined to any particular duties, but extended to every kind of relief that soldiers

---

since pursued him with alternate misrepresentations and solicitations for office."

might need. They aided in procuring furloughs for the sick and wounded and discharges for such as would not be able to serve again; in furnishing transportation at the expense of the state for such as had not means of getting home; in receiving the soldiers' money and distributing it to their families; in hunting up the descriptive rolls for such as had been long confined in hospitals, but for want of their rolls could not be paid or discharged; in visiting battle-fields, bringing home the wounded, and distributing sanitary stores. In some cases I directed the chartering of steamboats for the transportation of the sick and wounded, and in general instructed my agents to incur such expenses as were absolutely necessary to enable them to execute their mission. But notwithstanding all that has been done, I have to lament that the efforts have come far short of the mighty demand, that much suffering has gone unrelieved, and that many of our brave sons have languished and died among strangers, in destitution and neglect, with no friend present to soothe their last hours, or mark the spot where their ashes sleep.''

Morton also employed, at Washington, Louisville, Nashville, Memphis, Cairo, and Columbus, Ky., permanent agents, who rented houses where sanitary goods were kept, and other agents at Philadelphia, St. Louis, Keokuk and New York, for the relief of such Indiana soldiers as were carried to those points.

In February, 1862, Morton established the '' Indiana Sanitary Commission,'' under the charge of Dr. Hannaman, as military agent, and Alfred Harrison, of Indianapolis, as treasurer. Collections were made by soliciting agents and auxiliary societies, and the distribution of the supplies was made through the military agency. The Indiana troops were the first care of this commission, but applications for relief from others were not overlooked after they were provided for.

This separate action by a single state provoked unfavorable

criticism elsewhere. It was said of this organization that it was selfish, that it provoked jealousy and dissatisfaction, especially among the soldiers of other states, and thus interfered with the discipline of the army.[1]

But the Indiana commission did more efficient service than could have been accomplished by mere co-operation in the work of the United States Sanitary Commission, and Gover-

---

[1] The charge of selfishness is thus formulated by the author of the "History of the United States Sanitary Commission" : " The indiscreet zeal which was willing to recognize state lines, even in its ministrations of mercy on the battle-field, can hardly be too strongly condemned. It was only another development of that obnoxious heresy of state sovereignty, against which the whole war was directed, and its practical injury to the national cause, in creating disaffection among troops who were not recipients of its peculiar care, was scarcely less great than its violation of those sacred laws of humanity which make no distinction in the relief bestowed upon the suffering, except to seek first for those who most need succor. Against this stateish spirit the Sanitary Commission resolutely set its face at all times," etc. (See pages 150, 151.)

The Adjutant-General of Indiana, in his official report, thus considers the question: . . . "Men naturally prefer to trust those whom they know. And the six hundred thousand dollars contributed by Indiana are due largely to the fact that they were given by Indiana men, through Indiana agents, for Indiana's soldiers, at the instigation of Indiana's Governor. . . . . The magnitude of the operations of the National Commission required complicated machinery. In Indiana, every man employed was known to the commission. Its operations could be commenced at a moment's notice anywhere, and carried on without the hindrance of 'approvals,' 'orders' and 'requisitions.' There was nothing to gain by changing the State Commission to an auxiliary of the United States Commission. And there was something to lose—the home interest, the state pride, and the liberality incited."

Governor Brough, of Ohio, thus speaks of the Indiana commission, in his annual message in 1864 : " While extending our own operations, I have carefully watched those of our sister state of Indiana, and have found that her system merits the strongest commendation. It is simple in its character. Its central society at the capital, under the immediate care of the Governor, receives all the contributions from the various aid societies. . . . While the first care of the agent is for Indiana men, no other soldier in want or distress has ever, to my knowledge, appealed to an Indiana agency without having his wants relieved. The Indiana agents have frequently divided their stores with the agents of Ohio, and we have always tried to reciprocate the kindness."

nor Morton felt well justified in providing first for those whom his own exertions had called into the field.

This Indiana Sanitary Commission was Morton's special pride. He was never tired of devising ways and means to improve its efficiency.[1] Sulgrove, the editor of the *Journal*, tells us that often the last thing he would do before going to press would be to "trim up" for publication one of Morton's appeals for sanitary help, for which the Governor had left rough memoranda in his office late at night.

At no time were Morton's exertions for the welfare of the troops more earnest than after the battle of Shiloh. On April 9, only two days after that sanguinary struggle, he chartered steamers to bring home all the wounded who could be moved.[2] On the following day he sent a force of sixty surgeons and over three hundred nurses to take care of the sick and wounded on their arrival. They came in large numbers upon the hospital boats thus suddenly improvised, and the condition of the men improved greatly on the way home.

Morton himself went to the battle-field and, on several

---

[1] The last report of the president, Dr. Hannaman, thus referred to Governor Morton: "To no other person is the commission under so many obligations for help and encouragement as to the Governor of Indiana. In the midst of the accumulation of cares and labors which the rebellion has thrown upon his shoulders he has always found time to interest himself in whatever concerns the welfare of the soldiers of the Union, and he has, with uniform wisdom and patience, given his time and thought to the commission. His eloquent appeals have opened the hearts and pockets of our people; his influence has removed obstacles out of our way and broken the force of opposition; his steady and cordial co-operation has lessened our labors and divided our responsibilities, while his prompt and wise expedients have contributed to perfect our plans and secure our success."

[2] After all had been collected and the steamers were about to pull off, the major of a Kentucky regiment, who had a score of wounded men, sought out the captain in charge, and implored him to take these men also. "But my orders, sir, allow me to take only Indiana troops," replied the boat's captain. "But, damn it, sir," retorted the major, "isn't Morton Governor of Kentucky? If he can care for our state he certainly will protect you in caring for our soldiers." The boys were taken, and one of them related the incident.

subsequent occasions, visited the army. His presence there is thus described by General W. T. Sherman: "He remained with us during our advance on Corinth in May, 1862, frequently came to my bivouac on the extreme right, and rode with me during the day. He was a close observer of the practical details of camp life, sat his horse well, and was as impatient as the rest of us at our slow and methodical, if not timid, advance. We were short of wagons to bring from Pittsburg Landing the necessary supplies, and he wanted to send to Indiana for one thousand wagons and teams. The idea of war operations being delayed by the want of means easily procurable was a thorn in his side, and I believe that, had his advice been heeded, we would have taken Vicksburg that summer and turned eastward to do the work which had to be done two years afterwards. But the time was not yet ripe. We had to endure three more years of bloody battle, and I know that we at the front always felt the more confident because we knew that Oliver P. Morton was at his post in Indianapolis, multiplying his efforts in the days of reverses and cheering us on in success."

After the battle of Shiloh, Morton applied to the Secretary of War for permission to appoint two additional assistant surgeons to each regiment in Halleck's army. This permission was at first refused. But he was not to be put off, he sent by telegraph an appeal which the Secretary of War found too strong to resist, and seventy additional surgeons were dispatched to the Indiana troops. This movement led to an amendment of the law by which a third surgeon was added to each regiment.

Morton also superintended the establishment at Indianapolis of the "City Hospital," under the care of Drs. Kitchen and Jameson.

Indianapolis was a rendezvous for returning and departing troops. They needed a place for rest and refreshment. At first, quarters were procured at different hotels, and an agent was placed at the railway station to attend the arrival and departure of trains and furnish meals and lodging. But in June, 1862, Morton determined to established permanent quarters for soldiers passing through the city, and at his instance the Federal government paid for the erection of a building in a grove near White river, north of the railroads. The state government fitted it with necessary furniture. The expense of maintaining it (except the rations, to which the troops were entitled) was borne by the Indiana Sanitary Commission. These accommodations, however, soon proved too small, and a second building was constructed in the latter part of the same year, a third in the year following and two more in 1864.

Morton's care was not confined to the Union soldiers. The Confederate prisoners also received his attention. Camp Morton, which was at first established as a rendezvous for volunteers, was soon used for another purpose. When Fort Donelson was captured a great number of prisoners were taken and these had to be cared for. On February 17, 1862, Morton telegraphed to General Halleck that provision would be made for three thousand. They soon came in greater numbers. On February 22, five thousand arrived; eight hundred were sent to Lafayette, three hundred to Terre Haute and the rest remained at Camp Morton.

Colonel Richard Owen, who was then organizing the Sixtieth Regiment, at Evansville, was ordered by Morton to bring his incomplete command to Indianapolis to guard the prisoners. The buildings were turned into barracks and hospitals for the Confederates. The exposure to which these troops had been subjected was very great. The men were thinly clad, and unaccustomed to the rigor of a winter in the North, and they had been poorly fed. The day after they arrived there were more than four hundred under medical treatment. For the first month or more the sick list increased rapidly, and the mortality was alarming. But the condition of affairs soon became better. Morton, through the *Journal*, endeavored to inspire a kindly feeling toward these men, as the following extract bears witness: ''We have abundant cause for congratulation, none for boisterous exaltation over the fallen. What a proper sense of our position and cause requires, humanity doubly demands. These men, misled as many have been, were but a few months ago friends and neighbors. Let us bear a memory of the past, if they do not, and add no bitterness to their hard fate by unkind taunts or unfeeling treatment.''

Three hundred of these prisoners needed clothing. Morton telegraphed the Secretary of War and had them supplied. Buildings were hired outside the camp and turned into infirmaries. Many of the sick were removed to private residences. By means of a bakery established by Morton the prisoners secured fresh bread in place of the army hardtack, and the saving made in rations by the greater economy of this system went into a fund for the purchase of other articles not supplied by the government. Morton had an oven built where they might prepare corn-bread.

The prisoners generally spoke well of their treatment. Some of them wrote to the Governor thanking him for his kindness. There were occasional complaints, but these were the exception. A letter to the Governor was signed by great numbers of the prisoners, asking him to permit the men of the Sixteenth Regiment to remain on guard on account of their humanity and kindness. Colonel Owen, the commandant appointed by Morton, was highly esteemed by those in his charge.

A general exchange was effected in August, 1862. The camp was closed as a prison soon afterwards, and occupied as barracks by Federal troops. It was opened again later in the war under the control of the Federal authorities.[1]

---

[1] During the Vicksburg campaign of 1863 several thousand prisoners were sent to Camp Morton. From that time until the close of the war the number confined there ranged from three to six thousand. In 1891 a controversy arose concerning an article in the *Century* magazine, written by Dr. John A. Wyeth, a soldier in the Fourth Alabama Cavalry, who was

During the fall and winter of 1862, Morton busied himself
with many plans for the welfare of Indiana soldiers. On November 14 he published an appeal, asking aid for their fami-

---

there from October, 1863, to March 1, 1865. Dr. Wyeth declared that the
barracks at Camp Morton had been erected as cattle sheds, with wide
cracks between the weather-boards; that the prisoners slept without straw,
and with only one blanket; that the barracks were heated by four stoves
placed twenty feet apart; that only the strongest men could get near them,
and that many of the prisoners were frozen to death; that the rations were
insufficient to satisfy hunger; that rats and dogs were eaten, and men stole
from their comrades and took scraps from the swill tubs; that many died
from starvation; that letters containing complaints were destroyed; that
great cruelties were practiced and prisoners were wantonly killed; that
over fourteen per cent. perished during the confinement.

These charges were vigorously contested in an article by Wm. R. Holloway, Morton's private secretary, published in the *Century*, September
1, 1891 (page 757). Holloway stated that he had visited the barracks frequently; had eaten of the food; had seen the prisoners in good health,
and comfortably clothed. He declared that no complaints had been made to
him, nor to any one of whom he had ever heard; that the mortality was
caused by the sickness of the prisoners when they reached the camp; that
when they were exchanged their condition was better than that of the
men who guarded them. In answer to a statement of Wyeth that he had
counted eighteen dead bodies carried out upon a single day, Holloway
referred to the official reports, which, as well as the books of the undertaker who took charge of the bodies, showed that no more than nine had
died in one day. The undertaker was positive that none had died from
freezing. General Hovey, commander of the district, had inspected the
camp every week, and had heard no complaint. These matters all occurred
at the time when Camp Morton was under Federal supervision, and when
Governor Morton officially had nothing to do with it. Still Holloway
insisted that Morton would never have permitted the mistreatment of
prisoners had it come to his knowledge. During the legislative session of
1865 rumors reached the Governor that the prisoners at Camp Morton
were badly treated, and on the 14th of February he sent a communication
to the members of the legislature, calling attention to these reports and
asking them to go in a body to the camp and make a personal examination.
(*Century*, September, 1891, page 766.) They all went and were urged to
visit every part of the grounds and talk to the prisoners. They inspected
the arrangements for furnishing provisions, and looked into the quality of
the food. The prisoners made no complaint, and not a member of the
legislature had a word of censure for the management.

Dr. Wyeth, in his rejoinder to Holloway's article, corroborated his

lies.   Indiana had then nearly a hundred thousand men in the field.

On November 29, he addressed a circular letter to Congressmen, arguing, with great power and clearness, the necessity for an increase in the pay of private soldiers.

The foregoing facts are illustrations of Morton's watchfulness over the welfare of the troops whom he had called into service.   His constant care led them to consider him preeminently, "The Soldiers' Friend," a name which, however belittled and degraded by its subsequent application to undeserving demagogues, is still, in the hands of him who has fairly won it, a just title to lasting renown.

---

charges of cruelty by the statements of a number of prisoners. (*Century*, September, 1891, page 771.)

Holloway replied by showing in detail (*American Tribune*, March 31, 1892) that Wyeth's witnesses were unreliable.

No doubt there were individual cases of cruelty. A number of men were shot while attempting to escape, and it is probable that some suffered severely during the winter of 1863 and '64, when the temperature went down to twenty degrees below zero, but the charge of systematic cruelty on the part of the authorities in command of the camp is refuted by two circumstances.

First, the prisoners had many friends and sympathizers in the community around them. The peace Democrats of Indianapolis would have been only too willing to give currency to charges of mismanagement and to make the most of such charges for party purposes. Communication between the camp and the outside could not be prevented. The prisoners knew of the attempt made to liberate them in the summer of 1864. No effort would have been spared by the Knights of the Golden Circle and the Sons of Liberty to give publicity to charges of the mistreatment of these men, yet there was little complaint.

Second, Dr. Wyeth's charges were withheld for twenty-five years, until most of those who had taken part in the prison management were dead. The cruelties at Belle Isle and Andersonville were notorious at the time. Similar conduct at Camp Morton could not have been kept secret for so long a period.

CHAPTER XIV

ROCKVILLE SPEECH — WAR TAX — ARSENAL — MILITARY ASPIRATIONS

WE have seen that when Sumter fell all voices of sympathy with the South were stifled in a universal burst of patriotic enthusiasm. But later on this sympathy began to show itself, stealthily at first, in complaints and criticisms of those in power, afterwards more boldly and defiantly. These manifestations of discontent began in Indiana as early as the summer of 1861. Military appointments, it was said, had not been fairly divided between the parties. "If the Democrats are to be excluded from the offices of the army, then let Republicans find the privates in their own ranks." . . "Governor Morton manifested a liberal spirit at the outset, but he has changed his tactics." On July 27 a mass meeting of the Democracy of Putnam county condemned the conduct of Morton and of all others "who plunged us into this unnatural war with our brethren before every peaceable means had been fairly and honestly tried." John G. Davis, a leading pro-slavery Democrat, visited several of the western and southern counties, delivering speeches against the war and counseling a cessation of hostilities and a proposition for compromise. He pictured in lively colors the enormous burden of the war tax. He encouraged organizations to resist its collection. His favorite calculation was to ascertain the amount of tax paid for each foot of ground gained by the Federal army in Virginia, and the total amount at the end of the war. Davis lived in the neighborhood of Rockville, in

(171)

Parke county, and it was determined to hold a Union meeting at that place as a demonstration against his doctrines and the discord which they were likely to engender. This meeting was held on August 3. A vast multitude assembled and Morton made a speech. He began calmly and dispassionately, showing the need of submission to the constituted authorities, but he grew more stern and bitter as he proceeded in his denunciations of the men who were stirring up the spirit of dissension at home. His purpose was to overawe this growing sentiment of disloyalty. He thus answered the plea for compromise:

" I love peace as much as any man. Its sweets are as delicious to my taste as to that of any human being. But when I say this, I mean peace that is safe; peace that is crowned with liberty and the blessings of an enlightened civilization. I do not mean that peace which is the sleep of death, which is purchased by foul dishonor; nor that peace which is but another name for submission to tyrants and traitors. It is utter folly to talk about peace without pointing out some method by which it may be obtained. I know of but two conditions upon which peace can be had. The first is by submitting to the disruption of the Union and the destruction of the government. The second is by the submission of the traitors now in arms. And I appeal to you to-day to answer the question in your own hearts, upon which of these conditions do you demand peace? . . .

" We are told that unless we suspend hostilities an enormous public debt will be contracted, which will oppress the people for generations to come. A large public debt is undoubtedly a calamity; but there are greater calamities. What will it profit the people if they should gain the wealth of the world but lose their government and their liberties? . . . What is there to compromise but the integrity of the Union and the existence of the government? . . . The Southern commissioners sent to Washington last spring offered no compromise, and would listen to none. Their haughty demand was that we should consent to the dissolution of the Union. They said if this government would write its name on a blank piece of paper, and allow them to write over it the conditions upon which they would return to the Union, they had none to write. A proposition to compromise now is simply a proposition to surrender. We are fighting to preserve what our fathers fought to win. They established a republican government, and we will uphold it. If their cause was sacred, then is ours sanctified by their blood, and it should, if necessary, be sealed by our own. To concede the doctrine of secession is to concede the destruction of our political institutions. That doctrine is, that any state has a right to withdraw from the Union at pleasure. This being admitted, it requires no argument to prove that we have no government, but a mere voluntary association, with no higher sanction than a pleasure party from which any guest may retire at his own convenience. Carried to its consequences, it does not stop with the destruction of the national government, but is equally fatal to state and local institutions. Commerce must perish when one party can withdraw from a contract without the consent of the other. No other war ever involved such mighty interests, comprehending, as it does, the political and social existence of the nation, and if, while everything is thus at stake, we shall suffer ourselves to be distracted, and conquered by old prejudices and jealousies, the world may well pronounce final judgment that the experiment of self-government has failed, and that men can be successfully ruled only by an aristocracy or a monarchy.

"Much has been said in certain quarters about the right of free speech. I allow no man to be a more firm and consistent advocate of that right than myself. I have battled for it for many years, and shall ever uphold it as the very touchstone of liberty. It will be found, on examination, that those who are now making this clamor, mean, by 'freedom of speech,' the right to weaken our hands and strengthen the hands of our enemy, by distracting our counsels, by reviling our cause, by ignominiously proposing to lay down our arms, and by assailing the purity of the men who are laboring to uphold the honor and integrity of the nation. If any man in the rebellious states should utter in defense of the North a tithe of what men in Indiana are daily saying in defense of the South, he would not be permitted to live long enough to say his prayers. This freedom of speech is exercised in behalf of those who deny the right to all others, and who punish its exercise with death. The men who thus abuse this right of free speech are living monuments of the forbearance of our laws, and of the liberty and security of persons guaranteed by our institutions. While I will uphold freedom of speech, it is not improper to say that there are state and national laws defining and punishing the crime of treason, and that infractions of these laws will be punished with the utmost rigor.''

It is said that the cheering at this significant declaration "fairly shook the trees."

The effect of Morton's philippic upon the peace Democrats was extraordinary. They writhed and howled with rage. "What did his Excellency, the commander-in-chief of the army and navy of the state of Indiana, and head of the secret police thereof, mean by these declarations?'' asked the *Sentinel*. . . . . "A more devilish sentiment was never uttered by any despot.''

There were other signs of discontent with the government, but the Union feeling was so high that meetings opposing the war were often broken up by violence. At Centreville, a Democratic convention was held and a committee appointed to prepare resolutions. Lafayette Develin, Morton's old associate, attempted to speak, but he was interrupted by armed men who hissed and groaned and denounced him as a secessionist until he desisted, and the resolutions were not offered.

There was also trouble at the Democratic county convention held in October at Indianapolis. A man by the name of McClellan, suspected of being a disunionist, was chased through the streets by an angry mob.

But Democratic county conventions still criticised the administration, and opposed the war. The convention at Rushville, on December 28, 1861, resolved in favor of the Kentucky and Virginia resolutions, and declared that the Union could not be preserved by the exercise of coercive power.

The spirit of disaffection was expressed even more emphatically when the Democratic state convention met, on January 8, 1862. Thomas A. Hendricks was chosen to preside. His speech on taking the chair was filled with lamentation. "The pride and glory of the past," he said, "stand side by side with the humiliation and debasement of the present." "Fanaticism, bigotry and sectional hatred are doing the work of evil upon a great, generous and noble people." "Does not the sobbing voice of civil liberty, coming from out the ruins of a violated constitution, call us to the rescue?" . . . "Can we as patriots, without an effort to save it, surrender our country to a party whose history thus far is written in failure, corruption and public ruin?" He argued at length against the proposed emancipation of the slaves, and his speech contained expressions, which, to the minds of many, were considered to forecast a Northwestern Confederacy in close alliance with the South. "We are now being so crushed that if we and our children are not to become the hewers of wood and drawers of water for the capitalists of New England and Pennsylvania, we must look to the interests of our section, and for the first time in my life, I intend to speak as a sectional man. . . . . To encourage and stimulate the people of the South in the production of their peculiar commodities, that they may be large buyers from us, has been, and so long as 'grass grows and water runs' will be, the true interest of the Northwest; and the political party that would destroy that market is our greatest foe.

"Most earnestly, then, do I call upon the men of Indiana to consider what President Lincoln seems to favor, what Cameron urges, what the Republican members of Congress, in caucus, have determined upon, and what bills now pending in Congress contemplate, the freedom of the negroes in the rebel states, in a word the destruction of Southern labor and the ruin forever of our rich trade and the value of our products. . . .

"The first and highest interest of the Northwest is in the restoration and preservation of the Union upon the basis of the constitution, and the deep devotion of her Democracy to the cause of the Union is shown by its fidelity in the past; *but if the failure and folly and wickedness of the party in power render a Union impossible, then the mighty Northwest must take care of herself and her own interests.* She must not allow the arts and finesse of New England to despoil her of her richest commerce and trade by a sectional and selfish policy—Eastern lust of power, commerce and gain."

John G. Davis was a leading spirit in this convention. Referring to a visit to Richmond, Va., attributed to him, he said, that if he had made that trip he would have had it in his power to state that his old personal friend, Jefferson Davis, was in good health and sent his kind regards to his many friends in Indiana, whose names, perhaps, it would not be prudent to mention if he did not want them hanged; that the worthy president of the convention, Mr. Hendricks, might be one, and that so valuable a spoke to the wheel of the Democracy could not be spared. Davis believed the war would cost more than a billion dollars a year. Who was to pay this money? It must come out of the hard earnings of the tax-payers. The interest alone, at seven per cent., would be seventy millions a year.

Davis said that he would vote for no platform which would pledge the people to the unconditional prosecution of this war; that he did not believe the Union could be preserved by coercion.[1] The resolutions of the convention declared that the war had resulted from the fanatical agitation of the question of slavery and from the organization of a geographical party, producing its counterpart in the South; that in rejecting all compromises the Republicans acted in total disregard of the best interests of the country; that the suspension of the writ of *habeas corpus* and the seizure and imprisonment of citizens without warrant of law, were flagrant violations of the constitution and alarming acts of usurpation, which should receive the stern rebuke of every lover of his country.[2]

One thing is to be noted, that in the resolutions, bitter and aggressive as they were, there was no arraignment of Governor Morton's administration.

At the outbreak of the war, Indiana spent a large sum of money in equipping troops called into the service of the state. As these troops were transferred to the Federal government, the latter assumed the expenses. As early as July, 1861, Morton tried to procure the repayment of the amount then due. But the growing magnitude of the war soon made further taxation necessary, and it was thought best to raise part of the funds by direct imposition. On August 6, an annual tax of twenty millions was apportioned among the states. Indiana's share was $904,875.33. If

---

[1] Davis' speech in this convention was reported in the Richmond (Va.) *Dispatch* of January 25, and was received with great satisfaction at the South.

[2] The ticket nominated was as follows: For Secretary of State, James S. Athon; for Auditor, Joseph Ristine; for Treasurer, Matthew L. Brett; for Attorney-General, Oscar B. Hord; for Superintendent Public Instruction, Milton B. Hopkins.

12—MOR.

payment were promptly made, the state was to be allowed a rebate of fifteen per cent., and the tax might be paid by the release of any liquidated claim of equal amount against the United States. Morton at once opened a correspondence with the Secretary of the Treasury, and ascertained that the advances made by Indiana would be regarded as a '' claim,'' and admitted in payment of the tax to the amount which should be found due on settlement. In December, 1861, he filed with the Secretary a paper in which it was assumed that the state would pay her portion of the tax, and in which it was proposed to set off against it a like sum due to the state. The paper was accepted by the Secretary of the Treasury, who, therefore, declined to appoint the officers provided by law to collect the tax in Indiana.

The year 1862 opened with a succession of brilliant victories. General Thomas, in eastern Kentucky, defeated the Confederates on January 20, in the decisive battle of Mill Spring. Grant captured Fort Henry on February 6, and on the 16th Fort Donelson, where over ten thousand prisoners were ''unconditionally surrendered.'' Albert Sidney Johnston, who commanded the Department of the Cumberland, now found his positions in Kentucky no longer tenable. Bowling Green and Columbus were evacuated, and his new line was formed further south, along the Memphis and Charleston Railroad. West of the Mississippi Curtis defeated Van Dorn at Pea Ridge on the 8th of March, and the Confederate forces which had moved down that river to New Madrid were invested by Pope and compelled to evacuate that place on March 13. Meanwhile Johnston had collected from every quarter his scattered forces, which, on the 6th of April, he hurled against the troops of Grant at Pittsburg Landing. The struggle was sanguinary and doubtful, but Buell, with three divisions of the Army of the Ohio, arrived in time to save the day. Johnston was killed, the second day's battle was a victory for the Union army and the Confederate forces retired to Corinth. Meanwhile Island No. 10 had surrendered to Commodore Foote, who was co-operating with Pope upon the Mississippi, and Pope was directed to join Halleck and take part in the investment of Corinth, which proceeded with deliberation until the town was evacuated by the Confederates on May 30. In April Farragut had ascended the Mississippi from the Gulf and taken possession of New Orleans. Near the first of June, Fort Pillow was evacuated, and the Federal troops occupied Memphis. Kentucky was delivered. Tennessee was mainly in possession of the Union arms, and the Mississippi was nearly opened. While these encouraging events were taking place the enthusiasm of the North was unbounded. Troops could have been raised to any number required, but unfortunately, the government, believing that no more soldiers would be needed, had given orders to stop recruiting. Morton was opposed to any relaxation in the effort to subdue the rebellion so long as the South remained in arms. He was disappointed at this cessation in the work of raising troops, and the event proved the soundness of his judgment, for when, in the summer, disasters followed the successes of the spring, it was a harder matter to procure volunteers, and more of these were finally required.

But in equipping such troops as the government would take, in providing for them in field and hospital, Governor Morton was unremitting in his exertions.

He had continued to purchase arms until requested by the government to desist.

The Governor had established an arsenal at Indianapolis for the manufacture of ammunition. There was no law authorizing this, but to Morton that made little difference. In a speech to his fellow-townsmen, at Centreville, in 1864, he thus described the organization of this institution:

"This arsenal at Indianapolis was started by me on my own responsibility. When it became necessary to send Indiana troops into the field, I found that there was no ammunition with which to supply them. I would not send our soldiers forth without supplying them with means of attack and defense. I inquired if any person in Indianapolis knew the process of manufacturing ammunition. A man stepped forward and I gave him work. He at once employed six men to assist him. Soon the arsenal was established and the number of employes was increased to six hundred. . . . Besides providing for our own troops from this arsenal, we sent supplies to General Grant, and the government purchased ammunition of us at a lower price than elsewhere. When the accounts of the arsenal were settled it was found that there was a profit of seventy-five thousand dollars.''[1]

Morton's restless energy was ill content with a merely civil office in time of war. The palpable incompetence of many of the men who were conducting great operations provoked in him an eager desire to take the field in person. His natural gifts qualified him for military leadership. At a very early period he was convinced of the importance of dividing the Confederacy along the line of the Mississippi and of cut-

---

[1] The arsenal was the subject of bitter attack by Morton's opponents. They declared that its establishment was illegal, and there were charges of mismanagement. The Democratic legislature of 1863 appointed a committee of nine, which, after examination, made a unanimous report expressing their gratification at the economy and dispatch with which the business was conducted, and complimenting Sturm, the superintendent, upon the condition of his accounts and upon his energy in the enterprise. Another committee of investigation was also appointed by this legislature, the Republican minority of which reported in most complimentary terms, while the majority (composed of bitter partisans) failed to report at all. At the close of the session of 1863, a military auditing committee, composed of three Democrats and two Republicans, was appointed. This committee appointed Samuel H. Buskirk, a Democrat, to audit the arsenal account. He submitted monthly reports showing all expenditures. In regard to Colonel Sturm's management, Mr. Buskirk says (*Journal*, April 20, 1866), "If he committed any fraud or acted dishonestly, I have been unable to find it out, and I am sure that no one will do more to expose any fraud committed by him than I will."

ting off the territory west of that river from the rest of the seceding states. This was before the country realized the necessity of the immense armies which were afterwards required. Morton proposed to raise and command a force of ten thousand men for this purpose. William R. Holloway, his private secretary, went to Washington to lay the plan before the President. While they were conferring together, Seward entered the room and Lincoln asked him what he thought of it. They both appeared to approve of the proposition, and it was referred to the Secretary of War. No action, however, was taken.

In the summer of 1862, Morton's desire for a military command was again communicated to the President. A number of leading men from the West urged the consolidation of the troops in that section under Morton's command. But there was need of Morton's presence in a state where the political balance hung wavering, and where disaffection and treason at home made a strong hand necessary to watch and control them. So the President declined to grant the necessary authority, and Morton remained Governor of Indiana.

CHAPTER XV

As summer came on, the victories which had been gained by the Union arms were followed by reverses. The Peninsular campaign and the Seven Days' Battle before Richmond ended in an inglorious retreat to the James river. It was at this unfortunate time that a new requisition for volunteers had to be made. Lincoln was fearful lest a public call for troops would lead to a panic, and he, therefore, on June 30, addressed to Morton, as well as to other Governors of the loyal states, a letter asking for one hundred and fifty thousand men. But the Governors suggested that a greater number would be needed, and an address was prepared and signed by eighteen of them, asking the President to call for enough to fill up all regiments in the field, and to hold all cities and other places captured. The President's reply announced that he had decided to call into service three hundred thousand men, and later, in a private letter to the Governors, he urged them to send the troops at the earliest day possible. Not a moment was lost by Morton after the receipt of this solicitation. An impromptu war meeting was held in Indianapolis, on July 7, at the Bates House corner. Morton asked for an immediate response to the requisition of the President. Another meeting was held five days later. In the meantime, Morton was informed of a Confederate raid into Kentucky, and General Boyle, commanding that district, called for troops. It was not then possible to send them, but on the 11th, six

hundred men were dispatched to Louisville.   The meeting at
Indianapolis on the 12th was so large that it was necessary
to divide it.   Morton presided at Masonic Hall and made
the opening speech.   Kentucky, he said, was calling on us
again.   Marauding bands had infested that state, and Indiana was not deaf to her appeal.   He had just sent six hundred men.   But while we had been conquering, the forces
of the enemy had been concentrating.   The government
would not abandon the territory already conquered.   We
must relieve our forces, that our veterans might march on
Richmond.   It was for this purpose that the President had
made the call.   This was a crisis in which all was at stake.

Morton was followed by Benjamin Harrison, a young
lawyer, who had just been elected to the lucrative position
of Reporter of the Supreme Court.   Harrison had told Morton, some time before, that whenever it was necessary for
him to go, the Governor was to inform him.   Morton said
to him that now was the time.   He volunteered at this meeting as a private, though shortly afterwards a commission was
given him.

On the 14th Morton sent from the arsenal two car-loads
of ammunition for the use of the Kentucky troops in repelling the raid of the Confederates.   On the 17th four hundred men were dispatched to General Boyle.   On the 18th
the Confederates took possession of Henderson, a town on
the Ohio a few miles below Evansville, and a small band of
thirty-two men, under Adam R. Johnson, also attacked and
plundered Newburg, an Indiana town upon the river.   Information of the attack was telegraphed to Morton.

. A small force of mounted men proceeded to Newburg, and
steamers were also sent, but they arrived too late to intercept
the marauders.   At midnight Morton dispatched General
Love from Indianapolis with troops, arms and field artillery,
and on the morning of the following day he called for volunteers.   The men came with alacrity.   The Newburg raid had

aroused the people, and companies eager to fight were organized on a few hours' notice. The Governor now determined to send to Kentucky an expedition strong enough to drive the marauders out of the northern part of the state, and he started for the scene of the disturbance, arriving in Evansville on the 21st. A considerable body of Indiana men advanced into Kentucky, but the Confederates had disappeared.

This raid was only preliminary to a more formidable invasion. The Confederate government saw the need of anticipating the organization of the new troops that the President had called for, by prompt, aggressive action of their own. General Bragg had taken command of the Confederate forces. His right wing was at Knoxville, Tenn., under General E. Kirby Smith. It was determined that this force should invade Kentucky, destroy Buell's communications and bring his army back to the Ohio river. Bragg would then invade the state with his main force and, co-operating with Smith, would march on Louisville.

Meanwhile recruiting had been going on in Indiana to fill the President's call for troops. The response was prompt and satisfactory, and Stanton sent to Morton the laconic congratulation, "Well done, Indiana." Morton even went outside the state and aided in the work of raising troops in Ohio. On August 1 he attended a great meeting at Cincinnati, where he delivered an earnest address urging enlistment. "Our army," he said, "is in the condition of the man who built a house which he completed all but the roof, when he was compelled to stop. If the President obtains the men he has called for the rebellion is crushed, if he does not obtain them the government is lost."

But Lincoln's July requisition for three hundred thousand men was found to be insufficient, and on August 4 he called for three hundred thousand more to serve for nine months. If volunteers were not forthcoming by August 15, the deficiency was to be supplied by a draft. On the 8th of August,

Morton received from General Buell a dispatch announcing that another raid was anticipated, and requesting that re-inforcements should be sent to General Boyle. A few days afterwards Boyle himself announced an invasion of the state, and asked assistance. His appeal was of the most urgent character. He said: "I hope the patriotic soldiers of Indiana will not wait for bounties. Our state will be overrun if they do, and your own borders desolated." Morton had gone to Knightstown to spend Sunday when this dispatch was received at Indianapolis. The telegraph office at Knightstown was closed, and he could not be reached, but his secretaries dispatched orders to the commanders of the troops collected in different parts of the state to proceed at once to Indianapolis, and Colonel Holloway procured an engine and started for Knightstown. Morton returned immediately to Indianapolis, and the forwarding of troops began.

The mustering officer, Colonel Simonson, was careful, painstaking and methodical, but exceedingly slow. Morton asked the war department for a change. A new mustering officer was sent in the person of Colonel Carrington. He was brought immediately to the Governor and said: "Tell me where the troops are and let me go to work. Indiana shall have its quota first in the field, if the men are forthcoming." He was at once taken to Camp Morton, and at eleven o'clock on the same night he notified Morton that a regiment was ready for the field. The organization of troops went on with a speed never before known. Great numbers of men were sworn in at night by the light of torches, and before daylight were off for Kentucky. The Senate chamber was turned into a school-room, where officers were instructed by Carrington in the method of making out pay-rolls. The regiments now followed each other with great rapidity. The strain upon the railroads for transportation was immense. The arsenal established by Morton worked night and day, making three hundred thousand rounds of ammunition every twenty-four hours.

The following are some of Morton's telegrams announcing the departures of the troops:

"August 17. I send one thousand men to-night, seven thousand to-morrow and Tuesday."

"August 21. I sent another regiment last night; a battery will go to-morrow. The Sixty-ninth has started. The Seventy-fifth leaves at 6 P. M. and the Seventy-fourth at 9 P. M. to-day for Louisville."

"August 23. Will have at least seventeen additional regiments ready for arms, this time next week."

"August 26. The Seventy-ninth leaves Tuesday, will hurry others. Indiana has put 14,480 men in Kentucky up to Friday last; this will make it 19,296 by Thursday this week. This includes two batteries."

"August 27. Another regiment can leave to-morrow, one leaves this evening."

"August 30. The Eighty-ninth leaves this afternoon. The Eighty-first and Eighty-second will be armed to-day. Two regiments will start to-morrow, and five more will be ready next week."

"August 31. The Eighty-eighth is at the depot. The Eighty-seventh will be in Louisville to-morrow morning. Two regiments leave to-day and two more to-night."

A serious difficulty in forwarding these troops was found in the absence of money for bounties and advance pay. Many of the men had left their homes suddenly without, providing for their families, expecting to remit their bounties before going into the field.

Morton's action in this emergency was characteristic. He borrowed the money himself. He was a man of little property, but his credit at such a time and for such a purpose was unlimited. One morning he telegraphed to M. E. Reeves, a merchant in Cincinnati, asking that one hundred thousand dollars should be sent on that evening to pay the troops. The amount was borrowed within a few hours upon the personal responsibility of Mr. Reeves, and that evening a messenger was on the way to Indiana with the money. One day Morton went to one of the banks of Indianapolis and asked for thirty thousand dollars. "What have you got to carry it in?" inquired the president, and finding a market-basket near by, he placed the rolls of greenbacks in this, and Morton walked out with the basket and its unusual contents. The money to repay these loans was slow in coming, and Morton telegraphed to Stanton: "I have borrowed of various bankers for a few days two hundred thousand dollars to pay bounties. I have sent four regiments of the new levy to Kentucky and hope to get five off to-day. I hope, my dear sir, that you will see that the bounty-money, by which this may be replaced, may be sent forward promptly, that my credit may not suffer." Stanton replied: "The most peremptory orders have been given to supply you with funds. If it is not done I will dismiss the officer whose neglect occasions the delay, no matter what his rank."

On the morning of the 19th, it is said that Morton had thus borrowed five hundred thousand dollars. When the repayment was made the banks would accept no interest.

The Indianapolis *Journal* of August 21 voiced the exultation of the state at the result of its splendid efforts, in a leader entitled "What Indiana Has Done." "Fourteen thousand men," it said, "have been organized, equipped and sent to the field in four days. We do not believe this promptness has been equaled in any emergency by any state in the Union. The news of the invasion of Kentucky reached Governor Morton on Sunday. The necessity for a speedy accumulation of forces on the main lines of the rebel advance was obvious. Ohio could not be ready for a week. Men must be sent to arrest the advance, or the war would be transferred to our own border. Governor Morton determined that the men should be sent.

Enough of our regiments were full, but they were scattered all over the state, unorganized, undisciplined, and unarmed. They had to be collected, uniformed, equipped, armed, officered, paid and transported. . . . Everything had to be done that was necessary to change men just out of their shops and farms into soldiers. It was a task for a giant, but happily there were gigantic energies at the head of the government to undertake it. Since Monday morning this really formidable army, as large as that with which General Scott marched upon Mexico, has been collected, organized, paid, prepared, and sent into the field.''

One regiment was paid on the cars. One was actually paid upon the field, just before the disastrous battle at Richmond, Kentucky, between Kirby Smith and the Federal troops under General Manson.[1] When this battle was fought (August 30) the Indiana regiments, which constituted the bulk of the Federal troops, had been in service from ten to twenty days. They were utterly raw and inexperienced, and one regiment had no field officers, yet they fought during a great part of the day, re-formed their lines repeatedly, and distinguished themselves as raw troops have seldom done. But they were defeated at last and fled in confusion. Some four thousand officers and men were captured and paroled. The Indiana regiments lost heavily. This defeat took place at the same time as the second battle of Bull Run, and the two disasters led to great depression among the Union men.

General Boyle manifested his appreciation of the efforts of Indiana in the following dispatch to the President:

''The battle near Richmond was disastrous to us. Our troops, especially the Indianians, fought with the courage and gallantry of veterans. If Ohio and Illinois had supported Indiana, and had sent their troops on, the issue of the battle would have been different. Governor Morton has sent to

---

[1] General Nelson arrived on the field near the close of the battle and took command.

this state, since I have been in command here, over twenty thousand men.''

Morton now renewed his efforts and sent additional men to the field.   He went to Louisville the day after this disaster, and just before he started he telegraphed to General Buell: '' Two regiments left to-day and two more will go to-mor-row.''[1]   In the meantime Kirby Smith had pushed on to Lexington, and the Kentucky legislature had adjourned to Louisville.   On September 3 Morton visited the legislature. The members rose to their feet to receive him.   From Lexington the Confederates could attack either Cincinnati or Louisville.   Their first object was apparently Cincinnati. Kirby Smith moved northward to Cynthiana.   On the 5th of September Morton declared martial law in the river counties of Indiana, and ordered all citizens capable of bearing arms to meet for organization and drill.   The mayor of Cincinnati had telegraphed to the Governor of Ohio for artillery. The latter replied, directing him to make out a requisition and have it countersigned by the commanding general, saying that it would be duly honored.   But there was no time for delay. The mayor telegraphed to Morton, from whom the answer came: '' One battery ready, with two car-loads of ammunition.   Will send another train in two hours.''[2]   Morton went with his staff to Cincinnati.   General Lew Wallace was placed in command of the defenses.   He ordered that all places of business should be closed and that the citizens should work

---

[1] The speed with which he furnished troops was so surprising, that one day, while he was conversing with some friends in Louisville, a stranger thrust his head in at the door and said: "If you want soldiers from Indiana, all you have to do is to take some blue cloth and brass buttons, throw them into a hopper, put Morton at the crank, and they will come out a regiment."

[2] Morton sent twenty pieces of artillery, three thousand stands of arms, 31,136 rounds of artillery ammunition and 3,365,000 musket cartridges. These were forwarded by special train, and arrived in Cincinnati within fifteen hours after receipt of the requisition.

on the intrenchments south of the Ohio river. He was soon in command of forty thousand men, and within three days a formidable line of entrenchments had been constructed. In the meantime, General Heth, commanding the advance guard of Kirby Smith's troops, appeared within a short distance of the Federal lines,[1] but, in view of the preparations made to receive him, he was directed to wait until Humphrey Marshall, then near Mount Sterling, should be within supporting distance. But Marshall was slow in coming, and the preparations for resistance were so complete that the attack was abandoned.[2]

So grateful were the people of Cincinnati for Morton's help, that in 1864 the city council sent T. Buchanan Read to Indianapolis to paint a full-length portrait of the Governor for the council chamber. Read spent some weeks upon this portrait. "The painting," says Sulgrove, "was in his peculiar idealized style, in which all wrinkles and roughness were effaced, as if the subject had gone through the change of resurrection and nothing was left but the lines which ex-

---

[1] Morton's scouts were busy securing information of the advance of the Confederates.

[2] After the danger was over, Morton and his friends indulged in a little recreation, which Sulgrove thus describes: "Read, the poet; Murdock, the tragedian; Rogers, the sculptor; Brennan (author of the 'Harp of a Thousand Strings'); Eaton and Beard, the painters; Lane, Leslie Coombs, of old Kentucky fame; 'Buck' Terrell and I, with Morton as a sort of *magister morum* made up a lively company. One night the party got together in one of the basement rooms of the Burnet House. Tom Sanders supplied Longworth's catawba *ad libitum*. Brennan recited his 'Hard Shell Sermon' and Read his own verses. Murdock gave us 'Hamlet' and the 'Six Hundred at Balaklava.' Coombs told some of his tales of Fort Meigs and some jokes of later date, and Beard told his story of the 'Anatomical Venus.' Lane and Morton, Lew Wallace and I had little to say—enough to do to keep track of the rest, and the symposium lasted till Morton broke it up about 2 o'clock with the remark that he had work to do in the morning, and he meant to get some sleep. That was Morton's 'gala' night, though he was the only man who drank none of the Cincinnati champagne."

pressed the soul.'' The picture did not please Morton, but it long filled its place in the Cincinnati council chamber.[1]

---

[1] In 1865, after Read had completed this portrait, a complimentary entertainment was arranged for him in Indianapolis, at which he gave some recitations, introducing them by a short speech concerning Morton and the part which Indiana had taken in the war. In this he said: " There were no equipments; he had them made. There were no supplies; he procured them. His agents were busy everywhere, and they were men of such character and position as none but he could have commanded. He knew no rest, no hesitation, no failure. He was the right man in the right place at a time when the wrong man would have been ruin. When your troops reached their first field in West Virginia, his watchful eye saw the need of more numerous and more elastic agencies than the red tape of government regulations could allow. He led the way in the greatest of all the accompanying movements of the war—the establishment of stores of sanitary supplies and the appointment of agents to follow our armies to distribute such stores, and to care for the sick and wounded. Even he, I doubt not, had no suspicion of the sublime structure of benevolence that was soon to be erected on the foundation he had laid. What sanitary agencies and committees have since become I need not say. They have saved uncounted lives and untold suffering.

"As the war progressed, and fresh demands for troops were made, Indiana, spurred by the glory she had already won, and inspired by the zeal and genius of her Governor, was among the first to meet the call, and it became her pride to say, ' We have filled our quota without a draft,' while some states still lingered far behind. How much of this spirit was due to the people's patriotic impulse, and how much to the confidence that their efforts would be wisely directed, we can never know, but surely the most ardent patriotism would grow cold and slack if it saw its blood wasted and its spirit misdirected by an inefficient or dishonest executive.

" I do not propose to allude to the civil policy or acts of your Governor. But we may, without trenching upon the peculiar rights of parties, admire the energy and decision which could perform the labors created by the war, and meet new and embarrassing political problems and solve them with the promptness in which alone was safety. Without means, with the state's credit threatened, with the border alarmed, with treasonable conspiracies mining every section of your state, with his own life repeatedly menaced, what but a firmness, fearlessness and decision beyond my feeble praise could have ' plucked from this nettle danger the flower safety ' and have brought the state bravely through her perils, her credit unshaken, her institutions unimpaired, her peace undisturbed and her domestic enemies throttled into silence, if not into shame."

CHAPTER XVI

KILLING OF NELSON—REMOVAL OF BUELL—THE DRAFT

THE loss which Indiana had sustained in the battle of Richmond and in the surrender of Mumfordsville, which occurred about the same time, was keenly felt. Naturally, the chief share of the responsibility for these disasters was laid to the account of General Buell, who, with a large army in Tennessee and northern Alabama, had done little to prevent the invasion of Kentucky.

Another object of dissatisfaction was General Nelson. Buell had appointed Nelson to succeed Boyle in command of the forces sent to oppose Kirby Smith. When Kentucky was invaded, General Lew Wallace, although he had been a division commander, offered to serve under General Boyle, whom he outranked. This generous proposition was accepted and Wallace took command of the forces at Lexington and other places south of Louisville. But he was suddenly relieved of his command by General Nelson. Much dissatisfaction was caused thereby, and the ardor of the Indiana troops was greatly dampened. Nelson, in his report of the battle of Richmond, had cast the responsibility for the disaster upon General Manson, an Indiana man, a veteran of the Mexican war, who was greatly esteemed. Nelson was, in many respects, a good soldier, but he was brutal, passionate and overbearing. Morton had gone to Louisville, when that city was threatened, arriving there on September 22. Nelson was in command of the defenses. Bragg and Buell were hastening northward, each striving to outstrip the other. Nelson had put the city under martial law, had ordered the enrollment of every able-bodied man, and had hastily encircled the town with earthworks. Buell had ordered General Jefferson C. Davis to report to Nelson, which he did, and Nelson assigned to him the command of the citizen soldiery in Louisville. New men were arriving every day, and it was difficult, at any particular time, to know the exact number of troops under his command. Nelson's headquarters were at the Galt House, and, on Thursday, September 26, Davis called on him to confer with him in regard to the defense of the city. The previous interviews of these two men had been marked by the abrupt and dictatorial manner, which, unhappily, distinguished General Nelson. Nelson asked Davis how many guns he wanted. Davis answered, " about 2,500." Nelson sprang to his feet, and, glaring at Davis, exclaimed : " About ! Damn your 'abouts !' Don't you know how many men you have in your command, sir ?" Davis answered that he could not state the exact number; that he wanted to know where to get arms, and he would give the exact number when he made a requisition. Nelson answered with an oath, "You are a pretty general to tell me 'about' how many men; you are not fit to command. Get out of my sight. I will relieve you and send you to Cincinnati under guard, you puppy !" and Davis retired.

Four days after this Morton and Nelson were at breakfast together in the Galt House. Nelson had been galled by the criticisms of the Indianapolis *Journal* upon his overbearing conduct, and he threatened to sue the editor or give him a thrashing. They arose from the table and went to the office, where Nelson stood smoking. Davis came up and, requesting Morton to listen to what he had to say, he asked an explanation of the causes of his removal. Nelson interrupted him with, "What are you doing here? Get out of my way, you contemptible puppy," striking him in the face with the back of his hand, and turning fiercely to Morton, he said: "You came up to witness this insult, did you?" Morton answered: "General Nelson, you astonish me. I was standing here and he asked me to hear what he had to say to you." Nelson then strode away to his room. Morton met him again in the hall. Nelson had his hand in the pocket of his coat. Morton believed that he intended mischief, and, although unarmed, made a similar gesture. Nelson glared at him, but neither spoke. Davis, in the meantime, had procured a revolver, and, as he saw Nelson approaching, cried out, "Stop and defend yourself." Nelson came on. Davis fired and Nelson fell. There was intense excitement. Nelson was removed to his room, and in a few minutes he was dead. Davis was put under arrest. Nelson's men were filled with rage, for, much as they complained of the rough manner in which the general treated them, they were always anxious, when they faced the enemy, that "Old Bull," as they called him, should lead them. But General Davis' division had now reached Louisville, and were clamorous for his release. The feeling between Nelson's and Davis' men was very bitter until the battle of Perryville, but in the fellowship of that fearful carnage their friendship was re-established. Davis was afterwards released and ordered to join his command in Tennessee.

It was charged at the time that Morton was an accessory to the killing, that it was through his intrigues that the quarrel had taken place, and that he was present to witness it. But the circumstances were such a palpable refutation of this charge that these attacks required no answer.

Morton's opposition to Buell was well known, and when, early in October, he went to Washington, both the Louisville and Cincinnati papers announced that his purpose was to procure the removal of that general, and the Democratic press attacked him vigorously for his interference. On Morton's return to Indianapolis he telegraphed to Boyle that this report was untrue, and the *Journal* also denied it. His visit, it was said, was to secure the early exchange of Indiana prisoners. But although Buell's removal was not the object of his going to Washington, an earnest letter which he wrote to Lincoln at this time seems to point pretty clearly to Buell and McClellan. It is as follows:

"WASHINGTON, October 7, 1862.

"DEAR SIR—I could not leave the city without addressing you this note, and my intense solicitude for the success of our cause must be my apology.

"In my opinion, if our arms do not make great progress within the next sixty days, our cause will be almost lost. Our financial system must speedily end. The government may subsist for a time upon issues of an irredeemable currency, which the law has made a legal tender, but the time will come when the people will refuse to sell their commodities and receive this currency in payment, and when that occurs, financial embarrassment and ruin will overwhelm the country. The system may collapse in a single day, and should this occur before the termination of the war, it will of itself be sufficient to end the war against us. National and individual bankruptcy would be followed by public despair, and the war would be abandoned by common consent. The danger of foreign intervention is daily increasing. The time during which the rebels have maintained their government and the success of their arms are rapidly furnishing foreign nations with an excuse to do what they have desired to do from the first—to recognize the Confederacy, and to aid it in whatever way they can. You have now immense armies in the field, and all that they require to achieve victory is that they be led with energy and discretion. The cold professional leader, whose heart is not in the cause, who regards it as only a professional job, and whose rank and importance would be greatly diminished by the conclusion of the war, will not succeed in a contest like this. I would rely with infinitely more confidence upon the man of strong intellect, whose head is inspired by his heart, who, although he be unlearned in military science, believes that our cause is sacred, and that he is fighting for all that is dear to him and his country, rather than upon the polished professional soldier, whose sympathies, if he have any, are most likely on the other side. It is my solemn conviction that we will never succeed until the leadership of our armies is placed in the hands of men who are greatly in earnest, and who are profoundly convinced of the justice of our cause. Let me beg of you, sir, as I am your friend, a friend of your administration, and a friend of our unfortunate and unhappy country, that you will at once take up the consideration of this subject, and act upon the inspiration of your own heart and the dictates of your own judgment. Another three months like the last six, and we are lost—lost. We can not afford to experiment a single day longer with men who have failed continuously for a whole year, who, with the best appointed armies, have done nothing, have thrown away the greatest advantages, evacuated whole states, and retreated hundreds of miles before an inferior enemy. To try them longer, trusting that they may yet do something, would, it seems to me, be imperiling the life of the nation. You have generals in your armies who have displayed ability, energy and willingness to fight and conquer the enemy. Place them in command, and reject the wicked incapables whom you have patiently tried and found utterly wanting.

"I am, with sentiments of great respect,
"Your obedient servant,
"OLIVER P. MORTON."

The battle of Perryville, which was fought at this time between Buell and Bragg, although it resulted in a nominal victory for the Union arms, did not restore the confidence which had been lost by the previous disasters, and seemed to Morton to show bad generalship. On October 21 he telegraphed to the President as follows:

"An officer just from Louisville announces that Bragg has

escaped with his army into East Tennessee, and that Buell's army is countermarch:ng to Lebanon.   The butchery at Perryville was terrible, and resulted from a large portion of the enemy being precipitated upon a small portion of our troops. Sufficient time was thus gained by the enemy to enable them to escape.   Nothing but success, speedy and decided, will save our cause from utter destruction.   In the Northwest distrust and despair are seizing upon the hearts of the people.

"O. P. MORTON."

The President was dissatisfied with Buell's indecisive action, and on the 24th of October directed him to turn over his command to Rosecrans.   This action was extremely grateful to Morton who, in conjunction with Governor Yates, of Illinois, telegraphed to the President on October 25, as follows:

"We were to start to-night for Washington to confer with you in regard to Kentucky affairs.   The removal of General Buell and appointment of Rosecrans came not a moment too soon.   The removal of General Buell could not have been delayed an hour with safety to the army or the cause.   The history of the battle of Perryville and the recent campaign in Kentucky has never been told.   The action you have taken renders our visit unnecessary, although we are very anxious to confer with you in regard to the general condition of the northwest, and hope to do so at no distant period.

" RICH'D YATES, Governor of Illinois.
" O. P. MORTON, Governor of Indiana."

During these events Indiana had been busy filling her quotas of volunteers, called for by the President in July and again in August.   Finally a draft had to be ordered.

Under each call of the President, the share of Indiana had been fixed at 21,250 men, making in all 42,500 men.   The number of men to be drafted was apportioned among the townships, credit being given to each township for all the volunteers previously furnished.

Jesse P. Siddall, a Wayne county lawyer, and an old

friend of Morton's, was made Draft Commissioner, and assistants were appointed under him in the various counties.

An interesting question arose at the threshold of the proceedings. The draft was upon the militia of the state. The constitution of Indiana provided that no person conscientiously opposed to bearing arms should be compelled to do militia duty, but that such person should pay an equivalent for exemption. This clause had been inserted owing to the influence of the Quakers. The question at once arose as to the manner in which this provision should be enforced. Representatives of the Society of Friends had come to Indianapolis to lay their claims to exemption before the Governor, and Morton, anxious as he was to fill the regiments, was not unfriendly to a society whose members were strong supporters of the administration in everything save the performance of military duty. It was at last provided that members of any religious denomination which made opposition to bearing arms an article of faith should presumptively be entitled to exemption upon payment of such sum as should be thereafter fixed. This decision brought on a flood of criticism. Tenderness of conscience, it was said, would be produced where it had never been felt before. Men would suddenly " fall under conviction," and become spiritual.

The war department fixed the equivalent for exemption at two hundred dollars. Some three thousand persons established their claims, and many paid the commutation, but as the legislature had not fixed the amount, and as it was finally decided that the war department had no power to do so, the money was afterwards returned.

The draft took place on the 6th of October   Volunteering had been continued up to that time, and the number required reduced to 6,003. The draft was conducted without disturbance, except at Hartford City, in Blackford county, where the draft box was destroyed and the draft was stopped, but on the third day afterward it was completed

It was shown subsequently that, at the time the draft was

made, the state had contributed more than eight thousand men in excess of her proper share, and that the conscription was the result of an erroneous computation. Morton seems to have believed that Indiana had furnished her full proportion of troops, but he never sought to evade any demands which the Federal government made upon the state to carry on the war, and he was on this occasion quite willing that the townships which hung back and did not contribute their quotas of volunteers should be compelled to bear their share of the burden.

On the 3d of March, 1863, an enrollment act was passed by Congress under which troops were drafted by the general government instead of by the states.[1]

There was one feature of this act, to which Morton seriously objected, the commutation of three hundred dollars which it allowed. He sometimes endeavored to excuse this in his public speeches, but in his correspondence with the war department he vigorously protested against it.[2]

---

[1] The next call upon Indiana was in June, 1863, for four regiments of six-months men. No draft was necessary to supply this call. Even the *Sentinel* declared that Morton was entitled to consideration for what he had done in obtaining proper credits for Indiana, and avoiding a draft.

On the 17th of October, 1863, the President issued another call for three hundred thousand men. Morton had anticipated this call and had obtained authority, some three months before, to raise eleven new regiments. The work of raising these regiments was well under way when the call was made.

The *Journal* remarks with exultation, "We now occupy alone the proud position of offering volunteers to the government in advance of any call, while many of the other states are still behind, even with the draft."

This call was further increased in February, 1864, to five hundred thousand, and on March 14 to seven hundred thousand. These calls were also supplied by Indiana without resorting to the draft. On the 23d of April, 1864, a call was made for one-hundred-day men, and the state filled its quota. On July 18, 1864, another call was made for five hundred thousand men, under which the number of drafted men in Indiana was 12,476. On the 19th of December, 1864, the last call was made for three hundred thousand men, and under this 2,424 were drafted.

[2] On the 6th of March, 1863, immediately after the passage of the act, he thus wrote to Stanton on the subject:

"DEAR SIR—Public feeling has greatly improved in the West within

At a later period (February 1, 1864), he thus addressed the provost marshal, Colonel James B. Fry:

"It is generally thought in the West that the great states of New York and Pennsylvania, containing more than one-third of the population of all the loyal states, are largely delinquent, and the feeling is becoming quite strong that before any attempt is made by the government to draft in states that have regularly furnished their quotas, the government should first collect from those great states their arrears of troops. The

---

the last six weeks, but I fear the improvement is likely to receive a disastrous check from the construction given to the thirteenth section of the conscription act, which permits a drafted man to relieve himself from the draft by the payment of three hundred dollars. By this construction every man who can beg or borrow three hundred dollars can exempt himself from the draft, and it will fall only upon those who are too poor to raise that sum. I can assure you that this feature in the bill is creating much excitement and ill feeling toward the government among the poorer classes generally, without regard to party, which may, if it is not subdued, lead to a popular storm under cover of which the execution of the conscription act may be greatly hindered, or even defeated, in some portions of the country.

"Under this construction I am satisfied that the draft will not put into the ranks any Democrat who is not working with the Union party. Already movements are on foot in the secret societies of Indiana, and among the leaders of the disloyalists, to raise money to purchase the exemption of every Democrat who may be drafted and who can not raise the money himself; and already the boast is made that the government shall not have one more of their men for the prosecution of this war.

"From a careful reading of the section, I am of the opinion that a construction can be given to it without violence by which it is left discretionary with the Secretary of War to determine whether he will accept any sum in discharge of the drafted man, and that he may legitimately determine that he will not. In my judgment it is of the first importance that this construction, if possible, be immediately given to the act and published to the world before a current of feeling shall have set in against the government. In Indiana substitutes can not be procured in any number, if at all, for three hundred dollars and the rule should be that every drafted man should be required to serve unless he shall actually produce his substitute.

"I pray you to give this subject your immediate consideration.
"Very respectfully yours,
"O. P. MORTON."

burdens of the war should be made to fall, as nearly as possible, equally upon all the states. While this is done the people will bear them cheerfully, but if it shall become apparent that some states are avoiding their share of the burdens which are thus made to fall more heavily upon others, it will occasion great dissatisfaction, and must result disastrously to the government. . . . .

"What I have to say on this subject I say to the government and not to the public. I have labored, and shall labor, to keep down all discontent, and I intend, to the extent of my power, that Indiana shall furnish her quota, irrespective of what other states do.

"I know your opinion of the conscript law, and that the retention of the commutation clause is against your convictions of justice and sound policy. You understand this subject much better than I do; but you will be able to pardon the suggestions of one who has labored diligently in his sphere, and has but one great purpose, which is the support of the government and the suppression of the rebellion.

"I have not kept pace very accurately with congressional proceedings, but my impression is that the commutation clause will be retained in some form, which will substantially defeat the procurement of new troops within the time when they will be most needed by the government, and could be most useful for the speedy termination of the war.

"I dislike to trouble the Secretary of War in the midst of his great labors with my crude suggestions, but if he has time to hear you read this communication I shall be gratified.

"I am, very respectfully and sincerely, yours,

"O P. MORTON."

Morton's views at last prevailed. On July 4, 1864, commutation was abolished, except as to those who were exempted on account of their conscientious scruples.

CHAPTER XVII

THE POLITICAL CAMPAIGN OF 1862

WHILE Morton was at work night and day furnishing soldiers to the Federal government, and taking part in the defense of Kentucky, an important political campaign was going on in Indiana. The minor state offices were to be filled at the election in October, but more important than these, a new legislature was to be chosen, which would determine whether the state should maintain the aggressive attitude it had taken or should assume a position of lukewarmness or hostility toward the administration. And this legislature was to elect two United States senators.

Morton, at the outbreak of the war, had shown a disposition to disregard mere party preferences in his effort to unite the sentiment of the state in favor of the Union. In none of his acts was this more conspicuous than in his appointment of a United States senator to fill the vacant place of Jesse D. Bright, who had been detected in treasonable correspondence and expelled. The nomination of Bright's successor, up to the time of the next meeting of the legislature, was in the hands of the Governor. Morton was overwhelmed with letters urging the claims of a great number of persons, among them, men to whom he was bound by close ties. But he considered that it was more important that the Union sentiment of the state should be cemented by a nonpartisan appointment than that he should satisfy the demands of personal or political friends.

Joseph Wright had been a Democratic Governor of Indiana. He represented the more moderate element of his party. He had voted for Douglas in 1860, and had taken his part firmly and consistently on the side of the Union, supporting the war measures of the administration. This was the man whom Morton determined to appoint, and his decision was announced to the Senate on the 25th of February, 1862. On the evening of that day Wright delivered a speech at Indianapolis, declaring that he would stand upon no party platform and go into no mere party convention. What was needed, he said, was a united North. His platform was that the constitution was the supreme law and rebellion a monstrous crime. He had been told that he was not a Democrat because he would not approve of the infamous resolutions passed in the Democratic convention of the 8th of January, but whatever might be the opinion of his party friends, his conviction was that the rebellion must be put down at any cost. When he had finished, Governor Morton was called for and spoke in the same strain. On the following day Wright left for Washington.

Probably this meeting was an occasion prepared by the Governor for the purpose of securing from Wright such an explicit declaration as would be a guarantee of his future conduct in the Senate. Apart from his uncompromising devotion to the Union, Wright was a man of conservative opinions. He said, on the following day, to a representative of the Cincinnati *Enquirer*, that while opposed to secession, he entertained the kindest feelings toward the people of the South, and that so soon as peace was restored he stood ready to accede to a national convention, to consider any matters of grievance.

It was to be expected that such an appointment would create dissatisfaction. The radical Republicans, especially the friends of those whose "claims" had been overlooked, were not satisfied. The "peace" faction of the Democracy was still more displeased, and denounced Wright bitterly, attributing the appointment to discreditable motives. But the Union press of the North, with singular unanimity, approved of Morton's course.

The Indiana election was to take place in October. The sentiments expressed by the Democracy in the 8th of January convention aroused the indignation of the Union men of the state. Republicans and war Democrats united in a call for a "Union" state convention for the 18th of June, inviting the co-operation of all who favored a vigorous prosecution of the war. Meetings were held in every part of the state to select delegates, and on the day appointed the convention met in the state-house square. The Democrats who attended held a separate meeting in the morning and adopted resolutions favoring the union of all good citizens to support the administration in all necessary measures to crush the rebellion, and declaring that for this purpose they would cordially unite with any and all of their fellow-citizens, without regard to former party names or associations.

Governor Morton was made chairman of the united convention, which met in the afternoon. Hon. Henry Secrist, a Democrat from Mr. Voorhees' district, spoke in favor of sustaining the government. He justly observed that opposition to an administration in time of war inevitably resulted in opposition to the war itself. Governor Morton was next called for, and urged upon all the necessity of laying aside mere party considerations and of taking no action except that which was necessary for the salvation of the country.

The traitors, he said, expected aid and comfort from the North. They would array the Northwestern states against New England through the plea of mutual interest with the South. They urged that our market was at the South; that the natural flow of our trade was down the Mississippi; that we must cultivate amity with the slave states, and cut ourselves off from the East. There were many persons in Indiana who still cherished this wild and wicked dream.

Party spirit was the sunken rock on which other governments had been wrecked. He warned the men of Indiana to beware of all factions, of all secret organizations designed to embarrass the government. The administration, which had been so patient and forbearing, would not always overlook these things, but, if need be, would make short work in suppressing them. The evidence had come to him from several sources that there were secret associations of a dangerous character in the state. One of their avowed objects was to prevent the collection of the direct tax by the government. Such associations were treasonable in character, and came within the jurisdiction of the laws of the United States and of Indiana. He uttered a solemn warning that every citizen must keep aloof from such organizations.

The campaign proceeded under conditions most unfavorable to the Republicans. The pressure of military affairs prevented Morton from giving that personal attention to politics which he was accustomed to give. The disasters which had begun in the Peninsula continued with little intermission. Pope's army was beaten at Manassas, Washington itself seemed a second time in danger, Kentucky was again largely in possession of the enemy. Lee invaded Maryland, and though he had to retreat after the sanguinary struggle at Antietam, the conflict was undecided; the South was full of hope and the North of despondency. An enormous drain had been made upon Indiana in the withdrawal of a vast number of men who had volunteered under the two calls of the President in July and August. The votes of these men would be subtracted from the Union party. The draft was unpopular and much feeling had been excited against it. The political situation was further complicated by the President's proclamation of emancipation, which appeared in September, only a short time before the Indiana election. Indiana was a conservative state. The parties were closely balanced. There was a great deal of Union sentiment, but very little sympathy

with "abolitionism." Morton himself had been conservative upon this point, more so, no doubt, than Lincoln. In
the previous December, Morton, in response to a serenade in
Washington, had spoken in justification of the President's refusal to interfere with slavery. But when the step had been
taken he was one of the first to support this measure of the
President. Now that the die had been cast, there must be
no halting among the friends of the Union A few days after
the proclamation, a convention of the Governors of the loyal
states was held at Altoona, Pennsylvania, and we find Morton's name affixed to an address, signed by seventeen of
these Governors, indorsing the policy of emancipation.

Wise as this measure was, and successful in its ultimate
consequences, its immediate political result was disastrous.
Party conflicts, which had been smothered in the general enthusiasm, were now revived with great bitterness. There was
a violent protest that the administration had changed the war
for the Union into a war for the abolition of slavery.

In Indiana the burden of so many adverse circumstances
was more than the Republican party could bear, and the outcome of the election was the choice of Democratic state
officers and of a Democratic legislature. The Democrats
exulted greatly over their victory. They became bold and
insolent.[1] The Cincinnati *Enquirer* demanded the resignation of Governors Morton and Tod. "Let them imitate the
example of Magoffin. The people of Ohio and Indiana have
asked for a change." Morton realized what a severe blow

---

[1] On November 15, a Democratic jubilee was held at Cambridge City.
Vallandigham, Hendricks, Jason B. Brown, H. H. Dodd, George H. Pendleton and others addressed the multitude. Cheers for Jeff Davis and
curses for Abolitionists were heard. Vallandigham wondered if Morton
had heard the news? Some weeks before, on invitation of the citizens or
Wayne county, the speaker had visited that county to address the people,
when Governor Morton had sent his marshal and his police to violate the
hospitality of the state. Vallandigham wondered if these men knew that
their days were numbered .

had been dealt to the Union cause, but he knew that this was the time, above all others, when his presence in the executive chair was necessary. He felt sure that efforts would be made to tie his hands and cripple his power; that steps would be taken to develop that favorite project of Mr. Hendricks, the separation of the Northwest from the Northeast, and that a strong hand would be needed to keep Indiana in the line of the loyal states.

Morton believed that most powerful among the reasons which had contributed to the disaffection in Indiana was the belief that the interests of all the people living in the Mississippi valley were identical, and that so long as the seceding states controlled the mouth of that river, Indiana could not sever her destiny from theirs. The conquest of the Mississippi became, in his eyes, a matter of supreme importance. These considerations had been urged upon Mr. Lincoln, and an expedition down the river had been projected.

On the 21st of October General John A. McClernand was ordered by the Secretary of War to proceed to Indiana, Illinois and Iowa, and assist the Governors of those states in preparing for this expedition. On October 23 he had an interview with Morton, who co-operated in the undertaking It was in connection with this, and to strengthen the purpose of the President, that the following remarkable letter was written to Lincoln in elaboration of a plan which Morton had formed at a much earlier period in the year:

"INDIANAPOLIS, October 27, 1862.

"DEAR SIR: . . . The fate of the North is trembling in the balance. The result of the late elections admonishes all who understand its import that not an hour is to be lost. The Democratic politicians of Ohio, Indiana and Illinois assume that the rebellion will not be crushed, and that the independence of the rebel Confederacy will, before many months, be practically acknowledged. Starting upon this hypothesis, they ask the question, 'What shall be the destiny of Ohio, Indiana and Illinois? Shall they remain attached to the old government, or shall they secede and form a new one, —a Northwestern Confederacy—as a preparatory step to annexation with the South?' The latter project is the programme, and has been for the last twelve months. During the recent campaign it was the staple of every Democratic speech—that we had no interests or sympathies in common with the people of the Northern and Eastern states; that New England is fattening at our expense; that the people of New England are cold, selfish, money-making, and, through the medium of tariffs and railroads, are pressing us to the dust; that geographically these states are a part of the Mississippi Valley, and, in their political associations and destiny, can not be separated from the other states of that valley; that socially and commercially their sympathies and interests are with the people of the Southern states rather than with the people of the North and East; that the Mississippi river is the great artery and outlet of all Western commerce; that the people of the Northwest can never consent to be separated politically from the people who control the mouth of that river; that this war has been forced upon the South for the purpose of abolishing slavery, and that the South has offered reasonable and proper compromises which, if they had been accepted, would have avoided the war. In some of these arguments there is much truth. Our geographical and social relations are not to be denied; but the most potent appeal is that connected with the free navigation and control of the Mississippi river. The importance of that river to the trade and commerce of the Northwest is so patent as to impress itself with great force upon the most ignorant minds, and requires only to be stated to be at once understood and accepted, and I give it here as my deliberate judgment that, should the misfortune of our arms, or other causes, compel us to the

14—MOR.

abandonment of this war and the concession of the independence of the rebel states—Ohio, Indiana and Illinois can only be prevented from a new act of secession by a bloody and desolating civil war. The South would have the prestige of success; the commerce of the world would be opened to feed and furnish her armies, and she would contend for every foot of land west of the Alleghenies, and in the struggle would be supported by a powerful party in these states.

"If the states which have already seceded should succeed in their rebellion, our efforts must then be directed to the preservation of what is left; to maintaining in the Union those which are termed loyal, and to retaining the territories of the West. God grant that this contingency may never happen, but it becomes us, as men, to look it boldly in the face. Let us take security against it if possible, especially when by so doing we shall be pursuing the surest mode for crushing out the rebellion in every part, and restoring the Union to its former limits. The plan which I have to suggest is the complete clearing out of all obstacles to the navigation of the Mississippi river and the thorough conquest of the states upon its western bank. Between the state of Missouri and the Gulf of Mexico, on the western bank, are the states of Arkansas and Louisiana. Arkansas has a population of about three hundred and twenty-five thousand white citizens and one hundred and eleven thousand slaves, and a very large percentage of her white population is in the rebel army, and serving east of the Mississippi. Of the fighting population of western Louisiana not less than fifty per cent. is in the rebel army, and in service east of the river. The river once in our possession and occupied by our gunboats can never be crossed by a rebel army, and the fighting men now without those states can never get back to their relief. To make their conquest thorough and complete your proclamation should be executed in every county and every township and upon every plantation. All this can be done in less than ninety days with an army of less than one hundred thousand men. Texas would then be entirely isolated from the rebel Confederacy, and would readily fall into our hands. She has undoubtedly a large Union element in her population, and with her complete separation from the people of the other rebel states, could make but feeble resistance. The remaining rebel states, separated by the river, would be cut off effectually from all the territories and from the states of Mexico. The dangers to be apprehended from French aggressions in Mexico would be avoided. The entire western part of the continent now belonging to the government would be secured to us, and all communication between the rebel states and the states on the Pacific entirely stopped. The work of conquest in Arkansas and Louisiana would be easy and certain, and the presence of our gunboats in the river would effectually prevent any large force from coming from the east to the relief of those states. The complete emancipation which could and should be made of all the slaves in Arkansas, Louisiana and Texas would place the possession of those states on a very different footing from that of any other rebel territory which we have heretofore overrun.

"But another result to be gained by the accomplishment of this plan will be the creation of a guaranty against the further depreciation of the loyalty of the Northwestern states by the assurance that whatever may be the result of the war, the free navigation and control of the Mississippi river will be secured at all events.

"With high regard, I have the honor to be very respectfully, "Your obedient servant,

"OLIVER P. MORTON."

On October 30, Stanton telegraphed to McClernand: "I mean to give to the Governors of Indiana, Illinois and Iowa, latitude to raise, for operations on the Mississippi, all the force they can of artillery, infantry and cavalry outside of the calls heretofore made; but advanced pay and bounty are allowed only for those raised within the calls and pursuant to the previous orders. The local interest and feeling in favor of the Mississippi operations and your personal influence are relied on for the increased force, as the bounty funds will be exhausted by the previous calls.'' On December 12, McClernand announced that he had forwarded to the rendezvous more than forty thousand men.

The opening of the Mississippi continued to be one of the objects constantly sought by the administration, and the troops which McClernand had raised became incorporated at a later period in the armies of Grant and Sherman. Although the details of the movement were greatly varied, and the leadership of the troops was afterwards committed to other hands, yet the purpose was finally accomplished in the campaign against Vicksburg and the ultimate extinction of the Confederate power on the Mississippi river.

CHAPTER XVIII

THE PEACE LEGISLATURE—MORTON'S MESSAGE—HENDRICKS AND TURPIE ELECTED SENATORS

AT the opening of the year 1863, the military outlook had somewhat improved. The disaster of Fredericksburg, in the early part of December, had been succeeded by the battle of Stone river, in which the army of Rosecrans, althcugh suffering a loss of one-fifth of its entire force, remained master of the field, and the army of Bragg was so badly demoralized that West Tennessee and Kentucky were not again threatened by any formidable Confederate force. The capture of Arkansas Post by McClernand, on the 11th of January, was also reassuring. In both of these battles Indiana troops had taken an important part.

But the political outlook was gloomy. The bitterness between the two parties in Indiana was such as had never been known before.

The new legislature, which was about to convene, represented the peace Democracy of Indiana. It contained members whose avowed purpose was peace at any price, even the recognition of Southern independence; while some also favored the formation of a Northwestern Confederacy.[1]

---

[1] On January 1 the Democracy of Brown county resolved that, if the rebellion should be consummated by the recognition of the Southern Confederacy, their interests and inclinations would demand a withdrawal from political association with New England.

On the 3d of January the Indianapolis *Sentinel* declared that the policy of the party in power was to destroy the white race by servile insurrection and to make one-half the country a howling wilderness. On the same day Morton telegraphed to Stanton that he was advised that a joint resolution was to be passed acknowledging the Confederacy, and urging the Northwest to dissolve all relations with New England.

On January 8, the day the General Assembly convened, an inflammatory address from the Democratic State Central Committee was published denouncing the Emancipation Proclamation, and asking, "Will you submit to the abolition confederates and allow a degraded race to share the soil consecrated to the dignity and glory of the white race?"

From the first day of the session the Democratic members assumed an attitude of violent antagonism to Morton. Some came with the avowed purpose of taking from him all military power, and putting it in the hands of the Democratic state officers just elected. It was said that there was a plot for the seizure of the arsenal. The killing of Morton was talked of and predicted by the Knights of the Golden Circle. "We can easily dispose of him when the time comes. It will be an irrepressible assassination—that is all."

The Republicans were quite as belligerent. They believed that Hendricks, one of the candidates for the Senate, was not in favor of the war and would advocate a separate political union of the Northwestern states, as foreshadowed in his speech of January 8, 1862. They did not intend that he should be elected, unless with some pledge of loyalty, or upon resolutions which would require his support of the war. On the first day of the session, Mr. Claypool, a Republican, offered a resolution that the legislature would vote for no man who was not in favor of a vigorous prosecution of the war and unalterably opposed to the severance of any state from the Union. This resolution was referred by the Democrats to the Committee on Federal Relations, and the Republican senators, believing they had no guarantee of the loyalty of the men about to be elected, followed the example set by their Democratic brethren in the previous legislature and remained away, leaving the Senate without a quorum. On the 9th of January, during the absence of the Republicans, a communication was received from the House requesting the

senators to meet that body to hear the Governor's message.
It had been the custom in Indiana for the Governor to read
this document to both Houses in joint session. But as there
was no quorum, and the Senate did not come, the House
sent word to Morton that it could not say when it would
have the pleasure of hearing the message. He accordingly
sent it in writing.

Morton had prepared this message with great care. It
presented a comprehensive outline of the work of the state
government for the past two years, but the most important
parts of it were the dignified and noble sentences in which he
discussed the propositions for peace which had been urged
by the Democracy.

"Some there are," he said, "who profess to believe that
all we have to do, to bring about peace and a restoration of
the Union, is to lay down our arms and withdraw from the
conflict. Peace, temporary and hollow, might be had upon
such terms, but not a restoration of the Union. It would be
a dishonorable and shameful surrender, forever tarnishing the
character of the nation, and history would write down as infamous the instruments by which it was accomplished.

"Others say that we should re-construct the Union,
and that the New England states should be left out. But
what have the New England states done that they should be
left out? It is said we are paying heavy duties on imports to
sustain their manufactures, and are in that way oppressed. If
so, let us repeal these duties. The New England states are but
six, while the states of the Northwest alone are nine, with the
prospect of an indefinite increase. That, however, is not the
real objection. It is that their political principles are offensive, and the men who would turn them out desire to con-
struct a republic in which they can hold the power. Such a
project would be criminal to the last degree, if it were not
insane. The fortunes of parties are variable. The party in

power to-day is cast down to-morrow, and the victors are, in turn, overwhelmed, and so it goes on from year to year. The scheme of constructing a republic, taking in such states as are favorable and turning out such as are not, presents the last stage of partisan insanity. It would be forming the republic for the party, and not the party for the republic. A government founded upon such ignoble purposes could not stand, and would not deserve to. . . .

"I believe that the masses of men of all parties are loyal, and are united in their determination to maintain our government, however much they may differ upon other points; and I do sincerely hope that men of all parties will be willing to subordinate their peculiar opinions to the great cause of preserving our national honor and existence. And in conclusion allow me to express my confidence that your deliberations will be animated only by an ardent desire to foster the honor and interests of our beloved state, and to cherish and protect, at whatever cost, the power and the glory of the government of our common country."

But these earnest words fell upon heavy ears. Neither of the Houses of the General Assembly were willing to receive the message. The speaker of the House of Representatives ruled that it must be delivered to the legislature in joint convention, and since Morton had declined to appear in person the House refused to receive the message and returned it to the Governor. There was much foolish talk when the message was rejected. M. A. O. Packard insisted that the manner of transmitting it was an insult. Mr. Harney declared that the General Assembly was no mob to have the Governor's communication thrust in their faces by a clerk.

Jason Brown declared that his Excellency had, by one of his hirelings, a man whom he kept to sweep out his office, sent his message to be flung contemptuously on the speaker's desk, and on Brown's motion it was resolved that a commit-

tee from both Houses confer with the Governor and ascertain
at what time it would suit him to deliver his message. This
was evidently done for the purpose of putting Morton in the
ridiculous position of reading to the General Assembly a
document which had long since been communicated to them
and given to the public press.

Horatio Seymour, who had just been elected Governor of
New York, had, in his message to the legislature of that state,
on January 6, made an elaborate argument upon the subject
of state rights, had criticised the conduct of the war, denounced the Emancipation Proclamation, and declared his
belief that the Union was to be restored by the efforts of the
Central and Western states.

On January 13 Bayless W. Hanna offered the following
resolution in the Indiana House of Representatives:

"WHEREAS, His Excellency, Governor O. P. Morton, in
the midst of his arduous and patriotic endeavors as Commander-in-Chief of the military and naval forces of the state
of Indiana, has neglected to deliver his annual message to the
General Assembly, therefore

"*Resolved*, That this House adopt the exalted and patriotic sentiments contained in the message lately delivered to
the legislature of New York by his Excellency Horatio Seymour."

Pending the consideration of this insulting resolution, the
Senate entered the hall of the House of Representatives to
elect a United States senator, and Mr. Hanna's proposition
was informally passed over and was not renewed. But on the
following day a resolution was adopted, thanking Governor
Seymour for his message to the New York legislature, and
assuring him that the conservative people of Indiana looked
with confidence to his action, and believed that they would
find in it a firm and determined resistance to the encroachments of a despotic administration upon the liberties of the

American people, as well as a bold defense of the independent sovereignty of the several states.

But it so happened that Governor Seymour's own message had been delivered to the legislature of New York in the way that the General Assembly of Indiana had declared irregular and improper. So, on the 19th of January, Morton sent to the House of Representatives a communication, in which he adroitly availed himself of this fact in the following language:

"The point to which I call your attention is that in this resolution, *your honorable body have expressly recognized the message of Governor Seymour as having been delivered to the legislature of New York, although it was delivered only to the Senate, the House not being organized.*

"The action of the House, then, stands thus: On the third day of the session, after the complete organization of both the House and the Senate, the House, by resolution, returned my message, with the accompanying documents, on the ground that at the time of its delivery the Senate was not in session, and that there was no General Assembly, within the meaning of the constitution, to receive it.

"*This resolution was passed when the Senate was not in session.*

"On the 7th day of the session the House passed another resolution thanking Governor Seymour for his message, and expressly recognizing it as having been delivered to the legislature of New York, although it had only been delivered to the Senate, the House not having been organized.

"Having transmitted my message to the House in a proper and respectful manner, and it having been, in my judgment, unnecessarily and improperly rejected, I have nothing further to submit at this time."

Bitterly as the Democratic majority hated Morton, they found it impossible to oppose directly a resolution of thanks

for the care which he had manifested for the sick and wounded
soldiers   Efforts were made to stifle the matter in the Senate, but when the resolution came to a vote, no one had the
hardihood to oppose it, and it was unanimously adopted.
When it reached the House, Jason Brown moved to amend
it so as to read "for whatever solicitude and care the Governor has manifested." He was willing, he said, to compliment his Excellency according to his deserts, but not for
what he had left undone. "Render unto Morton the things
which are Morton's." This proposition was defeated, yet
the House, while not venturing to vote openly against the
resolution, succeeded in stifling it by referring it to a select
committee of five.

The withdrawal of the Republican senators, for the purpose of breaking a quorum and preventing the election of
Hendricks and Turpie to the Senate of the United States,
was a mistake. The Democrats had the undoubted right
to elect these senators. While Hendricks had not supported the war, he had not actively opposed it, and his
declarations in favor of the union of the Northwest made in
the convention of the 8th of January, 1862, were ambiguous.
He would be powerless in the Federal Senate to accomplish
any great evil in the face of the Republican majority, and if
his conduct became objectionable in the same way that Mr.
Bright's had been, he could be removed by the action of
that body. There was no need for the Republican senators
to assume the extreme position which they did at the outset
of the session. The real requirements for such action came
later. The Republican bolters were generally denounced.
Mr. Browne, of Randolph, a Republican, who had not withdrawn, offered a series of resolutions to compromise the
existing difficulties. These were intended to set forth the
conditions upon which the Republican members would take
part in the election of senator.

But the Democratic majority would listen to no terms. The resolutions were voted down, and, on January 14, Turpie and Hendricks were chosen senators by a vote of eighty-five to sixty-two, the Republicans having returned to their places without condition.[1]

---

[1] Some days after this election, a demonstration was held in Shelby county in honor of Mr. Hendricks, at which resolutions were adopted recommending a cessation of hostilities, opposing the conscription act and declaring that soldiers had been induced to enter the army by the false representation that the war was waged solely to maintain the constitution and restore the Union. Mr. Hendricks said: "Should our government go down in the vortex of this revolution, the responsibility is on the abolitionists. What has been the effect of the President's proclamation? Perhaps not one slave has been made free by it, but it has caused division in the North and stripped the soldier of his pride." Mr. Hendricks, however, opposed the efforts made by some of the more extreme peace men to induce soldiers to desert. He said: "Although I made no appeals to men to volunteer, as I would not say go, when I was not going myself, yet I must say to those who have voluntarily enlisted, you can not relieve yourselves by a breach of law, and you ought not to involve your friends in acts of violence, which will bring trouble upon them."

CHAPTER XIX

ATTACKS UPON MORTON'S FINANCIAL ADMINISTRATION— POLITICAL ARRESTS

BEFORE the legislature met there were hints of the misuse of public moneys by the Governor. It was declared by Democrats that he would shirk an investigation. But two days after the session opened, Thomas M. Browne, one of his close political friends, introduced in the Senate a resolution for an investigation of all public expenditures and for the exposure of fraud and corruption wherever found. This was a surprise to the Democrats. They were sure that it must be bravado. So, on January 19, the Governor was requested to furnish a statement of the military contingent fund in his hands. "If it comes," said the *Sentinel*, "it will form an interesting chapter in the history of public expenditures." The very next day the Governor sent the statement to the legislature. His critics could find nothing to object to, so they betook themselves to an examination of the accounts of the quartermaster's department, of the arsenal, of the Governor's purchase of arms, of his expenditures under the act for the defense of the state. Morton's friends insisted upon the fullest inquiry. It was not until January 31 that the enemies of the Governor could find anything. On that day the *Sentinel* declared that $828.78 had been taken from the treasury, after the battle of Richmond, Ky., in September, 1862, and had not been returned until the 2d of January, 1863, and it fiercely demanded, "In whose pocket was this money, by what authority and for what purpose?" To this

question Holloway, the Governor's private secretary, answered that the money had been deposited in bank until settlements could be made for which vouchers had not been received; that the money had gone into no man's "pocket";
that no interest had been received for its deposit; that not
one cent of it had been lost, squandered or stolen, and that
its payment into the treasury had been made as early as practicable. Apparently there was not enough in this discovery
to arouse the indignation of the people, and nothing more
was heard of it.

The claim was now made that certain items, charged by the
Auditor to the military account, should have been paid out
of the Governor's contingent fund, and Democratic patriotism
cried, "Let the whited sepulchre be thrown open." The Senate Finance Committee accordingly found that a loan of twenty-
five thousand dollars for equipping soldiers had been charged
to the wrong fund. Here was their chance, so they reported,
"the Governor has quietly put his hands into the treasury of
the military fund and paid this loan of twenty-five thousand
dollars while he had eighty thousand dollars of the Governor's contingent fund still in his possession." It was
perfectly evident from the facts stated in the report that he
had done nothing of the kind. If any mistake had been made
the Auditor was responsible. In fact, Morton had been absent from Indianapolis when the warrant for this money was
drawn, he had given no authority for the act, and did not
know of the payment. Even the Democratic members were
convinced of the injustice of this charge. The words incul-
pating Morton were stricken out by unanimous consent, and
this groundless attack came to an inglorious conclusion.

The remaining investigations were equally unsuccessful.
The accounts of the arsenal showed a large profit resulting
from economy and good management.

On March 7 Morton sent to the Senate a statement of
his proceedings under the act of 1861, authorizing the pur-

chase of arms and equipments. Toward the close of the session, a committee to investigate this subject was appointed, with authority to sit for forty days after the adjournment of the legislature. The committee pursued its inquiries in Indianapolis until nearly the end of these forty days, when the Governor asked them if they would make a report. Their answer was that they could not complete the investigation without going to New York to look into the contracts which had been made there, and that they had no money with which to defray the expenses of the journey. Morton supplied them with funds, and they went to New York and investigated the purchases, but could find nothing wrong.

Thus the threatened exposures ended in disappointment.

In the autumn of 1862, the President ordered that all persons discouraging enlistments, resisting conscription, or guilty of disloyal practices, which afforded aid and comfort to rebels, should be subject to martial law, and that as to them the writ of habeas corpus should be suspended.

In Indiana a number of arrests were made under this order, but on the 22d of November, 1862, the war department directed the release of those in custody.

The Democrats in the legislature wanted to use these arrests as a pretext for attacking the Governor, and a committee of inquiry was appointed, in which Jason Brown and Bayless W. Hanna were the leading spirits. This committee obtained leave to sit after the adjournment of the General Assembly, took a considerable amount of testimony, and finally reported a number of so-called "arbitrary arrests." This report is one of the curiosities of political literature.

At the time of the draft there was much disturbance in Blackford county and a number of arrests followed. The men taken were lodged, for a time, in the post-office building at Indianapolis, which now became, in the language of the peace Democrats, "the Bastile." In regard to these arrests the committee spoke as follows:

"Without the semblance of guilt, without a shadow of pretext, in the absence of all reason, forgetting all reverence for law and personal liberty, a few weak and misguided creatures, calling themselves the officers of the law, in the night-time, and acting under false pretenses, seize and carry away from their families and homes unoffending and peaceable citizens—citizens of character, of influence and position; and, after they are thus seized and dragged away, these irresponsible wretches hunt an occasion to appease their wicked and gangrened party malevolence, by exposing these kidnaped prisoners in the streets of Indianapolis, to the jeers and derision of a remorseless mob. . . .

"The United States marshal, when appealed to, folds himself more warmly in the flowing cloak of his own luxury, and, with a view to shift the responsibility, he wags his head ominously, and points these outraged citizens to the modern Caligula, and his willing satraps (!), who now inhabit the ancient metropolis of republican liberty. 'There,' he says, 'is my authority; I must obey—ask me nothing more.' . . .

"Citizens of Indiana were restrained of their liberty, and denied a trial. Why did not the Executive, made so by the constitution, and backed as such by the whole military power of the state, enforce the constitutional and unquestioned rights of these citizens? Was he ignorant of the fact that they had been trampled upon? That could not be. He does not pretend so much. One million of free Americans, of Anglo-Saxon-Celtic descent, ask the question, 'Where was he while these monstrous outrages were being practiced upon the liberties of the great people whose fortunes and destiny were the especial objects of his care?' . . ."

Bluford Mills was a man who had armed himself to resist the draft, and after a disturbance at Hartford City, had fled and hid himself in a swamp, and thus contracted a disease of which he died.

Of this the committee said: "Upon those who have been instrumental in taking the life of a valuable and intelligent citizen rests this terrible guilt. Anguish of soul will overtake them some time on account of it. If not before, they will feel it at last in that dark and melancholy hour, when, with feeble breath, they shall come to falter forth their last cry for mercy on an erring life."

The committee now extended its observations to other quarters.

"The last Congress," it said, "has been a disgrace to this nation. Its members—most of them—seem to have done everything they could to irritate the people and to destroy their liberties.

"When the nation was bleeding at every pore—when one million of our brothers were engaged in mortal strife—when hoof of fire and sword of flame were scourging the land and making our rivers run red and thick with blood, these remorseless plunderers and robbers were engaged in schemes of self-aggrandizement and in devising measures to increase our distractions in the states not in rebellion. Behold their record—the accumulated evidence that has been piled up mountain high against the thieving and jobbing villains that continually hang over the fallen, bleeding, struggling form of our liberties, like birds of evil prey, day and night, seeking some new quarry they may pounce upon and devour!"

Exactly what the committee had to do with this last Congress seems very misty. The report proceeded:

"Governor Morton has seen fit to pursue a very arbitrary and self-opinionated course in regard to the arrests made in Indiana. He has kept his lips sealed! But not one intelligent man, woman or child in the state doubts that he has been the sole cause of every arrest that has been made—at

15—MOR.

all events, that he could have prevented every one of them, and had all violations of law, if any had been made, corrected by the courts. . . . .''

The Republican minority of this committee made a report, in which they observed that those who were talking of *habeas corpus* needed more patriotism, and were not such friends of human liberty that that great boon could be trusted to *their* keeping.

The attempts to connect Morton with these arrests came to nothing. Certainly there is no reason to suppose that Morton would shrink from ordering the arrest of any one whom he might believe to be guilty of giving aid to the enemy, but in this case the proof was wanting. Indeed, it is evident that not one of the cases examined was thoroughly sifted, and that the purpose of the investigation was merely to prepare a campaign document.

During the session of the legislature a number of bills were brought in to punish ''arbitrary arrests,'' but they came to nothing.

Another matter that engaged the attention of the Democratic majority was injury to the property of various newspapers that opposed the war. A squad belonging to the Fifth Indiana Cavalry had broken into the office of the Rockport *Democrat* and destroyed some property. On February 5 a resolution was adopted asking the Governor by what authority these soldiers were stationed at Rockport, whether they had acted under any order, and whether they could not be removed to some other point, also demanding the punishment of the guilty. Morton answered: ''Ten companies of the Fifth Indiana Cavalry were stationed at points upon the southern border for the protection of the people from invasion by marauding parties from Kentucky. . . . The first knowledge I had of the alleged riot was obtained from this preamble and resolution. I have no knowledge of any order inciting or excusing the alleged out-

rage. . . . The interrogatory as to whether such cavalry
can not be removed to some other point I shall respectfully decline to answer. The attention of the proper military authorities has been called to the transaction, and they will, doubtless, make full investigation and bring all offenders to punishment.''

A bill was introduced ''to protect the liberty of the press,''
providing that where newspapers were destroyed by mob
violence, the parties injured might collect damages from
the cities, towns or counties in which such offenses occurred.
The measure came to nothing. The Republicans made great
fun of it. They said that it ought to work both ways—if a
party got a judgment against an editor for slander, and failed
to collect it, let him sue the county. Mr. Browne moved to
amend by providing that if a Democratic press were destroyed, the Republicans should be liable, and *vice versa*, all
damages to be recovered in an action of debt against the
guilty political party.

CHAPTER XX

CRITICISMS OF THE WAR—SOLDIERS' RESOLUTIONS—THE MILITARY BILL

MEANWHILE the General Assembly went on with its consideration of the war. Scores of grotesque and preposterous resolutions were tossed into the seething cauldron. There were propositions for an armistice, for a withdrawal of the Emancipation Proclamation, for peace conventions to consider impossible compromises. There were dismal wailings at the calamities of the war, at the overthrow of "sacred rights and liberties" by "tyrants and usurpers"—incoherent ravings against the President, the Governor, the abolitionists, the negroes, the Morrill tariff law, the Massachusetts Yankees— threats of "not another man, not another dollar"—mutual charges of treason and mendacity—a great tumult of words —much would-be Demosthenic eloquence, loud-mouthed, dissonant and ungrammatical. It is impossible for the chronicler to bring order out of such a chaos.[1]

---

[1] On January 13 Mr. Cobb offered a series of resolutions for the purpose of "binding together the several commonwealths in a union of brotherhood, never again to be shaken by the devices of secessionists or abolitionists." On January 14, Mr. Burton introduced a number of rambling declarations concluding thus: "While the President persists in his abolition policy . . . . Indiana will never voluntarily contribute another man or another dollar to be used for such a wicked, inhuman and unholy purpose." On January 15, Mr. Ferris introduced a resolution that the establishment of West Virginia betrayed the purpose of rearing upon the ruins of the Union a monarchical government. Mr. Humphreys submitted a plan for a suspension of hostilities. Mr. Cook offered a joint reso-lution succinctly described in the Brevier Reports "as condemning the

(229)

Propositions were passed denouncing the arming of negroes, demanding a withdrawal of the Emancipation Proclamation, and declaring that the President's scheme for compensated emancipation was a wicked defiance of the rights of the people. Mr. Hord offered a resolution declaring that the conscription law was subversive of state sovereignty, and that its enforcement should be resisted. The Democratic majority, emboldened by the success of their party in the late election,

---

war but not the rebellion." Mr. Burton presented a petition from Sullivan county against voting one dollar or one man for " this infernal abolition war." Mr. Lasalle introduced a proposition in favor of a national convention. Mr. Holcombe moved an instruction to congressmen, either to oppose emancipation or resign. Mr. Miller offered a resolution inviting the legislatures of Illinois, Kentucky, Pennsylvania and New York to join in propositions for a compromise. Mr. Burton submitted a document stating that Morton and Lincoln had lost all regard for the white men in the ranks and were giving their entire sympathy to the negroes.

Mr. Jason Brown introduced a joint resolution proposing a convention of all the states at Nashville. Mr. Blocher and Mr. Lasselle proposed a visit to the legislature of Kentucky. Mr. Packard moved an inquiry as to whether the state bank had not forfeited its charter by redeeming its notes in greenbacks. Mr. Wolfe introduced a resolution declaring that the war was a reproach to civilization, burdening the people with taxation and filling the North with a vagabond and worthless race.

Bills were introduced making negro immigration a felony and one sanguinary measure was succinctly described by the Brevier Reporter as "hanging every negro, he or she, who came into the state till he or she be dead."

The character of the Democratic majority in this legislature is also well illustrated by an incident in relation to the doorkeeper of the House, Mr. Benedict Burns. A committee was appointed to ascertain the number of men employed by him, but he refused to furnish the names of his employes, and the committee recommended his dismissal. He explained that he 'had lost heavily in his party's service,' and needed his post, that he had made promises in order to secure his election, and was beset by five hundred men clamoring for places, and had to disguise himself on leaving the state-house to go to his rooms. His appointments, he said, had been made at the suggestion of prominent Democrats, who had promised to sustain him. He believed that to the victor belonged the spoils. His employes were "all sound Democrats and a damned good set of fellows." The House accepted his excuses, but limited the number of his employes to fourteen.

evidently believed that they could go on in this extreme course without hindrance or molestation.

But the Governor had resources upon which they had not reckoned. Indiana had more than sixty thousand men in the field, and the Democratic majority at home was only about nine thousand. The soldiers were filled with rage at the action of the General Assembly, which they justly regarded as an attempt to cripple their efforts. Proofs of their indignation appeared at first in letters written home by single individuals. But their protests soon became general, and on the 23d of January the following petition and resolutions, adopted by the officers of twenty-two regiments and four batteries and approved by the soldiers, were sent from the Indiana troops at Murfreesboro:

"We ask that you will give this war a cheerful and hearty support; that you will strengthen and energize every department of the government so that this unhappy struggle may be pressed to a successful termination; that you will pour out the treasure of the state as your soldiers have poured out their blood on the field of battle to aid in the holy cause of restoring the Union of our fathers; that you will abstain from heated political discussions and violent party wranglings until the authority of the government is once more established; that you will resist the infernal spirit which would waste victory in humiliating compromise; . . . . that you will sustain all the officers of the state and general government in their efforts to subdue this unholy rebellion, and especially that you will sustain our worthy Governor, whose every energy during the past two years has been so entirely devoted to the cause of the government and its supporters. We appeal to you especially to sustain him for the reason that it is chiefly to his unceasing care and labor, exhibited in arming and supporting the troops of Indiana, that we have to attribute our present proud position among the loyal states of the Union; and for the further reason that he has demonstrated by acts that he is an honest and zealous patriot, devoting his time with untiring energy to the glorious cause for which we are battling.''

In conclusion the soldiers proposed that the legislature pledge itself, by appropriate resolutions, to preserve the Union, to prosecute the war, to sustain the state and national authorities with money and supplies, and to discountenance every faction tending to create animosities at home or to afford consolation and hope to the enemy; and they tendered to Governor Morton the thanks of his grateful friends in the army for his extraordinary efforts in their behalf, and assured him ''that neither time nor the corrupting influence of party spirit should ever estrange the soldier from the soldier's friend.''

These resolutions were the first of a series of like declarations made by Indiana troops in the field, and created much uneasiness among the opponents of the war. At first an effort was made to belittle the resolutions. The *Sentinel* insisted that Colonel Hunter, by whom they were drawn, was an abolitionist, and that Colonel Gooding, by whom they were supported, intended to run for sheriff, and that at the battle of Perryville he had hidden behind a stump and implored the rebels not to shoot. Mr. Wolfe insisted that these resolutions had been passed over a bottle of champagne, by officers who ''were getting a little too fast and saucy,'' and whom Mr. Shields called ''cowards and slanderers.''

But soon the Indiana troops in the Army of the Cumberland sent an address referring to their sacrifices, and declaring that the Governor of the state had so judiciously conducted its affairs that his praise was upon the tongue of the nation, and the gratitude of one hundred thousand soldiers was his reward. ''Some day,'' they said ''we expect to return, when we will remember and honor those who have aided us, and will visit those who have sought to defeat us with a retribution proportionate to the evil they have brought upon us and our country.''

Resolutions from Indiana regiments at Corinth said: ''We have watched the traitorous conduct of those members of the legislature, who, misrepresenting their constituency, have been proposing a suspension of hostilities—ostensibly to arrange terms of peace, but really to give time for the exhausted rebels to recover strength—and plotting to divest Governor Morton of the rights vested in him by our state constitution and laws; and to them we calmly and firmly say, 'Beware of the terrible retribution that is falling upon your coadjutors at the South, which, as your crime is tenfold blacker, will swiftly smite you with tenfold more horror should you persist in your damnable deeds of treason.'

''*Resolved*, That in tendering our thanks to Governor Morton and assuring him of our cordial support in his efforts to crush this inhuman rebellion, we are deeply and feelingly in earnest. We have left to the protection of the laws which he is to enforce, all that is dear to man—our wives, our children and our homes; and should the loathsome treason of madmen, who are trying to wrest from him a portion of his just authority, render it necessary, in his opinion, for us to return and crush out treason at home, we will promptly obey a proper order to do so; for we despise a sneaking traitor in the rear more than open rebels in the front.'

These resolutions provoked the rage of Democratic members, who declared that an effort was being made ''to mislead the army by the circulation of damnable lies,'' and the resolutions were returned as disrespectful.

On February 2 General Hovey and four colonels of Indiana regiments in Arkansas sent home an earnest address ''to the Democracy,'' and three days later, the Twenty-fourth Indiana Regiment sent a memorial. Two days afterwards came a statement from the officers of the Twenty-seventh Regiment declaring that in the resolutions of Messrs. Brown and

Wolfe they saw nothing less than treason, and recommend
ing that Governor Morton should make an example of these
men, and, if necessary, recall the Twenty-seventh Regiment
to do it.

The matter now began to look serious.   Mr. Harney introduced a resolution to ask the Governor whether he approved of these declarations of the soldiers, and whether any
officers had proposed to bring troops into the state to overwhelm the General Assembly.   A lively discussion followed.
"If we have a Cromwell at the door," said Mr. Given, "it is
time for us to know it."

On February 28 memorials from the Nineteenth and
Twentieth Regiments, containing specific charges of disloyalty against the legislature, were presented in the Senate.
Much feeling was displayed.   Mr. Dunning, the President,
declared that that body had been insulted, and that the statements were lies.

The legislature had sent a resolution of thanks to General
Rosecrans and his army for their conduct in the battle of
Stone river.   Rosecrans answered, "The unscrupulous despots in our front call us 'Lincoln hirelings,' and we hear that
this calumny has lately been repeated at home by some of the
men whose property and persons have been kept safe, by our
toil and blood, from the ruthless hands of Kirby Smith, Bragg
and Morgan.   Presuming on our absence, these men talk as
if we were not citizens, and speak mockingly of our patriotism.   They stab in the back the most generous, true-hearted
men of the country, who are standing guard in front of their
doors, and they prolong the war by encouraging rebels to
hope for divided counsels at our homes.   .   .   ."

Many other communications of the same tenor were made
to the legislature.   All these could not be ignored or rejected.
They were referred in the Senate, to the Committee on Federal Relations, and the report of that committee, adopted by
the Senate, shows what a deep impression they had produced.

This report proposed a resolution which was comparatively modest in tone. It urged that everything detrimental to the Union cause should be abandoned, and while it declared that the formation of West Virginia was unconstitutional, that arbitrary arrests were acts of tyranny, that the Emancipation Proclamation ought to be withdrawn, and that the Union could not be restored unless abolitionism were destroyed, yet it also declared that secession was a ruinous heresy; it did not ask for an armistice; it denounced secret organizations and paid a testimonial to the gallantry of Indiana troops. The effect of the soldiers' memorials was shown even more clearly in another report made by the same committee on March 7 as an answer to the troops. This document declared that the soldiers' words of counsel had been conveyed in the language of patriotism, and had been accepted by the Senate with the respect due to gallant men; that the soldiers in the tented field and the General Assembly in the legislative halls of the state were each endeavoring to put down rebellion and preserve the constitution; that the soldiers had heard much that was untrue, and that the Democracy had suffered from ungenerous accusations. The report continued: "We had no agency in inaugurating this war, none in carrying it on, none in directing its policy, none in the control of its armies, and it is not our design to interfere with it in any improper manner. Our duty is to pay taxes, to take care of the sick and wounded soldiers, to look and wait for the end of this cruel and bitter strife, to take care of our state affairs, and to hope that our beloved country will one day emerge from the clouds which hang over her, with the Union restored as it was, with all the states existing in harmony under the matchless constitution of our fathers."

The Republicans were jubilant. Mr. Mellett thanked the committee for the report and the soldiers for sending the petitions that produced it. "When we first met," he continued, "the talk was of an armistice, a cessation of hostilities, a peace convention taking the power out of the hands of the administration at once and stopping this bloodshed—that was the stock in trade. How is it now? Why, 'we have had nothing to do with this war; we did not commence it; it is our duty to pay taxes, to support the soldier and to feed and clothe the sick in hospitals.' That is the duty of the Democracy! How humble! My God, what a change!''

The change, however, was rather in seeming than in substance. The Democratic majority had found out that the public expression of their real designs and sentiments was inexpedient, but their purpose to cripple the government and aid the South remained as strong as ever.

All the tumult of debates and resolutions in the General Assembly might have gone on to the end of the session had it not been for a really dangerous conspiracy to take the military power of the state out of Morton's control and to put it in the hands of a board composed of state officers who were opposed to the war. A majority of these men were afterwards discovered to be members of the secret fraternities, the "Order of American Knights" and the "Sons of Liberty."

Even before the General Assembly convened there had been rumors of a state military board, to be controlled by Democratic officials, and as early as January 10, Thomas M. Browne, a Republican, introduced a declaration against such a board as one of the conditions upon which the Republicans would return to their seats and take part in the election of a senator. On the 5th of February, Bayless W. Hanna introduced a bill creating an Executive Council, to be composed of the Secretary, Auditor and Treasurer of State and the Attorney-General. This was considered a prelude to further legislation. The purpose of this measure, and of the Military Bill which followed, was clearly avowed. It was intended to ''have the lion shorn of his power.'' Finally, on February 17, the Military Bill was introduced by Mr. Hanna. Morton, in a speech at La Porte, in 1870, thus described it:

"It provided that the four state officers, the Treasurer of State, Secretary of State, Auditor of State and Attorney General, should constitute a military board; that they should have the appointment of all officers in the militia of the state of Indiana; that they should have command of the militia; that they should have the custody of the arms and munitions of war, thus placing the whole military power of the state in the hands of those four state officers. Now the command of the militia belonged to the Governor, as it does to the Governor of every state, necessarily and properly, as part of the executive power. The bill further provided that the Indiana Legion, which was then organized, and which was guarding the border counties against the incursions of the guerrillas from Kentucky, and was rendering valuable services, should be dissolved, and the arms delivered up into the hands of these four state officers, or their agents. It provided further, that the commissions of officers in the Legion, instead of being issued by the Governor, as the constitution requires, should be superseded by certificates issued by those four officers. The bill was unconstitutional in every particular,[1] it was simply revolution in the form of a legislative act.[2]

"Now, when that bill was brought forward I could not be-

---

[1] The Democrats, in defense of the bill, showed a rather adroit compliance with the letter of the constitution, while its spirit was subverted. Officers were still to be commissioned by the Governor, although these commissions now became a mere formality. The constitution had provided that the militia should be organized, officered and equipped in the manner provided by law, and the bill, it was claimed, made provision in literal accordance with this power. By the existing law, it was said, too much power was placed in the hands of one man, and "certainly four men, freshly elected by the people, were to be trusted as the advisers of the accidental Governor."

[2] One section of the bill provided that the militia might be called out on the warrant of a judge, mayor or justice of the peace, whose authority was defied, the warrant to be served upon the military commander, general or Governor, and the officer commanding the force to be subject to the civil officer requiring his aid. This would make the Governor subject to the orders of a justice of the peace.

lieve for a moment that it was their intention to pass it, it was so monstrous. I knew that, if passed, it would involve the state in civil war in twenty-four hours. The result would have been to take the state bodily into the rebellion, or, if that could not be done, to make her neutral, so as to furnish no aid to the government. I found before long that it was determined to pass it; that it had been resolved upon in midnight caucus, and that the bill would be enacted unless prevented by some bold and daring step.[1] I could have vetoed it, but under the constitution of Indiana a mere majority can pass a bill over a veto. Every hour that the bill was pending it endangered the peace of the state. It created alarm throughout all the loyal states, and excited the most intense interest on the part of the government. I knew that if the bill passed I could not afford to surrender my authority as Governor. I had taken an oath to administer my office according to the constitution, and I knew that the government of the United States would be bound to sustain me. I knew I could hold my position, but it would involve the state in civil war and our people would be cutting each other's throats

---

[1] Mr. Hanna moved immediately, upon its introduction, to suspend the rules and read the bill a second time with a view to its immediate enactment. A vote of fifty-two to twenty-seven, a little less than the two-thirds required by the constitution, supported this headlong policy. On the 19th of February it was read the second time and printed. On the 25th of February it was considered in committee of the whole and reported back to the House. Various amendments proposed by the Republicans were laid upon the table, and, under the operation of the previous question, the bill was ordered engrossed. Some Democrats had assured Morton that the bill should not pass, but these men had voted with their party for engrossment, which was carried by a vote of fifty-two to seventeen, and the final passage of the bill through the House might now take place at any moment. It was possible that this measure might be defeated in the Senate, but there was no assurance that it would be so, and the Republican senators having bolted once and been unsuccessful, it was very doubtful whether they could be counted on to bolt again. Morton did not intend to wait until the act went into effect. As the *Journal* expressed it, " If we must have war at our doors, let it come while we have the weapons in our hands."

in every county. I knew there was but one way to prevent
the passage of that bill, and that was to break up the legislature. The Republican members determined to withdraw
from the House. They did not commit the folly of resign-
ing, so that they would not be counted in making a quorum,
but quietly got on the cars and went to Madison, where they
could not be readily arrested.[1] Thus that legislature came to
an end. The passage of that bill was defeated.''

The Republican members afterwards published an address
to the people explaining their action and the reasons for it.
''The military bill,'' they said, ''had come from the midnight
caucus to the House; had been forced to engrossment without
the change of a word; all amendments had been voted down;
all reference to a committee had been refused; the previous
question had been sustained, and all debate cut off. Nothing was left but to sit by and see this measure passed and
civil war begun, or to retire and leave the House without a
quorum. If the military power were in the hands of the conspirators, it would be a matter of no importance what the
courts might decide. The path of duty was the path of
safety, and the minority had had no doubt nor hesitation as to
the course they should pursue. They had proposed in writing to come back and pass appropriation bills and all other
needful legislation, provided measures that were merely
political were abandoned. This proposition had been rejected and the Republicans had not returned.''

In the words of the *Sentinel*, the Indiana legislature 'died
without making a will. Its effects were in a strong box and
there was no key left to unlock it'.

---

[1] The Democrats declared that the minority were at Madison on a "big
drunk," and passed a resolution for meting out to legislators who abandoned their posts the same measure of condemnation as to deserters in the
army. The Republicans laughed at them, and recommended the use of
ice water.

ᴛwo men who have been referred to in connection with this legislature deserve special mention.   They were Jason B. Brown, commonly called "Bazoo Brown," the representative from Jackson county, a man of strong Southern sympathies, and his associate from Marshall and Starke, who rejoiced in the name of Marcus Aurelius Orestes Packard. These men were, perhaps, the most prominent members of the House of Representatives.   They worked together supporting and justifying each other, and between them they consumed a great part of the time of the House in attacks upon Morton and the administration.   This fact suggested to Morton the rhyme,

> " Brown and Packard, Packard and Brown,
>   One up and the other down."

which Sulgrove published in the *Journal*, and a day or two afterwards, he and Morton laughingly developed it into the following, which was published in that paper under the title "The Copperhead Brahma."

> " Brown and Packard, Packard and Brown,
>   One is up and the other is down;
>   One is nothing when t'other's not there,
>   The other is nothing anywhere.
>   Each is only a part of the other,
>   Yet each is as much as both together.
>   Take nothing from nothing and nought will remain,
>   Add nothing to nothing the sum is the same."

These rhymes were quite generally copied in the Republican press and were attributed to Sulgrove since they appeared editorially.   Morton was not suspected of writing verses.

It was during this session of the legislature that there occurred, in Morton's room at the state-house, a singular scene, which is thus described by Sulgrove: "Two old gentlemen, apparently well-to-do farmers, were shown in by the janitor.

They were Wayne county men, friends of Morton, Quakers, as I found from their speech. They were very anxious to get authentic news of the progress of the war and the outlook, and they listened to Morton's lucid summary with marked interest. When they had got what they came for, they rose to go and make room for other callers. The oldest, a man of seventy, I should judge, advanced to the Governor and laid his hand gently on the bald place on Morton's head, and in this attitude and with simple pathos invoked a blessing on the Governor's life and work. It was a beautiful and touching scene. There was no show or stage work about it, nothing but the honest faith of a gentle and manly nature breaking over the bounds of conventionality to express itself in the best way. Morton sat as quietly as a child, looking down and never moving an eyelid till the old man had closed the door. Then he looked at me and said, with deep feeling, 'That is a Christian, if there ever was one.' "

16—MOR.

CHAPTER XXI

POLITICAL MEETINGS—SPEECHES AT PIKE'S OPERA HOUSE
AND AT CAMBRIDGE—VALLANDIGHAM CAMPAIGN

BUSY as Morton was during this session of the legislature,
he found time to take part in several important political gath-
erings.   On the 14th of January a Union meeting was held
in Masonic Hall, at which the Governor gave a history of the
secret societies in Indiana.   One of their purposes, he said,
was to encourage desertions and demoralize the army.   He
spoke of the hopes of the Confederates, built upon dissensions
in the North, and of the certainty that a united sentiment at
home would speedily end the war.[1]

On the 24th of January Morton was present at a Union
mass-meeting at Shelbyville, where he denounced unsparingly
the Knights of the Golden Circle.

On February 23 he spoke in Pike's Opera House, at
Cincinnati.   The meeting had been called, he said, to give
assurance to the brave men in the field that they had not been
deserted at home.   He answered the arguments of those who
quoted the late election returns to show that the people were
opposed to the war.   Ohio, he said, had seventy thousand men
in the field, and the opposition majority was five thousand

---

[1] The *Sentinel* now declared that these societies were evidence of the
feeling against the war, and that there was no hope of ultimate success.
When Republicans organized to resist the formation of a Northwestern
Confederacy it was evident that there was danger of another revolution
more alarming even than the rebellion.   The men responsible for the anarchy which would follow were the Republicans who justified executive
usurpations.

only. Indiana had sixty thousand men in the field, and the opposition majority was only nine thousand. New York had one hundred and fifteen thousand men in the field, and the opposition majority was ten thousand. Pennsylvania had one hundred thousand men in the field, and the opposition at home had barely thirty-six hundred majority. The soldiers who were fighting for their country were all voters, while the submissionists stayed at home and played the game of politics.

"What would these men have?" he asked. "They propose an armistice. But what are the terms? One party may make war, but it requires two to make peace. What would we be required to do? To withdraw all our armies from the territory claimed and raise the blockade of all the ports. Then they would enter into negotiations. Suppose the peace convention met at Nashville. We would ask the terms. The rebels would say, 'acknowledge our independence.' Suppose that was agreed to, where would be the boundaries? Our commissioners would say, 'The southern line of Missouri, Kentucky, West Virginia and Maryland.' The rebels would say, 'No, you can not have peace on such terms; that is our territory. The Ohio and the Missouri must be the boundary. Suppose the submissionists should concede. The question would then arise about the navigation of the Mississippi. Our commissioners would say, 'Of course the navigation of that river will be free. You promised it in your convention at Montgomery.' 'No,' they would answer, 'We can not agree to that. The conditions upon which we offered free navigation were not complied with. We owe a thousand millions of dollars. We must have revenue to pay the debt. You must pay toll.'"

Morton next considered the demand of the peace party of the West for separation from New England. "New England's crime," he continued, "is that she has stepped forward and given assistance when the government needed money, that she owns the public debt.   What evil has New England done?   The tariff?   Let us repeal it to-morrow.   New England has but twelve votes in the Senate.

"New England's offense is this: she loves liberty too well [vehement and prolonged applause]. . . . From her we borrowed our school-houses, our free democratic government and—[the rest was drowned in applause] . . . In the war of 1812, the record of our gallant navy was made by New England men.   So in this rebellion the brilliant exploits of our gunboats on the Mississippi and on the Cumberland were performed by New Englanders.   Nineteen-twentieths of our sailors in the regular navy are Yankees.   And shall we turn New England out to let South Carolina in?"

Morton warned the people against the intrigues of the secret societies.   The One Hundred and Ninth Illinois Regiment, which had been recently disbanded by General Grant had been a "circle."   Its officers had been sworn members of a disloyal order.   The First, Second, Third and Fifth Indiana Cavalry had been affected, and an artillery company at Indianapolis had been destroyed by this agency.   It could not be tampered with.   It was a public enemy.   It must be throttled.

In the early part of April Morton delivered in Albany an impressive address.   On the 9th of that month a dinner was given in his honor at the Maison Dorée, in New York, in which he urged upon his hearers the necessity for the successful prosecution of the war.[1]

Two days later he spoke in that city at a mass meeting which had assembled for the purpose of commemorating the

---

[1] At the conclusion of the speeches a parchment roll, signed by many of the eminent men of the city, Mayor Opdyke, William Cullen Bryant, Cyrus W. Field, David Dudley Field, Alexander T. Stewart, Henry J Raymond and others, was presented to Morton.   It expressed the high regard of those who signed it and their appreciation of Morton's able and patriotic efforts to sustain the national government.

attack upon Fort Sumter. After his return to Indiana he addressed a great throng at Madison, arraigning the peace Democracy and the Knights of the Golden Circle, whose leaders, he said, were soon to be brought to punishment. Some "Butternuts" who were present slipped away during the speech, lest they should be pointed out as objects of his denunciation.

In the latter part of May it was announced that Vicksburg had fallen. The announcement was premature, but it created much enthusiasm. A multitude gathered in front of the Bates House and Morton was called for. He spoke, among other things, of emancipation. Slavery, he argued, had been the cause of the rebellion and there could be no permanent peace until it was abolished.[1]

But the most impressive of Morton's speeches at this period of the war was an oration delivered at Cambridge City, in his native county of Wayne, on the 4th of July, 1863. This was the time of the great battles of Gettysburg and Vicksburg.

The meeting was held in a grove near the town. The citizens of the neighborhood, without regard to party, had gathered in great numbers to celebrate the national birthday. Lafayette Develin, a peace Democrat, Morton's former associate at the bar, presided and introduced the speaker. Feelings of opposition to the war were very strong, and a considerable portion of Morton's audience was composed of the disaffected. He took advantage of the occasion to appeal to their patriotism. He said:

"Fellow-citizens: I appear before you under circumstances the most solemn and impressive. You have often before met to celebrate the independence of your country, but

---

[1] "He is for a new Union," sneered the *Sentinel*, "and a new constitution, a new Bible and a new God. Those who are for the old constitution, the old Union, the old Bible and the God of our fathers, are not good enough for the virtuous Morton."

never under conditions like the present. Many of our brave soldiers are doubtless bleeding to-day in defense of our country and her free institutions. Our fathers, brothers, sons and husbands are in the very front of battle, and almost every flash along the wires tells us of loved ones who have bravely fallen. Let us endeavor to realize the difference between them and ourselves. They are falling in the great struggle for the preservation of the freedom under which we are enabled to assemble in peace in remembrance of the sacrifices of our heroic fathers of the Revolution.

"Eighty-seven years ago to-day, a most illustrious convention of devoted men proclaimed the birth of our nation. What I have to say to you will be mainly a commentary upon the sacred instrument that has just been read. Such is the pressure of my public duties that I have had scarcely an hour's thought in preparation for this occasion, and I must speak to you as the truth is burning in my heart or I must not speak at all.

"For what, fellow-citizens, is that instrument especially distinguished? Apart from a long list of grievances, there are three or four important matters set forth in it to which I desire to call your attention.

"In the first place our fathers declared that all men were created free and equal, and entitled to certain inalienable rights, among which were life, liberty, and the pursuit of happiness. They announced the fundamental principles on which the new government was to be established. In this they addressed the conscience of the world—the common sense of mankind in reference to self-evident truths.

"What did they mean by the idea that all men are created equal? They did not mean equal in power, physical, intellectual or moral; but simply that all are entitled to the same rights, that the same justice presides over all, and that all should be held as 'equal before the law,' which should be no respecter of persons. . . .

"All are entitled to certain inalienable rights. This is the fundamental distinction between the theory of our constitution and that of the British government. The theory of Great Britain is that the people are entitled to no rights except those which may be granted to them by the crown. The lords at Runnymede extorted from the king the privileges of the Magna Charta, which are held to have been a grant from the crown. But we hold that the liberties of man are derived from God, and not from crowns, constitutions or magna chartas, and that they are inalienable.

"What is meant by inalienable in this connection? That these rights can not be sold or rightfully given up by the people or by any individual. They pertain to him as a man, and are essential to his existence as a man. No one has a right to sell himself, because he was born for certain duties and should be free to discharge them. No one can deprive himself, by any instrument, however solemn, of the privilege of exercising the liberties with which he was created.

"Our fathers also proclaimed, in the most solemn form, the principle that the colonies constituted but one nation. They did not act as thirteen independent colonies, but as one individual people. This vital and most important truth is announced in the first sentence of the Declaration: 'When, in the course of human events, it becomes necessary for one people,' etc. As one people they dissolved their connection with, and dependence upon, the British crown. And at the close of the instrument the same principle is declared.

"Thus it is evident that the first thought in the minds of the patriots of the Revolution was that they were acting, not as colonies, in separate municipal or civil capacities, but as an undivided people.

"The same principle was announced by the convention of 1787, the first words of the constitution being, 'We, the people, in order to form a more perfect Union,' etc. They were particular in stating that it was not in the capacity of the several states that they acted, but that the constitution was a compact of the people of all the states as one people.

"There are two theories in collision in this bloody contest. On one hand it is held that there is no such people as the American nation, but that there are thirty-four independent states, which have made a compact from which they can withdraw at pleasure. The other theory is that we are a unit, one and indivisible; that we are not separable into parts, but constitute a whole nation for common purposes clearly defined in the constitution. As the states are divided into counties, all of which constitute the state, so the nation is divided into states, all of which constitute the national government.

" When certain states undertook the treasonable work of secession they issued a declaration repudiating the fundamental principles announced by our fathers. They started out with, 'We, the deputies of the several states of South Carolina, Georgia,' etc., 'do ordain this constitution,' thus clearly implying that the fathers did act as one people, while the Southern States in secession act as separate governments. I allude to these things to show that this war is a war to subvert the principles which our fathers promulgated eighty-seven years ago; and that ours is now the great duty of maintaining and preserving the principles of human equality, human rights, and an indivisible nationality. . . .'"[1]

---

[1] In another part of this address Morton thus advocates the employment of negro troops : " If the rebels against the government can use the negroes for its destruction, shall we not be permitted to use them for our national preservation ?

"We hear much about the unconstitutionality of such a measure. Chief-Justice Taney has recently decided the blockade to be constitutional, and yet there is not a word in the constitution in reference to a blockade. So with many other things. The fathers did not deem it necessary to insert the laws of war in the constitution. The blockade is a right of war—it cripples the enemy. What constitutional right have we to destroy the mills of the enemy? The right of a belligerent. . . . The constitution protects commerce, but we blockade ; it protects mills and mules, but we seize the one and burn the other. So with the slaves ; they sustain the foe, let us turn them against him."

The effect of this address upon the audience was powerful. One who was present says: " I have frequently listened to Morton, have heard him when, as a young lawyer, he was making impassioned appeals to juries; when, as the nominee of a great party for the highest office in the state, he was in-spired by vast audiences and borne up by storms of partisan enthusiasm; when, as the acknowledged leader of that party, he stood, at the beginning of our state campaigns, and made his famous 'key-note' speeches, and when he was addressing regiment after regiment of departing or returning soldiers, but on no occasion did he ever exceed the brilliant and un-answerable appeal that he made for the Union cause on that memorable Fourth of July at Cambridge City."

There was no general election in Indiana in 1863, but in the neighboring state of Ohio an important political contest was going on. Vallandigham, who had been arrested, and afterwards required to leave the country on account of his disloyal utterances, had now become the idol of the peace Democrats, and, on the 11th of June, he was nominated for Governor by the Democratic convention. During the can-vass he issued an address from Canada, declaring that under the British flag he exercised rights which usurpers insolently denied him at home. If the war was to terminate only by the subjugation of the South, the infant of to-day would not live to see the end of it. He had not met one man, woman or child in that section who was not resolved to perish rather than yield to the pressure of arms.

This campaign involved the most important consequences, and Morton went to Ohio to take part in it.

The result was most encouraging to the friends of the Union. Vallandigham was defeated by the unprecedented majority of one hundred and one thousand votes. Secretary Chase, who had also taken part in the campaign, visited Indianapolis, just after this important victory, and addressed a large meeting.

He was introduced by Governor Morton, who, in a brief speech, alluded to the victory and its effects: first, on the nation, which it had saved from division and strife; second, on foreign powers, whom it would teach to believe in the preservation of our national integrity; third, on the rebels, to whom it would prove that their hopes of our dissensions were without foundation, and, fourth, upon the soldiers who would see in it the assurance that they were not to be abandoned.[1]

---

[1] Chase was, at this time, an active aspirant for the presidency. The story is told that he was driving with Morton through the streets of Indianapolis, and that he said suggestively, "If I were President I would make you Secretary of State." Morton made no answer.

CHAPTER XXII

"I AM THE STATE"

MORTON accomplished what had never before been attempted in American history. For two years he carried on the government of a great state solely by his own personal energy, raising money without taxation on his own responsibility and disbursing it through bureaus organized by himself.

The legislature, as we have seen, adjourned without making any appropriations. The state government and the benevolent institutions had to be provided for, and there was no money with which to do it. Morton had to make choice of one of three courses: first, he could call a special session of the legislature, which had just adjourned; second, he could close the state institutions and stop the government; third, it was just possible that by personal effort he could raise the money to carry it on. He had been able to borrow several hundred thousand dollars for a short time, for the purpose of equipping soldiers to oppose the invasion of Kirby Smith, but now a loan must be obtained for two years upon the doubtful contingency that the next legislature would sustain him in this perilous undertaking. Should he fail to get the money he would be discredited; should the loan not be repaid by the next legislature he would be bankrupt in purse and reputation. The responsibility was great, yet he did not hesitate. The other alternatives were fraught with public disaster. To call the legislature together was to invite a repetition of the scenes already enacted. The General Assembly

(253)

would make no appropriations except at the price of a military bill depriving Morton of all control of the forces of the state. Under no circumstances would he consider this alternative. Better that the state should be left unprovided for; that the criminals, the insane, the blind and the deaf and dumb should be turned out upon the highways than that, under the control of the sympathizers with secession, Indiana should become an ally of the Confederacy. But the operations of the state government should not stop, if the Governor could help it. He would risk all that he had and all that he hoped for to keep it going.

When the legislature adjourned the Democrats did not doubt that they could force him into submission. They did not believe he could carry on the government for ten days without an appropriation. "Does our noble Governor," they sneered, "intend to run the state on his own responsibility? We do not believe gentlemen of capital will thus invest money." Many of the Democratic members kept their rooms at the hotels and boarding-houses of Indianapolis, expecting to be recalled at once.

But Morton had resources upon which they had not reckoned. In the first place, a large sum had been made by the profitable management of the state arsenal. Money was due from the general government for ammunition furnished by this arsenal, and this money was paid to the Governor while he was in Washington, about the 1st of April. Morton proposed to devote it, as far as it would go, to paying the expenses of the state. The Democrats denounced him, insisting that the profits should be paid at once into the state treasury, where they would be securely locked up and useless.

The embezzlement act provided that if any officer should convert the money of the state to his own use, or loan, deposit or exchange it contrary to law, he should be deemed guilty of a felony; and Morton was reminded by his political adversaries of the pains and penalties provided in this act. But owing to the obstinacy of the late legislature the arsenal had, fortunately, not been recognized by law, and the general government could well claim that the proceeds of that institution were not state property. It was upon this theory that the money was paid to Morton. As the arsenal did not yet belong to the state the Governor insisted that he did not violate the embezzlement act in disbursing this money on his own account for state purposes.

Morton was not the man to flinch under threats of criminal prosecution. On April 18 he established a "Bureau of Finance," and appointed W. H. H. Terrell to be his financial secretary. The Governor also appealed to the people, to private bankers, and to the various counties of the state, asking for funds with which to carry on the government. He procured a safe for the keeping of these funds. The response was prompt and liberal. Many counties made appropriations ranging from two thousand to twenty thousand dollars each. Private citizens advanced considerable sums, among them one hundred of his old Wayne county friends, who signed a note for twenty thousand dollars, borrowed the money and sent it to him The Terre Haute and Richmond Railroad Company loaned him fifteen thousand dollars. On April 16 his enemies were further discomfited by news that a large sum had been sent to him from Washington out of the secret service fund of the war department.

He had now obtained money enough for carrying on the government until the meeting of the next legislature The benevolent institutions and the penitentiaries were managed with skill and economy at a diminished expense as compared with that of preceding years.

A more serious trouble was Morton's inability to pay for the arms he had purchased to repel the invasion of Kirby Smith. The Ocean Bank of New York had, before the meetting of the late legislature, advanced him the money for these arms, because it was believed that the General Assembly of 1863 would pay the bill. But that legislature adjourned without making any such provision. The arms, however, were of excellent quality and had been purchased at low prices, so the general government assumed the debt and took the arms, and Morton was enabled to meet the notes before they became due.

The other military expenditures of the state were also a source of great embarrassment. There were no funds on hand for the relief of sick and wounded soldiers, nor for the support of their families. There was no money with which to discharge the military claims against the state, or pay the surgeons who had been sent to the field, and the Indiana Legion which had been protecting the border. Moreover, new regiments could not be raised without large sums of money. And Morton's enemies soon devised fresh sources of embarrassment. Since they could not compel him to call a special session in any other way, they determined to bring him to terms by forcing a repudiation of the interest on the state debt.

As early as 1846 an act had been passed providing that this interest should be paid semi-annually in New York and for its payment the faith of the state was solemnly pledged. It was believed at the time that the act conferred sufficient authority for the payment of this interest out of the treasury, and for many years the Auditor drew his warrants and the Treasurer paid them without a specific appropriation. The legislature evidently considered such an appropriation unnecessary. In 1857 the legislature adjourned without making appropriations, and McDonald, the Democratic Attorney-General, advised Governor Willard that no further legislation was required to authorize the payment of the interest. The Governor, Treasurer and Auditor of State accordingly borrowed one hundred and sixty-five thousand dollars, and paid the July interest of 1858. In 1859 an act was passed, specifically directing the Treasurer to draw each year an amount sufficient for the payment of such interest, and to transmit the same to the place of payment in New York. This, too, was considered to be an appropriation.

Now, however, Mr. Hord, the Democratic Attorney-General, at the request of Mr. Ristine, the Democratic Auditor, prepared and published an opinion that the money could not be so drawn from the treasury.

It was believed that the purpose of this opinion and of the Auditor's refusal to draw a warrant for the interest was to compel Morton to call a special session. The Democrats wrote edifying homilies on "the honor of the state," and declared that the Republican Governor alone had power to redeem its plighted faith by calling the legislature together.

Morton, on April 23, addressed a letter to James Winslow (a member of a New York banking house, by which the money to pay this interest was afterwards advanced), containing an argument in answer to the opinion of Mr. Hord. He referred to the previous practice of the legislature and of the state officers, to the opinion of McDonald, and to the fact that in April, 1863, the Attorney-General had himself obtained from the Auditor, without a specific appropriation, a warrant for his own salary.

This letter was ridiculed by the Democrats and called "yaller kivered literature," and the Attorney-General published a reply in the *Sentinel*. Brett, the Treasurer of State, did not enter willingly into the scheme of repudiation. In order to secure his co-operation, Ristine and Hord determined to get an opinion of the Indiana Supreme Court confirming their views. A Mr. Talbot, one of Ristine's advisers and president of the Sinking Fund Commissioners, who held state bonds, brought suit for mandamus in the Marion Circuit Court, to compel the Auditor to issue a warrant for the July interest. The papers in the suit were presented to the clerk of the Circuit Court by Attorney-General Hord, on

17—Mor.

the 11th of May, with the request that a judgment, requiring
the issue of this interest-warrant should be at once entered
and a transcript made out for an appeal to the Supreme
Court. Hord said to the clerk that the case had been passed
upon. A transcript was accordingly certified before any
step in the cause had been entered upon the order-book of
the Circuit Court, and before any minutes had been read or
signed by the judge. This transcript was handed to the
Attorney-General, who said that he hoped to get the decision of the Supreme Court *in a few days.*

When Judge Finch, of the Circuit Court, read the entry of
judgment, he remarked that he had not been informed what it
contained, and that if he had known its character it would not
have been made, and he accordingly struck it from the record.
He then examined the pleadings and decided that the proceedings were premature, as the interest was not yet due.

From the last decision Talbot appealed.   The Supreme
Court received and retained *both records in the same case,* one
showing that a mandamus had been ordered and the other
that it had been refused.   The court considered both cases,
"brushed aside all other questions," and proceeded to decide
whether there had been any appropriation for the payment of
interest on the state debt.   Morton's letter to Winslow was
filed as a brief in both cases.

The Supreme Court was then in Democratic hands, and
political bias sometimes tainted its decisions. Judge Perkins delivered the opinion in the first case and Judge Hanna
in the second.

Perkins declared that the non-payment of interest "would
cover the state with dishonor," but that the constitution had
provided against this by authorizing a special session of the
legislature. His argument was long and rambling. He recited the safeguards of English liberty, Magna Charta, the
Petition of Right, the Habeas Corpus Act, the Bill of Rights
and the Act of Settlement. He quoted Macaulay, Hallam,

Adam Smith and the treaty with Mexico. The state officers, he said, must not assume doubtful powers, since this would be usurpation. Usage was not binding. The construction asked for in Morton's letter revived the worst habits of official discretion in the days of the Tudors and Stuarts."

Judge Hanna held that neither the act of 1846 nor that of 1859 was an appropriation.

The purpose of the suit was to compel Morton to call a special session. The Republicans denounced "the fraudulent appeal," and Morton himself, in his message to the legislature in 1865, said: "Without intending any disrespect to the eminent tribunal by which this case was decided I must be permitted to observe that the history of its origin, progress and conclusion was such as to deprive it of any moral influence, and that the principles upon which the decision was made have been since openly disregarded by the Auditor and Treasurer of state in the payment of large sums of money to the Public Printer."[1]

Despite the decision of the Supreme Court, Morton did not intend that the credit of the state should suffer if he could help it. He would raise the money with which to pay the interest on the bonds as well as to conduct the military operations of the state.

On June 9 the Republican members of the legislature and other prominent men in the party came together in Indianapolis for consultation. The opinion was unanimous against a special session. The Democrats now said that "nothing but legitimate business" would be transacted. But the Republicans asked "why should the legislature be called together?" It was, they said, the wickedest and most malignant body of the kind that had ever met. The promise that no political measures should be introduced had been given only the day before the attempt to pass the military bill. The Democrats were not to be trusted.

---

[1] J. J. Bingham, editor of the *Sentinel*.

The Democrats now urged a special session on another patriotic ground, "to provide for the needs of the Indiana soldiers." "No one knew," they said, "at what moment a rebel force might appear on the border and invade the state." But this exhortation was made to deaf ears.   Morton meant to provide for the soldiers but not by calling the legislature together.   He suddenly left Indianapolis, and it was given out that he was at Centreville.[1]

The fact was, however, that he had gone to Washington to get money to provide for the Indiana soldiers and to pay the interest on the state debt.   He first had an interview with the President.   Lincoln wanted to help him, but saw no way of doing it.   "I know of no law," he said, "under which I can give you the money."   Finally he referred Morton to Stanton, and the Governor betook himself to the War Secretary.

These men had been cast by nature in the same mold. They had become devoted friends.   Morton had called upon Stanton some time before on public business.   Stanton was brusque, irascible, repellent.   He had no time to listen to the Indiana Governor.   But Morton had staid till he was heard, and until his business was accomplished.   The intercourse thus born of common public aims had ripened into a firm and lasting

---

[1] "His Excellency," says the *Sentinel*, "after his arduous labors, needed a little time for recuperation, and he therefore betook himself, as did Washington, and Jefferson, and Madison, and Webster, and Clay, and all the great lights identified with American history, to feed his chickens and pigs, to watch the gambols of his flocks and herds, to cultivate his cabbages, his rutabagas, his beets, onions, parsley and parsnips; to see the wheat change to its golden hue and ripen for the sickle, or some modern patent reaping machine; to look upon the rich meadows as they mature for the scythe; to hear the corn crack as it springs from the earth under the influence of the heat and dews of the hot summer nights—in a word to enjoy all the felicities that a rural life affords. . . . Beautiful Centreville! Happy Morton! . . .

"P. S. We understand from a most responsible source that his Excellency has not been to Centreville at all, but that he has been paying court to the wise men of the East, and that yesterday, with majestic air, he was gracing the magnificent portals and corridors of the palatial St. Nicholas, in New York City."

friendship. Morton now laid his troubles before the Secretary, and asked for help. He told Stanton that Lincoln knew of no law under which he could aid him. "By God, I will find a law," said Stanton, and he did. An appropriation of two millions had been made by Congress in July, 1861, to be expended by the President in supplying arms to loyal citizens in states threatened with rebellion, and in organizing such citizens for their own protection against domestic insurrection. Indiana (so Stanton held) was threatened with rebellion. The terms of the appropriation were, perhaps, sufficient to cover the military expenses of the state, but they were hardly broad enough to justify the advancement of money to pay interest on the state debt. The need, however, was so extreme that Stanton was willing to take the responsibility. At his request Morton furnished him with an estimate that one hundred and sixty thousand dollars was necessary to pay the interest, and ninety thousand dollars to conduct the military operations of the state. Stanton laid the matter before Lincoln, and on June 18 Lincoln issued an order authorizing two hundred and fifty thousand dollars to be advanced to Morton, for which sum the Governor was to be held accountable.

When Stanton placed this order in Morton's hands, both these men appreciated the great risk they were incurring. "If the cause fails we shall both be covered with prosecutions," said Morton. "If the cause fails," said Stanton, "I do not wish to live." Morton was of the same mind. He took the order and departed.

He was deeply grateful for Stanton's help, and before leaving Washington wrote him the following letter:

"I could not leave the city without again expressing to you my appreciation and gratitude for the great service you have done my state. Heaven has endowed you with soul and ability to comprehend the times and grapple with the great questions presented. May you be preserved to your country, which will yet recognize your services, but can never sufficiently reward them."

Morton, thus provided with funds, went to New York. But he did not intend to use this money for the payment of interest, if he could help it.

J. F. D. Lanier, a prominent banker of New York, had spent his early life in Indiana, and was warmly devoted to the state. He was a man of wealth and patriotism, and the banking house of Winslow, Lanier & Co., of which he was a leading member, had conducted the financial affairs of Indiana in New York. He had already, on former occasions, loaned to Morton about four hundred thousand dollars, with which to arm and equip the Indiana troops, and these loans had been repaid. To this man Morton applied for money with which to pay the interest. He was successful. Mr. Lanier agreed to provide him with the needful sum, and Winslow, Lanier & Co. notified John C. Walker, Agent of State (the financial representative of Indiana in New York City), that they would pay the interest, and asked him to furnish from his books a list of the *bona fide* holders of the state stocks.

This list was made necessary by certain spurious certificates which had been issued by one Stover, a former Agent of State, many of which were still outstanding. The books of the agency would show which certificates were genuine and which were fraudulent. But Walker was a bitter enemy of Morton, who had caused his dismissal from the army for insubordination, and he could not forego this opportunity for revenge.[1]

---

[1] Walker had been a man of strong Southern sympathies, but, like Heffren and others, he had "yielded with reluctance" (as he afterwards expressed it) "to the persuasions of friends," had raised troops, besought an appointment, and been commissioned by Morton as colonel of the Thirty-fifth Indiana Cavalry. He was continually making trouble, and turned out to be a most pestilent fellow. A vacancy occurring in the lieutenant-colonelcy, in March, 1862, the Governor appointed to the place Major Balfe, the next in rank, a worthy and competent officer. Walker considered that Morton had insulted him by not appointing Captain Hughes, whom he had recommended, and he insisted that Balfe should not accept the appointment. He subsequently placed Balfe under arrest. He said that any one appointed by the Governor, when not recommended

He declined to furnish a list of the state's creditors, and refused access to the books of his office.[1]

by himself, "had better be in hell." He finally extorted Balfe's resignation.

In May, 1862, Morton, in conformity with instructions from the war department, ordered Lieutenant-Colonel Mullen, commanding the Sixty-first Regiment, to consolidate his command with Walker's regiment, and a number of appointments and promotions were made by Morton to fill vacancies. Walker refused to recognize the officers appointed. Morton communicated the facts to General Halleck, and Halleck dismissed Walker for insubordination. Walker applied for reinstatement, but in vain, and he was filled with wrath against the Governor. When the legislature of 1863 convened, Walker became a candidate for the office of Agent of State. His enmity to Morton was his chief qualification, and he was elected.

Some time later Walker addressed to the *Sentinel* a three-column article attacking the Governor. "His Excellency procured my removal upon a false charge lodged by himself. . . . He can not prove to the satisfaction of a court of justice or a court-martial that the charge made by him against me at Washington is not as false as his own heart is black, and as villainous as his nature is cowardly and infamous." . . . "He desired me out of the service because he was unable to purchase my friendship or poison my political principles." "The disposition manifested by the party in power to fasten a despotism upon this country by the destruction of the ballot-box may yet compel a people naturally forbearing and tolerant to rise in their might and teach our modern Neros and Caligulas that they can not be enslaved. They may live to see their party and themselves go down in a sea of blood to a dishonored grave."

On August 3, 1863, Walker, in another long letter to the *Sentinel*, said: "The means adopted by the Governor to create a vacant place for a cringing sycophant were cowardly and disgraceful, and show upon their front the impress of conscious felony." . . . "Has B. F. Mullen, who calls himself a Democrat, the name of Morton engraved upon the collar which he wears? It is humiliating, I confess it, to be compelled, in treating with the Governor, to kick away the hounds who form his body-guard. We should learn, however, not to be annoyed, as we sometimes are, by the yelping on our tracks of the dogs with which his Excellency has lately, at a small price, supplied his kennel."

[1] The following is the correspondence:

Banking Office of Winslow, Lanier & Co.,
52 Wall St., New York, June 24, '63.

John C. Walker, Esq., Agent of State of Indiana, New York:

DEAR SIR—It being now quite certain that the next July interest on the funded debt of the state of Indiana will not be paid for reasons publicly known, we have, at the earnest solicitation of Governor Morton and

Winslow, Lanier & Co. now proposed to Walker that he should pay the interest himself in the usual way by checks

---

other citizens of that state, agreed to pay the same to the holders of the certificates of indebtedness, to protect the credit of the state. To do this safely to ourselves we must take an assignment from each creditor of the amount of interest due, with power of attorney to collect the same when you are placed in funds to pay it. To enable us to do this satisfactorily, we must have a certified copy of your pay-roll for July, giving names of the holders, as also the amount of dividend due to each, etc.

We, therefore, respectfully request that you furnish us with the same at as early a day, prior to the day of payment, as your convenience will allow. We shall expect to pay you all expenses that may be incurred in and about furnishing the same.

We shall be pleased to hear from you as soon as convenient.

Yours truly,　　WINSLOW, LANIER & CO.

To this letter Walker answered:

Office Indiana State Agency,
New York City, June 25, 1863.

Messrs. Winslow, Lanier & Co.:

GENTLEMEN—Your favor of the 24th instant has been received and duly considered. In reply, I beg leave to say, that, in common with every citizen of Indiana, I am exceedingly anxious that the creditors of our state shall be promptly paid that which is due to them. The state has amply provided for them all. Her treasury is full and her tax-payers will keep it so for every lawful demand. All that is needed is that the legislature shall have an opportunity to make the appropriations to give the financial officers of the state authority to disburse the funds. I hope it is correct as you stated in your letter, that the reasons why the next July interest on the funded debt of the state of Indiana will not be paid at that time are "publicly known." The people of Indiana, with the issues before the country upon them, elected a majority of Democrats to represent them in the legislature of the state. To prevent the legislation demanded by the people, the Republican minority of the House of Representatives, instigated by Governor Morton, and in violation of their sworn duty, deserted their posts and left that body without a quorum to do business. By this revolutionary proceeding, the acts appropriating moneys to defray the expenses of the state, to carry on the benevolent institutions and to keep up the state prisons, failed to become laws. In consequence of this, there are thousands of creditors of the state at home who suffer already for their just dues, and, as you mentioned, the credit of the state abroad is also apt to suffer by the anticipated failure to meet the current interest on her funded debt. The majority of the legislature are ready and anxious to make those appropriations, not only to pay the class of creditors to whom you refer, but other creditors for a large amount, whose claims are equally just.

upon their banking house, which they agreed to honor, at the same time exonerating him from all personal liability. This offer was likewise refused.[1]

Through you, Governor Morton now asks me, as an officer of the state, whose duties the law prescribes, to co-operate with him and to furnish the records and facilities of my office, for what purpose? Not to facilitate the state to pay her interest or to add to her pecuniary resources, for the arrangement you propose is only to transfer some portion of the indebtedness to other hands. And you plainly state that you ask this, not as an individual about to buy and operate in the certificates of the state, in a business way (and as such reasonably entitled to information), but in connection with arrangements entered upon "at the earnest solicitation of Governor Morton and other citizens of that state." For an officer of Indiana, who has respect for his duty to himself and his state, to become a party to Governor Morton's real purpose in this claim is impossible. That object is not to "save the credit of the state," but to continue in his disastrous purpose to override the constitution and laws of Indiana; to arrogate to himself the functions of all departments of the state government, and to set at defiance the people and the legislature. Governor Morton, if he is faithful to the duties of his office, and to the wishes and interests of Indiana, will promptly convene the legislature, and let them, as they will do, if his friends will remain at their posts, appropriate the money for the payment of the demands of her creditors. The Governor prefers to rush into all sorts of temporizing expedients and shifts, bringing the good name and financial credit of his state into bad repute with every holder and hawker of claims against her. The honor and interest of Indiana require that her faithful servants and friends shall withdraw confidence from him in his mad career. The state does not need that creditors at home or abroad should be called upon to postpone their demands, nor, on the other hand, that individuals should be asked to advance the money. The party or parties who unnecessarily subject her to the shame of such apparent confusion, or who seem to sanction it as necessary, in fact only insult and dishonor her. Governor Morton has his partisan politics and his selfish ambition to prompt him, and I will not lend myself to the furtherance of his acts, which are revolutionary and ruinous. He has no right, after the people of Indiana have taxed themselves and filled their treasury for the purpose of paying their debts, still in his obstinacy to accept as a favor the advancement of funds from individuals to save them from dishonor. Without, therefore, intending disrespect to you, gentlemen, I must decline to render assistance to the Governor in his attempt to carry on the state government in defiance of law and without that legislation which the Supreme Court has decided to be essential in the premises. Truly yours, J. C. WALKER,
Agent of State of Indiana.

[1] The following is the correspondence:

Walker having thus for the time defeated Morton's arrangement, default in the payment of interest was made on the 1st of July. The value of the "state stocks" (as they were called) was, of course, affected, but steps had been taken to inform the creditors and the public of the fact that money had been provided to pay the interest, and of the reason for the default.

Banking Office of Winslow, Lanier & Co.,
52 Wall St., New York, June 26, 1863.

John C. Walker, Esq., Agent of the State of Indiana:

DEAR SIR—Your letter of yesterday in reply to ours of the 24th has been received.

We have nothing to say in reply, save to express our regret that the state should fail in paying the interest on her funded debt. As to where the fault lies in the premises, it is not for us to say. It has occurred to us, however, that we could shape our request in a manner that would meet your approbation. It is this: That you should, in the capacity of agent of state, go on and pay each creditor entitled thereto on your dividend book, taking the receipt of each in the usual form, you to draw your official check on our house, to the order of each party entitled thereto, expressing on the face of such check that it is given for the July dividend on stocks. These checks we will pay and hold the same as our vouchers until we are reimbursed. In this way the payment can be made in the usual manner, as the Agent has always heretofore paid, by drawing his checks on our house, or some other house of this city. As it is necessary for us to know whether or not we are to advance so large a sum of money by Wednesday next, we will thank you for an early reply.

Very respectfully,   WINSLOW, LANIER & CO.

Office Indiana State Agency,
36 Wall St., New York, June 26, 1863.

Messrs. Winslow, Lanier & Co.:

GENTLEMEN—Your letter of this morning is received. I regret to say that a sense of duty compels me to decline acceding to your proposition.

Respectfully yours,   JOHN C. WALKER,
Agent of State.

No. 52 Wall St., New York, June 27, 1863.

John C. Walker, Agent of the State of Indiana:

DEAR SIR—We yesterday received your reply to our second proposition. We should, perhaps, have said therein, that we did not propose to hold you responsible, in case you should agree to our requests. We now say so.   Yours truly,   WINSLOW, LANIER & CO.

To this letter it does not appear that Walker made any reply.

There was great indignation at Walker's action, and the credit of Indiana was not seriously impaired.

The Democratic newspapers, in order to justify Walker's refusals, declared that he could not pay the money without making himself and his bondsmen liable. They had not been informed of an offer of Winslow, Lanier & Co. to exonerate him from liability. "After they had all swallowed the bait, and were strung on the same string," said the *Journal*, "this last statement was published, which left them suspended like spoiled cat-fish on a hot day."

Morton, having now found that the money advanced to him by Stanton for the payment of interest was not necessary for that purpose, wrote to the Secretary on July 22, 1863, as follows:

"DEAR SIR—You furnished me the sum of two hundred and fifty thousand dollars, of which sum one hundred and sixty thousand dollars was to enable me to pay the interest on the state debt, and the balance to carry on the state government. The agent of the state in New York, a weak, bad man, who was the tool of the repudiators here at home, refused to avail himself of the money placed to the credit of the state by the house of Winslow, Lanier & Co., and suffered the interest to go unpaid. He also refused access to his books, so that I was unable to pay it by agents outside of his office.

"The credit of the state and of my administration has been saved by providing the money in New York with which to pay the interest, and the disgrace must rest upon a weak copperhead officer and his wicked advisers.

"The money which you so generously provided for this purpose is subject to your order, and is on deposit in a bank in New York.[1] I beg leave, however, to suggest that in the

---

[1] It might seem from this letter that there was some connection between the one hundred and sixty thousand dollars advanced by Stanton and the amount which Winslow, Lanier & Co. agreed to furnish. The Indian-

recent Morgan raid I incurred military expenses which I have
no means of paying, and that I am organizing the state troops
and putting them on a war footing for immediate service if
required. This is important to the government on account of
the draft, and in every point of view, but I have not a dollar
of money with which to do it unless I am allowed to retain
the one hundred and sixty thousand dollars for that purpose.
This, I suppose, would be within the letter and the spirit of
the appropriation.''   .   .   .

Stanton was willing that the money should be applied to
this purpose, so Morton retained it until the legislature met
in 1865.

The interest on the state debt remained, for some time,
unpaid, and Morton began to look elsewhere for a list of the
bona fide stockholders of the state.   Information upon this
point was contained in the records of the Auditor of State,
and the Governor applied to Ristine for access to those records.
Public opinion was very strong against the repudiation of the
interest.   It was now certain that the Governor did not intend
to call a special session of the legislature, whether the interest
was paid or not, and there was nothing to gain by further refusal.   Ristine accordingly permitted the Governor's secretary to take from the Auditor's books copies of the transfers
of the state stocks.   From these, and possibly other sources,
a satisfactory list of the holders of the state securities was at
last obtained, and in November, Winslow, Lanier & Co. gave
public notice that they would pay the interest which had fallen
due in July, and, afterward, that they would pay the interest
falling due on the 1st day of January, 1864.   These payments
continued until the legislature of 1865 made provision for the

---

apolis *Journal*, of June 28, stated that Morton had deposited with Winslow, Lanier & Co. one hundred and sixty thousand dollars, with which to
pay the interest on the state debt. The subsequent advancements made
by that firm, however, do not appear to have any connection with the
money furnished to Morton by Stanton.

reimbursement of the sums that had been advanced. The entire amount so paid was six hundred and forty thousand dollars.[1]

In December, 1864, a short time before the legislature met, Morton wrote to Stanton that there would be in his hands an unexpended balance of the sums advanced amount-

---

[1] Mr. Lanier, in his autobiography, prepared for the use of his family, thus states the circumstances which induced him to make the loan: "Governor Morton, most anxious to preserve the honor and credit of the state, applied to me to advance the necessary sums. Unless this could be done he felt that he could not justify, before his own state and the country, the position which his friends in the legislature had taken through his counsel and advice. The application was made at the darkest period of the whole war. I could have no security whatever, and could only rely for reimbursement on the good faith of a legislature to be chosen at a future and distant day, and on the chance of its being made up of more upright and patriotic members than those composing the one then in existence. If the great contest should turn out disastrously to the cause of the Union and of freedom, I could never expect to be repaid a dollar. I felt, however, that on no account must the debt of a great state be discredited, nor the position of its chief magistrate, the ablest and most efficient of all the loyal Governors, and the one who contributed most to our success, be compromised or weakened. No alternative was left to me but to advance the sums required. I would not allow myself to be responsible for the consequences of a refusal of his request. If the credit of the state in such a critical period should be destroyed, that of the other states, and even of the Federal government, might be so impaired as to render it impossible for them to sustain the immense burdens of the war. Another influence of very great weight with me was an ambition to maintain the credit of a state with which I had so long been identified, to which I was indebted for my start in life, and for whose credit in former times I had earnestly labored. The last, perhaps, was the ruling motive."

It would be supposed that a banking house which had thus assumed the interest on the state debt would be treated in Indiana with civility and respect. But this was not the case. It was hinted that there was a secret contract. "How much bonus were they to pay Morton to get their fingers into this thing and to advance so large an amount on profitable terms?"

"Winslow, Lanier & Co.," said the *Sentinel*, "might find it difficult to get their money returned. As a proper reproof to such audacious impertinence a prompt refusal ought to be given to the recognition of any part of this debt, so as to let Governor Morton and Winslow, Lanier & Co. know that it is better that they attend to their own business and let that of others alone."

ing to more than one hundred thousand dollars. This, he said, could be returned to the government and settlement made on vouchers for the money spent.

Stanton had suggested that the whole sum had better be charged to the state, and treated as an advance upon her account with the government. "This," said Morton, in his message to the legislature of 1865, "would undoubtedly be more equitable, with the distinct understanding, however, that the money did not come into my hands in that character, as in that case the law would have required me to pay it into the treasury at once."

The state did not, however, assume the debt, but at Morton's suggestion a joint committee, composed of members of both parties, examined his accounts and unanimously reported them correct, and on April 11, 1865, he paid the balance remaining in his hands into the United States treasury.

An incident connected with the refusal of the state officers to pay the interest on the state debt is graphically described by Morton in a speech made by him on February 23, 1864, at the Union State convention at Indianapolis. He said:

"There is another transaction connected with the refusal to pay the interest on the public debt, which must, if possible, increase the abhorrence entertained for it in the public mind. In August Messrs. Ristine and Brett, the Auditor and Treasurer, advanced to Walker, from the state treasury, the sum of fifty thousand dollars, to be invested by him in our war loan bonds or in the state stocks of which I have been speaking. Messrs. Ristine and Brett have also taken from the treasury the sum of fifty thousand dollars with which they have purchased Indiana five per cent. stocks, making in all the sum of one hundred thousand dollars taken from the treasury for that purpose. We are here presented with the remarkable spectacle of state officers deciding that there is no law by which they can pay the interest on the state stocks, but finding law to take money from the treasury for the purchase of the stocks themselves at a price depreciated by the failure to pay the interest!'' In this speech Morton also discussed another inconsistency in the conduct of the Democratic officials.

"I should fail to present the conduct of the state officers in its proper light," he said, "if I did not allude to their action in regard to the State Printer. It is difficult to see upon what legal or moral ground they could refuse to advance money for the support of the benevolent institutions and penitentiaries, and at the same time pay large sums of money to the State Printer, yet this was the case. When the Senate journal of the last day of the session (Monday) was read, it was found to contain a resolution, which the minutes showed to have been adopted, appropriating twelve thousand dollars for the payment of the State Printer.

"The Union members present declared that no such resolution had been read in their hearing, and that no quorum had been present to pass that or any other resolution. Be that as it may, it was but the resolution of one house. It was not a law, and had no force or validity whatever. Under the flimsy pretext of this resolution, warrants were issued to the State Printer for twelve thousand dollars, on which he drew the money. When this sum was exhausted, there was a little delay in the payments; but having become bolder, and the necessities of the editor of the *Sentinel* having become greater, they dispensed with all pretext or forms of law, and paid him large sums of

---

The *Sentinel* (February 27, 1864), thus explains this transaction: On the 13th day of March, 1861, an act was passed to authorize the war loan bonds and imposing a special tax of five cents on each one hundred dollars, and providing that the excess of money collected by said tax after paying the interest should be paid to the Sinking Fund Commissioners who should purchase these bonds, if they could do so on reasonable terms, and, if not, they should invest the same in other state stocks. This act, said the *Sentinel*, was an appropriation of the money derived from the tax.

money from time to time, in all amounting to about twenty thousand dollars. When asked to pay for the support of the benevolent institutions, they pleaded the absence of appropriations, and the terrors of the embezzlement bill. But when asked to pay the editor of a partisan newspaper, they laughed at the embezzlement bill as a good joke, and treated the plea of no appropriations as a clever thing in its way, but too trifling to interfere with the support of the newspaper organ of the party. I am informed that the Attorney-General gave an opinion to the effect that it was legal to pay the State Printer. I should have been surprised if he had not."

Another episode illustrates the bitter feeling of the state officers toward Morton. The law provided that the Auditor of State should make his annual report to the Governor, and that the Governor should cause this report to be printed. Ristine, however, without consulting Morton, printed and circulated a report criticising the Governor and charging him with all sorts of financial irregularities. Extracts from this document were published in Democratic papers for political purposes.

This document exasperated Morton, and he wrote to Ristine as follows:

"INDIANAPOLIS, February 13, 1864.
"*Joseph Ristine, Esq.:*
"SIR—I received this morning by the hands of your messenger a printed political document, purporting to be the official report of the Auditor of State. It has no convincing claim to the character of an official paper, and can not be regarded as such. O. P. MORTON."

Ristine wrote in answer a long letter filled with insulting language. Morton returned this letter without comment. Ristine denied that he had received it.

CHAPTER XXIII

BATTLE OF POGUE'S RUN—MORGAN'S RAID

THE battle of Pogue's Run was an engagement not mentioned in the Rebellion Records, nor in any of the histories of the war, yet few who lived in Indiana at that time will fail to recall the event with a smile, a shrug or a blush. It was announced that a great Democratic mass meeting would be held in Indianapolis on the 20th of May, 1863, and that Seymour, Vallandigham, Pendleton, Cox, Hendricks, McDonald and others would be present and would speak. The secret societies organized throughout the state for the purpose of opposing the war had determined to make this meeting the occasion of an armed demonstration, and had sent word to their members to come prepared for emergencies, with weapons concealed upon their persons. A small Federal force under General Hascall was in Indianapolis at the time. Information was given to him, as well as to Governor Morton, of these preparations and of the intention of those who directed them to attempt the seizure of the government arms, arsenal and stores. Hascall quietly organized some Union paroled prisoners who were at Camp Carrington, and placed them under command of Colonel John Coburn. These men, together with other troops, were stationed at various places in the city to protect the government property and suppress riotous demonstrations. There were several companies at the Circle, in the center of the town, two blocks distant from the state-house yard, where the meeting was to be

18—MOR.　　　　　(273)

held. A cannon was also placed in position to command the state-house.

On the day of the meeting special trains ran to the city from all parts of the state. The gathering was a large one, some ten or twelve thousand persons, and no less than three thousand of these were armed. But they were not organized, and the outcome of the demonstration was ridiculous. The mass meeting was a failure. Seymour and Cox were absent. Vallandigham had been arrested for inciting resistance to the government, and could not come. It was said that Pendleton was in the city, but that his friends thought best that he should not attend the meeting. Daniel W. Voorhees presided. His opening remarks were like the lamentations of Jeremiah: "Confusion and disorder darken the sky; the very earth is laden with the sorrow of our people; the voice of woe comes up from every portion of our distracted country; the angel of death has spread his wings on the blast, and there has been no sacred blood sprinkled upon the door-posts of our homes to stay the hand of the destroyer.   .   .   .
One man there would have been in our midst to-day, an invited and honored guest, one whom you all expected to see here upon this occasion, but he has fallen a little sooner, perhaps, than the rest of us, a victim to the base usurpation which has taken the place of public rights and of the constitution."

A committee on resolutions was appointed and speeches were made by a Mr. Merrick, and a Mr. Eden as well as by McDonald and Hendricks. Eden's speech was punctuated by shouts for Lincoln, from soldiers and other troublesome Republicans. McDonald counseled peace.

About four o'clock in the afternoon, while Hendricks was speaking, some eight or ten soldiers with bayonets fixed and rifles cocked entered the crowd and advanced slowly toward the stand. A great uproar arose. The multitude scattered in every direction. A high fence on the east side of the state-house square was pushed down by the rushing crowd. A squad of cavalry galloped along Tennessee street adding to the tumult. The soldiers who were moving towards the stand were ordered to halt by Colonel Coburn, who had been guarding the quartermaster's stores north of the state-house, but who came out when he heard the disturbance. He asked what they were doing. They said they were "going for Tom Hendricks," that he had said too much, and they intended to kill him. Coburn expostulated with them and they desisted. There was much confusion on the stand. Hendricks closed his remarks prematurely, suggesting that the resolutions be read and the meeting dismissed.[1] The resolutions declared that the Federal government had two wars upon its hands, one against the rebels and one against the constitution. The Republicans in the late legislature, who had

---

[1] The Indianapolis *Journal* gives a different version of the incident: "Thomas A. Hendricks was introduced. He asserted that the Democratic party had always been right, and was right now. Some one in the crowd shouted, 'That is a hell of a way to support the government.' Some friend of Hendricks attempted to strike the party who had spoken when a 'muss' ensued, and a squad of infantry came forward to quell the disturbance. The assailing party was taken out of the park and hurried to a place of confinement. . . . Mr. Hendricks kept one eye on the right of the stand, expecting to see a rush to the platform, and his speech was disconnected. There was a good deal of excitement in the crowd. Some one rushed on the platform and said they were coming to arrest Mr. Voorhees. Several of Mr. Voorhees' friends stepped forward and said, 'let them come, he was ready for them, and now was as good a time as any.' Mr. Voorhees assured them that there was no danger; they would not attempt to arrest him in so conspicuous a place. Quiet was again restored and Mr. Hendricks suggested that the resolutions had better be read and the meeting dismissed. Just then the chairman of the committee appeared with the resolutions, much to the relief of Mr. Hendricks, and as he was about to conclude his speech he was informed that one page of the resolutions was lost, and he must speak until it was found. He turned around in dismay and begged that they would hurry, for it would not do to keep the crowd much longer. He went on to declare his devotion to the restoration of the Union, and to charge the war upon the Republicans, when Judge Claypool, from the committee on resolutions, returned, and Mr. Hendricks was relieved."

broken the quorum, were denounced, and it was declared that the Governor could not clear himself from complicity, except by taking steps to prevent repudiation (*i. e.*, by calling a special session.)

When the resolutions were put great numbers shouted "no," and cheers were given for Lincoln, for the war and for the conscription act. General Hascall had given orders that all soldiers should stay away from the state-house. It was not easy, however, to restrain the men. Many of them went to the meeting and mingled with the throng. The torn flags of two Indiana regiments were upon the stand. The soldiers proposed cheers for the flags, for the government, and for the war, which were given with a will by the Union men present, while the others stood silent and angry. After the resolutions had been adopted the meeting adjourned, but a great number of Union men remained, took possession of the stands and made speeches. Toward the close of the day some young soldiers walked through the crowd, and, when they heard any one speak against the war, seized the culprit and marched him up the street with a great rabble following. In many cases, after they had marched some poor fellow a few squares and thoroughly frightened him, they either slipped away or told him that if he would behave himself they would let him go. A number of men were taken to the police court and charged with carrying concealed weapons, and about forty pistols were taken from those arrested. When the meeting was over and the trains were leaving the city a great number of shots were fired from the cars on the Lafayette and Terre Haute railroads. The intention to create an armed disturbance, although unaccomplished, now seemed clear, and the soldiers determined to give the remaining "Butternuts" a lesson. When the Indiana Central train left the station a gun was placed in front of it upon the track. The train stopped. A small body of soldiers were collected under General Hascall, and a policeman, accompanied by a few of these soldiers, demanded the surrender of all firearms by the passengers. Nearly two hundred weapons were given up. The train to Cincinnati was also stopped, many revolvers were taken and others were thrown in great numbers, by their owners, into Pogue's Run at the side of the track. Pistols had been given to many of the women, in the belief that they would not be searched. Seven were found upon a single woman. A knife nearly two feet long was discovered in the stove in one of the cars. In all, about five hundred loaded revolvers were taken from those who had attended the meeting.

Thus ended "the Battle of Pogue's Run," whose waters were filled, not with the blood of combatants, but with fire-arms prudently cast away that bloodshed might be avoided. The fact that a handful of men could disarm such a multitude aroused laughter and contempt. The Butternuts had come to the meeting armed for the purpose of making trouble, and not one of them had dared to strike a blow, not even in re-sistance of arrest and search.

The disgust of the "Peace and Pistol Democracy" at the outcome of their demonstration was very great. "It is with feelings of sorrow, humiliation and degradation that we wit-nessed the scenes of yesterday. . . . Indiana is as com-pletely under military rule as France, Austria or Russia," said the *Sentinel*, and then proceeded to denounce the gov-ernment in unmeasured terms. The *Journal* contemptuously retorted: "We implore you not to sit down in despair, and mourn as one upon whose cervical vertebrae the ferruginous heel of oppression has been ruthlessly deposited. There is a hope—a glimmer, a ray, a beam, a whole dawn of hope—if you would only open your eyes and see. Unassailable bul-wark of the freedom of disloyal speech, despairing advocate of the liberty to assist rebellion, did it not occur to you, when writing your denunciation of the government, that if you could publish it you were lying? Do you want any more liberty of abuse than you exercised yesterday morning?''

The Butternuts might rend their garments, and invoke the sympathy of the world, but the Union men had acquired valuable information. They had measured the courage of their opponents. ''Grant, for the sake of argument,'' said the *Sentinel*, ''that the Democratic masses of the state were made up of cowards, men who shrank from exposing their persons to hostile shot, was it politic to drive even cowards to the wall? Did the Republicans want the lamb changed to a lion?'' But the Republicans had little fear of such a metamorphosis. To the Union men of the state the Butternut was no longer an object of apprehension. He would not fight.

In the summer of 1863, General Burnside was preparing in Kentucky an army for the invasion of eastern Tennessee. The Confederates believed that he and Rosecrans would attack simultaneously the two armies of Bragg and Buckner, and it was resolved to create a diversion which would keep the troops of Burnside at home and cover the retreat of Bragg to Chattanooga. A raid through Kentucky was planned for this purpose. John H. Morgan was selected to command it. His success in such enterprises had been phenomenal, and his prestige was unbounded. Bragg directed him to confine his operations to Kentucky, but Morgan determined to violate his orders and invade Indiana and Ohio. A foray through these states, he thought, would keep a large force of Federal troops for weeks upon his track, and success would justify his disobedience. On the 2d of July he crossed the Cumberland with 2,460 men, and moved northward through Kentucky. It was believed in Louisville that he intended to attack that city, and the garrison were prepared to give him a warm reception. He learned this by tapping the telegraph wires. Louisville, however, was not Morgan's destination. Taking advantage of the concentration of Union troops in that city, he prepared to cross the Ohio at Brandenburg, some distance below. He marched with great rapidity, and, on the morning of July 8, arrived on the Kentucky shore of the river.[1]

A small advance guard which he had sent ahead had already captured two steamers at this place. Some troops of the Indiana Legion had collected on the north bank of the river and began firing on the Confederates, but they were driven away by Morgan's artillery, and two of his regiments were soon landed on the Indiana shore. A small wooden gunboat now appeared on the river and shelled the Confederate troops, but after an hour or two the gunboat retired, and by midnight Morgan's entire force had crossed the river.

At this time Indiana was stripped of national troops. All the available cavalry and artillery had been sent to Kentucky. The Legion was too feeble to offer effectual resistance. There were only a few hundred mounted men in the state, when Governor Morton learned that the Confederates were marching northward through Kentucky. He sent word to General Boyle that he would co-operate in any measures to arrest the

---

[1] Some time before this Captain Thomas H. Hines, one of Morgan's subordinates, had obtained authority to lead a scouting expedition north of the Cumberland. With a small band of eighty men he scoured Kentucky, then crossing the Ohio near Cannelton he passed swiftly into the interior of Indiana, where he exchanged his broken-down horses for the best he could find, claiming to be a Federal officer, and giving vouchers on the quartermaster at Indianapolis for the difference in value, which he always fixed at a satisfactory and liberal rate. But as he approached Paoli, the county-seat of Orange county, preparations were made to receive him, and he turned South. Some companies of the Indiana Legion started in pursuit, and another detachment headed him off on his return. A guide, whom he supposed to be reliable, but who was in fact a Union man, caused him great delay in selecting a practicable ford, and finally conducted him to Blue River Island, which was easily accessible from the Indiana side, but not from Kentucky. Hines and his little band having been caught in this trap, attempted to swim the river, but the steamer Isetta intercepted them, and they were all killed or captured, except three. Hines alone joined Morgan at Brandenburg, when the latter was preparing to invade Indiana.

invaders, and he asked where Morgan was. Boyle did not
know. On the 8th of July it was learned that Morgan was
on the bank of the Ohio preparing to cross. Morton telegraphed Boyle: "You have all our regular troops. Please
state what steps have been taken to arrest the progress of the
rebels." There was no reply. In the evening it was learned
that Morgan had crossed the Ohio. Next morning another
dispatch was sent to Boyle asking information. No reply.
To the third dispatch he answered: "Morgan is near Corydon, and will move either to New Albany or the interior of
the state. He has no less than four thousand men and six
pieces of artillery. General Hobson, in pursuit of him, is at
Brandenburg, and has sent for transports to transfer his forces.
Your cities and towns will be sacked and pillaged if you do
not bring out the state troops."

Morton went to work with his usual energy to arouse the
state. Word was sent to all the counties. Runners were dispatched from the county towns to the local neighborhoods to
alarm the people. The bells rang in every village. On the 9th
of July Morton published an order requiring all able-bodied
citizens in the counties south of the National road to arm
themselves and form into companies of at least sixty persons
each. They should be mounted whenever possible.[1] The
people in all other parts of the state were requested to form
military companies and hold themselves subject to orders.
Possession was taken of the railroads, and military business
took precedence of everything else. Burnside wanted to declare martial law, but Morton opposed it, and it was not
done.[2]

---

[1] Many amusing incidents occurred. A company was raised in Columbus for cavalry service, and the following dispatch was sent to Indianapolis: "We have a company of mounted men. Where shall we get
horses?"

[2] Morton also telegraphed to Burnside: "Indiana has repeatedly sent
all her troops to protect Kentucky. I now ask a return of some for our
own protection." And again he asks: "Can you not send some cannon

Everywhere the people responded with alacrity. Within twenty-four hours fifteen thousand men were on their way to the capital. Within thirty-six hours about thirty thousand had assembled, and before Morgan left the state sixty-five thousand had offered their services. These men were, however, utterly undisciplined; most of them were unmounted, and unable to follow the invader. It was not known in what direction Morgan was coming, hence it was impossible for any great body to concentrate and oppose him. It took some time to supply subsistence and ammunition. The military trains were all behind time, and the most contradictory statements were made as to Morgan's whereabouts.[1]

---

to this place, from Cincinnati or Columbus, to be placed in batteries immediately? We have nothing but small arms." To this dispatch Burnside answered : "Corydon is one hundred and twenty miles from Indianapolis, and if Morgan is disposed to go to Indianapolis it will take him two days from Corydon to do it, even if he meets with no resistance from home guards. I am pretty well satisfied he does not intend to go there, but intends to attack New Albany and Jeffersonville. . . . You may rely upon it, I will do all in my power to prevent disaster, but by scattering the troops in too many places I am rendered too weak to defend any one of them."

[1]On July 10 there came reports to the Governor that the Indiana forces had retreated through Fredericksburg, Orange county, at daylight, pursued by Morgan's whole command, six thousand strong ; that three thousand rebels had taken Paoli, and were advancing upon the Ohio and Mississippi Railroad at Mitchell ; that three thousand rebels had encamped the night before at Palmyra, and were moving towards Vienna ; that the rebels were north of Salem ; that Salem had been captured and burned. These dispatches were confusing enough, but those on the next day were worse. First, the news came that Morgan was at Vienna, and it was thought that he was trying to reach the Ohio river and cross at Madison Flats. At 2 o'clock it was reported that gunboats were engaging the rebels near Madison, and at half-past five, that Morgan was at Vernon, demanding its surrender. At half-past one in the afternoon of the 12th it was reported that Morgan was at Versailles ; at three, that he had suddenly turned, and was marching on Indianapolis ; shortly after, that he was skirmishing at Sunman's Station, on the Indianapolis and Cincinnati Railroad ; at eleven o'clock at night, that he was marching on Aurora and Lawrenceburg, and endeavoring to cross the Ohio at one of those places.

The fact was that Morgan advanced on the 9th to Corydon, driving before him the slender forces of the "Legion," many of whom he captured and paroled.   At this place he levied a contribution of one thousand dollars on each of the mills, and compromised on twenty-one hundred dollars from three of them.   Then he moved on to Salem, where he levied another contribution.   Everywhere he went his men burned bridges, tore up the tracks, exchanged their jaded horses for fresh ones, and plundered everything they could lay their hands upon.[1]   On the night of the 10th he reached Vienna, on the Indianapolis and Vincennes Railroad, tapped the wires, and learned of the preparations made to receive him.   Then he advanced to Vernon, where a considerable force was collected which he did not care to attack.   He sent a demand for the surrender of the place.   This was refused, but the officer in command asked for two hours in which to remove non-combatants.   Half an hour was granted, and Morgan improved the time by leaving on another route.   "Humane considerations," says General Duke (who commanded one of his brigades), "are never inopportune."   Morgan next passed through Dupont, where there was a large meat-packing establishment, and when the raiders left town each man had a ham slung at his saddle.   In many places there was a good

---

A dispatch from Mitchell thickened the confusion by reporting that General Buckner had crossed the Ohio at Brandenburg with sixteen thousand men, had burned Palmyra, and was advancing toward Indianapolis.

[1] General Basil Duke writes : " The weather was intensely warm, yet one man rode for three days with seven pairs of skates slung about his neck ; another loaded himself with sleigh-bells. A large chafing dish, a medium-sized Dutch clock, a green glass decanter, with goblets to match, a bag of horn buttons, a chandelier, a bird-cage containing three canaries, were some of the articles I saw borne off and jealously fondled. The officers usually waited a reasonable period, until the novelty had worn off, and then had this rubbish thrown away. Baby shoes and calico, however, were staple articles of appropriation. A fellow would procure a bolt of calico, carry it carefully for a day or two, then cast it aside and get another."

deal of consternation, at others the women and children staid at home, and the housewife, in answer to a question about the old man, would say: "The men hev all gone to the rally; you'll see 'em soon."

Morgan then passed through Sumanville, a station on the Ohio and Mississippi Railroad, and on the 13th he reached Harrison, where he entered Ohio. During his march he sent detachments in every direction to burn bridges and tear up railroad tracks.

When it was learned that Morgan had left Indiana there was a great feeling of relief in Indianapolis, and the last troops remaining in that city were dispatched to head off the Confederates at Hamilton. Five hours' delay, however, was caused by the intoxication of their commander. He was removed, and General Hascall, who succeeded to the command, arrived at Hamilton just too late. Morgan's forces marched very rapidly at night eastward between Hamilton and Cincinnati. They proceeded to the fords of the Ohio at Buffington's Island, near Pomeroy. These fords had been examined by Morgan's scouts some months previous. The river, however, had risen, and it was not now fordable. At this place his command was intercepted by formidable bodies of Federal soldiers and state militia. After a sharp engagement the greater part of his troops were taken. Morgan, with a few hundred men, escaped and wandered eastward. Some of his men swam across the river at a point further up the stream, and the remainder, with Morgan himself, were captured not far from the Pennsylvania line. Morgan was imprisoned in the Columbus penitentiary, but made his escape in November.

As soon as the Confederate troops had passed into Ohio, Morton offered to Governor Tod, of that state, the services of five thousand Indiana soldiers, and a considerable force was dispatched to Cincinnati. Morton also offered to send the regiments which he had forwarded to Lawrenceburg, but

Burnside thought them unnecessary, and the Indiana militia was sent home and disbanded.

In spite of his failure, Morgan's dashing exploit made him for a time extremely popular with the Confederates. The government at Richmond, however, could not overlook his deliberate disobedience of orders, and his command was taken from him. He engaged in another equally disastrous raid in Kentucky in the following June, and in September, when about to undertake a third, he was surprised and killed while endeavoring to escape.

But the most valuable result of Morgan's raid was the consolidation of public sentiment in favor of the Union throughout the states invaded. The demonstrations of disaffection made by the peace Democrats in Ohio and Indiana, and the intrigues of the "Knights of the Golden Circle" and "Order of American Knights," had induced Morgan to believe that he would receive substantial aid from many of the inhabitants of Indiana and Ohio when he was once in their midst. But the presence of a hostile force at their very doors aroused the people with a unanimity never before displayed except just after the fall of Sumter. Morgan had received accurate information of the places where valuable property could be found, of the men upon whom contributions could be levied, of the citizens who had arms, and of other facts to aid him in his scheme of plunder. But when he came, hardly a man could be found to join his ranks. The country was in arms against him. He was exasperated by this disappointment, and his men robbed with great impartiality, sparing the property of Southern sympathizers no more than that of Union men.

The Union men were much elated at the effect of the raid upon the public feeling of the state. "As rough a response as we may wish to give him," said the *Journal*, "we thank Morgan for this raid. It has evolved our patriotism; it has given us a marvelous unity; it has organized our state forces and rendered them efficient for any emergency; it has effectually cowed down sympathy with rebels, more than all it has taught the raider, who loves to plunder and lay waste more than he does to fight, that no part of the North is what Grierson found the South to be, a mere empty shell.''

Morton rejoiced greatly at this evidence of the loyalty of the people of Indiana. On the 15th of July he published an address to the officers and soldiers of the Legion and to the Minute Men of Indiana, in which he thanked them for the alacrity with which they had responded to his call and said that the wonderful uprising would exert a marked influence throughout the country.

Only a few days after Morgan had passed around Cincinnati, Governor Morton visited that city. He was always a welcome guest. A committee from the city council met him in the Burnet House and presented him with resolutions adopted some weeks before, asking him to sit for a portrait to be hung in the city hall.

He returned his thanks for the compliment and added: ''I trust that Cincinnati has been threatened for the last time during the progress of this war. Recent events have very much cleared away the gloom that lowered on the country, and I believe we may say, with some confidence, that the war is measurably over in the Mississippi Valley. The great event of the war, and one which is of special importance to the city of Cincinnati, has transpired—the opening of the Mississippi river. It is the beginning of the end. . . . .''

CHAPTER XXIV

IN September, 1863, Morton, foreseeing that another call
for troops would soon be made, sought and obtained leave to
raise eleven new regiments. A few days after this he asked
the war department for an order allowing any regiment to
come home and raise recruits whenever two-thirds of the men
would agree to re-enlist. This order, modified so as to require the re-enlistment of three-fourths of the men, was subsequently issued. He established camps in each congressional district. When the President issued his call for three
hundred thousand men much had already been done. Agents
were sent to the field to secure re-enlistments, and a constant
stream of veterans poured in ready for a new term of service.
The Governor offered a premium of six dollars to recruiting
officers for each man enlisted. On November 24, 1863, he
issued an appeal to those unable to volunteer. If each man,
he said, would attempt to procure one recruit, the ranks
could be filled and the state saved from a draft. Many
could support the family of a volunteer or provide an increase
of bounty.

There were persons in Indiana engaged in recruiting for
other states. Morton issued a military order commanding
them to desist.

The people of Jackson township, in Morton's own county
of Wayne, had asked him to make them a speech. He

(287)

promised to do this when that township had furnished its quota of volunteers. This was soon accomplished, and on January 4, 1864, he went to Cambridge City and addressed the people, speaking upon the subject of reconstruction, a theme which was already beginning to attract attention. "The government of the disloyal states," he said, "should be placed in the hands of loyal people."

Whenever the veteran troops returned Morton provided a fitting welcome. A warm luncheon was served to each regiment as soon as it had crossed the Ohio at Jeffersonville. Free entertainment was also given at Indianapolis, and meals were provided at the Soldiers' Home. The troops marched through the principal thoroughfares, where they were greeted by an enthusiastic multitude. They then assembled at the state-house, where the Governor and others addressed them. Day after day the newspapers teemed with accounts of these receptions.

As each regiment returned a statement was prepared of its history during the war, and of the engagements in which it had taken part. Morton referred to these records in his speeches. He declared that the noblest work done by the Indiana troops was their re-enlistment at this crisis. It would have been no reproach if they had refused. They might have served their terms and come home with honor. No man would dare to complain. They could have said to those who had remained behind, 'It is your turn, we have earned our right to rest.' But they had declared to the country that while rebellion lasted they wanted no rest nor peace. The enemy had not been prepared for this new evidence of enthusiasm, but had expected to oppose his veterans to our new levies. The Confederacy had been putting every man between the ages of sixteen and fifty into the army, but it would all be fruitless.

Our soldiers were welcome home. Their friends had never forgotten them. They would see the tearful eye and hear the broken voice, but there would be joy in all hearts at their return.

Those who had been at Shiloh, at Stone River, at Chickamauga and Mission Ridge, would have things to tell with pride to their children. The business of those who had staid at home would be to explain why they had not gone.

Those who would have peace on any terms forgot what had been sacrificed. They could not restore the thousands who had fallen. They could not heal the bleeding wounds at home. The sacrifices made for the Union were too great to allow it to be abandoned. It was not necessary to tell those who had marched through the Confederacy, bivouacked in the rain and lived upon parched corn, that their cause was a holy one. The soldiers had not complained. It was left for those who had staid at home and enjoyed the fat of the land to do the grumbling. The soldiers would pardon much. They had overlooked their short rations and insufficient clothing, but they would never forgive those who had been trying to prove that they had been fighting in an unsuccessful war.

When these regiments returned again to the field, the Governor was there to offer the new flags which were given to them and to bid them "God-speed."

But Morton was not content with efforts to recruit the veteran regiments and to fill the calls of the general government. He originated the "hundred days" movement. Campaigns had been undertaken which it was hoped would end in the overthrow of the rebellion. The generals in the field were anxious to have all the troops possible for active service, but a large number of men were necessary for garrison duty. Morton believed that if the trained soldiers, detailed for this purpose, could be released and new recruits put in their places, much would be gained. On April 6 General Sherman telegraphed to Morton to push forward all the troops he could "Three hundred men in time," he said, "were better than thousands too late. Every soldier should be at his place in the front." Governor Brough, of Ohio, was in Indianapolis when this telegram was received, and Morton laid before him a plan to call out troops for a hundred days. On April 11 messages were sent to the Governors of Illinois, Ohio, Wisconsin and Iowa, inviting them to meet at Indianapolis on the 22d. They were all there, and the outcome of the conference was a proposition to the President to furnish eighty-five thousand troops for one hundred days. On the following morning Morton issued his proclamation calling for Indiana's share. These troops were to be armed and paid by the United States, but were to receive no bounty.

The peace Democrats insisted that the withdrawal of so many men from productive industry would be disastrous. The plan, they said, was a sly Yankee trick to aid the stay-at-home patriots of the East. "Workingmen of Indiana," cried the *Sentinel*, "upon you fall the burdens and perils of the war." Morton called a meeting in support of this movement on April 29. At this meeting he said:

These men would enable fifty thousand veterans to go to the field and end the war. There were many in the North who wanted the war to fail. Within the civil organizations of the Sons of Liberty there was a military body, much more treasonable and dangerous. The leaders of the Democracy were not in it, but stood in the vestibule to avoid danger. If the summer campaign was disastrous this organization would try to take possession of the state. The twenty thousand men composing the hundred-day troops from Indiana would be an effectual reserve to check such a conspiracy.

The peace Democrats squirmed and protested, but the raising of the hundred-day men went on. Some sixty thousand volunteered, and did good service in relieving the troops in the field. On August 31 the regiments thus organized were mustered out, but many of the men afterwards re-enlisted under the last calls of the President.

Morton again aided Kentucky in resisting a raid into that state. Morgan, who had escaped from the Ohio penitentiary, invaded Kentucky in the latter part of May with about twenty-four hundred men by way of Pound Gap. General Burbridge telegraphed Morton, asking for four regiments. The Governor's answer was characteristic, "One regiment leaves to-night, one to-morrow and two others on Wednesday." The next advices were from the commanding officer at Louisville on June 8: "We are in pressing need of troops. This city and the Louisville and Nashville Railroad are almost defenseless. We hope for four or five thousand men from you for a few days. How many can you give us and how soon will they be here?" The next morning Morton forwarded the One Hundred and Thirty-ninth Indiana to Louisville, and called out the Indiana Legion in six counties. Morgan captured Mount Sterling, and on the 10th he entered Lexington. On that day the Forty-third Indiana arrived in Indianapolis from Arkansas on a furlough. This was a regiment of veterans who had been at the front for nearly three years, and had re-enlisted. But as soon as they were informed of the invasion of Kentucky they placed themselves under the orders of the Governor for immediate service, and marched to the relief of Governor Bramlette, who, with a small force, was confined to the fortifications around Frankfort, the capital of the state. Morgan proceeded to Cynthiana, which he captured. But on the 12th of June he was attacked by General Burbridge, and being defeated, hastened to Virginia, and the Indiana troops returned. On the 22d Bramlette sent to Morton a letter of thanks for his prompt assistance.

Who should be the Republican candidate for Governor? The eminence of one man settled this question as soon as it was asked. Morton had no competitor.

But at the threshold an inquiry arose, Was he eligible? Article V, section 1, of the Indiana constitution, had this provision: "The executive power of the state shall be vested in the Governor. He shall hold his office during four years, and shall not be eligible more than four years in any period of eight years." Morton had been elected Lieutenant-Governor. Three days after the beginning of his term Governor Lane had resigned, and Morton had performed the duties of the Executive during the rest of the four years. The Republicans claimed that the constitution prevented one thing only, to wit: two successive elections of the same man to the office of Governor; that it did not disqualify any one who had not been previously elected to that place. To say that Morton was ineligible was to say that his election to another office made him so.

But the Democrats did not want Morton. They insisted that the purpose of the constitution was to prevent the person who held the office from using his position to secure a re-election, and that this applied to Morton's case. The Republicans answered that at the beginning of the next term he would not have served four years. He would lack several days of it. During those days the constitution allowed him to be elected, and if he were elected at all, it could not be for less than four years. The constitution forbade more than one election in eight years, but it permitted one. Morton had never been chosen to the office which he held, and had, therefore, yet to exhaust his constitutional right.

The talk of Morton's ineligibility soon evaporated. Little was heard of it after his nomination. When the Union convention met, on February 23, Colonel Allen introduced a resolution endorsing the administration of Lincoln as well as that of Morton, and declaring these men the choice of Indiana for the places of President and Governor respectively. The question was at once put and carried "with a whirlwind of applause."[1]

---

[1] It was said afterwards that Morton had not intended that the convention should declare itself in favor of Lincoln's second term. The facts were

Morton was called for and delivered one of his most effective speeches. He upheld the duty of the government to set free the negroes in bondage. The President, he said, had the same right to pull down slavery that he had to pull down the fortifications of the rebels, to blockade their ports, destroy their railroads, burn their crops, or do any other act which would cripple the rebellion. In time of peace there was no power vested in the President or in Congress to interfere with slavery in the states. That power had been given to the President by the rebellion of the slave-owners. Their own hands had forged the bolt which was launched for their destruction.

Morton next spoke of the peace men, whom he characterized as "the guardians of slavery, left on duty in the free states, while the rebellion was seeking the destruction of the government."

That government, he continued, had, in a few cases, arrested and imprisoned persons, who, by speeches and writings, were striving to destroy it. These arrests had been made a pretext for an assault upon the administration, while the rebellion, with its horrors, had been utterly ignored. Thousands of Union men were languishing in Southern prisons, for no other crime than their adherence to the old

---

that, previous to the convention, an employe of the treasury department came to Indianapolis in the interest of Chase, and succeeded in winning the support of a number of Germans and other Republicans, who were of opinion that Lincoln had not prosecuted the war with sufficient vigor. These men desired that no instructions should be voted, and they asked a hearing before the committee on resolutions and the privilege of presenting the name of Chase, after which they agreed to abide by the action of the convention. Morton was willing that they should have a hearing, but he was not willing to take an active part in the contest beyond declaring that he was himself a supporter of Lincoln. When Allen offered the resolution nominating Morton and instructing the delegates to vote for Lincoln, it was put and carried before the friends of Chase could do anything. There was some dissatisfaction among these until after the nomination of McClellan, when they united with the other Republicans in favor of Lincoln.

flag. Were there no tears to shed over their sufferings? Did humanity exhaust its sympathies upon the few cases where Northern men had suffered brief confinement for the expression of disloyal sentiments and the encouragement of rebellion? Union men had been murdered upon their own thresholds; they had been cast into loathsome dungeons, where they had perished from disease or starvation; they had been hung like dogs upon trees and sign-posts, and their bones had been fabricated into jewelry, and worn as horrible keepsakes, as a savage would string upon his girdle the scalps of his victims. A member of the Kentucky legislature had declared that after the retreat of Kirby Smith, he had seen one grave in which were buried twelve Union men, with the halters still around their necks.

Where, among the politicians who talked of peace, was one who had raised his finger in suppression of the rebellion? Morton challenged his auditors to look through the state and find one, if they could. When the people had come together to consider the welfare of their country, these men had stood afar off with boding looks, with words of ill omen upon their tongues, and counsels of discouragement for those who were to enter the ranks of the army. When the country had talked only of vigorous, successful war, they had prated of compromise and had exonerated and encouraged the traitors by the declaration that Black Republicans had brought on the war. The army had been raised in spite of them. They had hung heavy upon the cause; they had assailed all who were urging it onward. While patriots thought only of saving their country, these men thought only of saving their party.

The great duty of the hour, continued Morton, was the suppression of the rebellion. The army must be recruited, the government upheld, the soldiers looked after with tenderest care, their families sheltered and provided for, and the people, rising to the level of the great occasion, must display a liberality, devotion and spirit of sacrifice, inspired by the conviction that, victorious, the country, liberty and honor would be saved, and that, defeated, all these would be forever lost.

This speech produced a profound impression, and its influence extended beyond the limits of the state. At the time it was delivered there was much despondency among the people of the North. One of the members of the National Republican Committee thus speaks of it: "It seemed as if a new dispensation had been given us. Hope was renewed on every side. This speech electrified the North, and the campaign went on with vigor to victory."

Morton's denunciation of the peace men filled the Indiana Democracy with unbounded rage, and the State Central Committee, after six weeks of preparation, published in the *Sentinel* a rambling tirade against the Governor, which they entitled "An Address to the People of Indiana."

This motley production, the body of which was written in the language of Billingsgate, concluded with copious extracts from the Scriptures. "My harp also is turned to mourning, and my organ into the voice of them that weep." (Job xxx: 31.) Well might the wise man say, "when the righteous are in authority, the people rejoice, but when the wicked beareth rule, the people mourn." Demoralization was spreading, as a leprous sore, through all the ramifications of society. Rascality and public plunder were rewarded, atheism and infidelity were seizing upon the public mind. "But how could it be otherwise," asked the address, "when the professed ministers of Him who was ushered into the world by a multitude of the heavenly host, praising God and saying 'Glory to God in the highest, and on earth peace and good will toward men' (Luke ii: 13, 14), forget the injunction to 'live in peace' (2 Cor. xiii: 11), and to 'follow peace with all men' (Hebrew xii: 14), and that 'blessed are the peacemakers, for they shall be called the children of God.' (Matthew v: 9.) 'They have become proud, blasphemers, . . .

unthankful, unholy, . . . false accusers, incontinent, fierce, . . . heady, highminded, . . . having the form of godliness, but denying the power thereof. From such, the people have turned away.' " (2 Tim. iii: 2, 3, 4, 5.)

"God," continued the address, "created the white man and the black man. The one he created superior, the other inferior. Our rulers are guilty of the folly of trying to make equal what the Creator made unequal. The consequence is the anger of the Lord has been kindled against the people, and he has afflicted us with war and pestilence, and he has burned and withered vegetation, for 'by the breath of God frost is given.' (Job xxxvii: 10.) That the Lord does thus visit the people because of the iniquity of the rulers, witness the plagues that were sent upon the people of Egypt for the obstinacy and wickedness of Pharaoh in refusing to let the people of Israel depart. (Exodus, chapters viii to xiv.) Witness the famine of three years for the sins of Saul. (2 Samuel, 21.) Witness the death of seventy thousand for the sin of David in numbering the people. (2 Samuel xxiv: 15.) Witness the smiting of Israel 'as a reed is shaken in the water' (1 Kings 14: 15), because of the sins of Jereboam. Witness the sore famine in Samaria (1 Kings xviii: 2), because Ahab did 'provoke the Lord' (id. xvi: 33), to 'forsake the commandments' (id. xviii: 18). Witness the Babylonian captivity, because of the sins of Manasseh (2 Kings xxiii: 26), and of Jehoahaz (id. 31), and of Jehoiachim (id. xxiv: 8–16). We, therefore, appeal to you, men of Indiana, to cast from your eyes the heavy mist that blinds you; rise out of the darkness of the slough of abolitionism into the light of liberty—the liberty of the white man."

Thus spoke the Indiana Democracy through its official representatives in answer to Morton!

At the beginning of 1864 a strong feeling in favor of the renomination of Lincoln had begun to show itself, but it was not yet unanimous. The principal centers of dissatisfaction were St. Louis and New York. The Radicals of Missouri had attached themselves to the fortunes of General Fremont and had denounced the administration with great bitterness, demanding the extirpation of slavery by congressional action, a measure of doubtful constitutionality. A convention of the disaffected was held at Cleveland. About four hundred delegates attended.[1] Fremont and Cochran were nominated. But there was not much support for this movement. The nominees saw that their candidacy was hopeless, and withdrew, and the feeling in favor of Lincoln's renomination became well-nigh universal. It was not a good thing, men said, "to swap horses while crossing a stream." The Republican National Convention met on the 7th of June in Baltimore. It had little to do. The Presidential nomination was already made. Andrew Johnson, Military Governor of Tennessee, was chosen as the candidate for Vice-President.[2]

On the 11th of June a ratification meeting was held at Indianapolis, and Morton spoke. Of Lincoln he said, that not within fifty years had a man received a more unanimous nomination. It was the voice of a great people speaking their confidence in one who had been sorely tried and found true.

The campaign was at first conducted by the Democrats with much recklessness. Harrison H. Dodd, Grand Commander of the Sons of Liberty in Indiana, addressing a Democratic meeting in Hendricks county on June 26, said that the real cause of the war was the breach of faith by the

---

[1] Lincoln, when he heard of this, reached for the Bible and read: "And every one that was in distress, and every one that was in debt, and every one that was discontented, gathered themselves unto him, and he became a captain over them, and there were with him about four hundred men."

[2] The Indianapolis convention of February had proposed his name for that office.

North in adhering to the original compact of the states. The Union was destroyed, the constitution was null and void, and the general government framed by it was also gone. In twenty-three states we had governments assisting the tyrants and usurpers at Washington to carry on a military despotism. The Democratic party would plant itself upon the solid rock of the sovereignty and equality of the states under a separate government. The Northwestern states would be united with those of the Gulf.

The frank expression of these extreme views gratified the Republicans. The peace Democrats, they said, were unmasking themselves. The *Sentinel* declared that Dodd's speech was merely the reiteration of the sentiments of Jefferson and Madison.

Our old friend Judge Perkins also broke forth into oratory. A few months before he had been in favor of "subjugating the South," but he seems to have become a grievous backslider. He was invited to Centreville, his former home, to address a Democratic meeting. He determined to electrify his audience. He had just learned, he said, that the public treasure of the state was in the breeches pocket of Governor Morton. The amount held during the last year had been nearly a million of dollars. The purse and the sword were in the same hand. This was the course of all usurpers. The Governor had seized the public treasure and, without giving bond, was spending it at his will. Thus did Cæsar, Cromwell and others. The judge trembled when he thought of this usurpation. It was an alarming precedent.

In reference to the general issues Perkins said: "Stop the war, procure an armistice, give time for passions to cool and for the people to reason, and to meet in national convention. Go back to the starting point."

Morton was much exasperated at this speech, which was published by the judge for general distribution over the state.[1]

---

[1] An article appeared in the *Journal* which bore strong internal evi-

He followed his accuser to the place where the speech had been delivered. In the early part of July he replied to the charges at Centreville.

He insisted that the peace Democrats were responsible for prolonging the war, by holding out to the rebels the idea that the North was paralyzed by dissensions. The speeches of Vallandigham at Hamilton, of Long in Congress, of Dodd in Hendricks county, and of Perkins at Centreville, said to them in substance, "We are your friends, and when we come into power we will end the war."

"Let not these men be surprised," he continued, "if the friends of lost ones who sleep in death on many a battle-field should lay at their doors the responsibility for thus protracting the struggle. If our people become angry, the Copperheads must not be surprised. They must remember that they are spilling our best blood, and if bitter oaths are registered against them in bereaved hearts, they must not be surprised."

Morton now read an extract from Perkins' speech, and continued: "This statement is made by Judge Perkins, of the Supreme Court of Indiana, a man of considerable note, well advanced in years, a man who ought to have some regard for truth. Not one word is true—not one word. And yet he comes before you, people of Wayne county, and makes these statements, as something just learned, as 'a fact just come to his knowledge.' He states that Governor Morton had seized the treasure and was disbursing the funds of the state, in a

---

dence that it came from Morton's pen. "It is scandalous," it said, "that such a diatribe, so utterly destitute of truth, should be uttered by a Supreme Court judge; and more scandalous still, that he should publish it. We wish we could believe, in charity, that these charges were made in ignorance of the truth; but they are too preposterous for belief by men of even less common sense than Judge Perkins. Morton has held a million dollars of the state treasure last year, has he? If so, where did he get it ? . . . If the public treasury of the state is 'in the breeches pocket of Governor Morton,' how came it there ? If he has seized the state treasure, where and how did he seize it ?"

most illegal manner.   It is all utterly false.   Governor Morton never seized one dollar, nor appropriated one cent of the funds of the state.   Judge Perkins places the amount which he says is seized at one million dollars.   Why has not Mr. Brett heard of this?   Why has it not been noised abroad that the treasury doors have been forced by armed guards? Because the story is false.''

Morton now detailed the circumstances which had led to the establishment of his financial bureau ; the failure of the legislature to make appropriations, the refusal of the Auditor and Treasurer to pay the expenses of the state government and the interest on the state debt, the decision of the Supreme Court and his own efforts to secure the money.

''It is for this,'' he added, ''that the peace Democracy, through Judge Perkins, have brought their charges against me in this very town.   I ask the men who thus assail me, wherein Indiana ever profited by their administration?''

The Democratic state convention was held July 12.   One man was considered by the party to be by far the most available opponent to Morton.   This was his friend Joseph E. McDonald, formerly Attorney-General.   McDonald was an experienced lawyer, an effective speaker, a man of unflinching integrity, clear intellect and good judgment, sturdy, unselfish and magnanimous.   His personal popularity was great, and it was deserved.   He had refused to participate in many of the extravagances of the ''Peace and Pistol'' Democracy.   He had opposed the scheme for repudiating the interest on the state debt.   He had invariably counseled obedience to law.   The Democracy felt that it was not safe, after the defeat of Vallandigham in Ohio, to nominate a man of the same extreme views in Indiana.

At first, when his party seemed likely to succeed, McDonald refused to be a candidate.   But as time wore on the outlook became darker.   The improved prospects of the war, and Morton's success in managing the affairs of the state gave the

Democracy cause to fear that the campaign of 1864 would not lead to the easy victory for which they had hoped. McDonald was now the man upon whom all eyes were cast. As early as April, it was announced that he would accept the nomination.

His only competitor was Lambdin P. Milligan, a man afterwards condemned to death by military commission, for his treasonable practices in connection with the Sons of Liberty McDonald received 1,097 votes in the convention and Milligan 167. David Turpie, Morton's competitor in 1860, was nominated for Lieutenant-Governor. Athon, Ristine, Brett and Hord were renominated for the offices of Secretary, Auditor, Treasurer and Attorney-General respectively.

The resolutions condemned the bolt of the Republican representatives in the late legislature—attacked Morton for establishing a financial bureau, squandering state funds, and borrowing money without appropriations—denounced the suspension of *habeas corpus*, the suppression of newspapers, arbitrary arrests and the failure to pay disabled and discharged veterans—thanked the soldiers of Indiana and pledged the party to the maintenance of personal and constitutional liberty. J. J. Bingham, editor of the *Sentinel*, was appointed chairman of the State Committee. Mr. Turpie, having accepted a nomination for Congress, declined the Lieutenant-Governorship, and the committee placed the name of General Mahlon D. Manson, a Democratic soldier, in his stead upon the ticket.

McDonald at once commenced his canvass. At Greencastle, about the middle of July, he delivered a speech assailing the administration of Morton. Morton followed him just as he had followed Perkins and made an address to the Union congressional convention at that place on July 27. It was an admirable presentation of the Republican case. He closed as follows:

"The seventh resolution in the platform, for cool audacity

and confident presumption upon the forgetfulness and forgiving spirit of the army, is a curiosity which should not pass unnoticed. It is a love letter to the soldiers from the convention, assuring them of its distinguished consideration and profound gratitude for their services, and earnestly hoping that the country would suitably reward them, and provide for their families. . . . In the very convention which indited this love letter, D. H. Colerick, a prominent member from Fort Wayne, uttered with applause the following infamous sentiment: 'Nine hundred and ninety-nine men of every thousand whom I represent breathe no other prayer than to have an end of this hellish war. When news of our victories comes, there is no rejoicing. When news of our defeat comes, there is no sorrow.' . . . .

"An examination of the books of the Indiana Sanitary Commission will reveal the fact that not one dollar out of every two hundred and fifty dollars contributed for the relief of Indiana soldiers comes from these men or from those in political fellowship with them. Their sympathies gush forth in fervent eulogies just before the election, but eulogies do not minister to the sick, nor bind up bleeding wounds, nor feed the hungry nor clothe the naked, nor soothe the dying hour, nor perform the last sad offices to perishing humanity.

"What is it that these men most desire? It is that this war shall be abandoned, the independence of the Confederacy conceded, the cause for which our gallant army has fought, dishonored, the public debt repudiated, the West separated from the East, the power of the government to reward the soldiers and provide for their families destroyed; and that the soldiers themselves shall become outcasts, the living remains of an unsuccessful and dishonored war."

CHAPTER XXV

DEBATE WITH MCDONALD AT LA PORTE

IT was not long after McDonald had been nominated that propositions were made for joint debates between him and Morton. Two were to be held in each congressional district. Morton selected half the places and McDonald the other half. Morton chose Republican counties and McDonald Democratic counties. The time was to be equally divided, and the right to open and close the debate was given alternately to each. Morton had the first choice, and he selected the town of La Porte, in Northern Indiana. At this place, on the 10th of August, the debates began. They have become historic. The speeches made at La Porte are given in full. Morton's opening argument was as follows:

"LADIES AND GENTLEMEN—I will state the order of this discussion. It is that I shall open in a speech of an hour, to be followed by Mr. McDonald in a speech of an hour and a half; then I have the privilege of closing in a speech of half an hour. I ask my friends that they shall give him a patient and candid hearing, and that all parties will preserve perfect quiet and order, and that every one will remain until the discussion is ended.

"These are peculiar times, and this campaign is a peculiar one. Much history has been written within the last three and a half years, and if there ever was a time when the people should divest themselves of all prejudice and passion, and listen temperately, calmly and dispassionately to the argu-

(303)

ments that may be presented for their consideration, to the end that they may act deliberately and thoughtfully for the good of the country, that time is now.

"Since I have been acting as Governor of Indiana my position has been one of great difficulty and embarrassment. I I have had much labor to perform that does not ordinarily devolve upon the Executive of this or any other state. It has been my duty, since the commencement of this war, to organize (including the troops of the United States and the Indiana Legion) one hundred and seventy regiments of men. To organize and equip these regiments, and appoint officers for them, has been a work of great labor and responsibility. The appointing power is one of great embarrassment, and while I, doubtless, have made mistakes in appointments of officers in the army during the progress of the war, I congratulate myself that the officers of the Indiana troops, take them as a body, are quite equal, in point of capability and intelligence, to those commissioned and sent forth by any other state, and that the Indiana troops that have gone to do battle for the Union have been certainly not below the average. It affords me great pleasure to be able to say that upon every field officers and men have behaved with a courage and devotion to their country that has not been excelled. I think that you will unite with me in saying that Indiana, from every point of view—from a military point of view and from a financial point of view—occupies a prouder position than she has ever occupied before.

"Not only have I had great labor devolving upon me in connection with the organization and equipment of troops, but my labors and responsibilities, from a civil point of view —in the ordinary administration of the government—have been greatly increased in extent over those of any former Executive. The last legislature of the state, which convened at Indianapolis in the winter of 1863, adjourned without making appropriations to carry on the ordinary machinery of the state government—to maintain the benevolent institutions, the penitentiaries, the superintendence of public instruction—to say nothing of the money required to organize troops, to carry on our recruiting service, or to do anything towards enabling Indiana to perform her part as a loyal and patriotic state in suppressing the rebellion and carrying on the war for the support of the government of the United States. This adjournment, without making these appropriations, grew out of a state of facts with which most of you are familiar. A few days before the time fixed for adjournment by the constitution of the state, the Union members of the legislature withdrew from that body. They withdrew to prevent the passage of what is known as the military bill; a bill in itself insurrectionary; a bill which, if it had been passed and had become a law, would have overturned the state government; a bill which trampled upon the constitution of Indiana, and would have resulted in the infliction of revolution and civil war upon the state.[1]

"To avoid the passage of that bill—to avoid all the calamities which you know must have resulted from its passage—the Union men withdrew from that body, and a few days afterwards the legislature adjourned. This adjournment, without making the indispensable appropriations, devolved a very great responsibility and embarrassment upon me as Governor of the state. I had one of three courses to pursue. The first was to call the legislature back in extra session; the second was to break up the benevolent institutions, to send home the blind, the deaf and the dumb and the insane—to turn out the inmates of your penitentiaries and cast them loose upon society; and the third was to endeavor to procure

---

[1] Morton had said in a speech at Greencastle, July 27: "The conception of this bill was a conspiracy, its introduction an insurrection, and its consummation would have been revolution and civil war in our midst."

20—MOR.

money from other sources for the purpose of carrying on these institutions.

"I had precedents for each of these courses.   In regard to calling back the legislature in extra session, the constitution of Indiana gave me the power to do that, but did not make it incumbent upon me to do it.   The power was discretionary with the Governor, to be exercised or not, according to his judgment.

"In 1857 the legislature adjourned, just as in this case, without making appropriations for carrying on the benevolent institutions.   Governor Willard had the power to call an extra session or to refuse to do so.   He refused to call the legislature back, and he put his refusal upon the ground that, from his knowledge of the men who composed that legislature, it would do no good to call them back; that it would incur useless expense to the state, with no prospect of accomplishing the desired object; therefore he declined to recall them.   The same discretion which Governor Willard had the right to exercise, I had the right to exercise.   I believed not only that it would do no good to call back the legislature, but that in calling it back I should endanger the peace and welfare of the state.   I believed it was my duty to take any and all responsibility rather than incur the risk of involving the state in revolution and civil war, which would certainly have been done if I had called the legislature together in extra session, and asked the necessary action at its hands in the matter of appropriations.

"I believe that in this conclusion I was sustained by every Union man in the state of Indiana, and I know that very many men who claimed to belong to the Democratic party justified me.   Now Governor Willard refused to call back the legislature in 1857 for the reason I have mentioned, and in that he was sustained by the subsequent action of his party. The Democratic convention which met in the June following indorsed his action.   The gentleman who is now my compet-

itor for Governor was renominated for the office of Attorney-
General by that convention. He went before the people as
Governor Willard's legal adviser in the refusal to convene the
legislature, and the ticket was re-elected. I do not insist
that that makes my case any stronger, but I do claim that it
places me in a position with which he has no right to find
fault.

"Having refused to call the legislature back, the next
course was to break up the benevolent institutions, to send
the deaf and dumb, the blind and the insane to their homes,
to turn them out of doors upon the charities of the world;
and for that also I had a precedent.

"In 1857 the legislature adjourned without making appropriations for the support of these institutions. There was
money in the treasury for their support, but no law had been
passed appropriating it, and the constitution declared that no
money should be paid out of the treasury except on appropriations made by law. Mr. McDonald was Attorney-General at that time, the adviser, legal and confidential, of
Governor Willard. Now, what was the action taken by his
advice? Rather than convene the legislature in extra session,
Governor Willard determined to break up the benevolent institutions of the state. He did so. They were closed. The
insane were scattered abroad to be taken care of by their
friends or to live or die unbefriended throughout the country.
The deaf, dumb and blind were sent abroad to live as best
they could. These institutions remained closed for six or
seven months. At the end of that time a change came over
the views and policy of Governor Willard and of Mr. McDonald. There was a strong feeling in the public mind that the
breaking up of these institutions had been unnecessary; that it
should not have been done. It was condemned by everybody. Then Governor Willard and Mr. McDonald, and other
officers of the state government, united in making a request
of Aquilla Jones, State Treasurer, that he should pay out of

the treasury the money necessary to reorganize these institutions.

"Mr. McDonald himself signed a written request which I will read in your hearing, asking Mr. Jones to take the responsibility of paying this money out of the treasury, confessedly in violation of the constitution of the state. Here is the request:

" '*Resolved*, That we advise the Treasurer of the State to advance, out of any money in his possession, belonging to the state of Indiana, sufficient funds to support the Indiana hospital for the insane and the institutions for the deaf, dumb and blind.'

"This was signed, as I have said, by Governor Willard, Mr. McDonald and the other officers of the state government.

"Now, if it was right for Mr. Jones to pay out, in September of that year, money for the purpose of carrying on these institutions which never ought to have been broken up, it would have been right in March before they were broken up. But public opinion had created a change in the policy of the state officials, and at last they asked Mr. Jones to pay out the money, confessedly in violation of the constitution of the state. The money was paid, the hospitals were reorganized and the inmates (as many of them as could be found) were called back.

"I had this example before me. I determined, so far as I was concerned, that I would not break up these institutions, and at the same time I would not, if I could avoid it, violate the constitution of Indiana, or any law of the state, in carrying them on, but would carry them on legitimately. I determined, if I could, to procure the money in a way that was legal. What was the excuse for asking Mr. Jones to pay the money in 1857 in violation of the constitution? What was the excuse given to Mr. Jones and the public by the Attorney-General (Mr. McDonald) and Governor Willard? It was the public necessity. It was said that public necessity, hu-

manity and sound policy required that these institutions
should be carried on; that the money was there to carry them
on just as it is in the treasury now, and, therefore, Mr. Jones
was asked to take the responsibility of violating the constitution and his oath. He did so, and in that he was sustained. As I have said, the Governor and all his associates
were subsequently indorsed by the state convention.

"I determined, if possible, that I would avoid the errors of
my predecessors, and, at the same time, avoid breaking up the
benevolent institutions of the state. When the legislature
adjourned, I did not know how the government was to be
carried on, but I soon found myself sustained in my endeavors to do the best I could. The people supported me in a
most unexpected and generous manner. Citizens of our own
and other states, one bank at least, railroad companies and
others came forward and proffered me money for the support of
our benevolent institutions, and not only for that, but for the
purpose of carrying on the recruiting service in Indiana, of
defraying the military expenses and of sustaining the penitentiaries, that the convicts who had been sent there might
not be turned loose upon society before their terms of service
had expired. In this way I was enabled to carry on the
government from that day to this, and I expect to be able to
do so until the next legislature assembles.

"But it has been said that I assumed the responsibility of
borrowing money upon the credit of the state without authority of law; that I have created a debt against the state where
I had no right to do so, and that I transcended my duties as
Executive. I can only say that if that were all true, the plea
of necessity is as good in my case as it was in the one I have
quoted. The plea of necessity is as good in 1864 as it was
in 1857. The argument is as good for me as it was for my
Democratic predecessors, and I am certainly no worse than
they. If I have sinned they had set me the example; I have

but followed in their footsteps.[1] I could offer that plea with truth and propriety, but I am not driven to that necessity. The persons and sources from which this money came had the right to furnish it to me. They came to me and said: 'Take this money; carry on these institutions; do your share in supporting the government. We do not want to see the state disgraced. We want Indiana to do her whole duty during the progress of this war, and we know that you can not do it unless you have the money.'

"Therefore, I say the money was furnished to me. They took the risk and responsibility. They relied upon the good faith of the state, knowing full well that I had no legal authority to borrow that money. But they advanced it cheerfully, relying, as I have said, upon the good faith of the state, confident that the subsequent action of the legislature would reimburse them.

"In this way I obtained money, not only for carrying on the benevolent institutions and penitentiaries, and all the ordinary machinery of the state government, but for paying the interest on the public debt. Here was a new source of trouble. After it was found that I could not be driven to calling the

---

[1] In Morton's speech at Greencastle, July 27, he caustically said: "An attempt has been made to break the force of McDonald's, Jones's and Willard's action by alleging that at that time there was no embezzlement bill, or, in other words, no law attaching a penalty for paying money from the treasury without an appropriation, and in violation of the constitution. Now this is going from bad to worse. It assumes that the constitution is not to be regarded unless a penalty for its violation has been prescribed by law ; that it is the fear of punishment, and not the obligation—the penitentiary, and not the oath of office, which should control political action. . . .

"Right here I wish it understood that I do not consider my position justified or strengthened from the precedent I have cited of the record of McDonald and Willard, and the indorsement of the Democratic party, but when my competitor assails me it is legitimate to present in answer his own history, and that of his friends and of the party which he represents, and to say to him that after he has plucked the beam from his own eye he can see more plainly whether there is anything in mine."

legislature together, it was suddenly discovered that there was no appropriation authorizing the payment of the interest on the public debt in the city of New York. This presented a very grave case. The credit of the state of Indiana was bound for the prompt payment of the interest on that debt. She had once been known as a repudiating state, by her failure to pay the interest on her debt, and it was discovered that she was in a fair way to repudiate again, there being no money set apart by the legislature for the liquidation of the interest. There had been a law passed in 1847 on the subject of the state debt. Under that law Governor Whitcomb had paid the interest, treating it as an appropriation. Then the constitution of 1850 had come in, and declared that the interest on this debt should be paid out of the first money secured, after payment of the ordinary expenses of the government. Under the same law that we have now, Governor Wright, Governor Whitcomb and Governor Willard paid the interest on the debt. Recently, however, my opponents found out that I could not pay the interest because there had been no appropriation. In 1857, when the legislature had adjourned without making appropriations, that question came up before Governor Willard. My distinguished competitor was the Attorney-General of the state. He gave to Governor Willard his official declaration that the Governor had a right, under the constitution, to pay the interest without an appropriation, and upon this advice Governor Willard acted, and paid the interest in 1858. Now in regard to the interest on the public debt and to the support of the benevolent institutions, the cases were just the reverse. There was money in the treasury to support the benevolent institutions, but no appropriation was made. In regard to the interest on the public debt there was an appropriation, but no money to pay out. My friend gave the opinion that the law authorized the payment of the interest, and that the appropriation of the money from the treasury, for that purpose, was constitutional. There was no

statute authorizing the Governor to borrow money for the
purpose of paying the interest on the debt.   But Governor
Willard did borrow the money—one hundred and sixty-eight
thousand dollars—out of the sinking fund, and borrowed it
in violation of the law establishing the sinking fund.   That
law required that the money of the sinking fund should be
loaned only upon bond and mortgage on real estate, and the
commissioners could not let the Governor have a dollar without violating the law organizing the sinking fund.   I am informed that my friend and competitor advised the commissioners of the sinking fund to loan the money to Governor
Willard.   It was loaned on the ground of public necessity—
that the credit of the state should be saved in the financial
world.   It was on this ground only that the commissioners
of the fund—the president of the board protesting—voted to
allow Governor Willard to have the money.   General Dumont
was president of the Board of Sinking Fund Commissioners at
that time, and although he acknowledged that public necessity
required that the interest be paid, he said he would not be a
party to such payment since it was in violation of the law,
and he entered his protest on the records of the board against
the loan of that money.   But Governor Willard got the money
and paid the interest.   I simply refer to these matters to
show that in every particular I have had the example of these
distinguished gentlemen, my predecessors in office; only that
in their case they went further than was necessary.   They
violated the law.   In borrowing the money to pay the interest in 1858, they did so in express violation of the law governing the sinking fund.   I am not here to find fault with
this to-day.   I presume they thought that sound policy and
the best interests of the state government required them to do
it.   But, after having done this, I have a right to insist that
they shall not come here to arraign me for going not nearly
so far as they went.

"Now, in my case, the money to pay the interest was in

the treasury. You had paid your taxes for the purpose of sustaining the credit of the state. The money was there, and there is money there now; there is more money in the treasury of Indiana to-day than at any previous time within my recollection. They are talking about buying a new safe, because the old one is full and running over. What was I to do? Was the credit of the state to be disgraced in my hands? I was just as proud on that subject as my political opponents had been; I felt as deep an interest as they could have felt in sustaining the credit of Indiana. I resolved that if I could get the money in any way, I would do so. A banking house in the city of New York, connected with the business of the state of Indiana, offered (without any agreement as to terms) to advance the money to me. That house, relying on the good faith of the state—believing that she would never voluntarily suffer her credit to be destroyed—that house came forward and advanced the money. It has made, up to this time, three payments of one hundred and sixty thousand dollars each—making, I believe, four hundred and eighty thousand dollars in all—and is preparing to pay the interest on the 1st of January, or until such time as the legislature shall provide for its payment. I have been able to do this without violating the laws. I do not say that I would not have done it in any case. I do not know what I might have done if I had been hard pressed. I might have gone as far as the Attorney-General went in 1857, but I did not feel called upon to do so. I was enabled to keep the machinery of the government of Indiana in motion, and to sustain the credit of your state (never so high as now) without violating any single law. But, if I had felt myself called upon to trample upon the law, I would have had the same excuse that these men had, who have gone before me—public necessity. I have spoken thus at length in regard to measures of state policy, because I deemed it necessary to give you a full and fair explanation on the subject. Having been intimately connected with the affairs of your state for the past three and a half years, it is proper that I should speak of these things. I do not speak of them in a spirit of egotism or vanity, but my friend Mr. McDonald made a speech in Greencastle lately, in which he reviewed my administration lengthily and harshly. If he can show that I have done anything wrong, it is his right, and I shall not complain. If, on the contrary, I can show that whatever he complains of he has been guilty of himself, then you can take his argument for what it is worth. He has a right to canvass my administrative record, and I have a right to canvass his record.

"I now propose to call your attention to the great national questions, which, in point of importance, overshadow all others at this time, and before which all others must appear to the patriotic mind trivial and insignificant. It is not for my friend to say that he will not define his position on national questions, because he is a candidate for the governorship—an office that he may say has nothing to do with national affairs. You understand that at this time, above all others, the position of Chief Executive of a state is of vast importance, much more so than at any former period in the history of our state or nation. If the Executive is not disposed to sustain the government by every means at his command; if his sympathies are not with the national government, he has it in his power to cast great difficulties, almost insuperable difficulties, in the way of the national government. Hence, it becomes your duty to know exactly how stands the man who solicits your suffrage for this very high and responsible position; hence, the question to be decided by you at the approaching state election is one of vast importance. I suppose you understand pretty well my position in regard to the war. I think I have taken part enough, said enough and done enough in regard to this matter, since the commencement of the war, to have every one understand exactly where I stand on this point. My position is easily defined. I am in favor of sustaining the national government, of restoring and maintaining the union of these states [applause] and of suppressing the rebellion by force of arms. [Applause.] I am for compelling the people of the rebellious states to yield obedience and allegiance to the constitution, laws and government of the United States. This is my position, and it is easily explained by me, and as easily understood by you. You will want to know from my competitor where he stands. Now, my friend made a speech in the convention, to which I beg leave to call your attention. I will read from it. He said: 'But the question has frequently been asked me whether I was in favor of a vigorous prosecution of the war. I now answer that to this war, as prosecuted under the ideas and policy of the administration, I am utterly opposed. I believe it is entailing upon the country unmixed evil, and I would be false to my country if I did not say so.'

" He says that to the war, as prosecuted by the administration, he is utterly opposed. This leaves the impression that it might be prosecuted on some other policy, of which he would approve. If he intended to leave that impression, he failed to tell us what his policy was. Now I say if there is any policy for prosecuting this war, other than that of the present administration, let him tell what it is, so that you may know whether his way or that of the President is the better. But he goes on to say that on the 8th of January the Democratic party of Indiana adopted this resolution:

" '*Resolved*, That we will sustain, with all our energies, a war for the maintenance of the constitution and the integrity of the Union under the constitution, but we are opposed to a war for the emancipation of the negroes or the subjugation of the Southern states.'

" To say that he is in favor of a constitutional war, prosecuted for a constitutional purpose, is to assert a general proposition, with which few would take issue, but which amounts to nothing unless it is explained and applied to the case in hand. It is much like saying that two and two make four. The proposition may be true enough, but unless an application is made it is clearly immaterial and amounts to nothing. Does he mean to say that he is opposed to the war unless it is so prosecuted as to preserve slavery in the rebel states? Or does he mean to say that if the President commits an unconstitutional act in the prosecution of the war he will, therefore, oppose the war and the government altogether and become a neutral, or take his stand on the side of the rebellion? Why, the rebellion is wholly unconstitutional, for the rebels have rejected the old constitution and made for themselves a new one. Such a position would not be consistent. Suppose the President is of the opinion that the destruction of slavery is an important instrumentality for the destruction of the rebellion, and suppose the gentleman differs with him on that point, which opinion is to govern? Lincoln is President and McDonald is not. Lincoln is acting under the oath of office and McDonald is not, and McDonald has no right to occupy the position of a neutral between the government and the rebellion.

"In fact, there can be no neutrals in this war. There is no half-way house. There is no place in the constitution where a man can stand midway between the rebellion and the government. The gentleman's proposition amounts to this: Because this war is prosecuted upon a policy which he does not approve, he is opposed to its further prosecution, is in favor of its abandonment, and of bringing upon the country all the consequences which attend defeat, dishonor and dissolution.

"When the gentleman says that he is opposed to subjugating the Southern states, it means that he is opposed to a war for the suppression of the rebellion; it means that he is opposed to subjugating, conquering, coercing or compelling the people of the Southern states to yield obedience to the constitution and laws of the United States. To say that he is in

favor of the preservation of the Union, but opposed to the
subjugation of the rebel states, is equivalent to saying that
he desires to preserve the Union, but is opposed to the use
of any means for its preservation.

"Now observe this singular union of propositions: 1st.
He is opposed to the subjugation of the Southern states. 2d.
He is in favor of peace at the earliest practicable moment;
and, 3d, he is in favor of peace, etc., on the terms of restoring
the Union.

"Now, if my friend is opposed to peace, except on terms
of restoring the Union, I want to know how he is going to
restore the Union. If he is not willing to carry on the war
for the purpose of restoring the Union, how does he propose
to restore the Union? Suppose we abandon this war, I want
my friend to tell you whether he believes that in that case
the rebel states will voluntarily return to the Union? If he
does not believe that by our abandonment of the war the
rebel states will return, I ask him how he is to restore the
Union by the abandonment of the war? Now, here is a
plain question: I want my friend to tell these people whether
he is in favor of the prosecution of this war, in any manner,
for the suppression of the rebellion? If he is not in favor of
prosecuting it for the suppression of the rebellion, he is in
favor of the abandonment of the war, and the acknowledgment of the rebel Confederacy. That brings upon us all the
evils and misfortunes to prevent which we have been fighting
for three years and more, shedding so much precious blood.
But he has told you he is opposed to subjugating the Southern states. Now I want to refer him to a little authority.
He is very fond of appealing to the law. There is a gentleman of high standing beside him upon the ticket—Judge
Perkins is his name. I suppose you have all heard of him.
He is candidate for Supreme Court judge. He wrote a
letter to Mr. McDonald nearly nine months ago, and in that
letter he said what I shall read. Now mark you, these gen-

tlemen stand side by side on the ticket that is to be voted for
next October.   The judge says:

"'I am, gentlemen, as I have been, most earnestly opposed to the civil administration of Mr. Lincoln, believing it
to be controlled by the radical Republicans, but I am for continuing to give a fair and efficient support to the vigorous
prosecution of the war, as prosecuted, and to that end I am
for aiding the government by all reasonable and proper
means, in raising the necessary volunteer soldiers, and in providing the funds required, to pay them promptly and liberally, more liberally than the private soldiers are now paid.'
And again: 'We shall conquer the South. We can annihilate her. If Deity does not prevent, twenty powerful states
can annihilate ten weak ones.'   The Judge says also: 'If I
were on board of a ship manned by pirates, and about to
sink, I would aid them in running into harbor.'   And again:
'The first job on hand then, disguise it as we may, is to
subjugate the South.   This is the point in progress at which
we have arrived, and this is one of those jobs, which, according to the old adage, "is well done, if 'twere done quickly."
The more dispatch the executioner uses the less the sufferings
of the victim.'   And finally, he said: ' I, then, am for a
speedy conquest of the South, so that war and strife may
cease, and peaceful scenes again abound throughout our land.'

"This was the position of Judge Perkins on the subject
eight or nine months ago.   Where he now stands I can not
tell you precisely, nor is it very material that I should.   But
as my friend is fond of legal authority, I simply read this to
show that the judge views the words 'subjugation' and 'conquest' of the South, in the common sense meaning of suppressing this rebellion, compelling the people of these rebellious states, by the power and armies of the Union, to submit to the government and authority of the United States.

"Now, my friends, it is time for Mr. McDonald to tell
you where he stands on this great national question.   I am

sorry to say that heretofore his language on the subject has not been such as to be entirely satisfactory to the people at large throughout the state. He has been a little on one side, and a little on the other, and not much on either. But it will be easy for him to tell you where he is, if he will only make up his mind to do so. If my friend is in favor of suppressing the rebellion and sustaining the government, he need have no difficulty in making himself understood. The English language is abundant for his purpose. He can find plenty of honest English in which to express himself; and if, on the contrary, he is not in favor of suppressing this rebellion—if he is in favor of abandoning the war and of giving up all we have been fighting for, in favor of acknowledging ourselves defeated and dishonored, it is easy for him to say that, and he is bound to tell you just where he does stand. You have a right to know it, and I have a right to know it. If ever men were called upon to vote understandingly upon a most important issue, now is the time. If you are for unconditional peace, if you are in favor of abandoning this war, and of giving up the rebellious states, giving up the Mississippi river, dividing the Union, you want a man who will carry out your views, and you want to know who and where he is. If you want such a man do not vote for me. [Applause.] Now, my friends, you want peace. We all want peace. There is no better peace man in the world than I. But I want a peace that shall be lasting. I do not want a peace, the effect of which will be to transfer the war from Georgia and Alabama, Tennessee and Virginia to Ohio, Indiana, New York and Pennsylvania. [Applause.]

"Suppose, my friends, we take the propositions of these peace men and abandon this war, and withdraw our armies. Suppose General Sherman should abandon the siege of Atlanta and retreat to Louisville; do you suppose the rebels would stay quietly in Georgia, with no foe before them? No, they would march upon Sherman's heels, and say that he was defeated and dishonored. They would not stop when they came to the Ohio river. They would cross into your state, with the determination to inflict upon Indiana the same desolation and ruin which war has inflicted upon Tennessee and Alabama, Georgia and Virginia. My friends, if you really want to have the war transferred from the rebel states to Indiana, just adopt the policy of these peace men and you will accomplish your end. There is no surer way of doing it, and I will guarantee the result, once the war is abandoned by the North. But, if you do not want such a state of things; if you want to keep the war away from the North, you have got to suppress this rebellion on Southern soil. [Cries of "we will do it."] As Judge Perkins says, 'we can conquer the South, and we must suppress the rebellion.'

"We have met with disasters since the commencement of the war, but look at what has been done. More than half of the territory first declared in rebellion has been seized, and is now held by us. We have our hold upon the throat of the Confederacy. We may not have choked it to death quite so soon as we hoped for, but General Grant and General Sherman have their hands upon its throat, and they will never let go until the monster is dead, unless they are pulled off by the peace men of the North, who seek to divide our people and sow the seeds of discord among them.

"I have endeavored to sustain the government from the beginning of the war. I have tried to do my duty. If my friend has done anything to restore the Union and suppress the rebellion he can tell you what it is. If his voice has been raised in favor of the government he can read you an extract from some of his speeches to that effect. But if, on the contrary, his influence has been against the government; if he has done all in his power to divide our people, and give aid and comfort to the enemy, then you have a right to know just what he has done. His record is public, and for it he is responsible to God and his own conscience, and he is also responsible to the people whose suffrages he solicits. Every man, in office and out of office, has had a great duty to perform since this war began. Every man has an influence, for the exercise of which he is responsible to his country and to his God. In proportion to the position he occupies in the state and in society, that influence is great or small, and the greater the influence the greater the responsibility. If my friend has rallied his friends and his party to put down this rebellion, then he should have credit for it; but if, on the contrary, his influence has been against the government, and in favor of the rebellion; if his influence has been exerted to divide us, to paralyze us in our efforts to suppress this rebellion, then he is responsible for that, and he can not avoid that responsibility.

"My time is not out, but I can speak no longer. I thank you, my friends, for your patient hearing. Mr. McDonald will now speak for an hour and a half, and I will speak for half an hour at the close of his remarks. I hope you will all remain to the close of the debate."

Mr. McDonald spoke as follows:

" FELLOW-CITIZENS—As you have already heard from Governor Morton, the object of our visit is to discuss before you the issues involved in the present political campaign in Indiana. I desire, fellow-citizens, to unite with Governor Morton in exhorting you, upon this occasion, that you will each consider the responsible position you occupy, and that nothing shall be done that is not becoming in free American citizens who have come together for the purpose of consulting for the common welfare of their country, and, therefore, I hope that the same good order which has characterized this meeting up to this point shall continue to prevail until the close. Although my name has been identified with the politics of Indiana for nearly twenty years, this is the first time I have stood in the face of an audience of La Porte county,

21—MOR.

and undertaken to address them upon political topics, and I am here under no ordinary circumstances. I well understand the deep and heart-felt interest that extends throughout this assembly, and I know the causes that have called up that interest. I simply ask my friends, if I can call you such, who stand opposed to me in political opinion, I simply ask you to grant me this request, that you shall believe that I have just as much at stake as you have, and that I have as earnest and ardent a desire for the general welfare of our common country as you have. Much as we may differ in political opinions our interests are the same. Those who compose the party to which I belong are not aliens, who by some strange mischance have come among you, but they are free American citizens, who possess in common with the rest of their fellow-citizens the right of controlling this country as the sovereign power in it. And it is in this light I desire you to look upon us and upon me this day, and if you do that, then I have no other favor to ask at your hands, except that you will scan well what I may say to you on this occasion.

"Governor Morton has presented his views, first, in regard to the policy of his administration in reference to the affairs of the state of Indiana, and second, in regard to that great national question which at this time is throbbing in the heart of every American citizen, growing out of the condition of our country involved as it is in civil war. I propose to take up these propositions in the order in which he has presented them. First, let me examine his official record. I desire to say that I am dealing with nothing this day in regard to Governor Morton except his political views. Personally, he and I have long been friends; we were friends when we stood shoulder to shoulder in the Democratic ranks, and we have still remained friends, although he has separated from me and my political household. I shall deal with his political views freely, and discuss them in that spirit which I believe is becoming in one who desires to present to an enlightened audience his views upon political questions.

"Governor Morton commenced by telling how the Indiana legislature adjourned in 1863 without making the necessary provisions for the administration of the state government. He undertook to tell you how it came to adjourn. Now, upon that point, we differ, and when we have each presented our views, it will be for you to decide who is right and who is wrong.

"Governor Morton insists that the Republican minority withdrew from their places for the sole purpose of defeating the military bill, which, he says, broke down the constitution of the state of Indiana, and inaugurated revolution. Now, my friends, let me call your attention to the political position of affairs in Indiana in 1863. In the fall of 1862 the people of Indiana had declared in favor of the Democratic candidates upon the state ticket, and had elected a legislature Democratic in both branches. Now, if I understand the principles of republican government—those we are professing to be governed by—they are that under the constitution—which is the common charter adopted by all—the majority shall rule. Therefore, when the people of Indiana in 1862 pronounced against Governor Morton and elected a Democratic state ticket, and placed in the legislative assembly a majority of Democrats, they expected that this majority would carry out their policy, and that the minority would yield, and not follow the bad example of the Southern states when they undertook to secede. But that legislature had not organized when the Republican minority in the Senate commenced bolting because the Democrats would not agree to elect to the Senate of the United States such a man as they thought proper to name. And the Senate was fully two days at the beginning of the session without a constitutional quorum because the friends of Governor Morton withdrew from their places and left the Democrats without power to carry on the government. That sort of bolting which they had inaugurated in the beginning continued throughout the session, until the 25th of February, when the Republican minority in the House of Representatives withdrew from that body never to return. When they withdrew on the evening of the 25th of February the military bill had been engrossed for a third reading, and was left on that evening among the unfinished business in the calendar of the House. The next day there was a mass convention held at Indianapolis by the friends of Governor Morton. What sort of counsels took place there was never disclosed, but the result was, that on the next morning thirty-six Republican members of the House of Representatives, in place of repairing to the representative hall, took their passage on board the cars and went to Madison, never again to return until the session had expired by constitutional limitation. They started south. They were certainly going in the right direction. [Laughter.]

"Now Governor Morton says the military bill was the sum of all iniquities. I have never examined its provisions with any care. I have contrasted them somewhat with the one that stands upon the statute book, placed there during the session of 1861, and I do not see that this bill is any more iniquitous than the one that is now governing state military matters. He says that it took from the Governor all military power. The bill under which he is carrying on our military affairs now vests in the Governor all power. It goes further, and authorizes him to legislate at will, and add to it any provisions he may see proper. I have no doubt that it suits his views of government much better than the one his friends bolted to defeat the passage of. But the principal objection that has been raised by the friends of Governor Morton to that bill is that it put the organizing power of the militia of Indiana into the hands of an executive council, and vested in the people who might organize under that law the power to elect officers, from colonel down.[1] They say it was unconstitutional to do this. Well, if it was unconstitutional, as he says, what harm could it do while we had courts open in which we could try the case? If it was unconstitutional, it is not to be presumed that the state courts would enforce it. As a matter of course, an unconstitutional law is void.

"I shall take up no time in discussing the merits of the law, because it was a mere pretext. I wish to show you that the fear of that law was simply a pretext to cover up revolutionary designs. When they bolted, that law had been engrossed for a third reading on the evening of the 25th of February, and left with other unfinished business. How stood the unfinished business? There stood before that bill, to be acted upon before it could be reached, eighty-two House bills that had been engrossed in their order, seventeen upon their second reading; and thirty-three Senate bills, ten of them on a second reading. Nearly one hundred bills stood upon the calendar of the House to be acted upon before this military bill could be reached. There was but ten days' time in which to take up these measures and pass them, and then this bill had to go to the Senate. To take it up out of its order for the purpose of putting it upon its passage, required a two-thirds vote,[2] so that it is plain that if the Republican members had not broken a quorum, but had staid in their places, they could have prevented its passage.

---

[1] In his Greencastle speech, Morton, after describing the bill in detail, said: "All these enormities were sweetly toned down by my competitor in the mildly-drawn phrase that the provisions of the bill 'amounted to simply this: the taking of the power of organizing and arming the militia out of the hands of the Governor and placing it in the hands of the people.' The people here described are the four state officers—the four new Executive heads of legislative manufacture. I am sure my competitor, in his cooler moments, will smile at the simplicity and scanty outlines of the garment with which he has tried to cover this revolutionary monster."

[2] This rule, however, could have been evaded by a determined majority in several ways. For instance, the previous measures might have been all temporarily laid upon the table by a bare majority vote.

"In replying to this portion of my argument, in a speech made a short time since, at Greencastle, the Governor said that there could have been other means used to defeat the bill.[1] He knows there were other means, and that by a strict exercise of legislative law the bill might have been defeated. What, then, was it that caused his friends to bolt? After they had remained five days away, a delegation from the bolting members, who were at Madison, as near the confines of Indiana, and as close to the realms of Jeff Davis as they could well get, in safety to their principles, waited upon the Democratic majority that still remained, and proposed terms of compromise upon which they would return. They said if the majority would agree to do so and so, they would come back again and pass certain bills necessary to carry on the state government.

"The propositions were ten in number, the last one of which was that the Democrats should pass no bill or joint

---

[1] What Morton said in his Greencastle speech was this: "After the introduction of the bill assurances were given by leading members of the majority in both Houses that there was no occasion for alarm or excitement, as the bill would not be passed, and had already been killed in party caucus. Quieted by these assurances, it excited but little alarm among Union members until the 20th day of February, 1863, when it was suddenly and unexpectedly ordered to be engrossed by a strict party vote. This vote in parliamentary proceedings is known to be the test. The determination to pass the bill was fully developed, and it became morally certain that it would be carried through both Houses and over the Governor's veto. Great excitement and indignation resulted at once from this action. The Union members complained bitterly that they had been deceived, and they determined that a solemn regard for their duties and the safety of the state demanded that they should at once arrest the further progress of this deadly enemy, which they did by withdrawing from the House and leaving it without a quorum. Mr. McDonald insists that this action was premature, and that the bill could have been defeated by other means, or at later stages, but the path of safety was the path of duty, and it was no time to take desperate chances or try dangerous experiments. The Union members felt that they had got quite as near to civil war and revolution as they desired, and they were not willing to be brought to the very edge of the fearful precipice, where by a bold *coup d'etat* they might be thrust over."

resolution of a political character. Now they demanded that before they would return and occupy their places in the House of Representatives, and pass these measures, and thus take from Governor Morton the trouble and responsibility he would otherwise have to assume—the Democrats should pass no bill or resolution, joint or otherwise, of a political character; that is, that the Democrats should do nothing displeasing to this minority that had seceded.

"It has been said that the Democrats did not intend to pass any appropriation bills, and that they had prepared none. Now, it was well known to the friends of Governor Morton that these measures were in process of preparation when the Republicans bolted; that the Committee on Finance had drawn up the bill and was daily adding to the list of expenditures such items as in their judgment would be necessary to carry on the state government. They would have made a report in ample time if these men had remained in their places. These appropriation bills, in addition to providing for the payment of the interest on the public debt, provided for the benevolent institutions, for the Executive mansion, for the military contingent funds for sick and disabled soldiers. One hundred thousand dollars was appropriated for the aid of sick and disabled soldiers, and the same sum for the support of the Indiana Legion and our defenses on the border. Now why was it that the Republicans would not pass the measure appropriating that one hundred thousand dollars for the relief of the sick and disabled? Simply because it provided that the money should be expended under the direction of the Secretary of State; because it was not placed under the control of Governor Morton. That is the only reason why his friends would not vote for it That is the reason why these men, when they found themselves at Madison, and had so far seceded from their duty to their constituents and the state—that is the reason why they would not come back. In these very propositions they

submitted one that there should be liberal appropriations made
for the same purposes as during the last session, to be expended by the Governor. Now there is nothing in the constitution of the state of Indiana that makes the Governor
the purser of the state, and places the funds of the state
under his control. There is an administrative branch of the
government formed by the Auditor of State, Secretary of
State and Treasurer of State, and until the friends of Governor Morton, in 1861, put into his care and keeping these
moneys and funds—until that time the extraordinary expenditures had always been made through other agencies. And
why? Because these other officers of the state are required
to give bond and security, and the Governor gives none.

"But the Governor says that, after the legislature had adjourned, he had to adopt one of three courses—first, to call
an extra session; second, to turn out the inmates of the asylums; or, third, to procure money in some way or other with
which to defray the expenses of the government.

"He says he decided not to call an extra session of the
legislature. He very correctly says that the power or discretion to call an extra session was vested in the Governor We
will not differ upon that point. But I contend that whenever
there is a failure on the part of the legislature to legislate,
and the state of Indiana is left without the necessary laws for
carrying on her state government, it is the duty of the Governor of the state not to legislate himself, nor to seize upon
the bureaus of the state government, nor to usurp the powers
of other branches of the government, but to call back the legislature and place upon its members the responsibility of
passing, or refusing to pass, the necessary laws. But he says
that Governor Willard did upon that subject as he did. I
say that there Governor Willard did wrong. I said so to
Governor Willard at the time, acting as Attorney-General for
the state of Indiana. I said to him, as his legal adviser, that
there was no law by which these asylums could be carried on

or the extraordinary expenses of the state paid, and that, in my judgment, it was his duty to recall the legislative assembly and leave upon them the responsibility to pass these necessary laws or not. He says that according to the precedent set by Governor Willard, another co-ordinate branch of the government may determine whether these men are worthy or not. He says the Executive may determine whether they are to be trusted or not. I say this is revolutionary. But he says that when Governor Willard refused to call the legislature together, I joined in a resolution requesting the Treasurer of State to advance the money to support the asylums, although it was contrary to law for him to do so. That much I did. When I could not prevail upon Governor Willard to recall the legislature, I then did subscribe my name to the resolution, and I told Mr. Jones that if he would advance the money to defray the expenses of these institutions I would stand by him I did so. But when Governor Morton desires to make me responsible for the executive action of Governor Willard, he attempts to make me Governor at that time, clothed with executive power. I acted then as I would have acted if I were Attorney-General under Governor Morton. I would have said to him, it is your duty to call back the legislature and throw upon them the responsibility of passing these laws.

"But again, what followed the action of Governor Willard? He was indorsed by the Democratic convention, it is true. But the people in 1858, although they elected a Democratic state ticket by a majority of three or five thousand, returned a majority of Republicans to both Houses; and, in that legislature, Governor Morton and his friends condemned the action of Governor Willard, and they placed upon the statute-book, during the session of the legislature in 1859 or 1860, their condemnation, in a law to which I shall call your attention. Governor Morton was one of the men who aided in placing that condemnation of Governor Willard's course upon the statute books of the state.

"Now, he says, he did not see proper to turn out the inmates of the asylums, as Governor Willard did. Governor Willard could not control that; Mr. Jones, the state Treasurer, refused to pay out the necessary funds. Governor Willard having refused to call an extra session of the legislature, at the end of six months, at the written request of the other officers of the state government, Mr. Jones took upon himself the responsibility of paying out the money. The difficulty with Governor Morton is this: when he is talking about one branch of the government, he seems to think that the power is all vested in that one branch. Governor Willard could not help closing these institutions. He was powerless. The funds ran out and he could do nothing until Mr. Jones furnished him with money. But Governor Morton says that *he* was determined not to close them. Then it was that he determined to take the third course, and procure the money to carry them on. He says that he met with unexpected and wonderful aid in procuring this money, and yet he got it in such a manner as to violate no law. Now let us call the Governor's attention to his own record on that subject. He says he never asked any one to violate a law. In 1859 the legislature of Indiana, a majority of them being Republicans, in condemnation of the course of Governor Willard, Mr. Jones and the other state officers who had a part in paying out the money without the necessary legal authority, passed a law by which they recognized the treasury system of the state and made specific provisions that the Treasurer of the state should pay no warrants, and the Auditor of the state should draw no warrants, unless there were funds for that specific purpose appropriated and unexpended. That law was approved by Governor Morton. It received his official sanction. In his address to the people of Indiana prefacing the report of his financial secretary, he makes this statement:

'The legislature adjourned without making any appropriations for defraying the expenses of the government.' Now what did he do? He says in this report:

" 'The Auditor and Treasurer of state, upon being consulted by me individually, after the close of the session, decided that not a single dollar, in the absence of legislative appropriations, should be drawn from the public funds for these objects.'

"Now, he says to you that he went to them and they refused to violate a law which he had signed. What higher compliment could he have paid to these officers than the one he has paid them right here. The action which he says was indorsed by the Democratic party in 1848 was condemned by the legislature, and he aided in its condemnation. Yet he says he went to the Auditor and Treasurer of state and asked them to pay that money in violation of law."

GOVERNOR MORTON—"I do not say so, Mr. McDonald."

MR. MCDONALD—"I will read it again: 'The Auditor and Treasurer of State, upon being consulted by me, decided that not a single dollar, in the absence of legislative appropriations, should be drawn from the public funds for these objects.'

"Well, in this same report, he goes on to say that he was very fortunate in obtaining funds. Here is the report of his financial secretary. Did you ever hear of any such thing in connection with the state government of Indiana as a financial bureau? Is there any law for it? Where does it spring from? How does it come into existence? It is simply called into existence by the political power of your Governor. No other authority can be found for it. Here is a list of the expenditures as furnished by the financial secretary. I have nothing to say against Colonel Terrell, the financial secretary of the Governor. If such an office existed I know of no one more capable of filling it than he. But that there should be such an officer grafted into the executive power is a thing that will in time be regarded as improbable, so improbable that men will hunt back through these records to find out where it came from and by whom it was authorized. But here is the report of Colonel Terrell, in which he says that Governor Morton has obtained from various sources $865,195.26, and that he has expended of that sum $617,299.14, leaving a balance in his hands at the time of this report, which was April 30, 1864, of $247,896.12. Now, Governor Morton says he had to borrow money. Let me read you what he says in his speech at Greencastle. It is in substance what he says now. Here it is:

"'McDonald further charges that, as soon as the legislature adjourned, Governor Morton at once seized the entire power of the state government, as by revolutionary authority, and has controlled the affairs of state up to the present hour, according to his sole will and inclination, and without any reference to the other branches of the government.' Here is his answer:

"'I must meet this broad statement by an absolute denial. It has not the slightest foundation in fact, and I defy Mr. McDonald, or any one else, to show where I have usurped a single power, or exercised any authority not conferred on me by law. He attempts to make out the case by showing that I procured money with which I carried on the penitentiaries and benevolent institutions and kept the machinery of the state government in motion. But there were persons and counties who came forward and tendered me the money with which to support all these institutions—not the money of the state, but their own money. They said: 'We are not willing to have the machinery of the state government stopped; we are not willing to have the state disgraced before the world as it was in 1857, and we, therefore, provide you with the necessary means, taking all the risk and responsibility upon ourselves. If the state shall hereafter, in a spirit of good faith, reimburse

us, well and good; if not, we prefer losing the money to
having the state dishonored. But upon that point we have
no fear and are willing to take the chances.' Now, when I
took the money and applied it to the purposes for which it
was contributed, what law did I violate? Upon what provision of the constitution did I trample? If the parties contributing this money had applied it directly to these purposes
without my intervention, the case would not have been different. It is simply the case of one man's paying another's
debts, against which there is no law, human or divine. If
the creditor accepts the money, the debtor may or may not,
in his own good pleasure, reimburse the friend who has paid
his debts, but surely the friend, by so doing, has committed
no offense.'

"Now Governor Morton says there was no money borrowed
on the credit of the state to carry on the government, but
these men voluntarily came forward to lend it to him, and
there is no obligation resting on the state of Indiana to refund
it. So far as legal obligation is concerned, I will grant it.
Now what did he do upon that subject? Let me call your attention to a few facts. Here is an order of the commissioners of Marion county, by which funds to the amount of ten
thousand dollars were placed in his hands:

'JUNE 15, 1863.

" 'Ordered that the sum of ten thousand dollars be and is
hereby appropriated out of the court-house revenue, as a loan
from the county of Marion to the state of Indiana, to be used
by the Governor in his official capacity. Such loan and such
reasonable interest as may be allowed, to be reimbursed and
paid to the said county of Marion by the state of Indiana,
and it is further ordered that upon the filing of the Governor's
receipt for the said sum of ten thousand dollars, the auditor
of the county shall pay the same,' etc.

"This is a voluntary loan, is it? It is not a loan to the state
of Indiana? The Governor says the terms are to be decided

by the legislature hereafter. How is the loan to the state of Indiana to be expended by the Governor in his official capacity, and to be repaid with such interest? Aye, interest. Usance, that is it. They could not say of the Governor what Shylock said of Antonio:

> " 'I hate him for he is a Christian,
>   But more for that in low simplicity,
>   He lends out money gratis, and brings down
>   The rate of usance here with us in Venice.'

"Contending that his friends in the legislature would come to his rescue, he has covered up this iniquity. But here is another order from the county of Decatur: 'It is ordered by the board that there be appropriated out of the county treasury the sum of seven thousand dollars to be loaned to the state of Indiana, for the purpose of defraying the expenses of the benevolent institutions of the state, and for the relief of the sick and wounded Indiana soldiers, and the auditor is authorized to draw a warrant for the same   The same shall be receipted for by the Governor in his official capacity.' That receipt we have not been able to obtain.

"I shall read one more of these orders. It is from Warren county, in response to 'a call.' But Governor Morton says 'these parties came forward voluntarily.' I say again there was no legal obligation, because he could not bind the state, that was all. Here is the other order: 'In response to a call, from the Governor of Indiana, for a loan from the counties of the state, for the purpose of carrying on the benevolent institutions of the state, etc., it is ordered that a loan of five thousand dollars be made to the Governor of Indiana, and that county bonds to that amount be issued, payable 1st of January, 1865, at the office of the treasurer of Warren county,' etc.

"Here is Governor Morton's receipt:

" 'EXECUTIVE DEPARTMENT, BUREAU OF FINANCE,
" 'INDIANAPOLIS, August 14, 1864.

" 'Received from the treasurer of the county of Warren, state of Indiana, five thousand dollars as a loan from said county, to be used by me in my official capacity as Governor in defraying a part of the necessary expenses of the benevolent institutions of the state, and of the Northern Prison, and for the relief of the sick and wounded soldiers of the state, said loan together with such reasonable interest as may be allowed, to be reimbursed and paid to the county of Warren, as may be allowed hereafter.

" 'O. P. MORTON,
" 'Governor of Indiana.'

"Now I have to call your attention to one other fact and then I will have done on that subject. Governor Morton says these are mere voluntary payments. He says there is no obligation to repay either principal or interest, yet in this respect it is shown he has paid to two citizens of Wayne county seventeen hundred dollars in interest. Altogether the financial report reminds me of the report of a road supervisor I once heard of. The supervisor had not been keeping any accounts. One day he was told that he must make out a report—that it was necessary for him to make out a statement of his receipts and expenditures. So he made one out in this way, after studying some time: 'All estimates paid in; all estimates paid out' That is the history of Governor Morton's record and that of his financial secretary.

"Now, my friends, the matter that brought up this discussion grew out of a declaration made by me when I accepted the nomination for this office. I said to the convention that nominated me, that if I should be elected Governor, I should take an oath to support the constitution of the United States, and of the state of Indiana; that I would endeavor to perform both branches of that oath, both to the United States and to the state. I said further, that I was a candidate for but one branch of the new government, which is divided into three co-ordinate branches, and that, if elected, I would undertake to discharge the duties of but one office. If the legislative and judicial branches disregarded their duty, I said that, after I had done all I could to see the laws enforced, if there was a failure, its responsibilities should rest on other heads than mine. I repeat here now that if you want your state carried on by the one man power, don't elect me. [Applause.

"Now, my friends, I propose to come to the other branch of this discussion. I shall speak to you of that just as frankly, and I hope as satisfactorily, as I have of that which relates to our state affairs. I know that each one of you understands exactly where I stand in regard to these; I have no doubt you will as fully understand me on the other branch before I close. I never come to the discussion of a question, springing from this civil war, but my heart feels ready to bleed with the thought that a great country like ours—the greatest the sun shines on—should be rent in civil feud, drenched with fraternal blood. We have now progressed far into the third year of this terrible struggle. The pictures that rise before the imagination grow still more horrible than they were in the beginning. There is enough to make any man that loves his country hang his head in sorrow, and weep for the desolation that has been sweeping over this land.

"I said, on a former occasion, that the causes of this war were by no means hidden. I believe the historian will be compelled to say they have sprung out of an unwise and fanatical agitation between the Northern and Southern states of the question of domestic slavery, contrary to the principles of our constitution, which confine the Federal government simply to the exercise of Federal powers. This government, framed by the wisest men that have ever lived, might otherwise have continued through all time. But it has been the intermeddling by one section with the affairs of another section that has divided our country into parties, separated by geographical lines, until the election of a sectional President transferred this controversy from the political arena to the arena of arms. I believe this will be the record of history, and I will now show that it has not been my judgment alone on that subject. I wish to read the first resolution ever adopted by a national Democratic convention on the subject of slavery agitation. The convention which met at Baltimore in 1840 adopted this resolution:

" '*Resolved*, That Congress has no power under the constitution to interfere with or control the domestic institutions of the several states, and that such states are the sole and proper judges of everything appertaining to their own affairs not prohibited by the constitution; that all efforts of the abolitionists or others, made to induce Congress to interfere with the question of slavery, and to take incipient steps in relation thereto, are calculated to lead to the most alarming and dangerous consequences, and that all such efforts have an inevitable tendency to diminish the happiness of the people and endanger the permanency and stability of the Union, and ought not to be countenanced by any friend of our political institutions.'

"That was the record of the Democratic party in 1840, when my friend and I stood together. In every Democratic convention, from that time to this, that resolution, in all its force and meaning, has been re-indorsed and re-enacted by the Democratic party. Now let me read to you a resolution adopted by the Whig convention in 1852, in the last great effort made by that party to maintain itself. Here it is:

" '*Resolved*, That the Whigs of the United States declare as a fundamental article of political faith an absolute necessity for avoiding geographical parties. The danger so clearly discovered by the father of his country has become fearfully

Mor —22

apparent in the agitation now convulsing the nation, and must be arrested at once, if we would preserve our constitution and our Union from dismemberment, and the name of America from being blotted out from the list of civilized nations. '

"That is what the Whigs said on the subject of fanatical agitation. But in 1854 a new organization sprang up in this country, which my friend entered. In 1858 it nominated its candidate for the Presidency, and in 1860 it succeeded, and upon its success civil war came upon this land. I do not say the South was justified in secession, but I do say that the election of a sectional President was the superinducing cause. At this point my friend will say that in 1849 I occupied ground which sustained this agitation.

"On a former occasion[1] he read you a letter written by me in that year, when I was a candidate for Congress. I am glad he did so, and I hope he will read it again to-day. I am not going to take up a great deal of time in talking of myself, because in these times men are but atoms compared to the great principles at stake throughout the land. But I say that I am glad that letter has been brought up by my friend, because by it he proves I have been a consistent man for fifteen years. That is one-third of my whole life, and more than one-half of my entire manhood. I have nothing to say in regard to that letter. If any man in Indiana has been misled by it to unite his destinies with a sectional party endangering the peace of the country, to that man I owe an humble apology, and I shall ask his pardon in any terms he may dictate.

"In 1850, being in Congress, I took my stand on the question alongside of Henry Clay, Daniel Webster, General Cass and a whole band of conservative men who stood against the sectional strife between the North and the South. Now, all I have to say to my friend is this: If he fell off from

---

[1] At Greencastle.

the faith in the Democratic party on account of my letter of 1849, let me kneel to him and ask his pardon. If that was not the cause of his backsliding, I ask him, in God's name, not to put on my old clothes. [Laughter.]

"But this war has come upon the country. After the election of Mr. Lincoln, I believe the war might have been avoided. Mr. Lincoln was elected in November, and Mr. Morton became Governor of Indiana in January following. From that time to June, I ask him to state to you what steps he took to avert this dreadful calamity which was then hanging over his country. Did he use words of conciliation? Did he try to reason on the subject? Did he attempt any compromise of the difficulties? If he did he knows what steps they were, and to use his own language, applied to me, 'he has no difficulty in making himself understood.'

"When this war came upon us, there was no man who, more than myself, took pride in that prompt and patriotic effort that was made by the volunteer soldiers of this country to save it, when its statesmen refused to reach forth their hands to do so by the arts of peace. The volunteers of Indiana, as well as of other states, acted upon patriotic impulses and sought to save by the sword that which these men might have saved by the pen. The question was submitted to these politicians whether they would lose their party and save their country, or save their party and lose their country, and they chose the latter alternative. They preferred their party to their country.

"But this war has now been raging for three years and a half, and I am now asked what kind of a war I am in favor of. Well, theoretically I am in favor of no war. I wish those men who came upon earth to preach 'peace on earth and good-will to men' would exercise that power now, and still the waves of strife that are breaking over this land. Governor Morton says there is no difficulty in understanding his position on this question. Now let us see what our positions are on that subject. I have said from the beginning, and it is unalterably fixed in my mind, that this country shall not be dismembered. [Applause.] I believe this country was made for one government and one people, and I have never yet seen the day nor the hour when I should be willing to give up our claim to the people of the South as our fellow-citizens. It is our land, from the Atlantic to the Pacific, and from the Gulf to the Lakes, and we can not give it up. He says that I had undertaken to answer the question, but, according to his views, did not answer it. Let me call your attention to that for one moment. I think I can show that I made my position then much clearer than he has made his to-day. I said (and when my friend undertook to quote me he did not quote me exactly right, although I think this was only an inadvertence)—I said: 'But the question has been frequently asked me whether I was in favor of a vigorous prosecution of this war? I now say that to this war, as prosecuted under the ideas of the abolition minority that rules this administration, I am utterly opposed.' In reading this my friend made me say: 'To this war, under the idea and policy of the administration, I am utterly opposed. I believe it is entailing unmixed evil, and I would be false to my country if I did not say so.' Then I went on to the question of the resolution of the Democracy of Indiana, adopted by a convention of which I was a member. I was one of the committee that presented the resolution, which was:

" 'That we will sustain with all our energies a war for the maintenance of the constitution and the integrity of the Union under the constitution, but we are opposed to a war for the emancipation of the negroes, or the subjugation of the Southern states.'

"I stand there now. I stand there to-day. Then, says my competitor, you are for no war at all, because any war will subjugate the Southern states. There is where we differ. The states—what are they? They are not the people of the states. It is against the states as states, and against their domestic institutions, that I say the government has no right to make a war. We may attempt to put down the men who are in arms against the government and resisting its authority, but the Federal government has no right to infringe upon the institutions of any state. Therefore I say that I am opposed to any war for the subjugation of states.

"And my competitor, in reply to this part of my speech at Greencastle, undertook still further to define my position by quoting from a speech delivered by me in December, 1862. I will not say that he intentionally garbled my remarks, but he did not quote me correctly. I will call his attention to it, that hereafter he may make full and complete correction. He says:

" 'But by going back to an address which he delivered before a Democratic association in Indianapolis, on the 25th of November, 1862, reported in the *Sentinel* of the next day, we shall gain a little light upon his true position. In that address he declared that the abolitionists, his former political friends and associates, had forced the war upon the South; that the South could never be conquered, and his motto was, "No war for the subjugation of states or the emancipation of slaves." ' "

"Right here, now, let me call Governor Morton's attention to what I did say. You will find that if he had read the entire paragraph he would not have made the inquiry he did. I said the Democratic party, while dissenting from the civil politics of this administration, had obeyed the laws because they were laws, and there is no other party in this country that would have done it except the Democratic party. If the party of my friend had had all its political opinions trampled under foot, and its views of what is right completely disregarded, it would have been at war before this day with the Federal government; but the Democratic party has not regarded these abuses as furnishing any ground for revolution. It has been a law-abiding party, and is now. I used in that speech the sentiment which I here reaffirm and reiterate : 'In the meantime let us illustrate our devotion to the constitution by a course of conduct which shall close the mouth of the slanderer. Let us show that we are for our country and our whole country, and while we stand by the country in the future as in the past, let us insist that there shall be employed all just measures of conciliation, as well as the strong arm of power, to hasten the day when the authority of the government shall be recognized throughout the land. Let our motto be, "No war for the subjugation of states or the emancipation of negroes, and no peace that looks to a dismemberment of the Union." ' If Governor Morton had read the whole of that paragraph he would have no occasion to parade me as in favor of a dissolution of the Union.

"This country was made for one people. But after having tried this war for three years and a half, I say it is time to try some other remedy.

[Here the audience became vociferous in their demand for "the other remedy." They were finally quieted by Governor Morton's earnest appeal for the preservation of order and a patient hearing of Mr. McDonald.]

"I say it is time to try some other remedy. In the speech I made then I said, as I say now, that I am opposed to a war for the subjugation of states, or to interference with state laws, local institutions or state authority, whether that covers the institution of slavery, or what it covers. I am for insisting upon the enforcement of Federal authority over those who deny it. I am for saying to this people : 'We simply ask to enforce the constitution among you, and we want you to yield obedience to the legal authority of the United States.' I am for carrying these terms as the olive branch of peace in every move we make. If that had been done in the beginning, and constantly persevered in, the Southern armies would long since have wasted away, and we would have no rebels to fight now. I said in the speech from which my friend has attempted to quote, when I accepted the nomination in the state convention: 'At the same time I am for peace at the earliest practicable moment, but peace on the terms of the restoration of the Union under the Federal constitution, with all its rights and guarantees to the several states, North and South.' I have already said that I recognize the power of the Federal government to put down those who attempt to resist its authority. But I deny that the government of the United States has any right to overthrow the institutions of any state under the pretext that it is in rebellion. That is the distinction. It is the one that Governor Morton and his friends have always refused to make. It is the one that always induced me to believe that Governor Morton and his friends would suppress the rebellion by force of arms, but that they had no other plan but force of arms. They have adopted the maxim of the old Roman emperor, who said he would create a solitude and call that peace.

"Now, my friends, I don't think any fair-minded man can go away without fully understanding my position on this question. I have no doubt many will go away saying they do not understand me; but it is not my fault, it is theirs. I have undertaken to place my views fully and plainly before you. I have said that if this war had been prosecuted for the single and sole purpose of the restoration of the Union, it would have been over long ago. Our victories at Fort Donelson, at Vicksburg, and at other points, would not have been wasted as they have been. But the policy of the administration, portrayed in that letter of Abraham Lincoln, 'To all whom it may concern,' has divided the people of the North and united the people of the South.[1] Here are his terms, 'To all

---

[1] The circumstances leading to this letter are well known. Horace Greeley, editor of the New York *Tribune*, had been persuaded that Confederate commissioners, with full power to treat for peace, were at Niagara and he had urged the President to invite them to exhibit their credentials

whom it may concern.' Whom does it not concern that there shall be peace in this country? It concerns every man who has in the war a relative, a friend or a brother. It concerns any one that can mourn, and if you can find any one on this broad green earth who can not, let him pass away into solitude. Let him be regarded as one blighted by Heaven. But here is what Mr. Lincoln says: 'Any proposition which embraces the restoration of peace, the integrity of the whole Union, and the abandonment of slavery, and which comes by and with authority that can control the armies arrayed against the United States, will be received and be met by liberal terms, in other substantial and collateral points.'

"The proposition for peace and the integrity of the Union is well enough. That far I go. But the abandonment of slavery—what is that? Simply that he is to overcome the people of the South, and their institutions, and compel them to give up the rights vested in them by the constitution. Upon a question of that kind I can not agree with him. It is in violation of a pledge made by him when he went into the Presidential chair on the day of his inauguration, when he said he had neither the power nor the purpose to interfere with slavery in any state.

"I will close my remarks by asking my friends to remain and give my competitor a patient, calm and deliberate hear-

and submit their ultimatum. Lincoln had little faith in this project, but offered safe conduct to any one who had a written proposition from Jefferson Davis embracing the restoration of the Union and the abandonment of slavery. Greeley went to Niagara with the safe conduct, but the Confederate commissioners had no credentials. They declared that they could get credentials if they could be sent to Richmond, armed with the preliminary correspondence. When Lincoln, on July 18, wrote the letter to which McDonald refers, it was bitterly criticised by the Democrats, not only on account of the slavery clause, but because it was claimed to be a withdrawal on Mr. Lincoln's part of the unconditional authority to convey commissioners to Washington to treat for peace. Greeley himself criticised the President, and in a private letter asked him to grant an armistice for one year, a thing which would at this time have been utterly disastrous to the Union arms.

ing, while he replies and closes this debate. Let it be said once more in Indiana that discussion can take place, reason can control, and that the men of the state are again themselves, calmly deliberating on their rights, knowing what these are, and determined to maintain them as freemen.'' (Applause.)

Morton's rejoinder was as follows:

'' LADIES AND GENTLEMEN—I desire your attention but for a few moments. In the first place I desire to ask each candid person in this assembly if, from what my distinguished friend has said here to-day, he can tell where my friend stands on the war question? He reminds me of a piece of poetry once made about Martin Van Buren:

> '' 'He wires in and wires out,
> Leaving the people still in doubt
> Whether the man that made the track
> Was going South or coming back.'

'' Now, my friends, he tells you in one breath that he is opposed to making peace except upon the terms of a restoration of the Union. He tells you in another breath that he is opposed to the subjugation of the Southern states by war; and he tells you we have tried war for three years and a half and it has failed, and he is in favor of some other remedy. [A voice—''We want to hear about his other remedy.''] Now I ask you, gentlemen and ladies, if you can tell where he stands? It is not for lack of ability that he fails to make himself understood, for he is one of the ablest men in his party. He could tell you very easily and in very few words, if he felt disposed. Why is it he shrinks from doing so? He tells you, finally, that having tried war for three years and a half, and having failed with that, we must try some other remedy. The question came up from this vast audience, What is that remedy? Did he tell you?

''I asked my friend this plain question: Are you in favor

of prosecuting this war in any manner for the suppression of this rebellion? He did not answer that question. I then asked him: If we should end the war and make peace, do you expect the rebel states would voluntarily return to their allegiance? If not, how do you expect to restore the Union by abandoning the war? These questions he could have answered in two minutes if he had felt inclined, but he has not answered them.

" My friend has alluded to his letter of 1849. He and I were together then on political matters. In that letter he said:

" 'I am opposed to the admission of any more slave states. I believe Congress has the power to exclude slavery from the territories, and should do so. I am in favor of abolishing slavery in the District of Columbia, and if that can not be done, I am in favor of removing the capital from the District of Columbia to free soil.'

" He says he has been a consistent man for fifteen years. That carries him back to 1849, when he wrote that letter, and if he has been consistent for fifteen years he is still in favor of the propositions just quoted. When he talks about my wearing his old clothes, let me say that upon my word I would rather wear his old ones than his new ones. I think his new ones need washing a great deal more than the old ones.

"But my friend was in the state convention of 1849. I was there too. That convention declared unanimously that slavery should be excluded from all the territories by act of Congress. That was the first action of the Democratic party of the state of Indiana on that subject that I know anything about. I stood by the party till 1854. Then my friend joined the party which began agitating the slavery question. He approved of the introduction of the Nebraska bill repealing the Missouri Compromise. I was opposed to that bill. I said I would not stand by any party that indorsed it. I

bolted from the party but not from my principles. My friend
bolted from his principles but stood by his party. [Ap-
plause.]

"Now I want to come to a few matters upon the subject of
state affairs. My friend talks about my garbling his speeches.
I do not think he would intentionally garble anything, but he
was so anxious to see something to complain about that he
finally thought he saw it. I have proved, and he has con-
fessed, that he advised one State Treasurer to violate the constitution of the state of Indiana. He tried to prove that I
did likewise. Here is what I said on that subject in my
report: 'The Auditor and Treasurer of State, being consulted
by me immediately after the close of the session, decided that
not a single dollar, in the absence of legislative appropriation,
should be drawn from the public funds for these objects.' I
will tell you why I consulted with them. I knew that one
State Treasurer, under precisely similar circumstances, had
paid money out of the Treasury to support these institutions
by the advice of my distinguished friend, and I did not know
but the present incumbent might do the same. But I was
deceived; in other words, there was not a Democratic Governor at that time. There was a Union man and the case was
quite different.

"Now, my friend says I have violated the law by borrowing money on the faith of the state. He reads these receipts,
and really I am surprised that he should try to make a
case for me out of them, as he certainly has done. I told
you that every man that advanced this money did so with
the clear and perfect understanding that I had no legal power
to borrow it. I did not pretend that I had any power in the
matter. It was all referred to the future action of the legislature. It is simply a question of good faith on the part of the
state. I told them 'if the legislature shall make provision for
paying you, well and good, if not, you have no remedy.' It
was a perfect understanding. It makes no difference whether

the word 'borrow' or 'loan' was used.   These receipts bear
out the truth of what I say.   'To be reimbursed to the said
county of Marion, by the state of Indiana, as may be provided by law hereafter.'   I could not control the action of
the state legislature, and did not say I could.   Nobody was
deceived by anything I told him on the subject.   Here are
two of the orders which my friend has read, and what is said
in them is simply this: 'That this amount, with such reasonable interest as may be allowed, shall be reimbursed to said
county, as may be provided by law hereafter.'   These county
officers will tell you that the representations I made to them
were just what you see in this receipt.

"But, suppose I am guilty of all the gentleman charges,
suppose I have borrowed this money and pledged the credit
and authority of the state for it, what was it for?   It was to
support the benevolent institutions and carry on the penitentiaries, and no man can say that twenty-five cents of it has
been wrongfully expended.   If I had done all the gentleman
says I have done, it would be no disgrace.   But how can my
friend, having admitted that he advised the Treasurer to violate the constitution in paying out money for the purpose of
carrying on the benevolent institutions, blame me for taking
the money of other people, that did not belong to the state
and which they had a right to give me for that purpose?   He
says he did advise Mr. Jones to pay the money because Governor Willard had refused to call the legislature back.   Because Governor Willard would not do his duty, therefore, he
advised Colonel Jones to violate the constitution of the
state.   The whole thing depended on this, that it was important to carry on these institutions, and therefore he advised Mr. Jones to pay the money.   If the officers now in
the state department had done the same thing, they would
have been justified by public opinion.   So the very papers
he presents against me make out a case in my favor.   I
gave no pledges, but told everybody that the matter would

be referred to the legislature for its action. My friend says
he had some trouble in getting these receipts. If he had
called on me I would have got them for him at any time,
without any trouble to him whatever.

"My competitor says that Mr. Lincoln might have avoided
this war if he had felt disposed. He further says that it has
been brought on by the agitation of the slavery question. I
can only say that if the agitation of the slavery question has
been the cause of the war, then my friend is very guilty. He
commenced agitating in the first place on the anti-slavery
side, and went further than I did. He then commenced, in
1854, on the other side, and became an ultra pro-slavery man.
Now, having tried both sides, I should like to know which
side he likes best. [Laughter.] His judgment now, owing
to his great experience, is entitled to great consideration.

"Now one word in regard to the assertion that Lincoln
commenced this war. In October, 1859, more than one year
before Mr. Lincoln's election, Mr. Floyd, the Secretary of
War under Buchanan's administration, issued an order sending one hundred and fifteen thousand muskets to the Southern
arsenals, and during the progress of that administration orders
were frequently issued sending guns to Southern forts and
arsenals, and placing them where they could be seized. In
October, General Scott informed Mr. Buchanan that preparations were being made to seize the forts and dock-yards in the
South. During the time of Mr. Buchanan's administration,
before Mr. Lincoln came into office, eight states seceded.
During the time of Mr. Buchanan's administration, the Montgomery constitution was formed and Jefferson Davis was inaugurated as President of the Southern Confederacy.

"Mr. Davis himself had said before Lincoln came into
office: 'The time for compromise is past, and if they resist
secession, we will make them feel Southern steel and Southern
gunpowder.' On the day of Lincoln's inauguration, there
were more than thirty thousand men under arms in the South,

while we had less than five thousand. On the 6th of March, the rebel Congress passed a bill to increase the rebel army to one hundred thousand men. Four days before Mr. Lincoln's inauguration, every shipyard, dock, mint and custom-house in the South had been seized, and almost every fort, except Sumter. All this was done during Buchanan's administration. Remember that eight states had seceded during a Democratic administration, when you charge that secession has been caused by Republican fanaticism. The rebel constitution was adopted while we of the North had a Democratic administration. And yet, for the purpose of dividing the people of the North, we are told that Mr. Lincoln made this war, when it is a matter of public history that the preparation for the rebellion had been going on not only through Buchanan's administration, but for thirty years before it. When the ordinance of secession was passed in South Carolina, Mr. Ingalls, in the South Carolina convention, said: 'It is the work of years.' Mr. Keitt said: 'I have been engaged in this war all my life.' Barnwell Rhett said: 'We have been engaged in this war more than thirty years. It is no consequence of Lincoln's election nor of the failure to execute the fugitive slave law; we have been engaged in this war for more than thirty years.' That was true, and the same declarations were made in Georgia, Alabama and other Southern states. Yet we are still told that Lincoln made this war, and that he might have avoided it if he had been so disposed. If there ever was a time when we were called upon to deal truly and honestly with the people, it is now. We have no right, as we are men and as we love our country and our homes and our families—we have no right to deal unfaithfully and untruly with the people. My friend should not let his party prejudices lead him so far aside from the path of duty and the truth of history. You have heard him denounce my administration and you have heard him denounce Mr. Lincoln's administration. I want to know if any man in this assembly has heard him say one word directly or indirectly against the administration of Mr. Davis? Has he said one word against these men who are endeavoring to kill your brothers and sons on Southern battle-fields? Has he said one word against those men who shed the blood of the gallant Colonel Hathaway of your own county? Not a single syllable. Has my friend no indignation except against the brave men who rally around the old flag, and are true to the cause of the Union? Has he no sympathy except for those who are opposing the government? Is there nothing to be said against these men who are shedding the best blood of the land? I speak for our brave men. In their name I denounce the rebellion as wicked and infamous—against the best government in the world—it is a rebellion against liberty, against God, and against humanity. And I call upon all truly loyal and patriotic men to unite with me in denouncing that cause.

''Now, before I conclude I want to say one word about the military bill. My friend says he never examined that bill very closely. I advise him to examine it immediately. It is now about eighteen months old. The constitution of Indiana says the Governor shall be the commander-in-chief of the militia, but this bill took the entire power out of the hands of the Governor and put it into the hands of the Treasurer, Auditor and Secretary of State and the Attorney-General—four new commanding major-generals—four new executive heads unknown to the constitution. It gave them control of all the arms and accoutrements of the state. It gave the Governor a sort of control of the men, but none whatever of the arms and ammunition. To enable the Governor to command the militia he must have control of the arms as well as the men. If he has not, the power to command the militia does not amount to much. A militia without arms will not do very effective service. But this bill put all the arms and ammunition under the control of four state officers. The Governor was not vested with the power to put a single musket or cartridge into the hands of the militia. Why was this? Had I abused the military power of Indiana? Why was that power to be taken from me? It was for the purpose of revolution, bloodshed and civil war. Again, the constitution says the Governor shall commission every officer in the militia, but this bill provided that if the Governor refused to commission officers according to the will of the four state officers, then their appointment in writing would stand in lieu of a commission. But he says if the bill was unconstitutional it could not do any harm. Well, my friend, if my acts are unconstitutional they can not do any harm. But the idea that a military bill, which was insurrection in itself, should be passed, and that it should be left to the courts to determine its validity, when there was strong reason to believe that the courts were in the insurrection!

"Now, my friends, find out if you can where Mr. McDonald stands on the war question. If you are for peace, and think he is a peace man, vote for him. But if you want to vote for a man who has tried to stand by the army and the soldiers—who believes that this Union must and shall be preserved—then vote for me."

When Morton concluded the Republicans were wild with enthusiasm. Three rousing cheers were given for "Morton, old Abe and the army," while McDonald retired unattended.

The discussions between Morton and McDonald, like those between Lincoln and Douglas in Illinois, show very clearly the excellence of this Western method of joint debates. There can be no final judgment in a court of law until both parties have been heard. In politics the joint debate has the same relation to the one-sided political speech that an open trial bears to an *ex parte* proceeding. There is no room for imposition. The arguments which can not bear investigation are withheld, and the good sense of the people can be safely trusted to form a just conclusion. The applause of the multitude in the La Porte discussion was generally in the right place. Undoubtedly the weakest point in McDonald's argument was his reference to the "other remedy," to be tried after three years and a half of war. He could not state it and the vociferous demand that he should do so showed that the audience penetrated the vital defect of the Democratic position. On the other hand the applause which greeted McDonald's declaration that if elected he proposed to administer nothing but the executive branch of the government was an expression of the law-abiding instincts of the people. On this occasion Morton had the advantage of opening and closing the discussion. He was not at the time in good physical condition, but a sympathetic audience, in a county of his own choosing, was more than sufficient to overcome this drawback. It would appear from the reports that through all these joint discussions the Republicans sustained the Governor more loyally than the Democrats upheld McDonald. Wherever he spoke, Morton did not lack the support of enthusiastic partisans who gave the utmost effect to all that he said.

23—MOR.

CHAPTER XXVI

THE relations between Morton and McDonald through this campaign, as at every other time, were cordial. Neither of them ever failed in personal courtesy toward his antagonist. After Morton had been elected he procured a portrait of Mc-Donald and hung it in his office where it remained while he was Governor. When they became colleagues many years afterwards in the United States Senate, they were still warm friends, and they so remained until Morton's death. Indeed, had it not been for these excellent personal relations there could have been no joint campaign at all in 1864. The bitterest feelings had been aroused between the two parties. Great numbers of men upon both sides came armed to the meetings. At South Bend, the determination shown in the faces of many in the great audience foreboded evil. As they sat side by side upon the platform, Morton said to McDonald: "I am told a great many of your friends have come here armed." McDonald answered: "I have no doubt three-fourths of that audience are armed, but you and I can control these meetings, and so long as we do not lose our heads there will be no trouble." Morton answered that there was no danger in that quarter, and the debate went on without disturbance.

During these discussions new questions were constantly arising. The Democratic State Central Committee, of which J. J. Bingham (one of the "Sons of Liberty") was chairman, published on August 15 an address to the people of Indiana, insisting that in view of apprehended attempts of those in authority to interfere by military power with the freedom of elections, the constitutional right of the people to keep and bear arms should not be abandoned, and that it was the duty of all good citizens to co-operate in open and lawful organizations for the protection of this freedom and for the preservation of order as well as for defense against invasion. The address recommended thorough organization for these ends.   Morton understood perfectly the meaning of this circular.   It was intended as a signal to the Sons of Liberty to take up arms.   He instantly issued his proclamation to the people containing the following:

"The assumption that those in authority in this state will interfere by military power with the freedom of elections is absolutely and wickedly false.   .   .   .

"So far as my administration is concerned, I can safely defy the authors of this document to point to a single act giving color to this infamous charge, or to show a single instance in which I have failed to exercise the executive power for the protection of persons and property, and of social and civil rights, without regard to parties or politics.   While serving as Governor of Indiana, I have endeavored to act for the whole people and not for a party, and will so continue to do, regardless of all assaults or aspersions.   At the same time I will not hesitate to vindicate legitimate authority, no matter under what pretense or by what method it may be assailed.   So far as the approaching elections are concerned, they shall, to the extent of the power vested in me, be open and free, and every legitimate voter shall be protected in the unrestrained and deliberate exercise of the elective franchise.   This is my purpose, nor has there ever been any reason to doubt it; and I can not, under the pretext that I am about to violate my duty, tolerate the formation of any dangerous or illegal military organizations, the true purpose of which is to resist the state and Federal authority, overawe the people, control the elections, and thus accomplish the very thing against which it is hypocritically pretended they are to guard.   .   .   .

"Need I argue to an intelligent people that the things recommended by this document would inevitably lead to collisions and civil war, the end and consequences of which no man can predict? While it purports to be addressed to the people of the state generally, it is intended only for those who belong to the political organization which its authors assume to represent. Should its recommendation be followed men belonging to other political organizations would feel their personal and political safety endangered, and would be driven, for self-defense, to resort to similar means. Then we should have two or more political parties in the state, armed and organized into military bodies, and all hope of preventing collisions and preserving order would be lost. Military organizations must be under the control of the constituted authority of the state. All others are illegal, unauthorized and dangerous.   .   .   .

"I do, therefore, solemnly warn the people of the state not to accept the evil counsel they have received, but to keep themselves aloof from all military bodies contemplating resistance to Federal or state authority and from all organizations tending to compromise them in their allegiance to the government. The men who would inveigle them into such schemes or combinations are powerless to protect them, and would be the first to desert them in a moment of peril."

This address and proclamation at once became the subjects of discussion in the joint debates. On August 16 Morton and McDonald met at Brownstown. The weather was inclement. There was no house in the village large enough to hold even a considerable fragment of the vast audience, and so anxious were the people to hear the champions of the two parties that they stood for three hours in the rain without flinching. The speakers occupied an uncovered stand, and were only partially protected by umbrellas held over them while they addressed the audience. McDonald justified the address of the Democratic committee. There were grounds for apprehension that the authorities would interfere. "In 1863," he said, "in Indianapolis on election day, before 10 o'clock, the polls were seized by armed forces from the camps around the town. From that time, Democrats, if they voted, did it at the risk of their lives. The Seventy-first Regiment went to the polls with their guns upon their shoulders."[1]

At the meeting at Brownstown a number of new questions were discussed. McDonald asked Morton what would be done with the hundred and fifty thousand negro soldiers who had been called into the field. Were they to be made equal fellow-citizens?

Morton answered: "It is not for me to decide what their fate will be, but I trust that they will be forever free; that the men who have gone forth to fight for the Union will never be enslaved again. As to whether they will enjoy political equality and the right of suffrage, that will depend upon the laws of the state where they live. Indiana has her laws, and I will not ask to change them. But I want to ask a question. Does Mr. McDonald insist that we shall fill up the ranks with

---

[1] Such were his words as reported by the Cincinnati *Commercial*. The *Sentinel*, the organ of Mr. McDonald's party, thus reported them: "At one election, the Seventy-first Regiment marched to the polls, and, against orders, they voted. At 10 o'clock no Democrat dared approach the precinct. One of the proprietors of the *Sentinel* had been driven away. He was pleased to hear that such scenes were not to be re-enacted, but that they had happened was too well known to be contradicted." This criticism of the conduct of the Seventy-first Regiment was bitterly resented. W. D. Carter, the major of this regiment, wrote to McDonald from Marietta, Ga., a letter declaring the statement to be "a foul slander on the regiment." The soldiers who visited Indianapolis on that day, he said, were unarmed and were accompanied by officers. The regiment did not leave its camp, and had never violated the purity of the ballot-box.

On August 22 a citizens meeting, held at Indianapolis, called upon McDonald to retract the statement. McDonald, in an answer to John W. Ray, the chairman of the meeting, denied that he had used the words imputed to him.

white men instead of using the negroes? I have heard a good deal from Democrats against negro soldiers, and the provost marshal says that Democrats were the very first to put in negro substitutes."

To this McDonald replied: "I have been opposed to making soldiers out of negroes, not because I am not willing that they should stand in place of white men in battle and camp, but because I do not believe any people ever made use of a servile race in war that did not suffer from it. The negroes are an inferior race. I have always looked upon this government as made for the white man. I am not in favor of slavery or equality.

Morton asked: "Are you in favor of enforcing the conscription law?"

McDonald answered: "I regard that law as odious, and if I had been in Congress I would have voted against it. I hope the day will come, and very soon, when it shall be repealed. But while it is a law I stand ready to obey it."

The running commentaries of the press upon these joint debates throw occasional side lights upon interesting episodes connected with them. Morton had much the advantage of McDonald in these contemporary chronicles. We are told by the *Journal* that at Bedford McDonald's humorous allusions to the financial bureau "occasioned no smile save one that passed in a southerly direction across the broad disc of the orator's face. So Joe (as an old fellow in the crowd familiarly called him) tried 'some other remedy.' He was more successful in his next effort, which was to show that there were three branches of the state government—the executive, legislative and judicial—and also in what followed, where he proved that the Governor had procured money to keep the government going, and to provide for the soldiers. No sooner had he shown this than he was encouraged by shouts, 'That was right,' and 'Three cheers for Governor Morton,' who courteously rose and requested that his friends would keep silence. . . . Alluding to Morton's assertion that he had bolted from his party but adhered to his principles, McDonald called him, ironically, a fixed star. And Morton answered: 'I will not call *him* a star; he is a *moon*, rather. In his first quarter he was an abolitionist; in his second he was merely a Douglas Democrat; in his third a Breckinridge Democrat, and in his fourth quarter we behold him surrounded by a beautiful "Golden Circle." He may not belong to the order, but those who do are his friends and supporters.'"

Democratic criticism is less graphic. McDonald's closing speeches, it was said, were a series of sledge-hammer blows upon his opponent, who ought, perhaps, to be addressed as Lieutenant-Governor. The Irishman's definition of "left-tenant" was one who had left off being a tenant and lived in a house of his own. This definition suited Morton's case. He had left off being a tenant of the people and owned the state himself.

At one meeting (says a Republican commentator) an Irish Democrat was talking with a friend near the outskirts of the crowd. The Governor said: "I have borrowed a great deal of money for the purpose of carrying on the state government, which they charge I have done without law and against the constitution." And Patrick said, "Indade you have— without law and against the constitution." But as Morton went on to vindicate his course and show the necessity which drove him to it, the Irishman turned to his friend and said: "Jim, wouldn't the striped mackerels up at Michigan City[1] have been let out, if the old Governor hadn't broken the constitution?"

On the way to Lawrenceburg, Morton and McDonald were riding on the same train. They went together into the forward car to smoke. The train leaped from the track and rolled down an embankment. There was no way out except

---

[1] One of the state penitentaries is at this place.

through the windows, which were now on top. Morton crawled out followed by McDonald.

In the debate at Lawrenceburg there were several sharp encounters. McDonald proposed, in respect to the secret societies which Morton had criticised, that they should both unite in an address to the people, warning them of the danger of such bodies and urging them to abandon all organizations, and to lay aside their arms. The Loyal League, he claimed, was an armed political organization and ought to be disbanded. Morton, in his reply, proceeded with great vigor to draw a comparison between the Sons of Liberty and the Loyal League. The Sons of Liberty, he said, was a treasonable, oath-bound organization of the most dangerous character. If the Grand Commander issued an order for assassination, the member to whom that order was given was bound to execute it. If he commanded revolution, every member was bound to obey. It was an organization inimical to the government, recognizing the right of secession, and revolutionary in its purposes. The Loyal League was not secret. It was pledged to sustain the Union, the constitution and the old flag. It had been dragged in by McDonald to excuse and defend the Sons of Liberty. In some of the border counties the League might have provided itself with arms, but they were for use against the enemy, not against their neighbors, and God helping him, he would never consent to place the Loyal League on an equal footing with McDonald's treasonable order. At this declaration the Union men in the audience leaped to their feet and cheered for several minutes. There had been no such excitement since the opening of the canvass. Morton now spoke of the seizure of arms belonging to the Sons of Liberty within the past few days at Indianapolis. They were worth seventy-five thousand dollars. Where had the money come from? Not from Indiana. It had been provided by the rebels. Mr. McDonald was not a member of the order, but members had nominated him for Governor.

There were cries from the audience, "Name them," and Morton said, "I will. There is Joseph Ristine, candidate for Auditor of State on the ticket with Mr. McDonald, he is a member. There is Oscar B. Hord, candidate for Attorney-General, and James S. Athon, candidate for Secretary of State. One-half the ticket are members of this treasonable organization."

Morton added that if his friend wished to escape responsibility, he must dissolve his relationship with members of this order. Even if McDonald's proposition were accepted it would accomplish nothing. McDonald was not in command of the order. Vallandigham commanded it. If McDonald would say that it was under his control that would put a different form on the proposition.

Morton determined, if possible, to provoke his competitor into some definite declaration in regard to the war, so he propounded, in writing, the following question: "If an armistice were granted and negotiations were pending, and the rebel states should say that they would not return to the Union nor make peace except upon the condition of the recognition of their independence, would you then be in favor of resuming the war, or of making peace upon terms granting their independence?"

At this meeting the tide of enthusiasm had set in so strongly in favor of Morton that nothing could be done to stem it. McDonald's reply was short and spiritless. He could with difficulty command attention. He did not then attempt an answer to Morton's question. Lawrenceburg was the county seat of a Democratic county. It was a place of McDonald's own choosing. He had the opening and close of the debate, but he was unable to stay the tide of patriotic feeling that swept over the audience.

Up to this time the Democrats had had no national platform and no Presidential candidates. They could attack the administration at their pleasure, but were themselves not yet exposed to hostile criticism. Throughout the country there was great depression among the Republicans, although, thanks to Morton's vigorous campaign, there was less of it in Indiana than elsewhere. Grant's battles in the Wilderness, at Spottsylvania and at Cold Harbor had thus far led to no result, and the loss of life among his troops had been frightful. The raid into Maryland and Pennsylvania, and Mr. Greeley's peace negotiations at Niagara, had added to the discontent. Henry Winter Davis and Benjamin Wade had attacked the President in the New York *Tribune*. The supporters of the administration were lukewarm. Lincoln himself despaired of re-election. He said: "We have no adversary and seem to have no friends."

But there were great weaknesses in the opposition. The war Democrats and the peace Democrats could not agree. The former were led by the delegation from New York which insisted upon McClellan as the candidate. The peace Democrats were led by Vallandigham, who had returned from Canada. Mr. Lincoln knew of the conspiracy of which he was the chief, but with wise forbearance did nothing to hinder him from coming to take part in the Democratic convention. This body met at Chicago on the 24th of August. Governor Seymour was made chairman. Vallandigham was a member of the Committee on Resolutions and wrote the celebrated clause in the platform declaring that after four years of failure to restore the Union by war, immediate efforts should be made for the cessation of hostilities, with a view to a convention of the states or other peaceable means to the end that peace might be restored on the basis of the Federal Union. The war Democrats were so intent on nominating McClellan that they consented to the platform, and this clause was unanimously adopted. McClellan was nominated, and Pendleton, an extreme peace man, was chosen candidate for Vice-President.

Scarcely had the convention adjourned when Atlanta surrendered, and a public thanksgiving for this event was the answer of the administration to the demand for peace.

After the Chicago convention the joint debates between Morton and McDonald naturally turned upon the Democratic platform and candidates. Morton called attention to the fact that Dean Richmond had ineffectually offered a resolution in the convention favoring the resumption of war if peaceable means failed to restore the Union, and he again asked McDonald, whether, upon the refusal of the rebels to return, he would favor the resumption of the war, or the recognition of the independence of the South. Vallandigham, said Morton, had declared, in a speech at Dayton, that the platform meant an abandonment of the war. As he had written it, he ought to understand it. As McDonald had voted for it, he ought to know what it meant. As to McClellan, what was he? He owed his position to Lincoln. Lincoln had made him, and he was the poorest job Father Abraham had ever turned out. The army of the Potomac had won victories in spite of McClellan's blunders, and yet this military failure had been put forward for the Presidency, as a war man. Pendleton had opposed the war. These men were on a peace platform. The action of the Chicago convention was a piece of double dealing with the people. There was nothing about the ticket or the platform which (in the words of Judge Taney) "a white man was bound to respect."[1]

---

[1] After McClellan had accepted the nomination, Morton in another speech declared: "My competitor stands with one foot on the platform and the other on McClellan's letter. One-half of him is on the war footing and the other half on the peace establishment. Now, I have seen a man riding two horses in a circus, but both horses were running in the same direction. If the horses ran in different directions he could not stay on long without an indefinite extension of his legs."

[2] The progress and result of these joint debates was well summarized in the following extract from the Wabash *Express*, written a few days after the November election: . . . .

"With a majority of ten thousand against him two years ago, he comes out of this contest with more than twenty thousand majority over his

McDonald replied that if, after proper overtures of peace, the South would not come back into the Union, he would favor the resumption of coercive measures.

But it was now too late to strengthen by concessions the palpable weaknesses of the platform and candidates of the Chicago convention, and at the close of these remarkable discussions it was evident to all who could be influenced by argument that Morton had overcome his competitor. [2]

A great number of the voters of Indiana had gone to the war. The constitution of the state provided that these men must cast their ballots in the precincts in which they respectively resided, and no law could be passed, as in other states, allowing them to vote in the field. The political views of the Indiana soldiers were, no doubt, the same as those of the soldiers from other Northern states; that is, they were Republican by a very large majority. The Democrats, however, contended that most of these men were of their own faith, and in order to outbid their adversaries for the soldiers' vote the Democratic candidates requested Morton and the other Republican candidates to unite with them in applying for furloughs for all legal voters.

Morton answered: ''Your proposition meets with my hearty approval and concurrence. As early as April last I made application to the authorities at Washington, substantially in the form proposed by you, to permit our soldiers to come home and vote at the ensuing election. On my late visit to Washington I renewed the application. The influence of your names in connection with my own and those connected with me on the Union state ticket (who, I am advised, fully concur in the propriety of your suggestions), in

---

competitor. No other man could have achieved more—who could have accomplished so much? This great change in popular opinion is owing more to the masterly manner with which he handled the thrilling issues of the day, than to anything else. Wherever he spoke, a flood of brilliant light followed him which could be plainly seen by the unwilling.''

an effort to secure to the brave men from Indiana, who are now serving in the armies of the republic, the privilege of returning to their homes to cast their votes in accordance with our constitution and laws, is especially gratifying to me, and, with your permission, I propose to forward to the Secretary of War a copy of your communication, with a copy of this reply, to the end that definite arrangements may be made.''

As Morton stated, he had been to Washington twice to make application for the return of all Indiana soldiers possible, in order that they might vote at the election. Stanton willingly co-operated with him, and on one occasion they went together to see the President. A gentleman who was present at this interview declares that Morton expressed his belief that the votes of these soldiers were necessary to save the state to the Republicans, and that if Indiana went Democratic, she would be withdrawn from the column of loyal states and would no longer furnish any substantial aid to the government. But Lincoln answered: '' It is better that we should both be beaten than that the forces in front of the enemy should be weakened and perhaps defeated on account of the absence of these men.'' Morton, as a last resource, suggested that all the troops who were unfit for service should be sent home and not be kept in hospitals out of the state. To this suggestion Lincoln assented.

There was another peril which confronted the Republicans. A draft had been ordered for the latter part of September. The Indiana election was to be held on the 11th of October. The draft of 1862 had been the cause of much bitter feeling, which it was believed would be renewed and increased if another conscription were to take place in such a crisis as the present. Morton had asked Lincoln to suspend the draft until after the election, but the President had refused. The Governor determined to make another effort, and in connection with the Republican members of Congress from Indiana, and with other persons, he addressed to the Secretary of War, for transmission to the President, the following letter:

"To Hon. Edwin M. Stanton, Secretary of War:

"SIR—Assembled from the different parts of Indiana, and practically familiar with the influences now at work in each congressional district of the state, we express it as our profound conviction that upon the issue of the election that occurs within a month from this date may depend the question as to whether the secession element shall be effectually crushed or whether it shall acquire strength enough, we do not say to take the state out of the Union, but practically to sever her from the general government, so far as future military aid is concerned.

"We further express the gravest doubts as to whether it will be possible for us to secure success at the polls on the 11th of October unless we can receive aid—

"1. By delay of the draft until the election has passed.

"2. By the return, before election day, of fifteen thousand Indiana soldiers.

"As to the draft, we propose an informal delay only, of which no public notice need be given. Reason sufficient will suggest itself in the time necessary to adjust the local quotas of townships, towns and cities, without the careful settlement of which, great dissatisfaction, even among the loyal, can not be avoided.

"Volunteering is going on rapidly at this moment, and we have no hesitation in expressing the confident opinion that if the draft be delayed, and fifteen thousand Indiana troops be ordered home before the election, with suitable arrangements for recruiting, Indiana's entire quota can and will be filled by volunteering within two weeks after election day. She is at this time ahead, after filling former quotas, fully fifteen thousand three years' men.

"Thus the government will obtain the recruits it has demanded about as soon as by pressing compulsory measures at once, and it will secure itself against the possible loss of the power and influence of the state for years to come.

"If the draft is enforced before the election there may be required half as many men to enforce it as we ask to secure the election. Difficulty may reasonably be anticipated in from twenty to twenty-five counties. If the draft goes on immediately after the election, the soldiers will be on the spot to secure its being carried into effect, should that be necessary. But we are confident that if our propositions are adopted no draft will be needed at all.

"The case of Indiana is peculiar. She has, probably, a larger proportion of inhabitants of Southern birth or parentage—many of them, of course, with Southern proclivities—than any other free state, and she is one of the few states in which soldiers are disfranchised.

"It is not on the score of Indiana's past deserts that we ask this assistance. All such considerations must give way before the public good. We ask it because the burden of this political contest is heavier than we can bear. Nor have we asked it before exhausting every effort which loyal men can make for their country. We ask it for that country's sake. We ask it, because we feel absolutely assured that in this way more readily and more speedily than in any other can the general government accomplish the object it proposes.

"If it were possible that you could see and hear what we, in the last month, each in his own section of country, have seen and heard, no word from us would be needed. You would need no argument to prove that a crisis, full of danger to the entire Northwest, is at hand.

"We do not expect any general commanding, engrossed with vast military operations, to realize this. And therefore, while of course we do not urge any withdrawal of troops that would imperil the situation in Georgia or elsewhere, we suggest that a mere request to General Sherman, or other commander, to send home, or not send home, the troops in question, as he might think best, unaccompanied by an expression of the urgent desire of the government in the premises, and a view of the vast interests at stake, would be of no avail. No commander willingly diminishes his command. To what extent it may be prudent or proper to make the order imperative, we, not having the entire situation before us, can not judge. We hope you will see, in our most precarious condition, cause sufficient to do so.

"The result of the state election, whether favorable or unfavorable to the government, will carry with it, beyond a doubt, that of the Presidential vote of Indiana.

"All which is respectfully submitted,

"O. P. MORTON.

"E. DUMONT, 6th District.

"GODLOVE S. ORTH, 8th District.

"C. M. ALLEN, 1st District.

"THOMAS N. STILLWELL, 11th District.

"RALPH HILL, 3d District.

"JOHN H. FARQUHAR, 4th District.

"JAMES G. JONES, A. A. P. Marshal-General.

"W. W. CURRY, 2d District.

"J. H. DEFREES, 10th District.

"S. COLFAX, 9th District.

"JOHN L. MANSFIELD, Maj.-Gen. Ind. Legion.

"JAMES PARK, Capt. P. Mar. 8th District Ind.

"CHARLES A. RAY, Judge 12th District.

"A. H. CONNER, Postmaster, Indianapolis, Ind.

"J. T. WRIGHT, Ch. St. Cent. Com.

"INDIANAPOLIS, September 12, 1864."

As the result of these different efforts Lincoln wrote to General Sherman as follows: "Anything that you can safely do to let these soldiers, or any part of them, go home to vote

24—MOR.

at the state election will be greatly in point.   They need not remain for the Presidential election, but may return to you at once.   .   .   .   This is in no sense an order, but is merely intended to impress you with the importance, to the army itself, of your doing all you safely can, yourself being the judge of what you can safely do. ''

Many Indiana soldiers came home, though the bulk of them remained at the front.   The draft was not postponed, but it created less dissatisfaction than had been feared.

The election resulted in a majority of twenty thousand for the Republicans, Morton running ahead of his ticket in nearly every county.   Indiana had been saved to the Union cause.

On October 14 a meeting of congratulation was held at Indianapolis by the Republicans, and Morton spoke.   He had the satisfaction of knowing, he said, that in all the counties where he had met McDonald in joint debate and had had a chance of defending his administration before the people, the Republicans had made large gains.   The election had dealt the rebels a staggering blow.   Their hope had been, not in the defeat of our armies, but in carrying the elections in the North.   And where had they had greater hope of success than in Indiana?   They had expected to win.   They had depended upon cold arithmetical calculations, and had not comprehended some of the factors which had brought about the result.   They had not understood the sympathy between the soldiers and the soldiers' friends.   He had experienced this in the joint discussion.   While McDonald had been regarded merely as the representative of a party, Morton had met with a friendship from the fathers, brothers, sisters and mothers of soldiers in which there was heart and soul.   The most melancholy fact was that the Democratic candidates who had been proved to belong to the secret military organizations lately exposed had been allowed to remain on the ticket.   But it was for the good of the Union party that these candidates had remained.   They had weighed down the ticket like lead.

The Democrats attributed the result of the election to quite a different cause, and their state central committee issued a proclamation announcing the most stupendous frauds. "At almost every point," they said, "where voters could be transported, the lines of railroad might be traced by the increase of the Republican vote."

The Republicans retorted by proofs of fraud in Democratic counties. It is, of course, impossible at this time to determine how much truth there was in these charges and counter-charges. There were certainly illegal votes cast, but not enough to have changed the result. Morton was undoubtedly the choice of the people.

So far as Indiana was concerned, the result of the election in October settled the matter of the Presidential election in November. Morton felt so secure that he found time to go to other states to aid the Republicans. He visited New York, New Jersey and Pennsylvania, speaking in many places at the solicitation of the Republican National Committee. On the 26th of October he delivered an address at the Cooper Institute, in which he considered the fatal consequences which would follow the policy recommended in the peace resolution of the Chicago convention.

In the November election the October states increased their Republican majorities. McClellan received but twenty-one electoral votes (from New Jersey, Delaware and Kentucky), two hundred and two being cast for Lincoln. The last substantial hope of the Confederacy had failed.

CHAPTER XXVII

KNIGHTS OF THE GOLDEN CIRCLE

THOUGHOUT the foregoing narrative allusions have been made to the secret societies in Indiana, especially the Knights of the Golden Circle and the Sons of Liberty. It is now time to retrace our steps to the beginning of these organizations and follow their history down to the period of their overthrow.

The absurdities of knight-errantry, as laid bare in the pages of Don Quixote, were no fitter subjects for satire than the manufactured solemnities of these latter-day knights, their mystic conclaves and absurd ritual, their midnight initiations in the woods of Martin county, the "Storming of Fort Dodd," the warlike Sunday-school literature for the conversion of Hoosiers and the proposed establishment of a Northwestern Confederacy under the leadership of men who had neither the ability to organize nor the courage to fight. But their conspiracy to overthrow the government was planned at a time when our national existence hovered between life and death, when a formidable foe hung upon the borders of the state and invaded its soil. It was a time when a straw could turn the balance, and that which, at other periods, would have been only a subject for scornful jest, became dangerous, and demanded additional energy from those who had already expended the strength of Hercules in the effort to subdue an armed rebellion. It was fortunate that there was at this time at the head of affairs in Indiana a man whose resources were equal to every emergency, whose autocratic

(373)

will supplied everything that was lacking in a disloyal legislature and a partisan judiciary, a man who could hold as a plaything in his hands a conspiracy that aimed at his own life, and could even coerce it into his service. No one can read the history of the secret organizations in Indiana and not feel that, wide-spread as they were, there was not an instant in which they were not securely within the grasp of the "War Governor."

In the narrative of these organizations his name does not often appear. It was ostensibly by others that they were exposed and overthrown, but many of the secret agents employed were his emissaries, and those who have examined the reports made to him at each step in the plot can understand how completely these organizations were under his control, how he played with them as a cat with a mouse, how he even permitted them to grow and develop that he might fasten conviction more securely upon them and overthrow them utterly when the time should be ripe for their destruction.

The history of the conspiracies in Indiana has never been better told than in the words of Morton himself in the United States Senate on May 4, 1876:

"The state was honeycombed with secret societies, formerly known as the Knights of the Golden Circle, but later as Sons of Liberty. They claimed in 1864 to have forty thousand members in the state, were lawless, defiant, plotting treason against the United States, and the overthrow of the state government. In some counties their operations were so formidable as to require the militia to be kept on a war footing, and throughout 1863, and until the final explosion of the organization in August, 1864, they kept the whole state in uproar and alarm. So bold were their demonstrations in the summer of 1863 that General John Morgan, of Kentucky, was induced to invade the state with his forces, in the belief that there would be a general uprising in his support.

In 1864 so numerous were these treasonable organizations, and so confident were they of their strength, that they matured a plan for a general uprising in the city of Indianapolis, on the 16th of August, under cover of a mass meeting of the Democratic party, attended by members of these organizations from all parts of the state. The plan, as shown by the subsequent confessions of some of the leading conspirators, was to release on that day about seven thousand rebel prisoners confined at Camp Morton, to seize the arsenal and arm these prisoners, overturn the state government, and take possession of the state. This plan was discovered some three weeks before the time fixed, and was abandoned by the leading conspirators, and orders were issued countermanding the march of their forces upon Indianapolis. Subsequently, the seizure of arms and ammunition collected at Indianapolis for treasonable purposes, and of the records and rituals of the Sons of Liberty, as well as the arrest of eight of the ringleaders, had the effect of breaking up and destroying the power of the organization. I regret to state that in the list of the principal members of the organization were found three of the state officers into whose hands the legislature of 1863 had attempted to place the whole military power of the state. On the trial of these ringleaders before a military tribunal, appointed by the President under the act of Congress, some of them turned state's evidence and disclosed the full character and extent of the conspiracy. Four of them were convicted and sentenced to death. One of them was pardoned outright by President Johnson, and two others, Bowles and Milligan, had their punishment commuted to imprisonment for life, but were afterwards released by a decision of the Supreme Court of the United States, to the effect that a military commission had no jurisdiction to try them."

With this for the text let us develop somewhat more in detail the history of these secret political societies.

The first was called the "Knights of the Golden Circle."

It had been organized in the South before the war, and had members in Indiana at the outbreak of the struggle. Another society existed for a short time called the "Circle of the Mighty Host." We hear of some of its lodges as early as 1861. Then followed the "Mutual Protection Society" and the "Knights of the White Camelia," and in 1863 the "Circle of Honor." Then came the more extensive "Order of American Knights," which had an armed organization throughout Indiana, Ohio, Kentucky, Illinois and Missouri. The ritual of this last order was made public, and the society was then merged into the "Sons of Liberty," an organization larger and more definitely insurrectionary than its predecessors.

How did these associations begin? It is said that in 1855, one Charles C. Bickley, a native of Boone county, Indiana, living in the South, who ardently espoused the cause of slavery, endeavored to bring to a more perfect state of organization the "Southern Rights" clubs, which existed in various parts of the slave states. After a constitution, by-laws and ritual had been formed, he christened the new order "The Knights of the Golden Circle," and he subsequently became its commander-in-chief. The several divisions were called "castles." There were subordinate castles and state castles, the latter being represented by delegates in the "Grand American Legion," from which body emanated the "Articles of War" governing the order. Military drill was required. The organization was at first intended to foster filibustering schemes. Its constitution set forth the annexation of Cuba, Mexico and Nicaragua as among its objects. A slave-holding empire around the Gulf of Mexico, which should become to the New World what the Roman Empire had been to the Old, was the dream of these adventurers. They were outspoken in favor of a Southern Confederacy. The order was insignificant in point of numbers. Even its existence was not generally known, but some of the wealthiest men of the South belonged to it. In 1858 the Knights became more thoroughly organized. The "Castle" was divided into the "Outer and Inner Temples," and new members were admitted only after a probation sufficient to determine whether they could be trusted. The association now began to acquire great antiquity. Regalia were provided. A close helmet surmounted by a crescent set with fifteen stars represented the growing Confederacy. A skull and crossbones threatened death to abolitionists. There was a temple to the "Sunny South," with the image of the noon-day sun beneath the dome.

Castles sprang up in the border states, and Northern men with Southern feelings knocked at the doors. Some citizens of New Albany desired to establish a castle, but the Knights at that time thought that as their order was exclusively a Southern one, it would be better not to extend it into Indiana. There were now three degrees, military, financial, and governmental. In the first, the candidates were told that the field of their operations was to be in Mexico, and that it was proposed to raise a force of sixteen thousand men to take the field under the command of Manuel Doblado, Governor of Guanajuato, with whom they had made a treaty on February 11, 1860. The members of this degree were called "Knights of the Iron Hand."

In the financial degree, composed of "Knights of the True Faith," it was declared that the headquarters were to be at Monterey, where stores and munitions were deposited.

Into the third degree, the "Knights of the Columbian Star," none were admitted unless born in a slave state, or if in a free state, the applicant for admission must be a Protestant and a slaveholder. The object was to organize a government for Mexico. No Knight must admit that he was a member of this degree except to a brother. Among the obligations was this: "I will do all I can to make a slave state of Mexico, and as such I will urge its annexation to the United States; otherwise, I will oppose it with equal zeal.

All civil places of prominence shall be given to the Knights of the Columbian Star, and when these are supplied, to the Knights of the True Faith, and then to the Knights of the Iron Hand. . . .'' A plan for the conquest of Mexico was revealed in the instructions to neophytes, and the Knights were to cross the Rio Grande by the first of October, 1861.

But before that time the advocates of the extension of slavery were busy about other things, and the original purpose of the order was lost sight of in the conflict between the North and South. The Knights took an active part in the Presidential campaign of 1860. They used their influence in favor of the rupture in the Democratic party which led to the separate nomination of Breckinridge. At this time there were a number of Northern politicians in the order, and the Knights were anxious to find out how many Northern men sympathized with the South. They believed that the vote for Breckinridge would show this, and that many of those who supported him could be counted upon as soldiers for the Southern army. A letter from Madison, Indiana, to Jefferson Castle in Kentucky, promised a thousand men who would fight Northern aggression to the death. One from Evansville promised that Vanderburg county would be good for a regiment. A letter from Washington, Indiana, said that there were thirty thousand men who would never compromise with Black Republicanism, and it was thought probable that the whole of Indiana south of the National Road would unite its fortunes with the South. The organization now rapidly extended. Members were sent in all directions to establish new castles. These were organized everywhere—in court-rooms, stores and barns. Preliminary degrees were instituted to try the soundness of the opinions of the neophytes, who then entered the outer temple, where they were received according to a ritual adopted in October, 1860. But the agents sent into the free states to establish castles found the time unfavorable and their mission dangerous. The order had to confine its efforts to the South. The ritual was by no means uniform; it was modified to suit the demands of the locality. In the border states, the initiatory steps were more gradual than in the extreme South. Members in the North were to act as spies, and were to raise companies of militia for the Confederate service. This effort was not successful. Still there were a number of castles, with about five hundred members, in Southern Indiana and Illinois, as shown by the list in Jefferson Castle, Kentucky. At the outbreak of the war, when the news came that Sumter had been fired upon, and the North was one blaze of patriotism, there were several centers of disaffection in Indiana, where sentiments favorable to the South were freely spoken. Prominent among these were Orange and Washington counties, in the southern part of the state; rough, hilly regions, where civilization was half a century behindhand—neighborhoods where the roads were almost impassable, where even to-day the traveler hears stories of outrages by local banditti, who find their refuge in caves and hidden places in the forests—uncanny regions where streams lose themselves in subterranean recesses and wander for miles under the earth and where the waters of the springs, impregnated with sulphurous deposits, are said to restore health to the afflicted, but are certainly filled with noisome and unsavory ingredients for those who are whole. Among these regions the French Lick Springs have acquired much local celebrity. They are situated at a place which, at that time, was distant from railroad communications—a wild and inhospitable neighborhood. Here lived Dr. W. A. Bowles, a man of some wealth, who had served as an officer in the Mexican war, and had acquired an unenviable reputation in connection with the retreat of the Indiana troops at Buena Vista. He was a member of the Knights of the Golden Circle. His house was a rendezvous for those who sympathized with secession. He had married a Southern wife. She was in Louisiana just after the fall of Sumter, and he

wrote to her of his fears that the Douglas wing of the Democratic party would go with the Black Republicans. "If so,"
he said, "our fate is sealed. Kentucky will go out, but too
late to help us in this state. If Kentucky had gone out at
the proper time, Southern Indiana would have been with her
to-day, if not the whole state." On May 3, 1861, he wrote
again: "If things do not change very soon we will have
fighting here in our midst, for many persons, whom I supposed to be true to the South, have been silenced and are
afraid to open their mouths in favor of Southern rights.
Ayer, Charles Dill and many others have come out for the
North, and call all traitors who do not espouse the cause of
the North. God knows what I am to do. If I leave and
join the Southern army, my property will all be confiscated,
and besides that my health is such that I fear I could render
no service; but I have already sent some who will do service,
and I expect to send more." Later he became discouraged
about Kentucky, and wrote: "Louisville is in a perfect tumult. The abolition party is very strong, and I think the
worst consequences are in store for Kentucky under her policy of armed neutrality, which is a humbug. It is reported
that a battle has been fought at Fortress Monroe and that six
hundred abolitionists were killed and fifty on the Southern
side, but I fear it is too good to be true. When the fighting
commences I think I shall go South." But Bowles did not
go South. Either restrained by fear of the confiscation of
his property, or believing he could be more useful if he
remained in Indiana, he became one of the leading spirits in
the subsequent conspiracies.

As the war went on and the armies of the North suffered
defeat, these centers of Southern sympathy became more numerous, and the voices of the disaffected bolder and louder.
The Knights of the Golden Circle now spread their organization over many parts of Indiana, and the project of a union
of the Northwestern states (which had been obscurely

suggested in Hendricks' speech at the Democratic convention in January, 1862) was warmly advocated by the members of the order.[1]

In May, 1862, the Grand Jury of the United States District Court at Indianapolis reported that the Knights numbered some fifteen thousand; that lodges were instituted in various parts of Indiana and that among the signals was one invented for members drafted into the army, whereby the soldiers on the other side were reminded of their obligation not to injure the person giving the signals. The report further stated that the members had bound themselves to resist the payment of Federal taxes and to prevent enlistments, and that it was observed that in neighborhoods where the organization existed there had been a failure to furnish volunteers.

Some members of this grand jury, having learned the signals of the order, went to Camp Morton, at Indianapolis, where they found that these signals were recognized by the Confederate prisoners. The report of the jury was afterwards bitterly denounced by the peace Democrats as having been made in violation of their oath of secrecy, and it was said that members of the jury were making speeches over the state retailing what they had discovered. Subsequent developments showed that the facts reported had been rather understated than exaggerated. This report, published August 4, 1862, excited much alarm.

About the first of December it was discovered that the Order of the "Golden Circle" had been introduced into the Federal camps at Indianapolis. This created much anxiety and vigorous measures were taken to eradicate the order from the army. The witness who first made known its existence in the camps disappeared and was never heard of again.

---

[1] These designs seem to have been understood in the South. The Richmond *Enquirer*, of February 16, published a telegraphic dispatch from Mobile headed, "Grand Programme for Forming a Northwestern Confederacy."

After the election of 1862 the Democratic majorities in both Houses of the General Assembly were bitterly hostile to the administration and to the further prosecution of the war.[1] An attempt was made by the Republicans in this legis-

[1] Resolutions passed in Democratic meetings and conventions favored many of the objects for which the Knights of the Golden Circle were contending.

On January 1, 1863, a meeting, in Carroll county, declared against the war and the Emancipation Proclamation. A meeting in Brown county resolved: "Our interests and inclinations demand of us a withdrawal from political association with the New England states. . . . We demand an immediate armistice, preparatory to a compromise of existing difficulties."

A meeting on January 23, in Martin county, resolved "We have given the last man and the last money we are willing to give for the prosecution of the present abolition war."

A meeting on the 24th, in Lawrence county, resolved against the prosecution of the war.

A meeting on the 25th in Starke county declared for a cessation of hostilities and a national convention.

A meeting in Scott county, on the following day, announced its opposition to the war.

A meeting on January 31, in De Kalb county, declared: "We will not give one cent, nor send one single soldier to the present contest, while it is conducted for its present unholy purpose."

A convention on the same day in Rush county declared: "We are unqualifiedly opposed to the further prosecution of this abolition war, and believing that in its continued prosecution there awaits us only the murderous sacrifice of legions of brave men, ignominious and certain defeat, shame and dishonor at home and abroad, public ruin and the serious endangerment of our liberties, we unhesitatingly declare that we are for peace, the cessation of hostilities, an armistice, and the settlement of existing difficulties by compromise, or negotiation through a national convention."

A meeting in Shelby county on February 5 demanded a cessation of hostilities and opposed the conscription act.

On February 7, at a meeting in Bartholomew county, an armistice was favored and conservative men were invited to co-operate to bring about a termination of the war.

On the 19th of February, a meeting in Jackson county declared its conviction that the Union could never be restored by war.

On February 21 it was resolved at a meeting in Putnam county that there should be a cessation of hostilities, and that not another soldier and

lature to investigate the secret political orders in the state, but after long discussions the resolutions of inquiry were laid upon the table by a party vote.

While the legislature was debating, the Governor received information that many of the Knights were armed, and were talking of war at home. Even before the General Assembly met a plot was reported to seize the arsenal. A project for the assassination of Morton was also conceived.[1] The Governor received letters warning him of this plot. One was written in a woman's hand. It contained a correct plan of Morton's house and of the room on the ground floor in which he slept. The writer declared that her husband had been led into the scheme by wicked men, who had held meetings at her house to accomplish their purpose. Upon the insistence of Mrs. Morton the Governor now changed his sleeping room.

The project of putting Morton out of the way was not un-

---

not another dollar ought to be furnished for the further prosecution of the war.

A meeting on February 23, in Clay county, recommended a cessation of hostilities until a national convention could be assembled.

A meeting on February 27, in Green county, opposed the further prosecution of the war, and the furnishing of another man, gun or dollar for such a hellish and unchristian crusade.

A meeting March 7, in Warren county, opposed the conscription act.

A meeting on March 20, in Wayne county, declared that the further prosecution of the war would result in the overthrow of the constitution, of civil liberty, and of the Federal government, and resolved in favor of an armistice and a national convention, predicting that if the administration went on with its arrests blood would flow.

It was resolved in a convention in Allen county, on August 3, that the proposed draft was the most damnable of the outrages perpetrated by the administration, and that the honor, dignity and safety of the people demanded that they should give to themselves that protection which usurpation and tyranny denied them.

[1] Wesley Trantor afterwards testified in the "treason trials" that in the early part of 1863 one Stone, a leader in the organization, said to him that a visit would soon be paid to Morton, and that the Governor had not much longer to live.

known in the South.   The "Atlanta Confederacy" of January
24 remarked that the accomplishment of this project was a
probable event.

These threats of an "irrepressible assassination," as it was
called, turned out to be something more than idle words.
The attempt was actually made.   Morton was often at work
in the state-house until late at night.   On one occasion he
left the building, as usual, by the Market street entrance,
where there was a pathway running north, and then two or
three steps descending to a gate.   He had just gone down
the steps when a shot was fired at him from a wooden outhouse at the northwest corner of the state-house yard.   The
ball whistled close to his head.   He went to the Bates House
and aroused General Carrington, but did not speak of the
matter at home for fear of alarming his wife.   On the following day he told Sulgrove of the occurrence, but charged him
neither to publish nor mention it.   No clew was ever found
to the man guilty of this cowardly act.

In various parts of the state the lodges of the secret orders
did their best to embarrass the government by resisting the
draft, shooting enrolling officers, and preventing the arrest of
deserters.

About the time of the adjournment of the General Assembly some Indiana soldiers had been sent to Illinois to capture
deserters.   The latter had been assured that the Knights of
the Golden Circle would not permit them to be taken.   Judge
Constable, of Clark county, in that state, ordered the arrest
of the soldiers as kidnapers and released the deserters.   When
Morton heard of this he was furious.   He said to Carrington
"I want protection for these soldiers.   I want you to use the
utmost power of the government to rescue them and to punish
those who have prosecuted them."   Carrington went with a
small body of troops and surrounded the court-house where
the trial for kidnaping was in progress.   The proceedings
were stopped and Judge Constable was himself seized and

brought to Indianapolis, where he was held for some time, but finally discharged.

On the 26th of March, Morton, by telegram from Washington, informed Carrington that large shipments of arms to Indiana were being made from New York for insurrectionary purposes. Carrington at once issued a military order prohibiting the importation of weapons for secret organizations and restricting the sale of arms.

The legislature having refused to investigate the doings of the Knights of the Golden Circle, Governor Morton determined to make the investigation himself. It made no difference to him whether he was authorized by statute or not. Treason was lurking in the state, and he intended to drag it to the light. On April 18, Louis Prosser, a Democratic representative in the legislature and a leader of the Knights in Brown county, killed a soldier and was himself mortally wounded by Captain Cunning, a volunteer officer. Morton appointed a commission to inquire into the affair. Union men testified to a state of anarchy in Brown county. Their neighbors, they said, had been driven from home by threats of Southern sympathizers; houses had been fired into and one had been burned to the ground; the lives of Republicans had been threatened, soldiers had been shot, and bands of armed men had been seen drilling and passing through the country. The agency of the Knights in these proceedings was clearly shown.

All through the state, wherever disloyal feeling existed it was naturally attributed to this secret order. Thus, when, on May 2, 1863, one hundred men galloped through the town of Centreville, shouting for Jeff Davis, and a telegram was sent to Morton that armed "Butternuts" were parading the streets, public rumor at once connected this with the Knights of the Golden Circle. General Hascall sent a detachment of soldiers from Indianapolis, and sixteen men were

25—MOR.

arrested. A number of the leaders were compelled to mount a platform used for a pump in front of the court-house and take an oath of allegiance and loyalty, wholly unknown to the statutes, which was prepared and administered by Lewis D. Stubbs, justice of the peace, who had come over for the purpose from Richmond.

In some parts of the state the Knights of the Golden Circle did not immediately assume that name. We find organizations with other names, created for the same purpose and with a similar ritual. One of these was called "The Circle of the Mighty Host."

The disaffection inspired by these orders reached an absurd culmination in the battle of Pogue's Run, already described, when large numbers of men who came armed to Indianapolis with the intention of exciting an insurrection were deprived of their weapons by a handful of soldiers. It was largely due to the encouragement which these orders had offered that General John Morgan invaded the state in July, 1863. Morgan did not, however, meet with the assistance he expected. The Knights were silenced, and the whole state was soon in arms to resist him.

CHAPTER XXVIII

ORDER OF AMERICAN KNIGHTS AND SONS OF LIBERTY.

THE disturbances created by the Knights of the Golden Circle early in the war were of little account by the side of the widespread conspiracy set on foot by the later associations, the first of which was called the "Order of American Knights," while the last was known as the "Sons of Liberty." The Knights of the Golden Circle accomplished little, but the members of their "castles" were afterwards brought together in these later and more formidable bodies, and the "Golden Circle" ceased to exist in the fall of 1863.

The first grand council of the "Order of American Knights" in Indiana was organized by one P. C. Wright, editor of the New York *News*. There were meetings as early as August, 1863. In September Harrison Dodd was elected grand commander and William M. Harrison secretary. A "military bill" for the government of the order was prepared, and the state was divided into four districts, each under command of a "major-general." These appointed "brigadiers" and the "brigadiers" appointed "colonels."

Harrison Dodd was a man of romantic disposition, fond of mystery. He had been an active member of the Know-nothing party, and one of the chiefs of the "Sons of Malta," whose initiations, conducted by him, are described by surviving members as "most impressive."

The ritual of the order of American Knights was turgid and rhetorical, and gave play to Mr. Dodd's peculiar talents. There were three degrees, each with a separate initiation.

(387)

In the vestibule, or lowest degree, the Warden of the Outer Court gives the signal of the neophyte's approach. Thereupon the Knight Lecturer demands—"Who cometh? Who cometh? Who cometh?" And the Warden of the Outer Court answers: "A man. We found him in the dark ways of the sons of folly, bound in chains, and well-nigh crushed to death beneath the iron heel of the oppressor. We have brought him hither, and would fain clothe him in the white robes of virtue, and place his feet in the straight and narrow path which leads to truth and wisdom."

The Knight Lecturer then addresses the candidate as follows:

"Man, thou art now in the vestibule, and if found worthy, will hence be ushered into the consecrated temple, where Truth dwells amid her votaries. Let thy soul be duly conscious of her presence, and go forth in exalted desire for her divine influence."

Then follow long colloquies written in the same strain and equally meaningless. But a little political instruction is imparted in the following words:

"The government designated 'the United States of America,' which shall blazon the historic page, and shed its light along the path of future ages, was the transcendent conception and mighty achievement of wisdom, enlightened patriotism, and virtue, which appear to have passed from earth amidst the fading glories of the golden era, which they illustrated with immortal splendor. That government was created originally by thirteen free, sovereign and independent states, for their mutual benefit, to administer the affairs of their common interests and concerns; being endowed with the powers, dignity and supremacy (and no further nor other) which are distinctly specified, warranted and conferred by the strict letter of the immortal compact, 'The Constitution of the United States.'"

Sponsors—"Amen."

"Man, under the influence of sublime truth, and the inspiration of the Divine Presence, which thou didst invoke on thy approach to this altar, how wilt thou respond to the declarations, which thou hast just heard? Answer to thy conscience 'ay' or 'no,' for so it will be recorded. Amen "

Answer—"Ay."

"Listen to the words of thy sponsors."

Sponsors—"I would advance onward and upward, even to the temple where Truth dwells serenely. I would fain worship at her shrine through all of life to me on earth."

Friend—"Sayest thou so?"

Answer—"Ay."

"So be it! Thou shalt advance."

"Thy sponsors will deliver thee to the Warden of the Temple, who will conduct thee to the Most Ancient of Sages, who will instruct thee in wisdom, and will give unto thee a new name," etc., etc.

The instructions to the candidate for the second degree contain an edifying homily upon the subject of slavery. In the third degree of the order this is further amplified as follows:

"In the divine economy, no individual of the human race must be permitted to encumber the earth, to mar its aspects of transcendent beauty, nor to impede the progress of the physical or intellectual man, neither in himself nor in the race to which he belongs. Hence, a people upon whatever plane they may be found in the ascending scale of humanity, whom neither the divinity within them, nor the inspirations of divine and beautiful nature around them, can impel to virtuous action, and progress onward and upward, should be subjected to a just and humane servitude, a strict tutelage to the superior and energetic development until they shall be able to appreciate the benefits and advantages of civilization. . . .

"The Caucasian or white race exhibits the most perfect and complete development of humanity. Hence, the noblest efforts of that race should be directed to the holy and sublime work of subduing, civilizing, refining and elevating the wild and savage races wheresoever found, nor should those efforts cease until the broad earth shall bloom again like Eden, and the people thereof shall be fitted to hail the dawning light of that millennium which the inspiration of that Divinity within us has pictured to our hopes, and whose transcendent glories are even now glowing upon the vision of calm, serene, undoubting faith.''

The following is included in the obligation of the third degree: ''I do further solemnly promise and swear, that I will ever cherish the sublime lessons which the sacred emblems of our order suggest, and will, so far as in me lies, impart those lessons to the people of the earth, where the mystic acorn falls from its parent bough, in whose visible firmament Orion, Arcturus and the Pleiades ride in their cold resplendent glories, and where the Southern Cross dazzles the eye of degraded humanity with its coruscations of golden light, fit emblem of Truth, while it invites our sacred order to consecrate her temples in the four corners of the earth, where moral darkness reigns and despotism holds sway. . . . Divine essence! so help me that I fail not in my troth, lest I shall be summoned before the tribunal of the order, adjudged and condemned to certain and shameful death, while my name shall be recorded on the rolls of infamy. Amen.''

One of the most important pass-words of the order was Nu-oh-lac, or the name of Calhoun spelled backward. This was employed upon entering a temple of the first degree. There were signals of danger, pass-words, ciphers, badges and all the insignia and paraphernalia of foolish mysticism which attract the superstitious and uncultured mind.

This order, like its predecessor, the ''Knights of the Golden Circle,'' encouraged desertions, harbored and protected deserters, discouraged enlistments, resisted the draft, circulated publications in favor of the South, gave intelligence to the Confederates, furnished arms and aided recruiting for the

South, destroyed government and private property, and co-operated with the enemy in raids and invasions. It also contemplated the establishment of a Northwestern Confederacy.

At the state council of the order, held in Indianapolis in November, 1863, Dr. Athon, Secretary of State; Mr. Ristine, Auditor of State, as well as Lambdin P. Milligan, Dr. Bowles and J. J. Bingham, editor of the *Sentinel*, were present, together with delegations from some thirty counties. At the meeting held on February 16, 1864 Horace Heffren was elected deputy grand commander.

But the secrets of the "Order of American Knights," like those of its predecessors, the "Knights of the Golden Circle," were revealed to government officials by detectives and renegades,[1] and it was found necessary to reorganize the associa-

---

[1] One hundred and twelve copies of the ritual of the order were captured in Terre Haute early in August, 1864, in a room which had been occupied as a law office by D. W. Voorhees, then a member of Congress. Mr. Voorhees denied that the office belonged to him at the time of the capture. He said, in a speech delivered on August 6, that he had had no office for more than a year, and that he had never seen a copy of the ritual till he saw it printed in the Indianapolis *Journal*. He asserted that he had no knowledge of the character of the documents seized, and he demanded of General Carrington, by whom the seizure was made, a retraction of the charge that these papers had been found in his office. To this General Carrington, on August 16, 1864, published an answer containing the following:

" The gentlemen who found 'these papers' told me that they were found in your office.

" The following are some of the circumstances that led me to think they were correct in the supposition: Your law library and office furniture were in the office where 'these papers' were found. You had declined a renomination for Congress, and the office was reported as not for rent, as late as April, 1864. The ritual had been issued in the autumn of 1863.

" Your congressional documents were in the office where 'these papers' were found. Your speeches, up to March, of your entire congressional career were in the office where 'these papers' were found.

" The correspondence of Senator Wall, of New Jersey, under his frank, enclosing a proposition to furnish you with twenty thousand stands of Garfield rifles, just imported, for which he could vouch, was in the office where 'these papers' were found.

" The correspondence of C. L. Vallandigham, from Windsor, C. W., as-tion with new ritual, signs and pass-words. Thus began the order of the "Sons of Liberty."

---

suring you that 'our people will fight,' and that 'all is ready,' and fixing a point on the Lima road at which 'to meet you,' was in the office where 'these papers' were found.

"The correspondence of Joseph Ristine, Auditor of State, declaring that 'he would like to see all Democrats united in a bold resistance to all attempts to keep ourselves a united people by force of steel,' and that 'this was a war against the Democracy, and our only hope was the successful resistance of the South,' was in the office where 'these papers' were found.

"The correspondence of E. C. Hibben, who assured you that 'the Democracy is fast stiffening up and when this war is to be openly declared as being waged for the purpose of freeing the negro, this will arouse another section of the country to arms,' and declaring 'that Lincoln bayonets are shouldered for cold-blooded murder,' was in the office where 'these papers' were found.

"The correspondence of J. Hardesty, who 'wants you to have those one hundred thousand men ready, as we don't know how soon we will need them,' was in the office where 'these papers' were found.

"The correspondence of J. J. Bingham, who asks you 'if you think the South has resources enough to keep the Union forces at bay,' and says 'you must have sources of information which he has not,' was in the office where 'these papers' were found.

"The correspondence of John G. Davis, informing you that the managers of a certain New York journal 'are wonderfully exercised about secret anti-war movements, and tremble in their boots in view of the terrible reaction which is sure to await them,' was in the office where 'these papers' were found.

"The correspondence of W. S. Walker, who 'keeps out of the way because they are trying to arrest him for operating in secret societies,' enclosing the oath of the K. G. C. prior to that of the O. A. K., was in the office where 'these papers' were found.

"The petition to C. L. Vallandigham, D. W. Voorhees and Benjamin Wood, in favor of two republics and a united South, was in the office where 'these papers' were found.

"The correspondence of Campbell, who says the 'Democracy were once not afraid to lay their purposes out to daylight, but that now it is deemed best to work in secret,' and asking your counsel, was in the office where 'these papers' were found. . . ."

On the 26th of August Voorhees replied:

"I was nearly a thousand miles away, a political enemy had possession of my desks and drawers, and all you had to do was to apply the burglar's art, prepare false keys and pick my locks and you at once had access to my

This last and most important of the secret political societies during the war was organized in the early part of 1864, and at a grand council in New York on the 22d of February of that year, Vallandigham was elected supreme commander. The political principles of the Sons of Liberty were more definitely stated than those of the earlier fraternities. They are thus set forth in the ritual:

"The government designated 'the United States of America' has no sovereignty, because that is an attribute belonging to the people in their respective state organizations, and with which they have not endowed that government as their common agent. It was, by the terms of the compact, constituted by the states, through the expressed will of the people thereof severally, such common agent to use and exercise certain specified and limited powers. . . . .

"Whenever the officials to whom the people have intrusted the powers of the government shall refuse to administer it in strict accordance with the constitution, and shall assume and exercise power or authority not delegated, it is the inherent right and imperative duty of the people to resist such officials, and if need be, to expel them by force of arms. Such resistance is not revolution, but is solely the assertion of a right.

"It is incompatible with the history and nature of our system of government that the Federal authority should coerce, by arms, a sovereign state, and all intimations of such power or right were expressly withheld in the constitution, which conferred upon the Federal government all its authority. . . .

private, confidential correspondence embracing a period of seven years. I have every reason to believe that you read it all, letter by letter. You took your time, and like the furtive, thieving magpie, narrowly inspected each line and word to find, if possible, some expression of opinion which your servile political creed holds to be disloyal. . . . ."

To this, on the 29th, Carrington answered:

"*Yet they were in that office where the ritual was found.* Grave offense! As well might a thief find fault that the stolen goods were found in his possession. As well might the burglar complain that the instruments of his craft were abstracted from his den. . . . ."

"In a convention of delegates elected by the people of a state is recognized the impersonation of the sovereignty of the state. The declaration of such a convention upon the subject-matter for which it was assembled is the ultimate expression of sovereignty. Such convention may refer its action back to its constituents, or the people may reverse the action of one convention by the voice of another. Thus sovereignty resides in the people of each state, and speaks alone through their conventions."

Those who are familiar with the theories and formulæ of the secessionists will recognize in these declarations the doctrines set forth by Calhoun and followed by Jefferson Davis and the other leaders of the Confederacy.

In other places the ritual was only a little less bombastic and puerile than that of the Order of American Knights. It is thus described by a contemporary commentator:

"Among the rubbish we find schedules of their first degrees, their second degrees, their third degrees, their oaths, obligations, invocations—a strange medley of blasphemy and innocence, past credulity. Who, for instance, can imagine that a man of reasonable sense, consenting to initiation into the Order of the Sons of Liberty, would stand up after the mysterious three raps at the subterranean wicket and hear his sponsor, in answer to the sepulchral, 'Who cometh? Who cometh? Who cometh?' gravely respond, 'A citizen we found in the hands of the sons of despotism, bound and well-nigh crushed to death beneath their oppression. We have brought him hither, and would now restore him to the blessings of liberty and law.' How many of the thousands in Indiana who have, by the official report, gone through this mummery, ever imagined they were in the hands of the 'sons of despotism' until some impudent demagogue informed them of the alarming fact? Not one, we venture to affirm, of all who have gone through this miserable form, standing in the 'vestibule of the temple,' the right hand under the left arm, the left arm under the right, the fore-fingers over and the thumb hidden under the right arm, or with his 'hands crossed on his bowels, representing the belt of Orion.' . . . We do not propose to follow the initiated through all this drivel.

"Allowance must be made, of course, for the assorted lot of ninny-hammers and ignorant zanies, to be found in all communities, whose heads are emptier than an idiot's skull, and should be bored for simples. These fellows are excellent material to work up into under-ground dark-lantern conspirators. But we can not be persuaded that the sensible, intelligent men of the country—and they are yet in the majority, we hope—can be persuaded into any such subterranean scheming. The open way is the best and most honorable. It is the way in which free men will travel. Therefore, we believe the apprehension aroused by the recent disclosures is in a great degree groundless. So far as known, the men whose names figure conspicuously as the leaders of this Confederate, Democratic carbonari are politicians who needed but this exposure to put the final blow to their political influence, and consign them to the graves that have gaped these many years for their carcasses.''

While the order of the "Sons of Liberty" was a mere continuation of the "Order of American Knights," the colloquies, lessons and obligations were somewhat changed, and members of the old order were not admitted unless they were considered reliable. Those who joined the new organization, however, were not required to take new obligations. The order spread widely. It had an extensive membership in Ohio, Kentucky, Indiana, Illinois and Missouri. New York, Pennsylvania, Delaware and Maryland were also represented. During the spring of 1864 it began to work more actively. It was claimed by Vallandigham that in the summer of that year its membership in Indiana was not less than forty thousand. The figures given by Harrison, the Grand Secretary for Indiana, were, however, not nearly so large. In February, reports for seventeen counties showed five thousand members; in September, reports for forty-five counties showed eighteen thousand.

Heffren was Deputy Grand Commander of Indiana and Harrison was Grand Secretary. Judge Bullitt, of the Kentucky Court of Appeals, was Grand Commander of that state, and Felix Stidger (a United States detective) was elected Grand Secretary. There were two organizations, one within the other. One was a civil organization, to which the mass of the members belonged, the object of which was to insure the success of the Democratic party. The other was military, and had for its object the separation of Ohio, Indiana, Illinois, Wisconsin and Kentucky from the Eastern states to make a Northwestern Confederacy, and, failing in this, to join their fortunes with those of the South.

Many of the members did not belong to this second organization, but the leaders of the movement belonged to both. Active steps were taken to organize the military department in Indiana. Bowles, Milligan, Humphreys and Walker were "Major-Generals" commanding the four districts into which Indiana was divided. The efforts of the organization to procure arms were unremitting, and were rewarded with considerable success. As early as March, 1864, it was estimated that there were in the possession of the order in Indiana six thousand muskets and sixty thousand revolvers, besides private weapons. Considerable sums of money were subscribed by members for the purchase of arms. At a single lodge meeting the sum of four thousand dollars was subscribed. These arms were sent from the East to Indianapolis, and then distributed to the different counties. The boxes in which they were enclosed were marked " pick-axes," " hardware," "nails," "household goods," etc. A cipher was used to designate the kind and number of arms in the hands of the different lodges. If a member subscribed for the Cincinnati

Enquirer, it meant that he had a revolver; if for the Chicago *Times*, that he had a shot-gun; if for the Louisville *Democrat*, that he had a rifle.[1] General Carrington estimated that in February and March, 1864, nearly thirty thousand guns and revolvers entered the state. This estimate was based upon the actual inspection of invoices. At a later period a much larger quantity of arms and ammunition was imported. Some of the military schemes of the order were fantastic enough. Dr. Bowles proposed companies of lancers, armed with a hook "to punch with," and a sickle "to cut the horses' bridles with," so that the enemy, when they had no way of holding their horses, "would be easily mashed up." Among the devices of the order was the so-called "Greek fire," invented by R. C. Bocking, of Cincinnati. There were hand-grenades and machines with clockwork for setting boats and government buildings on fire. The Greek fire could be so prepared that it would ignite after three or four hours, and "nothing could put it out." It was said that certain government stores and two boats were burned at Louisville by this "Greek fire."

The military department of the "Sons of Liberty" was to be controlled by a secret committee of thirteen, appointed by the grand commander. The names of the members of this committee were to be known only to him. At a meeting on June 14 a plan of organization was reported, and it was recommended that the order should equip as rapidly as possible. The question arose as to how they were to be armed Some proposed to raise the means by taxation among the members; others by subscriptions, and others preferred that the members should arm themselves. They finally came to the masterly conclusion that each sub-district should arm as

---

[1] Arms were also marked in columns headed corn, beans, etc., meaning shot-guns, pistols, etc., respectively.

best it could.[1] Bowles claimed that he had his command organized and divided into regiments and companies, except in one district, and that they were drilling at "such snatched times as they could get."

These regiments, however, did not appear when the hour came for action.

---

[1] This was before they received two hundred thousand dollars from the Confederate emissaries in Canada.

CHAPTER XXIX

THE NORTHWESTERN CONSPIRACY

THE most important project of the Sons of Liberty was a conspiracy for an armed uprising throughout Ohio, Indiana, Illinois and Missouri, in which the Confederate prisoners in Cincinnati, Indianapolis, Chicago, Rock Island, Springfield and elsewhere were to be released, the state governments of Indiana and Illinois overthrown and provisional governments established with the ultimate purpose of organizing a Northwestern Confederacy. This purpose was not known to all the members of the order. It was confided only to those who took part in the military organization.

A mere reading of the testimony given at the "Treason Trials," in which this plot is detailed by detectives and by various members of the Sons of Liberty, gives a very inadequate impression of its character. The absurdities of the ritual and of many of the military schemes would lead to the belief that the conspiracy could not be as extensive as it really was. The light is thrown on in flashes, giving glimpses of small fragments of the organization. A little company meets at "The Pinnacle," a vacant house in the woods. Some men go down a railroad track and find ammunition, which they hide in a barn and cover with threshed oats. Some ignorant members say that they were sworn into the service of Jeff Davis. We hear of bands drilling once or twice a month in groves and woods. A witness tells us of a lodge organized "in Isaac Decker's barn." Another speaks of a meeting "in the kitchen at Oxenriders." Hundreds of pages are filled with testimony of this description. The full scope of the plot is best seen by looking into the Confederate authorities. The most important of these are the report made to Jefferson Davis by Jacob Thompson, one of the Confederate commissioners in Canada, and the articles written for the *Southern Bivouac* by Captain Thomas H. Hines, who was appointed to aid the commissioners, and who describes the negotiations between the Confederates and the Sons of Liberty, as well as the development and final issue of the conspiracy.

In the spring of 1864 the outlook for the South was dark and discouraging. Vicksburg had fallen. The states west of the Mississippi had been severed from the main body of the Confederacy, and Tennessee had been abandoned. Lee had recoiled from Gettysburg, the armies of Grant were closing around Richmond, and the resources of the South were becoming exhausted. The only hope seemed to be in an uprising in the North, which would release the Confederate prisoners, turn back the Federal forces for the protection of their own territory, and recruit the armies of the Confederacy in the border states.

The disaffection in the North was well known to the authorities at Richmond, and the time seemed ripe for stirring up an insurrection.[1]

Jefferson Davis accordingly appointed Jacob Thompson, C. C. Clay and J. P. Holcombe commissioners to visit Canada and negotiate for peace "upon the basis of Southern independence." But peace was not the only thing they were to seek, and Captain Hines, who had escaped with Morgan from the Ohio penitentiary, was detailed to collect such Confederate soldiers as were willing to re-enter the service, and, with their assistance, to release the prisoners confined at different places in the North. The Confederate

---

[1] It is curious to observe how accurate was Morton's knowledge as shown by his speeches of the condition of the South and of the reliance of the Confederates upon the peace party in the North.

government left to his judgment the means for effecting "any fair and appropriate enterprise of war," consistent with British neutrality.

At the time of Captain Hines' appointment (March 16), Holcombe was in Canada, and the other commissioners, Thompson and Clay, left Richmond on the 3d of May to join him. The instructions to Thompson were that, if he failed in his efforts for peace, he should adopt measures calculated to cripple the Federal government, by destroying stores, and hindering the forwarding of supplies. A large sum of money was provided for the use of the commissioners.

Upon his arrival in Montreal, on the 30th day of May, Thompson endeavored to induce influential newspapers to urge a cessation of hostilities, but the press was unfriendly to the project, and little could be done.

Then followed the negotiations with Horace Greeley. On the 9th of June Hines was sent to confer with Vallandigham at Windsor, and on the 11th Thompson himself met Vallandigham. They discussed the disaffection in the North, and the organization of the Sons of Liberty. Vallandigham represented that the order was three hundred thousand strong. The members, he said, desired that the war should cease; that the Federal army should be withdrawn from the South and that measures should be adopted to bring about an early peace.

Some of the leaders, he said, desired to establish a Northwestern Confederacy, but this wish was by no means universal. Thompson encouraged the idea, and urged it strongly upon those "who seemed most sensible to the stimulus of personal ambition." Vallandigham stated that he intended to go to Ohio at an early day, and thought that he would be again arrested, and that this would lead to an outbreak. The forbearance of Lincoln doomed him to disappointment.

The 20th of July was the day first fixed upon for an up-

26—Mor.

rising in Illinois and Indiana, in which the state officers were to be deposed and provisional governments organized. Councils of the Sons of Liberty were held at various places to prepare for this movement.

But as the day for the uprising drew near, the leaders of the order found that they were far from ready. Sixteen delegates met at Chicago. Dodd, Bowles and Walker from Indiana, Bullitt from Kentucky, Barrett from Missouri, and other prominent members attended the meeting. There was some difference of opinion as to whether the order should act at once or wait until Confederate forces were sent into Kentucky. A committee from this conference met the Confederate commissioners on July 22 at St. Catherines, and the time for the uprising was then fixed for the 16th of August. This uprising was to be general in Ohio, Illinois, Indiana and Missouri, and as far as possible in Kentucky. The Confederate commissioners and officers were intrusted with the secrets of the order, and asked to give all needful information to the South. Thompson had strong hopes of success, and distributed some half a million of dollars to procure arms and ammunition for the order. Dodd and Walker received the money for Indiana. It was estimated that one hundred thousand dollars was given to each.[1] Ohio was to be cared for by Vallandigham. In Indiana Dodd was to give his orders to the "Major-Generals" of the several districts. These were to send "runners" into the counties, and the counties were to notify the townships. The forces in southern Indiana were

---

[1] It would appear from the correspondence of Commissioner Clay with John C. Walker, Agent of State, that the latter had already used public funds for the purchase of arms. He said that he had bought arms to the value of seventy-five thousand dollars, and begged Clay to send the money promised. He added: "It has been very difficult for me to arrange with the fund in my office to prevent trouble. I shall expect you to send me a draft to Indianapolis. . . . This I wish you to send immediately to square my account. My reputation is involved in this, and I trust that you gentlemen in whom I have confidence will not leave me to suffer."

to meet under Bowles, near New Albany; those in Illinois at Rock Island, Springfield and Chicago, from which places they were to march on St. Louis; the forces in central Indiana were to be concentrated at Indianapolis. The capture of the state capital was left to Dodd, who proposed to call a political meeting at some place of resort for Sabbath-school picnics, east of Camp Morton, to which the members of the order were to come in wagons, with arms secreted in the straw. Some one was to propose that they should drill without arms, so that each man would know where his place was. Upon a given signal the men were to seize their arms and march on Camp Morton. The fences and buildings were to be fired, the released prisoners were to join in the uprising, and the Federal soldiers who guarded them were to be surrounded and overcome. The prisoners were then to be armed and the guards were to be held as prisoners. A detail was then to be sent to seize the Governor and the arsenal. The railroad to Jeffersonville was to be captured, and the released prisoners were to be sent to New Albany and Louisville. Morton was to be held as a hostage, and Dr. Athon, Secretary of State, was to be installed as Governor. If Morton could not be captured he was to be otherwise "taken care of," and a committee of ten was selected to make way with him.

Early in August Dodd communicated this plan to his friends. He suggested that Bingham, as chairman of the Democratic State Committee, should call a mass meeting at Indianapolis on the 16th of that month. But revelations of the conspiracy had just been published, members of the order had been arrested, success seemed doubtful, the enterprise was dangerous and Bingham refused to call the meeting.[1]

---

[1] Prior to this time Bingham had denied the existence of any conspiracy in the columns of the *Sentinel*, and in answer to an exposure in the *Journal* he had published a satirical "Exposé of the Loyal Legion, a

The matter had also come to the knowledge of McDonald, who said the thing must be stopped, and Michael C. Kerr,[1] a Democratic Congressman (afterwards Speaker of the House of Representatives), came up from New Albany and said, "The devil is to pay in our section. The people have caught the idea that a revolution is impending. Farmers are selling their hay in the field, and their wheat in the stacks." Kerr also related to Bingham the scheme for the uprising, and said that Dr. Athon was involved in it. Athon was visited by Bingham and Kerr, but he pretended to know nothing of the matter.

A meeting of prominent Democrats was held in McDonald's office. Kerr said he had come up on purpose to stop this revolutionary scheme; that if it could not be stopped in any other way the authorities should be informed of it. Walker and Dodd were present and insisted that "the government could not be restored without a forcible revolution," but before the conference broke up all agreed that the uprising should go no further, although the authorities were not to be informed of it. This was, however, quite unnecessary.

---

secret dog-fennel Republican organization, whose head is Abraham Lincoln, and in Indiana one O. P. Morton."

Judge Bullitt, grand commander for Kentucky, had been intrusted with large sums of money by Jacob Thompson to aid the uprising in that state. On arriving at Louisville he was arrested, and a large amount of gold together with drafts upon banks in Montreal were taken from him. This arrest was made as the result of a conference held on the 30th of July by General Burbridge, Colonel Farleigh and Governor Morton. With Bullitt, some twenty-four others were arrested, among them Dr. Kalfus, who had formerly commanded the Fifteenth Kentucky Regiment, and had been dismissed for disloyalty. The chief of the fire department of Louisville was also arrested. A fire in that city in which government property had been destroyed was attributed to him. Members of the order in Missouri were also arrested shortly after this, and Green B Smith, the grand secretary for the state, was examined in August, and made a partial statement of the conspiracy.

[1] Kerr had been initiated into the order by Heffren in a harness shop at New Albany.

"The authorities" knew all about it. Morton and Carrington had long been upon the track of these secret enemies, and an elaborate detective system had been established.[1]

A number of men had been appointed to attend each of the meetings of the conspirators. None of these men had been informed of the employment of any of the rest, and each was expected to report on the doings of the others, as well as on the conduct of the *bona fide* members of the order. The reports were made at different places. There were several offices at Indianapolis to which Morton was accustomed to go to receive the statements of his detectives. This secret service was fraught with no little danger. On one occasion a young man employed by Morton visited a meeting held at a house in Indianapolis, and was never seen again. The inference was strong that he had been killed, though the proof was not sufficient to justify a prosecution.[2]

---

[1] For more than two years Morton's correspondence bristled with letters and dispatches like the following to Joseph Speed, July 19, 1862: "I wish you would send me a detective immediately, I want him to smoke out a nest of traitors—Knights of the Golden Circle."

[2] One of the most skillful among the agents employed to ferret out the doings of these secret orders was a man named Coffin, who had been a client of Morton's in Wayne county, a man of loose character, but full of courage and cunning. He had been employed for a long time and had furnished accurate reports of the doings of the Knights of the Golden Circle and the Order of American Knights. He was not suspected until the early part of June, 1864. A conference of the conspirators was then held at Louisville, in Dr. Kalfus' office, at which it was decided to have Coffin put out of the way. Felix Stidger took a message from this conference to Dr. Bowles to the effect that Bowles ought to be the man to do this work, as it had been he who had brought Coffin into the order. Bowles answered that he would put men on Coffin's track, but that he did not consider him dangerous.

Stidger himself was a detective. He had sent word to Coffin of the intention to murder him, and had communicated the matter to Morton and Carrington, to whom he also gave the ritual, constitution and cipher of the order, all which had been confided to him by Dodd.

At the conference of the state council of the Sons of Liberty, on June 14, at Indianapolis, Coffin's case was discussed, and it was decided that he

So complete was this system of espionage that Morton and Carrington often knew the most important plans of the order

---

must be killed. On the following day there was to be a meeting at Dayton, Ohio, to be addressed by Vallandigham. It was thought that Coffin would be present, and Dodd asked what members would volunteer to go with him and put Coffin out of the way. Most of the members did not know Coffin. McBride, of Evansville, knew him, but was so situated just then that he could not go upon this errand. Bowles and Dodd went, but Coffin was not to be found. Afterwards Ristine, Auditor of State, showed Stidger a letter from Richard Bright, warning the order against Coffin. At Ristine's request Stidger remained at the Auditor's office all day in order that Ristine's son might point Coffin out, so that Stidger could make way with him.

Stidger was the most valuable of all the government detectives. He was a Kentuckian who had been sent to Carrington about the beginning of May. He was instructed in the vestibule degree of the order by another detective on the 5th of that month. On the 9th of May he visited Dr. Bowles, at French Lick Springs, and Bowles talked with him freely in regard to the secrets of the order, without testing him to ascertain whether he was a member. He had two interviews with Heffren at Salem. He was instructed in the third degree by Secretary Harrison in June, and displayed such zeal for the work that he was elected grand secretary for Kentucky under Judge Bullitt.

Another important detective was Dr. Henry M. Zumro, who had joined the association at the suggestion of Colonel Slack, "who had talked with Morton about it." Zumro was doubted by some of the members, and for the purpose of disarming suspicion, Carrington ordered his arrest and examination on the charge of conspiracy and disloyal practices; but the proof failing, he was soon discharged. This restored him to confidence.

The same course was pursued with Edmund Klamroth. At one time the members lost faith in him and threatened to hang him for betraying them. Carrington now had him arrested, put in irons and tried by a court-martial. This rehabilitated him in the order, and several members testified in his behalf.

When General Morgan invaded Kentucky by the way of Pound Gap, in 1864, the first information of the fact was sent to the Sons of Liberty. But the dispatches were given to messengers who were in the service of the government. The messages were steamed, opened and transcribed, and copies were delivered to Morton before the originals were sent to their destination. The correspondence on both sides was thus examined in several other cases before it was delivered to the parties interested.

One of the delegates to a Chicago conference, who went with a proxy from Deputy Commander Heffren, fell into the hands of a detective, who secured the proxy and attended the conference in his stead.

before they were communicated to the members who were expected to take part in their execution.

Reports of the proceedings at the night meetings of the conspirators were often in Morton's hand on the morning of the following day. On one occasion the Governor was visited at the state-house by an old acquaintance, a judge of one of the courts of Indianapolis, who had repeatedly assured him that no such an association as the Sons of Liberty existed. He now said: "I am sure if there were such an organization I should know something about it. No one would insult me by asking me to belong to it, but I could not help knowing that it existed." Morton opened a drawer of his desk, took out a file of papers and proceeded to read a stenographic report of a meeting of the order held the evening before, at which a speech had been delivered by his visitor, in which the Governor was bitterly denounced. The old man sank into a chair and became as pale as death. He finally raised his arm above his head, as if to shelter himself from the words to which he was listening, and, without a word, he tottered, rather than walked, out of the room.

When it was agreed by Dodd and Walker, in the conference at McDonald's office, that the uprising should be stopped, these men had no intention of giving up their project. A short postponement was all that they meant to concede. On the 11th of August some Confederate officers were at the Bates House in Indianapolis, on their way to Chicago to take charge of the prisoners who were to be released by an uprising in that city. Walker had a conference with these officers, which he reported to Bingham. On the 13th of August the Democratic State Committee, of which Bingham was chairman, in an address to which reference has been made, urged the citizens of Indiana to arm and organize. It was said that this address was the result of a compromise between the leaders of the Sons of Liberty and those who opposed the uprising, and that the intention of the conspirators was to bring on the insurrection at another time and place.[1] So the Confederate commissioners in Canada were now informed that the uprising would take place at Chicago on the 29th of August, when the Democratic convention would meet in that city.

It was found hard to buy arms in any great quantity without being caught. Money was given by Thompson to "reliable men" in different places to be spent for this purpose in such a way as not to attract attention but much of this money was wasted. Some of the agents, like Judge Bullitt, were arrested with the funds in their hands. Others diverted these funds from the purpose intended, and applied them to other things, to getting substitutes for drafted men, and sometimes to supplying their own personal wants.

Even in the cases where the arms were bought they were sometimes seized by the authorities. This was done at Indianapolis. About the 20th of August Governor Morton received the following letter from a lady in New York, dated the 17th of that month:

"SIR—The facts here stated have come to my knowledge in a manner and from a source such as to leave no doubt, in my mind, of their reliability. The Copperheads of Indiana have ordered and paid for thirty thousand revolvers and forty-two boxes of fixed ammunition, to be distributed among the antagonists of our government, for the purpose of controlling the Presidential election. On August 5 the steamer Granite State landed in New York forty-two boxes of revolvers and ammunition; on August 6, the steamer City of Hartford landed twenty-two boxes of ammunition, destined for Indianapolis. Thirty-two boxes of the above have been forwarded to J. J. Parsons, Indianapolis, via Merchants' Dispatch, and marked 'Sunday-school Books.' The balance is stored at

---

[1] The address of the Indiana State Committee, urging Democrats to arm and organize, was perhaps intended as a cover to furnish reason for the distribution of arms which were to be used, not at the election in Indiana, but at the uprising in Chicago.

No. —— ——— St., New York, waiting for the Copperheads
to pay for the same before shipping.''

Morton placed this information in the hands of the police
authorities. The railroad station was visited, but nothing
was found. A drayman was intercepted, however, driving
back to the station. He stated that he had brought some
''Sunday-school books'' to the printing office of H. H. Dodd
& Company. A detail of soldiers was sent to this office and
found thirty-two boxes, containing four hundred navy revolvers and one hundred and thirty-five thousand rounds of ammunition. They also seized, at the same place, the great
seal of the Sons of Liberty, the official list of the members,
several hundred copies of the ritual, and Dodd's private correspondence, including some compromising letters from
Bright, Walker, Develin, Vallandigham, Wright and others.
The facts concerning this capture, together with the correspondence found, were published. There was great excitement at the discovery.[1]

The public indignation led to a mass meeting in the Circle,
on Monday evening, August 22. Speeches were made and
vigorous resolutions passed denouncing the conspirators.
Morton was called for, and said that for eighteen months past
the people had been told repeatedly that immense quantities
of arms and ammunition had been coming into Indiana to be
used in resisting state and Federal authority; but because
there had been no visible evidence of these things, no deep
impression had been made upon the popular mind. The
same thing was still going on in other portions of the state.

---

[1] The *Sentinel* attempted to make light of the matter. The people had
a right, it said, to bear arms in their own defense. This seizure was a
"tempest in a teapot." The revolvers were doubtless shipped by detectives in the employ of Morton, Carrington and Company to compromise
the Democratic party. "The last time we saw Mr. Dodd," continued the
Sentinel, "it was in affiliation with his Excellency. They took each other
cordially by the hand. They sat side by side, and who can say they are
not equally guilty?"

A central committee, claiming to represent the Democratic party, had come forward in a public address and had called upon the Democrats of the state to organize an army. This was the beginning of civil war, rebellion and bloodshed. The time was a solemn one.

Morton regretted that so much had been said about Mr. Dodd. There were more wicked men in Indianapolis than he; men who were using him for their own advantage; men who held up their hands in horror at the bare mention of any participation on their part in the doings of the Sons of Liberty. Yet these men had knowingly affiliated with the members of that order; had gone into secret caucus; and had stood side by side with them in the most intimate political relations, and such men could not say that they were not equally guilty.

Morton next discussed the secret political correspondence which had been seized. "Look," he said, "at some of these letters. As an example, take one written by the present Auditor of State, a candidate before the people for re-election. The letter was written three years ago, before the inauguration of Mr. Lincoln's anti-slavery policy, which these men now assert to be the great source of dissatisfaction. What does he say to his friend, Mr. Voorhees? 'Our salvation is in the success of the Southern arms. If they are crushed then woe betide us.' What think you, my fellow-citizens, of that, coming from the Auditor of this State? . . . And let me say to you that the sentiments of Mr. Ristine are the sentiments of the men with whom he has associated himself in a political capacity.

"My fellow-citizens, it is time for us to consider where we are standing, and it is time for us to act. . . . . If you would secure your homes, your wealth, your business from the torch and the robber, you must take time by the forelock.

"The question has been asked me this evening what money it is that has been expended in the purchase of these arms and munitions of war, and where it came from? In answer to that question I must say that I do not know. . . . . I believe, however, and am as confident of the fact as I am of any other fact of which I have not positive and indisputable evidence, that the money, with which these operations are carried on in Indiana, has been supplied by the rebellion, either directly by the Confederate authorities or by their authorized agents in New York. . . . . .

"It is all one thing to Jefferson Davis whether we fail by means of a defeat at the coming elections or by the overthrow of the Union arms in the field. If we elect a candidate for the Presidency, who is in favor of withdrawing our armies from the field, and recognizing the independence of the Southern Confederates, they will gain their object just as effectually as if they had annihilated the last Union army.

"Look at the composition of the Democratic state ticket, now before the people. Five men upon it are members of the Sons of Liberty, one-half of the whole ticket. This secret order, however, is but the nucleus. It does not embrace all the traitors, nor indeed the principal traitors. It probably embraces the greater part of the rank and file of those who are willing to go into this movement, but the men who expect to enjoy the fruits of this revolution, these it does not include. . . ."

Public opinion ran so high against the Sons of Liberty, that the candidates upon the state ticket, who belonged to the order, Ristine, Athon, Hord, Napoleon B. Taylor and William Henderson, saw that something must be done, and they published in the *Sentinel* a card in which they said (rather ambiguously), that they never had been members of any society of a *treasonable or disloyal* character, nor had they entertained any purpose to inaugurate any movement of a *treasonable or revolutionary* character against the Federal or state government, and they had no knowledge of the purchase or shipment of any arms or ammunition into the state.

In the meantime, Walker, Dodd's fellow-agent of the Confederate commissioners, with incredible presumption addressed from Chicago (to which city he had gone to prepare for the postponed "uprising"), a demand upon Governor Morton for the evangelical literature of which Dodd had been so unceremoniously deprived.[1]

Let us now return to the plots of the Confederate commissioners in Canada. In August the Federal garrison in Chicago was considerably increased, and many pretended to believe that the Democratic convention would be forcibly interfered with. This was thought a sufficient ground to justify the assembling of a large body of men to resist interference. The county commanders of the Sons of Liberty were to bring members to Chicago to attend the convention. Ample means of transportation had been furnished by the Confederate com-

---

[1] It is as follows:

"CHICAGO, August 25, 1864.
"*To His Excellency, O. P. Morton, Governor of Indiana:*

"SIR—A few days ago, I purchased, in the city of New York, a few hundred pistols, with accoutrements and ammunition, and shipped them to Indianapolis for the purpose of supplying the orders of friends in Indiana.

"I am now informed that on the 20th or 21st of this month, this property was seized by the military authorities at Indianapolis. No law was violated by the purchase or shipment of this property.

"The constitution of Indiana guarantees to the citizen the right to bear arms for the defense of himself and the state. The arms in question were intended and would have been used for this purpose only.

"In your Excellency's proclamation of the 16th inst., you promised to the people without distinction of party protection to their persons and property, and in their social and civil rights.

"Having the legal right to the custody of the property which has been forcibly and illegally taken from the possession of my consignee, I now call upon you, the chief executive officer of the state of which I am a citizen, to fulfill your promise to the people, obey the requirements of your oath of office, and see that the laws are faithfully executed.

"Hoping that you will feel it to be your duty to rebuke the attempt made to subordinate civil to military power, and in the protection of citizens to vindicate the honor and dignity of the state, I am,

"Respectfully yours, etc.,
"J. C. WALKER."

missioners. Sixty Confederate soldiers in Canada, under the command of Captains Hines and Castleman, had been selected to co-operate with the Sons of Liberty in releasing the Confederate prisoners at Camp Douglas. These soldiers were, many of them, men of great cunning and daring. On the 27th and 28th of August they went to Chicago, traveling in small parties and stopping in that city at places agreed upon beforehand. They believed that with any sort of co-operation on the part of the Sons of Liberty, during the excitement of the convention, they could successfully attack Camp Douglas, and that with its five thousand prisoners released and armed, and with seven thousand more from Springfield, in addition to the Sons of Liberty, a formidable force could be organized. Information had been conveyed to the prisoners of the intention to set them free. Chicago was thronged. The officers of the Sons of Liberty met Hines and Castleman at the Richmond House the night before the convention. About one hundred and fifty persons were present. But the men employed to bring the members of the order together had failed, and the courage necessary for the outbreak was wholly wanting. Even those who had come to Chicago were scattered everywhere over the city, and could not be brought together, organized or controlled. The conference was adjourned until the 29th, when even greater timidity and irresolution were apparent. When a count was taken of the number of members who could be relied upon, there were so few that the attempt was abandoned.

Hines and Castleman now proposed that the leaders of the order should furnish five hundred men to liberate the prisoners at Rock Island and to take possession of that town. Castleman was to command the expedition, capture a passenger train for Rock Island and cut the wires, in the hope of surprising the place. But the "major-generals," "brigadier-generals," "colonels," and other officers of the Sons of Liberty, had immediate business at home, and this project also collapsed.

Dodd, who had gone to Chicago, now returned to Indianapolis, and although he had been not only a chief conspirator but also one of the agents for the distribution of Jacob Thompson's money, he had the effrontery to publish in the *Sentinel*, on September 5, a card declaring that the conspiracies charged upon the Sons of Liberty had no existence, and asking the people to suspend judgment and not to be imposed upon by unfounded rumors and the machinations of malicious tricksters. "I shall shrink from no mob," he said, "and flee from no arbitrary arrest."

The secret "Committee of Thirteen," appointed by Dodd, of which Walker was the leading member, now issued an address. They had requested the editor of the *Sentinel* to publish it, but public indignation had, by this time, apparently overcome Bingham's courage, and he declined. The communication was in Walker's handwriting, and was afterwards printed and circulated in pamphlet form. Before it finally appeared, Dodd had been arrested and Walker soon made his way to a neighborhood of greater safety than that of Indianapolis. This curious tract thus sought to explain and justify the purposes of the "Sons of Liberty."

AN ADDRESS BY THE COMMITTEE OF THIRTEEN.

"*To Whom it May Concern:* . . . The sensational charge that the order of the Sons of Liberty is engaged in a conspiracy against the government, with a view to the establishment of a Northwestern Confederacy, is 'absolutely and wickedly false.' *Whatever may be the views and wishes of individuals, the object charged is not comprised in the purposes of the organization. A Northwestern Confederacy, it is true, is not an impossibility, but its establishment would be the effect rather than the object of an uprising of the people;*

an event which a continuance of the acts of tyranny of the party in power will certainly produce. . . . ."

The address went on to declare that the *immediate* purposes of the *Sons of Liberty* and the *Democratic party* were identical. It rehearsed at great length the grievances of the Democracy; peaceful citizens "dragged from their firesides and weeping families" and compelled to take strange oaths "dictated by lawless oppression"; Democrats hunted like wild beasts; a prominent citizen led through the streets of La Porte with a halter around his neck; the destruction of Democratic printing presses; the "wanton murder of the lamented Prosser"; the disturbance at the Democratic mass meeting of 1862;[1] the confinement of citizens in "bastiles"; the impossibility of a free ballot at Indianapolis with soldiers at the polls and "honest men" driven away; the unnecessary presence of Massachusetts and Pennsylvania troops in that city; the unlawful seizure of the arms and ammunition at Dodd's printing office, and the illegal arrest and imprisonment of Dodd himself, who was soon to be tried by court-martial.[2]

In conclusion the address declared that the people would resist these acts of tyranny:

"Many years ago the ancestors of our countrymen, who had not yet enjoyed the privileges of a constitutional government, protested against the personal wrongs inflicted by their sovereign from year to year, until at last, when peaceful measures failed of effect, they arose in their strength and wrung

---

[1] On the occasion of the "Battle of Pogue's Run."

[2] For months past, said the address, the Sons of Liberty had been closely followed by detectives. These detectives had been the victims of marvelous stories relating to 'plots and conspiracies' which had involved the 'capture' of the governor, and the 'crucifixion' of the great 'Letter Thief' of Indiana (General Carrington). Although the indulgence of these 'practical jokes' might have been unwise, they had been provoked by the espionage of the authorities, and generally had the desired effect of unsettling the nerves of those for whom they were designed. . . . ."

from an unwilling despot the Magna Charta of civil liberty—
the right of *habeas corpus* and of trial by jury. The descendants of those heroes in this new world, rebelled against the
mother country on a principle, and after seven years of war
established the independence of the American colonies, and
formed a government for a Federal Union, under a constitution which guaranteed to the people full protection in their
persons and property. The children of the men who established these free institutions—dear as life to all who appreciate civil liberty—have lived, in these degenerate days, to see
their constitutional and personal rights trampled under
foot by that ribald jester and canting hypocrite whom the
people, in an evil hour, intrusted with the management of
the affairs of the Federal government. They have submitted,
under protest, to the waste of their resources, to the desolation of their country, to the sacrifice of their sons in a fruitless
war, to the unlawful arrest and imprisonment of citizens, to
usurpation and despotism in all their forms. Through three
long years of bloodshed and anguish, while desolation has
swept across the land and the angel of death has lowered his
fatal wing upon every household, the people have waited, en-
during the gibes of the wretch who sits enthroned at Washington on the ruins of their liberties, hoping for the time to
arrive when, through the mode prescribed by the constitution,
they should restore peace and wise counsels to their distracted
country. They have waited, while the war has 'dragged its
slow length along' through seas of blood and years of grief,
until, as the time draws nigh for the fruition of their hopes,
they see, staring them in the face, that 'handwriting on the
wall,' which discloses the terrible fact that bullets may be required to restore the rights to which madmen, 'whom the
gods destroy,' seem determined to deny the efficacy of ballots. . . .

"If the men of these days, who have suffered wrong and
endured oppression, and waited, and hoped, are deprived, at

last, of peaceful means of redress, they will not be found less self-sacrificing, less courageous, less patriotic, less worthy of a name than their heroic ancestors   Let the emergency come —as seems predestined—and the people will rise in arms, Titanic in the majesty and strength of a just cause, moving forward like the ground swell of the earthquake, and the fanatics, the bigots and petty despots encountered will be swept away like rubbish before the Alpine avalanche.

"COMMITTEE OF THIRTEEN.

"September 8, 1864."

27—MOR.

CHAPTER XXX

THE TREASON TRIALS

WE must pass rapidly over the final scenes of the grotesque drama. In these the principal roles were played by the ministers of public justice, and the Sons of Liberty were most unwilling actors. The order had been exposed. The thing to be done now was to make an example of those who had taken the leading parts in its schemes of insurrection. General Carrington, who had collected the evidence against the accused, was in favor of trying them in one of the Federal courts, but Secretary Stanton and Governor Morton determined that more drastic measures were required. It was necessary to strike terror into the hearts of the conspirators and prevent a repetition of plots which, however awkwardly they might be managed, were a continual source of danger in the midst of the struggle for national existence. So it was determined to resort to a military commission. General Alvin P. Hovey took charge of the department of Indiana and on the 17th of September he instituted a tribunal for the trial of Harrison H. Dodd, who had just been arrested. The trial began on September 22. The defendant objected to the jurisdiction of the court, claiming to be a citizen not connected with the army, and not subject to military authority. Major Burnett, the judge-advocate, supported the jurisdiction of the tribunal by the President's proclamation of September, 1862, ordering insurgents and their abettors to be tried by courts-martial. The charge was that of conspiracy in organizing secret societies for the purpose of overthrowing the government, seizing the arsenal, releasing Confederate prisoners, co-operating with rebels, inciting insurrection and resisting the draft. Dodd was thunderstruck when he found that the principal witness against him was Felix Stidger, a man with whom he had been in close confidence, and he now learned for the first time that this man had been a detective employed by the government. Several witnesses had testified for the prosecution, when the case came to an abrupt termination. Dodd had asked General Hovey to be allowed to occupy a room in the third story of the post-office building instead of being confined in a military prison, and he was permitted to do so. About four o'clock in the morning of October 7, the prisoner, who had promised to "flee from no arbitrary arrest," escaped by means of a rope conveyed to him with the aid of a ball of twine which had been left by his friends. The street lamps were darkened and he slipped off unseen. He remained hidden for some time in Indianapolis, and finally made his way to Canada. This escape was effected a few days before the October election and the Republicans improved to the utmost the advantage which it afforded them. Not only Dodd himself, but the order which he represented and the Democratic party with which that order had been so closely connected were held up to the public gaze as objects of ridicule and contempt. In their subterranean councils, it was said, these men had ruminated the most ferocious plots, and in imagination had waded in blood. But when the evidence had been gathered, and the arrest of the grand commander had been made, all their ferocity had disappeared and the man whose every hair was to be protected by so many thousand armed Democrats had made his exit through a window by night.

On October 8th General Carrington issued the following address to the people: "The exposure of the Sons of Liberty has been made. Every word is true. Harrison H. Dodd, grand commander of Indiana, has been on trial. Proof was overwhelming. Dodd was released from a military prison upon his parole of honor not to attempt to escape and night before last was granted quarters in the United States court building. He escaped from the third story by a rope. Only one man was in the room with him. That man was Joseph J. Bingham. Innocent men do not do so. The act confesses his guilt. Citizens, every day shows that you are upon the threshold of revolution. You can rebuke this treason. The traitors intend to bring war to your homes. Meet them at the ballot-box, while Grant and Sherman meet them in the field.''

On October 10 General Hovey also issued an address setting forth the objects of the conspiracy and appealing to the people to aid in suppressing the "unholy combination."

The guard which had been placed over Dodd in his confinement had not acted with much vigilance at the time of his flight. It was afterwards charged in Democratic papers that the arrest and escape were parts of a scheme concocted between him and Morton for political purposes,[1] and that Dodd

---

[1] The following is from a special dispatch to the Chicago *Times*, dated Indianapolis, October 22, 1864:

"Mr. Dodd, who was on trial in this city, and 'escaped' is no criterion of the purposes of the order. He was acting in concert with Governor Morton to endeavor to get up a show conspiracy against the government, to be exposed upon the eve of election, and afford a fund of political claptrap to assist the Republicans in carrying the state. He has fulfilled his contract as far as he could, has received his reward, and is now at large under an 'escape,' arranged with the authorities and executed under their supervision. . . . The guards neglected to search the room, and singularly enough, Dodd found a rope there long enough to reach the ground, and down he went. The sentinel saw him descending, and singularly enough did not fire as is the custom when prisoners are escaping, but on the contrary ran down the stairs to the door, which he found locked. The soldier did not realize that he could break it down with a good blow from his musket. It would have been a pity to have spoiled the paint on the door. The building was surrounded by a chain of sentries, but, from the side upon which Dodd descended they were singularly absent, and the sentry inside, very strangely, did not make the least noise to alarm them. In short, there was a combination of strange coincidences about that

was well paid for it!   It was even said that Dodd lay hidden in Morton's house the three days following his flight![1]

Bingham, the editor of the *Sentinel*, had been arrested just before the escape of Dodd.   Morton was then out of the

---

escape which could not have occurred without some arrangement with 'the authority to control armies' in and around Indianapolis.   These co-incidences, the fact that Dodd made money very rapidly, and his strange conduct—for it would have been strange in a fool—show conclusively, even in the absence of more convincing proof, that he was in complicity with Morton." . . .

On November 22 Dodd denied these charges of complicity in a card to the editor of the Cincinnati *Enquirer* from Windsor, Canada West. His answer contains the following:

"This unfounded assault upon my character originated with some irresponsible correspondent of the Chicago *Times*, at Indianapolis, and has since been made the basis of editorial comments in the *Sentinel* and *Enquirer*, and thus, intentionally or otherwise, you are giving credence and publicity to the 'complicity with Morton' dodge, gotten up by a coterie of 'Sons,' who have seen fit to take the benefit of the 'baby act.'"

"To charge me with being a 'spy and informer,' or that I would become a decoy to lure unsuspecting associates into the boiling cauldron of 'crime, hatred and malice,' all for the 'effigies of the President and Secretary of the Treasury,' is to charge me with a heinous crime against mankind that I can not permit to be laid at my door. . . . The charge that I violated a parole is, like all the rest, utterly false.   I was in solitary confinement every moment from the time of my arrest until the escape."

[1] So far did these fictions go that in the following year Vallandigham made a speech at Dayton from which the following quotation was made by the *Journal* of October 11, 1865:

"But within the last three months I have been informed by men who were said to be in this alleged conspiracy, whereof Dodd was the head, that this same Governor Morton had been selected by them, with his consent, to be president of the Northwestern Confederacy, in case the conspiracy should prove a success. . . . . The conspiracy, of course, failed, and after Mr. Dodd had mysteriously made his escape, Governor Morton proved his loyalty by hunting and hounding Democrats all over the state of Indiana, and to-day, three gentlemen of that party who may have done wrong, but yet are entitled to arrest by due process of law, and to trial by jury in a judicial tribunal, are in the penitentiary of Ohio for a political offense, while, if what those men say be true, Morton himself was the greatest offender "

If Mr. Vallandigham used this language words can not do justice to such statements from such a source.

state, and had no knowledge of the arrest until afterwards, but he was charged (naturally, perhaps) with being the prime mover in it, and all Indianians who respected liberty were exhorted to cast their votes against him.

On the 6th of October Bingham caused to be published an address to the people, which was dated the day of his arrest. It contained the following:

"To-day I was arrested by order of Major-General Hovey, the military governor of Indiana, and confined in a military prison, upon what accusation I know not. Faithfully and earnestly, in public and private life, I have endeavored, according to the convictions of my judgment and conscience, to preserve peace and maintain law and order. I am guilty of no crime, unless it be criminal to differ from the principles and policy of the party in power. . . . I am cast down but not destroyed—a victim of arbitrary power. I am a military prisoner. From a cell I urge every true man of Indiana, as he values constitutional liberty, freedom of thought, of conscience, of speech and the press, and the blessings and privileges of constitutional government, to return, in the rapidly-approaching elections, a conservative party to power, as the only hope of restoring and maintaining our free institutions, the constitution and the Union. If such is not the verdict of the people at the ballot-box next Tuesday, farewell to civil and religious liberty."

These protestations of Bingham's innocence, patriotism and peaceful character contrast strangely with his previous editorials and his subsequent testimony in the trials of the other conspirators.

The authorities believed that they could make better use of him as a witness than as a defendant. He was soon released, and gave valuable evidence against his former associates.[1]

---

[1] He still remained chairman of the Democratic State Central Committee, and editor of the *Sentinel*, which paper, on October 31, 1864, and on February 6, 1865, reproached the authorities for not sooner arresting the parties engaged in the conspiracy!

W. A. Bowles, Andrew Humphreys, Horace Heffren, Lambdin P. Milligan and Stephen Horsey were now arrested. Bowles had boasted that he had assembled a large number of men, and could successfully resist any attempts to take him, but he was quietly seized early one morning at his home at French Lick Springs and removed to Indianapolis. A new commission was detailed for the trial of these men and it was convened on October 21. The charges preferred against them were the same as the charges against Dodd. The conspiracy was very clearly shown by the testimony of the detective Stidger, as well as by that of Clayton, a *bona fide* member, of Harrison, the "grand secretary," and of Bingham. There was a general stampede of all who had been connected with the order. Every one seemed anxious to preserve the integrity of his own skin by giving evidence to convict his associates. The "grand commander" had slipped down a rope and run to Canada, and the rest proposed to purchase safety as best they might. But a great surprise was still in store for the remaining defendants. Heffren, the "deputy grand commander," had been sitting with the others and taking part in the defense. In the afternoon of the 4th of November the Judge Advocate said that all proceedings against him were withdrawn, and he was released from arrest. He was immediately placed upon the stand as a witness for the prosecution. He was evidently much terrified and eager to save his life at the expense of his comrades. His appearance was explained by his own testimony that on that morning, just before dinner, he had had a conversation with Governor Morton and General Hovey, which was "confidential."[1] Heffren had sought the interview with Ho-

---

[1] The release of so many important defendants, in consideration of testimony against their associates, is perhaps explained by the significant words used in the report of General Hovey to the Secretary of War, August 10, 1865: "Bingham, Wilson, Heffren and Harrison were used as witnesses in the trials of Dodd, Bowles, Milligan and others, not only to prove the conspiracy, but to convince the public mind."

vey because, to use his own words, "he wanted to get out of
the scrape," and he was base enough to testify to conversa-
tions held with the other defendants while they had been in
prison together. The scenes attending his testimony were
dramatic. The crowded court-room was silent with astonishment while Heffren told of the ten men who had been selected
"to make way with the Governor," and it became evident
that there had been a deliberate plot for Morton's assassination. This project had not been given up even when "the
uprising" was abandoned.[1]

One evening, during the progress of the treason trials,
General Hovey received a telegram stating that some men had
left Niagara on a certain train for the purpose of killing Morton
and himself and warning him to be on his guard. Hovey
sent Captain Warner to the train on which these men were
expected, and upon their arrival, about midnight, they were
arrested and sent to Camp Morton. But there was not sufficient proof to put them upon trial and they were afterwards
discharged. Morton frequently received letters threatening
his life. He showed a number of these letters to Hovey.
Most of them were consigned to the flames, but on one or
two occasions Morton permitted them to be published. One
which was sent from Cincinnati while Morton was absent in
New York was as follows:

"INDIANAPOLIS, October 24, 1864.

"SIR—'The Sons of Liberty,' having organized themselves
into a 'court-martial'—the only kind of court now deemed of
any account—have condemned you to death, under certain

---

[1] The intention "to take care of Governor Morton" seemed to have
been pretty well understood throughout the order. Other witnesses testified to it, though not so explicitly as Heffren. On August 13 a letter
from Thomas King, of Fairland, Shelby county, to Lindsey Gannin, one
of the soldiers of the Seventieth Indiana, declared that a squad was going
to Indianapolis to kill Governor Morton. "If we can not get him out we
will shoot him through the window, and then we will elect our own Governor and have things our own way."

contingencies. We are, or have been, private citizens. We, each of us, know you by sight. We have tried you for the crime of depriving citizens of their liberty without due process of law, and of subjecting them to condemnation to the penitentiary or the gallows, through testimony given in accordance with your own will, or that of those you serve. Our court is as arbitrary as yours, perhaps more so, for it is self-constituted. Yours acknowledges an authority foreign to the constitution of the United States. Ours owes its origin, not even to the 'Temple of the Sons of Liberty.' We have constituted our own court. Its edicts are as legal and shall be as binding as that which pretends to have tried H. H. Dodd.

"You are required to liberate, within two weeks of the mailing of this letter, J. J. Bingham, Dr. Bowles, A. Humphreys, L. P. Milligan, H. Heffren, W. H. Harrison, S. Smith and Dr. Carter.

"We hold you responsible for the arrest of these gentlemen, and we know that you have the power to release them, or to procure their release.

"If you fail, we have sworn to kill you. And, so help us God, we will do it. A bullet or knife will reach you wherever you are, no power on earth can save you, and your crimes forbid your presuming to appeal to God.

"One of us is by you now. One of us will be by you until these men are released or you are a corpse. This is no idle threat. Your life is measured if you fail to do what is herein ordered. Should you procure the release of the men named within the time specified, no human mind will know what is herein written.

"On the vow of a

"SON OF LIBERTY AND ONE OF THE TEN."

The participation of Bowles and Milligan in the conspiracy was shown conclusively. The case against Horsey was not so strong, and the evidence against Humphreys was weaker still. Jonathan W. Gordon made an elaborate argument against the jurisdiction of the court. Mr. Ray discussed the facts in behalf of Humphreys and Bowles. For Humphreys he made a strong case, denying complicity in any military or insurrectionary schemes, and claiming that the order itself was not a conspiracy. For Bowles he was able to do little more than to make a plea in mitigation of the sentence, and commend his client to the mercy of the court as a man broken in age.

All the members of the commission, except two, voted that it had jurisdiction. The defendants were found guilty. Bowles, Milligan and Horsey were condemned to death and Humphreys to imprisonment for life. In the case of Humphreys, the general commanding the district substituted for the sentence "confinement within the boundaries of two townships in his own county." The attorneys and friends of the men condemned to death visited Mr. Lincoln to persuade him not to confirm the judgment. Before he had taken any action he was assassinated, and Andrew Johnson became President with the determination of "making treason odious." He approved the judgment of the court and ordered the execution of the prisoners, though Horsey's sentence was soon afterwards commuted to imprisonment for life. Petitions for a writ of *habeas corpus* were prepared, addressed to the United States Circuit Court, which court certified to a difference of opinion between the two judges composing it as to the jurisdiction of the commission. Judge Davis, of the Supreme Court, was in favor of issuing the writ. Judge Drummond dissented.

Bowles and Milligan were to be hanged on May 19. President Johnson postponed the day of execution until June 20, but all efforts to secure a commutation of the sentence were unavailing. General Hovey had been instructed from Washington to pay no attention to writs from any civil court, but to proceed with the execution unless orders staying it were received from the administration. It was said that the condemned were preparing written statements of the conspiracy which would implicate prominent men not yet connected with it, and there was much anxiety. Milligan wrote to his wife to prepare for the worst. The gallows was erected by Confederate prisoners from Camp Morton. Bowles displayed a good deal of courage during the hours which he supposed were to be his last. "Well," said the old man, "they can't deprive me of many days," and he talked with Colonel Warner concerning the merits of the mineral waters of French Lick Springs.

Meanwhile, Judge David Davis visited Indianapolis and had a long and earnest talk with Governor Morton during a ride with him one Sunday morning. The judge thought it was clear that the commission had been illegal since the courts of Indiana had been open and martial law had not been declared. Morton had hitherto taken no part in the effort to save the lives of the prisoners, but he now determined that he would not have the blood of these men on his hands if they had been unlawfully convicted. President Johnson had notified him that an application for pardon had been made, and Morton at once wrote to Johnson advising him to commute the sentences to imprisonment. He sent several communications to this effect, one by General Mansfield, another by the wife of Milligan.[1] Finally John U. Pettit, then speaker of the Indiana House of Representatives, was dispatched to Washington by the Governor for the purpose of preventing these executions. Pettit thus describes the circumstances: "I learned that Governor Morton desired to see me. I called on his Excellency at once. He was quite abrupt, and we remained

---

[1] This letter, dated May 22, 1865, was as follows: "This communication will be handed to you by Mrs. Milligan, wife of one of the persons condemned to be executed at this place. I have no hesitancy in reiterating the recommendation made in my former communication on the same subject that the punishment of L. P. Milligan and William A. Bowles be commuted to imprisonment for the reasons stated in that communication."

standing after greeting. 'Have you heard of the President's orders for the execution of Bowles and Milligan?' said the Governor. 'Yes,' I replied. 'What do you think of them?' he continued. I said: 'I do not see where the military commission has its authority. We have lived through the whole war with the courts open. A military court exists only by necessity, when civil courts are subdued. . . . Now at the beginning of peace the President ought not to pick out this, as the first of all the states, and have a military execution in our midst, as if we did not know how to administer the law.' Morton replied with much feeling that these were exactly his sentiments, and added that he had remonstrated with the President against the execution of these sentences, but in vain, and that he desired me to go at once to Washington to bear his last appeal to Mr. Johnson. I begged to be excused, but the Governor insisted, saying, 'These men are our citizens and entitled to the care of our laws. It is as much your duty to go as mine.' I gave my consent, telegraphed my wife, and made other rapid preparations as the train left in a few minutes. The Governor wrote an open letter to the President, the closing words of which, in bold characters, were: 'I protest against these executions.'

"On reaching Washington I sought the President at once. The interview was unsatisfactory, but he intimated that a second one could be arranged. At the second visit he said: 'I think I shall say no, but will not do so now, lest I change my mind, and I do not wish this answer to stand in the way.' Two or three more unsatisfactory interviews followed. On the day of the commutation I met the President in the morning, when he agreed to give me a final answer at five in the evening. He appeared to be distressed, and struggling for a sense of right judgment. I called at the appointed time, and was told that the President had gone to Bull Run to review some troops. While I was standing at the window looking at the Potomac an orderly appeared bearing a message, which proved to be the commutation of the sentence. The President had forgotten to leave the document, and had sent the orderly back from Alexandria with it. I at once telegraphed to Governor Morton.''

This commutation aroused the wrath of the more extreme and radical Republicans. President Johnson and Governor Morton were bitterly denounced for cheating the gallows, and the more violent went so far as to declare that their action was the result of corruption. Bowles was very wealthy, it was said, and money had saved the necks of these men from the halter. Some even pointed out a fine house built by Mr. Hasselman, on Meridian street, which was to be transferred to Morton in consideration of his services. But a better sentiment soon prevailed, and these idle stories were heard no more.

Morton thus referred to the reasons for his action in a speech delivered at Richmond, September 29, 1869:

"These men were convicted and found guilty and sentenced about the 10th of December, 1864. The papers were immediately laid before Mr. Lincoln for his approval. He refused to take action upon them. I never had any communication with him on that subject, directly or indirectly, but he refused up to the time of his death to take any action in the case, and gave assurance to the counsel for the defendants that upon the return of peace he would pardon the prisoners and turn them out upon society. After Mr. Lincoln's death these cases were brought before Mr. Johnson, who issued an order for the execution. It was after the war was over, after the military necessity for their death had passed, and the question now came up, what was my duty in the premises?

"I was the man whose life they had sought. They had conspired against me and against the state of Indiana to seize the state arsenal and release the rebel prisoners.

They had appointed a commission of ten to dispose of me. All their schemes had been baffled and detected; the ringleaders had been arrested and put in prison. I had outlived it all. The rebellion had been put down. The great peril had passed by. I felt that, if they had been executed, it would be said that I might have saved them, and that, as I was the man whose life had been imperiled, it would be becoming in me to ask the President to spare their lives, and I did so.''

The appeal in the *habeas corpus* case brought by the prisoners finally came on for a hearing in the Supreme Court. David Dudley Field volunteered his services in their behalf. Elaborate arguments were made upon both sides, and in April, 1866, the court decided that the military commission had no jurisdiction. So, after an imprisonment lasting in all nearly eighteen months, Horsey, Bowles and Milligan were set free.[1]

In the spring of 1868 Milligan brought suit against the members of the Military Commission for damages for his imprisonment. The case was tried in May, 1871. Thomas A. Hendricks was the leading counsel for Milligan, and Benjamin Harrison for the defendants. The trial was a long one, and a great part of the history of the Sons of Liberty was given in evidence. Judge Drummond charged the jury, that owing to the two years' statute of limitations the defendants would not be liable for any act prior to March 13, 1866, but that they would be liable for any imprisonment subsequent to that time, which was the result of the previous trial and conviction. The jury evidently had little sympathy with Milligan, yet recognized that the law required that some

---

[1] Indictments were afterwards found against Bowles, Milligan, Horsey, Humphreys and Dodd. Milligan was arrested upon his return to Indianapolis, in May, 1866, and compelled to give bail, but the cases were never pressed and were afterwards dismissed.

damages must be given. They made the amount as low as possible, bringing in a verdict for five dollars. And with this verdict the history of the secret organizations in Indiana, the conspiracy and the treason trials comes to an end.

CHAPTER XXXI

WHEN, on the 6th of January, 1865, Morton stood before the two houses of the General Assembly to read his message, the surroundings were such as to awaken in him feelings of the liveliest satisfaction. Two years before he had been met by a hostile legislature, which had contemptuously rejected his message, assailed his administration, and sought to take away from him all military power. During these two years he had carried on the government single-handed. Now after his great labors he found his work ratified by the people, not only in his own re-election, but in the return of a legislature prepared to co-operate heartily in his policy, to assume on behalf of the state the liabilities he had incurred, and to relieve him of much of the burden he had borne alone. The clamor of disaffection had been hushed. The audience listened with deep attention to the message.

This message was characteristic of Morton. Sulgrove, who was now his private secretary, says: "He dictated it to me, and it was made up of patches prepared just as he happened to think of the subjects." He began without introduction, giving in detail the number of men who had gone into the military service from Indiana. These amounted in all to 165,314. He next asked the legislature to demand relief for those who had enlisted in veteran regiments with the understanding that they would be mustered out when the terms of these regiments should expire, but who were being held for three years. He paid a tribute to the Indiana soldiers, and spoke of the gratitude due them which should be shown by the care of their families and the education of their children. He requested such an investigation of the Indiana Sanitary Commission as would establish its merits or enable its enemies to point out its defects. He urged that steps be taken to amend the constitution so as to permit soldiers to vote in the field. He praised the efficiency of the Indiana Legion, and recommended that the families of those who had fallen in its service should be placed upon equal footing with the families of volunteers. He referred to the raid of John Morgan, and recommended that a commission should be created to appraise the damages sustained by citizens in consequence of this raid, and that an appropriation be made to pay these damages. Morton then gave a brief history of the arsenal. It had yielded, he said, a net profit of $71,380.01, which had been used in defraying the expenses of the state. He urged the necessity for a Normal school, recommended the acceptance of a gift of land from Congress for an agricultural college, and favored the establishment of a bureau of immigration. The State Board of Colonization, he said, ought to be discontinued since more than eight thousand dollars had been paid out in salaries and only one man had been sent to Liberia. The statute which excluded negroes from testifying should be repealed. There should be an enumeration of the inhabitants of the state and a proper apportionment for legislative purposes. The Governor described his efforts to offset against the direct tax imposed by the Federal government, the expenses of enrolling, arming and paying the Indiana troops, and asked the approval of the General Assembly. He set forth the manner in which the state institutions had been kept going with moneys borrowed by him, and gave an account of his military expenditures and of the sums he had received from the general government, which he recommended should be returned. He spoke of the payment of interest on the state debt by Winslow, Lanier

& Co., and urged the legislature to reimburse them. He referred to the conspiracy of the Sons of Liberty, whose schemes had been exposed and baffled, and closed his message by a discussion of national issues, which contained the following passage:

"Whatever it may cost us to preserve the Union, we may be assured it will cost us everything to lose it. A refusal to prosecute the war because it is expensive would not be unlike the case of the man who should resolve to die because the employment of a physician would embarrass his financial affairs. Nor would it be less absurd to refuse to sustain the government and prosecute the war upon the pretense that, by so doing, constitutional rights and personal liberty would be endangered, when we know perfectly well that if the rebellion succeeds, civil and religious liberty and constitutional rights, of whatever kind, will be overwhelmed in one common ruin."

On the 9th of January the votes for Governor and Lieutenant Governor were canvassed, and Morton and Baker were inaugurated. Morton's inaugural address was filled with the spirit of congratulation and hopefulness.

"While we are called on to shed bitter tears over the graves of many of our fellow-citizens who have died that their country might live, we have still many causes for thankfulness and rejoicing. Good health has generally prevailed, labor has had a liberal reward, bounteous harvests have repaid the farmer's toil. Manufactures have increased and prospered, and commerce has brought to us its richest returns. . . . Indiana shows signs of prosperity and power she never knew before. . . . Our fidelity to obligations of every kind is recognized at home and abroad. Our military, political and commercial importance is more conspicuous than ever, and in consequence, the current of immigration and wealth is setting towards us. Indiana is increasing in population more rapidly than at any previous period. From every part of the state comes the intelligence that our

towns are filling up. New lands are being brought into culti-
vation, and new enterprises in manufactures and commerce
set on foot. It is indeed a strange anomaly, beyond human
foresight, that in the midst of a desolating civil war our state
should have unusual prospects of prosperity and power.''

While the legislature, as a whole, showed a disposition to
co-operate with Morton in his efforts to uphold the general
government and to preserve the credit of the state, there
were still some members, now fortunately belonging to the
minority, who did all they could to throw obstructions in the
way.

A bill was introduced to refund to Winslow, Lanier & Co.,
with interest, the sums advanced by them. Francis B. Hord
declared that this bill ''covertly enfolded a revolutionary principle,'' and there was a good deal of opposition to ''paying
strangers a bonus for assisting Morton.'' But the bill passed
by a large majority, and Winslow, Lanier & Co. were repaid.

On the 6th of February the Governor sent to the legislature the joint resolution of Congress proposing the thirteenth
amendment to the constitution, abolishing slavery. The opponents of the amendment attempted to organize a ''bolt,''
but it failed and the resolution passed by a vote of twenty-
six to nine. Then the retiring members came back and asked
leave to record their votes and make additional speeches, and
a day was contemptuously set apart by the majority for listening to the harangues of the discontented upon a resolution
already passed.

As the session drew near its close it became apparent that
many important measures would be crowded out.

Most of Morton's recommendations, however, were adopted.
His offset of the claims of the state upon the Federal govern-
ment against Indiana's share of the direct tax was ratified.
The agency for the colonization of negroes was discontinued.
A bill was passed for the relief of Indiana soldiers and their

families. The grant of land for an agricultural college was accepted. A joint resolution was adopted urging Congress to place upon the pension rolls the men wounded in the service of the Indiana Legion, and the families of those who had been killed; also a memorial to Congress urging the discharge of the men who had enlisted in veteran regiments with the understanding that their terms of service would expire with those of their regiments. A joint committee was appointed, which investigated and approved the accounts of the Governor,[1] and money was appropriated to pay the one hundred and thirty-five thousand dollars, which Morton had borrowed from counties, towns and individuals to carry on the state government. But there was great opposition to the Governor's recommendation that the state should assume the payment of the two hundred and fifty thousand dollars received by him from the general government, and no provision was made for the assumption of this debt.[2] A bill to pay the claims of those who had suffered from Morgan's raid was also the subject of much wrangling and failed to become a law. A bill to admit the testimony of negroes in courts of justice was unsuccessful, and a proposed constitutional amendment providing that the votes of soldiers might be cast in the field also came to nothing.

---

[1] This committee found the books and vouchers correct, and reported that there had been great care in the disbursement of the moneys borrowed to carry on the state government. The Governor had received—

In cash advanced from the United States	$250,000 00
In sums loaned by counties and individuals	135,000 00
Profits of the arsenal	71,380 00
Cash for the Third Volunteer Cavalry	1,150 51

Making in all...$457,530 51
Detailed accounts were submitted showing the expenditure of this sum, except $124,265.23, which still remained in the Governor's hands deposited in bank.

[2] Morton therefore accounted to the Federal government, as its agent, for the money which he had spent in equipping troops, and paid the balance remaining in his hands into the Federal treasury,

Morton did not consider these omissions as of sufficient importance to justify him in calling a special session at this time, and it was not until the following fall that the General Assembly was again convened.

The war was now rapidly drawing to a close. It was just after the re-election of Lincoln that Sherman started upon his march to the sea. Before Christmas, Savannah had been taken, and about the middle of December Thomas crushed the army of Hood at Nashville. While the Indiana legislature was still in session, the captures of Fort Fisher and of Wilmington were announced to them. Sherman was marching northward through the Carolinas.

Lincoln began his second term by the inaugural containing the memorable words, "With malice toward none, with charity for all." Grant was tightening his relentless grasp upon Petersburg and the Confederate capital. The final blow was delivered at Five Forks, and, on the 9th of April, Lee's army surrendered at Appomatox. This event was celebrated with great rejoicing. At Indianapolis a meeting was held in the state-house yard. Morton spoke, and on the following day he issued a proclamation inviting the people to assemble upon the 20th to return thanks to God for the victory.

The war was over. Every face was radiant with the hope of the coming peace.

About two o'clock on the night of the 14th of April Morton was awakened from his sleep. A little messenger boy brought in a telegram. The boy was weeping. Morton saw it. He took the telegram, and before he opened it he had a foreboding of a danger which had been often before his eyes. He said, "Lincoln is killed!"

And so it was. The hearts which had been beating high with enthusiasm were now crushed with sorrow. No one who lived at that time can ever forget it. The flags which had decked the city for rejoicing were now at half mast and edged with black, while every citizen had some sign upon his person of the grief which had overtaken all. A deep gloom overhung the city. A few miserable creatures declared their joy at the assassination, and they were hung up to trees and lamp-posts by their enraged fellow-citizens and cut down again only when life was nearly extinct. Morton asked the citizens of Indianapolis to close their places of business and to meet at noon in the state-house square. The Rev. Mr. Burgess made a prayer with tears streaming down his face. Then Morton spoke simply and feelingly of the great calamity.

Among those who had been invited to the meeting were McDonald and Hendricks. McDonald was filled with the deepest sorrow. In this universal grief, party differences were forgotten. Heretofore, he said, there had been no personal differences between him and Governor Morton, and hereafter there should be no political differences. But the sentiment in that assembly was not one of sorrow merely, but also of deep and bitter rage, not only against the miscreants who had committed the great crime, but against all who had shown sympathy with the cause which they were believed to represent. When Hendricks arose to speak the multitude was stirred with an uncontrollable fury. Men rushed toward him, brandishing weapons and screaming, "Kill him! Hang him!" "Don't let the traitor speak!" with other cries of dreadful menace. Terror seized his friends, and many thought that the blood of the senator from Indiana would be added to the deeds of violence which the frenzy of that time had provoked. Morton sprang to his feet, "raised his hand, and with his terrible eye and ringing voice" (so says the biographer of Hendricks) "commanded and besought and quelled the crowd." Morton said that he himself had invited Hendricks to speak, and he asked the people to pause and listen. Quiet was restored, and Hendricks proceeded. "I, too," he said, "will support the successor of Mr. Lincoln just as far as I can, always saving my conscience void of offense."

The day which had been set apart for thanksgiving was

changed to one for humiliation and prayer. Business was
generally suspended. Lincoln's remains, which had been
exhibited in state in several of the eastern cities, came west
for final interment at Springfield. The Governor and his staff
met the funeral cortege at the Ohio line, and the body lay in
state at the capitol during Sunday, the 10th of April, and at
night it was sent westward to its final resting place.

Lincoln had died just at the moment when the new problem of reconstruction was unfolding itself. Andrew Johnson,
an untried man, was now the most important factor in the
solution of this problem. Morton had strong convictions upon
the subject, and he determined that his views should be laid
before the new Executive.

On Saturday, the 22d of April, a delegation of citizens
from Indiana, headed by the Governor, called upon Mr. Johnson at his rooms in the Treasury building. The new President was much esteemed by the Republicans of Indiana.
They had admired his courageous course as the military Governor of Tennessee. He had aided them in the political
struggles of their own state, and the feeling between him and
Morton was very cordial. The Indiana delegation was received in a most friendly manner, and Morton delivered to
the President an address upon the subject of reconstruction.

"As we approach the end of this mighty rebellion," he
said, "the great question of re-adjustment will force itself upon
your mind and upon that of the public, and the principles of our
government will be presented for new consideration and application. We hold that no state had a right to secede from
the Union, neither had it the power to work such a result indirectly. The constitution provides for the admission of new
states, but when thus admitted and incorporated into the mass
of the nation, there is no provision or method by which they
can be withdrawn or expelled. The rebellion can be viewed
by the government only in its individual aspect. . . . .
Every act looking to resistance or secession was unconstitu-

tional and void, and could have no legal effect whatever except upon the political and civil rights of the individual committing it. Each rebel is politically and criminally responsible for his action, without regard to the number who may have united with him. Nor is there any power to punish rebels collectively by reducing a state to a territorial condition, or declaring its municipal character forfeited.

"As the crime of treason is individual in its character, so must be its punishment. Rebels have the power to forfeit their personal rights, civil or political, but they have no power, directly or indirectly, to work the destruction of a state. The disorganization of a state government does not affect the existence of the state. Suppose, if you please, that every officer connected with the government of the state of Indiana should be assassinated to-day, would the existence of the state thereby be lost? Certainly not. The powers of the state government would be in abeyance only until new men could be called to the exercise of those powers. There is in every rebel state a loyal element of greater or less strength, and to its hands should be confided the power and duty of reorganizing the state government, giving to it military protection until such time as it can, by convention or otherwise, so regulate the right of suffrage that this right will be intrusted only to safe and loyal hands. . . . . ''

The President in reply, after denouncing treason and declaring that traitors must be "punished and impoverished," concurred in Morton's view of the impossibility of destroying states. Their life-breath had been only suspended. No matter how small the number of Union men, if there were enough to man the ship of state, he held it his high duty to protect them and secure to them a republican form of government. The duty of again putting the government in operation must pass into the hands of its friends. The President declared that he might well have adopted Governor Morton's speech as his own.[1]

On the 4th of July Morton delivered an oration on the battle-ground of Tippecanoe, near Lafayette. He had intended to prepare a formal address, but he was ill during the time he had allotted to that purpose, and his remarks were entirely extemporaneous. "In 1783," he said, "when Great Britain was about to acknowledge our independence, a letter of authority executed by the court in London to the commissioners at Ghent empowered these commissioners to acknowledge the independence of certain colonies therein named. Our commissioners rejected that acknowledgment. 'You must acknowledge,' they said, 'the independence of the United States of America.' The British commissioners were compelled to return to London to obtain the power to make that acknowledgment, and it was made. . . . Again in 1787, when our fathers formed the present constitution, they began by declaring that it was established, not by states, but by the people of the United States, and that this constitution and the laws and treaties made in pursuance of it were to be the supreme law of the land." Morton referred to these historical landmarks for the purpose of showing that from our earliest infancy the unity of the nation had been acknowledged and that the doctrine of state sovereignty had its origin long after the time when our fathers had done their work and transmitted the constitution to their children.

---

[1] The views of Morton at this early period were sustained three years later by the decision of the United States Supreme Court in Texas *v.* White (7 Wallace 700), where Chief Justice Chase, in pronouncing the opinion of the court, declared that the ordinances of secession were absolutely null, that the seceding states did not cease to be states, although they might have no government, and that by virtue of the constitutional obligation to guarantee a republican form of government to each of the states, it became the duty of the United States to provide for the restoration of a state organization and to hold elections for that purpose. All powers for the accomplishment of this object would be implied.

The Governor now took up the subject of the war. Mr. Lincoln, he said, had always held there was but one salvation for this government, and that was to crush the rebels by force of arms. "Upon one occasion," Morton continued, "I saw him take out of a private drawer a little paper in his own handwriting, which he had compiled from the census of 1860, showing how many men we had and how many they had; how many horses we had and how many they had; how much corn, how much pork, and so on, showing how we and they were respectively situated as to the resources with which war is carried on. He showed that our resources were so much greater than theirs that if we kept on we could wear them out. 'We never shall triumph,' said he, 'until we have worn them out.'"

Morton thus concluded:

"We have had four long and bloody years. My faith never deserted me, though sometimes I was unable to see how we would triumph. When defeat had settled upon our armies, and thousands were clamoring for peace and the abatement of the contest, sometimes I had dark hours. My heart was heavy within me. But we struggled on, until finally our victory came, suddenly, completely, perfectly. It was as if the heavens had been overspread with clouds, and as if these clouds had been suddenly rolled back by a great wind and the sun of power and hope and glory had burst upon us."

CHAPTER XXXII

ABOUT the 1st of June the veterans began to come home, and many regiments, one after another, passed through Indianapolis. Morton determined that not one of them should be without its public reception. On each of these occasions the gun was fired at 8 o'clock in the morning, the ladies of the city prepared breakfast at the Soldiers' Home, and the veterans then marched to the state-house, where there was a speech by the Governor and another by General Hovey or some one else in authority, and "an original song" by Chaplain Lozier, who possessed what was called by contemporary journalism, "a fatal facility for rhyme, with lungs of steel and a voice like a thunderstorm."

The soldiers took kindly to the reception ceremonies, inhaling the incense burned for them with evident satisfaction, but without that extravagant enjoyment with which they would have received the same testimonials three years before. Morton's speeches were given in detail in the columns of the daily papers. He extended the thanks of the state to those who had preserved the Union. How different, he said, was their home-coming from that of the men whom they had conquered. These men had gone back without banners, without triumph, without hope. The Union veterans returned as conquerors. The Confederacy had died suddenly—died like the gourd of Jonah in a single night.

Morton exhorted the soldiers to cherish the principle that

this Union was one in all its parts. It would become larger in time. Louis Napoleon had taken possession of Mexico, but he had brought upon himself serious and fatal embarrassments. We would absorb that country as certainly as we would die. Canada, too, would finally come into the fold, but not by war. England had made indecent haste to recognize the rebels as belligerents. She had fitted out pirate ships to prey upon our commerce, and had shown a desire to overthrow our institutions. Canada had harbored the miscreants who had plotted robbery, assassination and other monstrous atrocities. But a change had lately come over the spirit of her people, and over all the Canadas there might be heard clamors for annexation. To what were we indebted for these things? To the armies of the Union.

At the commencement of the struggle the reputation of the Hoosiers had been a little under par. There had been many who were ashamed of Indiana, and when they had spoken of their nativity they had made it convenient to be born in Kentucky. But now these men were all born in Indiana. They had been "born again."

Speaking of reconstruction, Morton said that if the country could be restored in as short a time as it had taken to crush armed treason he would be content.

He would gladly crown all who returned with laurels and decorate them with medals, but this was impossible. All he could do was to give them, in behalf of the state, thanks, heartfelt and earnest, for their inestimable services.

A prize banner had been promised by the Indiana State Sanitary Commission to the county contributing the largest sum for the relief of sick and wounded soldiers during the year 1864. Wayne county won the prize, and the banner was presented by Morton at a meeting of the citizens in Richmond on the 29th of September, 1865. He took this occasion to speak at length upon the question of reconstruction.

In this speech he compared the plan adopted by President

Johnson with that set forth by Lincoln in his message of December 18, 1863. The oath of allegiance prescribed was substantially the same. Lincoln had proposed to exclude certain classes of persons from the benefits of amnesty. Johnson excluded all these and eight additional classes. His measures were more stringent. In neither plan could those who had been concerned in the rebellion come back to office. Lincoln's scheme had been submitted to his cabinet and approved by every one of its members. Lincoln had died holding out to the nation his policy of amnesty and reconstruction. Johnson had faithfully tried to carry out the policy bequeathed to him by the man around whose grave the whole world gathered as mourners.

But the burden of Morton's speech was upon the subject of negro suffrage. Of this he said, that it had been proposed to exclude from Congress members from the Southern states until these states should incorporate negro suffrage in their constitutions.

There was also another plan, founded upon the theory that these states were out of the Union, and held as conquered provinces, like unorganized territories, in which Congress had the power to call conventions, prescribe the right of suffrage, and then determine whether the constitutions offered by these conventions should be accepted.

Morton contended that from the beginning of the war every message of the President, every proclamation, every state paper, and every act of Congress had proceeded upon the hypothesis that no state could secede from the Union and that this war was an insurrection, not of states, but of individuals.

Upon this hypothesis we had put down the rebellion. But it was now proposed that we should admit that the Southern states had seceded; that they were out of the Union; that a government *de facto* had been established, and that we held these states as conquered provinces, just as we should hold Canada if we were to invade it and take possession of it. As a consequence of this doctrine Jefferson Davis could not be tried for treason, because he had been the ruler of a conquered province. We would have no more power to try him for treason than to try the Governor of Canada, in case he should fall into our hands during a hostile invasion of his territory.

Another consequence which would grow out of the admission of this doctrine was that we would be called upon to pay the rebel debt. If we should admit that those states had for one moment been out of the Union it would be insisted that when we took them back we should take them with their debts, as we would take any other conquered province.

Morton continued: ''In regard to the question of allowing the freedmen of the Southern states to vote, while I admit the equal rights of all men, and acknowledge that in time all men will have the right to vote without distinction of color or race, I yet believe that in the case of four millions of slaves just freed from bondage, there should be a period of probation and preparation before they are brought to the exercise of political power. Let us consider for one moment the condition of these people in the Southern states. . . . Perhaps not one in a thousand can read, and perhaps not one in five hundred is worth five dollars in property of any kind. They have no property, personal or real. They have just come from bondage, and all they have is their own bodies.

''Their homes are on the plantations of their old masters and they must depend for subsistence on the employment they receive. . . . Can you conceive that a body of men, white or black, who, as well as their ancestors, have been in this condition, are qualified to be lifted immediately from their present state into the full exercise of political power, not only to govern themselves and their neighbors, but to take part in the government of the United States? Can they be regarded as intelligent or independent voters? The mere statement of the fact furnishes the answer to the question. To say that such men—and it is no fault of theirs, it is simply their misfortune, and the crime of the nation—to say that such men, just emerging from this slavery are qualified for the exercise of political powers, is to make the strongest pro-slavery argument I ever heard. It is to pay the highest compliment to the institution of slavery. . . .

"In what condition is Indiana to urge negro suffrage upon South Carolina, or any other state? Let us consider the position we occupy. We have, perhaps, twenty-five thousand colored people. Most of them can read and write; many of them are very intelligent and excellent citizens, well-to-do in the world, well qualified to exercise the right of suffrage and political power. But how stands the matter? We not only exclude them from voting, we exclude them from testifying in courts of justice. We exclude them from our public schools, and we make it unlawful and criminal for them to come into the state. No negro who has come into Indiana since 1850 can make a valid contract; he can not acquire title to a piece of land, because the law makes the deed void, and every man who gives him employment is liable to prosecution and fine. I sent out the Twenty-eighth Indiana colored regiment, recruited with great difficulty and at some expense. It has been in the field two years. It has fought well on many occasions, and has won the high opinion of officers who have seen it. Yet according to the constitution and laws of Indiana, more than one-half of the men in that regiment have no right to come back again, and if they do come back they are subject to prosecution and fine; and any man who receives them or employs them is also liable to punishment. . . . With what face can Indiana go to Congress and insist upon giving the right of suffrage to the negroes in the South ! . . . ."

Morton next discussed the speech of Charles Sumner at a recent state convention at Worcester, Mass. Sumner's prop-

29—MOR.

osition was that all persons connected with the rebellion should be excluded from suffrage, and that the negroes should be enfranchised. Morton discussed the effect of this policy. If every man concerned in the rebellion were disfranchised, twenty out of every twenty-one white men in most of the Southern states would be excluded.

If the negroes were enfranchised, there would be twenty negro votes to one white vote. The effect of this would be to erect colored state governments. "Suppose," continued Morton, "they send colored senators and representatives to Congress, I have no doubt you will find men in the North who will be willing to sit beside them, and will not think themselves degraded by doing so. I have nothing to say to this. I am simply discussing the political effect of it. In every state where there is a colored state government, a negro for Governor, and a negro for Supreme Court judge, white immigration will cease. You can not find the most ardent anti-slavery man in Wayne county who will go and locate in a state that has a colored state government. You will shut off at once all emigration from the northern states and from Europe. These states will remain permanently colored states. The white men who are now there will move away. They will not remain under such dominion. . . .

"In such case the colored states will be a balance of power in this country. . . . As three hundred thousand slaveholders, bound by a common tie, were able to govern this nation for a long time, so four millions of people, bound together by a much stronger tie—despised by the whole world as they have been—would constantly vote and act together, and their united vote would constitute a balance of power that might control the government of the nation.

"I submit, then, that however freely we may admit the natural rights of the negro, colored state governments are not desirable; that finally they will bring about a war of races. . . . I would give these men, just emerged from slavery, a period of probation, I would give them time to acquire a little property and get a little education, time to learn something about the simplest forms of business, and to prepare themselves for the exercise of political power. At the end of ten, fifteen or twenty years, let them come into the enjoyment of their political rights. By that time, the Southern states will have been so completely filled up by emigration from the North and from Europe that the negroes will be in a permanent minority. Why? Because the negroes will have nothing but the natural increase of the race —while we will have emigration from all the world and natural increase besides. Thus, by postponing the thing until such time as the negroes are qualified to enjoy political rights, the dangers I have been considering will have passed away.''

Morton proposed, instead of negro suffrage, the apportionment of the political powers of the states, not according to population, but according to the number of voters. The North, he claimed, would not consent that the white men of the South should exercise double political power, by reason of their disfranchised negroes. Heretofore, three-fifths of the negro population had been represented in Congress in accordance with a clause which had been put into the constitution on account of slavery. Now, there was no reason why representation should not be determined by the number of voters. Such an amendment would finally drive the white men of the South to confer suffrage on the negroes for the purpose of enlarging their own political power.

At the time it was delivered this speech excited widespread comment. President Johnson said it was the ablest defense of his policy yet made public. The sentiments expressed in it found favor among moderate Republicans, but the radical members of the party, especially those who had been prominent in the anti-slavery agitation of former years, were greatly dissatisfied.[1]

The Richmond speech marks an important step in the progress of Morton's views from the Democratic conservatism of his youth to the radicalism shown by his final efforts for the adoption and enforcement of the fifteenth amendment. These successive changes corresponded roughly in point of time with the general opinion in the Republican party which demanded at the outset free territories, afterwards emancipation and finally enfranchisement. It was "first the blade, then the ear and after that the full corn in the ear."

At a later period when his views had undergone further modifications, this speech was persistently thrown in his face. and it was charged by his critics that his friends were endeavoring to collect and destroy all copies which could be found. Morton insisted that his change of views was a natural evolution—that changed conditions, and the failure of the effort to reconstruct the South upon the basis of "a white man's government" made it necessary to confer suffrage upon the negro at an earlier period than would otherwise have been desirble.

---

[1] Democratic opinion was also divided. The Cincinnati *Enquirer* said that Governor Morton had expressed himself in the main very well and "had planted himself squarely upon the Democratic platform." The Indianapolis *Sentinel*, however, called the speech a "Yankee dodge," whose final object was the accomplishment of negro suffrage, and insisted that there was no difference between Sumner and Morton, except upon the question of time.

CHAPTER XXXIII

PARALYSIS—MESSAGE TO THE SPECIAL SESSION—JOURNEY TO EUROPE.

DURING the summer of 1865 it became evident that Morton's health was seriously impaired. He came often to the receptions of the veteran regiment so haggard and careworn that he could hardly deliver the speech of welcome expected of him, and sometimes he had to stay away.[1]

Morton, himself, thus described his condition: "I felt an indisposition to read or study. I did not care to read so much as a newspaper. My mind felt dull and clouded, and I found many things escaping my memory. I was confused easily, and took little or no interest in what was going on about me. Even the duties of the state no longer engaged my close attention. These feelings continued until the 10th of October. I never shall forget the day. It was a beautiful one, the air was crisp, and I walked a long distance. In the evening I retired somewhat fatigued, but in other respects ap-

---

[1] Early in August he went to Niagara for his health. From this place he thus wrote to his wife:

"MY DEAR WIFE—I reached here Friday night feeling better than I have done for many weeks. Yesterday and to-day I have been entirely free from pain in my back, and can hardly realize the sudden relief on account of it. The atmosphere is very bracing, the soft moist breeze from the Falls is delightful, and the place is as charming as ever, but I am lonesome. There is not now here a man, woman or child I ever saw before. This morning it is raining, and I am very apprehensive that the day will be a long one. I have two dispatches saying Ollie is better. The news was very grateful to me, and I am impatient to see him and his dear mother."

(453)

parently in my usual health. The next morning I woke early, but as I attempted to get out of bed, I discovered that I was unable to lift my limbs.[1] Again and again I made the effort, when it flashed through my mind that I was paralyzed.[2] I felt no pain, but from my hips downward I was unable to move. My head seemed as clear as a bell, and I recalled to mind incidents I had forgotten.''

His first feeling was one of despair. He believed that his hour had come. He sent for his physician and for a lawyer to make his will, but neither then nor in his final illness did he call for a clergyman.

Thus came the disease which afflicted him during the remainder of his life, which made it impossible for him to walk without assistance, which broke down his vigorous frame and entailed continued suffering, but which seemed to increase rather than diminish the power of his intellect and will. His physicians prescribed absolute rest, but this for Morton was impossible, and it was not long before he was again at work.

He had convened the legislature to meet in special session on November 13. It was his duty to lay before the General Assembly a message stating the causes for which he had called it and recommending such measures as he deemed necessary for the welfare of the state. In spite of his illness Morton prepared for this occasion one of his ablest and most elaborate messages.

When the legislature convened to hear this document, the Brevier Reports contain the significant statement that when the Governor had ascended the speaker's platform he "excused himself for sitting." From this time to the close of his life, nearly all his speeches were thus delivered.

---

[1] The morning newspapers had been brought to him and he had read them as usual before he arose. He had then attempted to leap out of bed but found he was unable to do so.

[2] His father was a paralytic in his later years, and an aunt had been similarly stricken.

In his message he gave the legislature a history of the public debt, and urged that provision be made for its payment, and that the trust funds of the state be invested in its own stocks. He recommended a new enumeration and apportionment of the inhabitants for the election of state senators and representatives. He advocated the institution of houses of correction for juvenile offenders. He asked for a revision of the act for the relief of soldiers' families, and proposed the establishment of a soldiers' home. A bureau of immigration, he said, should be created. Indiana ought to take part in the world's fair at Paris. A state normal-school should be set on foot. Damages sustained in the Morgan raid should be adjusted and paid. An enumeration should be made of the colored children, and a portion of the school fund set apart for their education in separate schools. Negro testimony ought to be received in courts of justice. Indiana had the bad eminence of being the only state in the North which excluded it.[1] Referring to negro suffrage in the South he said that he considered education and the right to testify more important than the right to vote.

He recommended the President's views on reconstruction.

The war, he said, had established the high character of the American soldier, his valor, patriotism, endurance and humanity. He had taught the world a lesson before which it stood in amazement; how, when the storm of battle had passed, he could lay aside his arms, and go back with cheerfulness to the pursuits of peace, thus showing that the bravest soldiers could become the best citizens.

The preparation and delivery of this message had been against the earnest remonstrances of Morton's physicians. They insisted that he should withdraw absolutely from the du-

---

[1] Most of these recommendations were adopted. An act was passed to enumerate the voters, another to adjust the state debt, the Sinking Fund Commissioners were authorized to invest their funds in Indiana state bonds, a normal school was created and negroes were allowed to testify.

ties of his office, and that a change of scene and climate was needful for his recovery. He had been told of the success of Dr. Brown-Sequard, of Paris, in the cure of paralysis, and he made up his mind to go abroad and seek the aid of this celebrated physician. Sumner had recovered under his treatment, why not Morton? The message had been delivered on the 14th of November, and on the afternoon of the 17th he announced his intended departure. Resolutions of regret and sympathy were adopted. On the same day he left Indianapolis for Washington. Political bitterness was forgotten in view of the Governor's affliction, and not only his friends, but many of those who had opposed him, paid a tribute to his high qualities.

It was about this time that he received from Chief-Justice Chase the following letter:

"WASHINGTON, Nov. 10, 1865.

"MY DEAR GOVERNOR—I think it is the right of men who have ably and faithfully served their country to know that their labors are appreciated So I will not deny myself the pleasure of telling you that Secretary Stanton was with me last evening, and we, naturally turning our minds to the past, fell to talking of you. We agreed that no Governor had rendered such services or displayed such courage or ability in administration, and we agreed that your recent services were the most meritorious of all, because rendered under circumstances of personal risk of health and life which would have been by almost any man regarded, and by all accepted, as good reason for total inaction.

"I have seldom heard Stanton express himself so earnestly. I hope you will derive some satisfaction from this little relation. The talk gave much to me.

"Cordially your friend,   S. P. CHASE."

The state government was left in the hands of Lieutenant-Governor Conrad Baker. Morton's physicians thought his recovery doubtful. Morton himself did not know whether he would ever come back, and his parting from his Indianapolis friends was affecting. McDonald was present to see him off. There were tears in the eyes of both when they separated. McDonald had never allowed himself to cherish an unkind thought of his antagonist, and Morton warmly returned McDonald's friendship.

From Indianapolis the Governor went to Washington, where he had an interview with the President. On this occasion Johnson confided to him a secret mission to the Emperor of the French. This was not communicated to the French minister in Washington nor to the American minister in Paris. The purpose of it was to secure the withdrawal of the French troops from Mexico. The demand for this action through the regular diplomatic channels would be accompanied with embarrassment to the French government, which, on October 18, had demanded a recognition of the government of Maximilian as a condition precedent to the recall of the French army. President Johnson, therefore, asked Morton to intimate informally to Louis Napoleon that it would be impossible for the administration to withstand the pressure of public opinion in America for the expulsion of these troops if their withdrawal were postponed much longer, and to suggest that it would be easier for the French government to remove them at once voluntarily rather than later after a formal demand.[1]

---

[1] Hon. R. R. Hitt visited Morton during his last illness. Morton drew him to the side of the bed and said: "I want to tell you about that mission to Paris. There is not a word about it in writing. I was asked by President Johnson to have an interview with the Emperor, and to secure the removal of the French troops from Mexico. Bigelow was minister at the time, but he knew nothing of it. Rothschild procured the interview. The purpose of it was to show the Emperor that it was to his interest to withdraw the French troops; that the American people were insistent; that nothing would prevent a war unless the troops were speedily removed, and that if this were done without any formal request the French

Morton spent a week in Washington.   He received more
than three hundred callers at his rooms.   From Washington

government would escape the humiliation of yielding to official demands,
and the good feeling between the two nations could be preserved."

Morton's ostensible mission was to investigate the systems of sanitary
police, of transportation and of subsistence in the armies of France, Germany and Italy, and the following letters constituted his credentials:

" WAR DEPARTMENT, WASHINGTON CITY, ⎱
                    " November 30, 1865.   ⎰

" SIR—It is the desire of the President that during your contemplated
trip to Europe you should perform certain duties of a special nature, that
are deemed important for the benefit of the military service, and which
your long experience and observation will enable you to discharge with
advantage to the government, namely :

"First.   To make yourself acquainted with the sanitary regulations
connected with the military service in Germany, France and Italy, and to
collect all the information upon that subject which may be accessible to
you, and transmit the same in a report to this department.

" Second.   To examine into and collect information in relation to the
system of transporting troops in the several countries above mentioned,
directing your attention to the collection of statistical information in regard to the speed and cost of transportation, the number of troops that
can be transported at given times, and the distances.

"Third.   To examine into the general mode of subsisting troops in
camps, garrisons and *en route*, and into the quality and quantity of rations supplied to the troops under the different exigencies above mentioned.

"Fourth.   To direct your attention to any other matters connected with
the military service upon which useful information can be collected by
you.

"On these subjects you will from time to time make such reports as your
information may permit, to this department, giving to each subject as much
minuteness of detail as may be in your power.

"To defray your necessary expenses in performing these duties, a reasonable compensation, to be fixed by the President, will be allowed.

        "Very respectfully your obedient servant,
        (Seal)   "EDWIN M. STANTON,
"His Excellency, O. P. MORTON."   "Secretary of War.

                    "WAR DEPARTMENT, Washington City.
"*To All to Whom These Presents Shall Come:*
"His Excellency, O. P. Morton, Governor of Indiana, has been appointed by the President of the United States of America, Special Commissioner, to make such inspections and acquire such information in
reference to the sanitary police of the military service and matters per-

he proceeded to New York in a special car furnished by the Secretary of War. At the latter city his wife and his son John joined him, also Berry Sulgrove, who had been editor of the Indianapolis *Journal*, and at a later period the Governor's private secretary.

A few days later Morton sailed on the Scotia. He appeared in better health than he had been for some time. A physician, detailed by the Secretary of War to attend him, had faith in his recovery. Many of his friends were upon the wharf to say good-bye.

Captain Judkins, of the Scotia, gave the Governor his room. The voyage was uneventful, and Morton arrived in Liverpool the day before Christmas. He passed that anniversary in the old town of Chester, and proceeded to London, stopping only two days in that city. He then went to Paris, where he remained until the 1st of February. Here he had to undergo the ordeal of the "moxa." Previous to the operation he had an audience with Louis Napoleon in pursuance of an appointment made through the agency of Baron Roth-

---

taining to military transportation and subsistence as shall be accorded to him by such governments and military authorities in Europe as he may visit.

"This department takes pleasure in commending him to the hospitality and courtesy of all military and civil authorities in foreign countries, as a gentleman of high personal character and attainments, and requests that such courtesies and facilities may be afforded to him as are usual to accredited agents of friendly governments.

"In testimony whereof the seal of this department is hereto affixed this thirtieth day of November, 1865, at the City of Washington.

    (Seal)   "EDWIN M. STANTON,
                            "Secretary of War."

    "EXECUTIVE MANSION, WASHINGTON, D. C.,
                       December 11, 1865.

"His Excellency, Governor O. P. Morton, of the state of Indiana, has been intrusted by the government of the United States of America with important business in Europe. As the executive of one of the states of the Union, and as a citizen possessing the confidence and regard of his country, he is cordially recommended to the kind consideration of all whom it may concern.   ANDREW JOHNSON."

schild, to whom Morton had brought a letter of introduction
from August Belmont. Morton delivered to the Emperor
the message of President Johnson. The Emperor spoke
regretfully of a speech which General Logan had delivered
in Congress, demanding the expulsion of Bazaine. The
Emperor said that it had never been his purpose to retain
permanent possession of Mexico, and that his only object had
been to secure the rights of French creditors and residents,
and to leave the people of the country free to make their
choice of rulers.[1] The interview was followed by a formal
invitation to a reception at the Tuileries. Morton wanted to
go, but to do this he must wear a court dress and sword. At
first he determined to do it. He went with Sulgrove and
picked out a costume that fitted him, but he disliked to wear
it and believed that to stand for a long time on his feet at a
court reception would be hurtful to his health, so he made
up his mind to stay away, and Mrs. Morton went to the reception without him.

He did little sight-seeing in Paris. He visited the Louvre
and other places, which were interesting to him on account of
historical associations—the court-room where the trials took
place during the Reign of Terror—the Conciergerie, where
Louis XVI and Marie Antoinette were imprisoned, and the
cemetery of Pere la Chaise.

"The day the 'moxa' operation was to be performed," says
Sulgrove. "Morton asked me to stay and be ready to help
him if he needed help. But his wife was there, and I feared
I would do more harm than good, so I begged to be let off.
I couldn't bear to see him suffer under the torture of the
cautery, or burning with white hot iron, which I supposed
would be the process employed. I stayed away till I was

---

[1] The Emperor's address to the Corps Legislatif, on January 22, declared that the French expedition to Mexico had reached its limit, and
the date of the departure of the French troops was soon afterwards fixed
for April, 1866.

sure that all was over. When I came back Morton was in bed, weak from pain, but recovering a little, and relieved by anodynes. He kept his bed for two or three days. Then he said he felt a change for the better, and he was up, most of the time in the parlor, where he told me about the operation. The doctor did not use the "actual cautery" or hot iron, but applied caustic potash in two places, close to the backbone. The "actual cautery" would not have needed more than a minute to each perforation. The caustic potash required, I think, about eight minutes. It ate two holes in the back, one on each side of the spinal column, and each big enough for a man's finger. It was more painful because more protracted than the burning with hot iron. Morton was not a man to whimper and fret. After a while he became satisfied that the operation was not going to do him the service it had done to Sumner. Once clear upon that point he let the whole affair go, with his pain, his crutches, his cane and his general helplessness."

Morton while abroad had a conversation with Baron Rothschild in regard to the internal improvement bonds of Indiana, issued in 1836, of which Rothschild was a large owner. These bonds had been compromised by the Butler bill in 1846. The Wabash and Erie canal had been surrendered to the creditors for half the debt, and five per cent. bonds had been issued for the other half of the principal, and two and a half per cent. bonds for the unpaid interest. The bondholders had lost heavily. The canal had turned out to be worthless. Rothschild claimed that the state was bound in honor to compensate the holders of the old bonds for their losses, since the state's permission to build competing railways had destroyed the value of the canal. Morton argued that the progress of the age and the necessities of commerce made railroads indispensable, and that the state was no more liable for the injuries which these might inflict upon old methods of transportation than for the damage which might be done by a flood or a tornado.

When Morton left Paris he intended to pass the winter in Italy. He went to Geneva, but by this time he had become convinced that his paralysis could not be cured. He had grown restless over his absence during the stirring political events which followed the first efforts at reconstruction. There was work for him at home, and there was nothing to be gained by staying away. His son John had already gone back to America.

President Johnson had offered to Morton the Austrian mission, if he felt able and disposed to assume its duties. But a diplomatic service of this kind had no attraction for him at that time. He decided that he would not go to Italy, but would return at once. After a sail on Lake Geneva he parted company with Sulgrove, and went with his wife to London. Here he listened to some debates in the House of Commons, in which Lord John Russell, Disraeli and John Bright took part. Morton considered Bright the orator of England.

The voyage home proved a stormy one. The bulwarks of the steamer were crushed, a fire broke out, and the vessel was for a time in imminent danger of destruction, but at last Morton arrived safely in New York.

CHAPTER XXXIV

FIRST STEPS IN RECONSTRUCTION—MASONIC HALL SPEECH

WHEN Morton returned from Europe the reconstruction question was reaching a crisis. President Johnson and the Republican majority in Congress had come to the "parting of the ways." The problem of restoring to their normal relations the states that had been in arms against the government, would have been, under any circumstances, extremely difficult, and it was made doubly so by reason of the egotism and obstinacy of the President. The differences between him and Congress soon took the shape of a personal quarrel, and it became clear that there could be no reconciliation.

In 1863 Mr. Lincoln had recommended a plan for the reconstruction of each state under a constitution adopted by a vote of such of its former electors (with certain specified exceptions) as would take an oath of allegiance to the Federal government, provided these electors amounted to one-tenth as many as those voting in the election of 1860. This scheme, however, was not then acceptable to Congress, and when, after Lincoln's death, a plan not very different was adopted by President Johnson without consulting that body, a great deal of opposition arose in the Republican party. While the conservatives of that party believed that reconstruction could be accomplished under the direction of the Executive, the more radical members insisted that this work must be done by Congress. President Johnson declined to call a special session.

He had kept in office the members of Lincoln's cabinet.

Three of these, Stanton, Harlan and Dennison, were thought to favor more radical ideas of reconstruction, while McCullough, Welles and Speed were conservative. The decisive voice, as it turned out, was that of Seward, a man whose personal influence over the new President was very great, and whose magnanimous spirit insisted upon the earliest possible reconciliation with the South. Under Seward's persuasions the President forsook his sanguinary purpose of "punishing and impoverishing traitors," and adopted the policy of restoring the seceded states to political rights with few conditions and with guarantees of future conduct such as Congress afterwards considered insufficient. One of the first acts of President Johnson was a general proclamation of amnesty to all who had taken part in the rebellion, upon the simple condition that they should take an oath of allegiance to the government. From this amnesty, however, thirteen classes of principal offenders were excepted. On May 29 the President appointed a provisional governor of North Carolina, to whom he intrusted the work of reconstructing that state and of calling a state convention to be composed of members chosen at an election in which no citizen should vote unless he had been an elector under the former constitution and had also taken the oath of allegiance. The thirteen excepted classes were not allowed to take this oath.

Proclamations were soon issued for the reconstruction of the governments of Mississippi, Georgia, Texas, Alabama, South Carolina and Florida in a similar way. In Louisiana, Arkansas and Tennessee the so-called "ten per cent." governments recommended by Lincoln were recognized. In Virginia an organization which had existed during the war, with its headquarters at Alexandria, was continued. The whole scheme of reconstruction was in operation by the middle of July, three months after Lincoln's assassination.

Seward and the President believed that their liberality would be reciprocated, but the Southern states soon showed, by the legislation of their "reconstructed" governments, that they were not yet prepared to accept the issue of emancipation decided by the war. A nominal assent to the thirteenth amendment, necessary to secure for their representatives admission to Congress, was accompanied by laws regulating "apprenticeship," "vagrancy" and "taxation," which practically deprived the negro of liberty.[1]

During these events Congress had assembled. There was a large Republican majority, and the Republicans were in no mood to forsake the men whose freedom had just been secured at so costly a sacrifice. A joint committee on Reconstruction was appointed. The President's message sketched the progress of his reconstruction measures, and urged that the question of suffrage be left to the states. Thaddeus Stevens was the leader of the House of Representatives. He considered that the states lately in rebellion were conquered territories, subject to the will of the conquerors. Congress might re-admit them, but the separate action of the President had no such effect. He insisted, as a condition of reconstruction, that unless negro suffrage was allowed negroes should be excluded in estimating the population of the Southern states for representation in Congress. In the Senate Sumner de-

---

[1] In Alabama " refractory servants " were declared " vagrants," and might be " hired out " for six months by public outcry, a punishment that could be repeated whenever desired. Minors, whose parents failed to support them, were to be apprenticed to some suitable person. The former owner of the parents should have the preference, and whoever should entice such apprentice from his master, or furnish him food or clothing without his master's consent, should be heavily fined. No negro could, without an expensive license, pursue any employment except that of husbandry or domestic service. Similar statutes were enacted in other states. Excessive poll taxes were laid upon the poor, and in default of payment the services of the delinquents might be sold at auction. Men without means of support were compelled to labor upon municipal and public works. Other oppressive laws were passed for the evident purpose of again reducing the negro to a condition little better than that of slavery.

manded, as requirements for restoration to the Union, general enfranchisement, an organized system of education, repudiation of the Confederate debt and the proved loyalty of all electors, together with other conditions. The Democrats came to the support of the President, insisting that the moment the rebellion was suppressed the states were at once restored to their original rights, but the Democratic Congressmen were in a minority of less than one-third.

Congress passed a bill to enlarge the powers of the Freedmen's Bureau, providing that where ordinary civil rights were denied to freedmen, or where they were subjected to punishment different from that provided for white persons, military jurisdiction should be extended. The President vetoed this bill on February 10, and Congress was unable to pass it over his veto.

The resolutions which led to the fourteenth amendment to the constitution were now introduced and debated. In February the President began that series of harangues, full of personal vituperation and attacks upon members of Congress, by which he forfeited the confidence of many who would otherwise have approved of his policy. The first civil rights bill was introduced by Mr. Trumbull, vetoed by the President and passed, notwithstanding the veto, on the 9th of April.

It was on the 7th of March, 1866, during these events, that Morton landed in New York. He did not proceed at once to his home at Indianapolis, but remained in the East for more than a month. One of the Republican senators met him in New York and gave him the details of the President's quarrel with Congress. Morton had been on confidential terms with Johnson, but saw the unfortunate tendency of his present policy, and, proceeding to Washington, he had a long interview with the President and urged him to sign the first civil rights bill, just passed. Johnson was unwilling to do so. Morton told him that unless he did, this would be the rock upon which the President and the Republican party would separate. Johnson was laboring under great emotion. Large beads of perspiration stood on his forehead. He was stubborn and seemed to think he was strong enough to build up a new party. Morton argued that new parties could only be organized on great questions, that the pending issues must be fought out by the organizations then existing, that "all roads out of the Republican party led into the Democratic party," and that if the President did not sign the bill, Morton would feel, when he left him, that they could not meet again in political fellowship. When Morton left the President he believed that the latter was lost to the Republicans, and he so informed several members of Congress whom he met later in the day.

He reached home on the 12th of April, looking better than his friends had expected to see him after his fruitless journey. He found the Republicans in Indiana apathetic, despondent, and demoralized. They had been much embarrassed by the course of the President, who had many warm friends in the state, and while the mass of the party favored the policy of Congress, Johnson's supporters could not, in view of the slender Republican majority in Indiana, be safely spared. The Republican convention, which had met on February 22, had sought to please both sides, and had adopted a platform which was weak, inconsistent and even ridiculous. The Democrats were hopeful and aggressive. They attacked Republican officials and the party itself for corruption, usurpation and all sorts of misdeeds, and they took a decided and affirmative stand with President Johnson against the Republican majority in Congress. An air of triumph breathed through all their speeches, editorials and resolutions. They felt that in Indiana, at least, they were sure to win.

But Morton was in no humor for defeat. He did not propose to see the government of his own state fall into the hands of those whom he considered the enemies of the Union. He had, moreover, strong personal motives for extraordinary

effort. The legislature to be elected was to choose a United
States Senator. By common consent Morton would be the
man. And the Indiana Democracy had now exasperated
him beyond measure by the violence of its personal attacks.

For many long months, both before Morton's affliction had
fallen upon him, and since that time, the voice of slander had
been raised against him by his political enemies. Every sort
of charge had been made. He had placed in the heart of Indianapolis, it was said, his arsenals and pest-houses, whence
proceeded the dangers of gunpowder and disease. He had
sold surplus recruits to Massachusetts, and made them the
"victims of Lincoln's slaughter pens." Horses, coaches,
farms, bank-stock and innumerable perquisites were affluently
bestowed upon him by Democratic imagination. "A magnificent residence in Indianapolis" was given to him no less
than six times by reports in Democratic newspapers. "The
Indiana arsenal had made many rich." "Flannels intended
for cartridges had gone to cover billiard tables." "Many
Christians had been deeply wounded by Morton's disregard
of the Holy Sabbath in distributing election tickets on Sunday." All sorts of accusations, from those that were ridiculous to those that were infamous, were repeated with dismal
monotony from day to day.[1]

After Morton had been home a few weeks he called a
meeting of fifty prominent Republicans from different parts
of the state. They discussed the political situation and decided to issue an address to the people, hoping to arouse Republicans from their apathy and warn them against impending
dangers. A committee was appointed to prepare the address. The following afternoon a member of the committee
brought to the Governor a rough draft of what had been pre-

---

[1] "Perkins, Bingham and the leaders of the Democratic party generally,"
said the *Journal*, "seem to have Governor Morton on the brain. They
talk, write, lie about him incessantly and dream about him when sleeping.
If any one of them receives a kick he jumps up and shouts 'Morton!' . . ."

pared. "That evening," says Mr. W. R. Holloway, "Morton handed me the manuscript and asked me to read it to him. I had not read five minutes, when he said: 'Stop, the committee have made a failure of it. They do not seem to know what is needed. We don't want a political essay. We must remind the people of the Democratic record, and arraign that party for the crimes and infamies it has perpetrated against society and the government during and since the war. Sit down at the table, and let me try my hand at it.' He then and there dictated, without stopping, the terrible indictment which afterwards appeared as a part of his celebrated Masonic Hall speech. After he had finished, he said, 'How do you like it?' I replied: 'That is the best thing you have ever done, and it is far too good to be sent out as an address by a committee. If you want to arouse the people of Indiana why don't you make a speech?' He said he would think about it. The day following a number of friends were called in and the arraignment was read to them. They were filled with delight and enthusiasm. I repeated my suggestion, and they all agreed that the Governor ought to make a speech at as early a date as possible."

The speech was delivered on the 20th of June at Masonic Hall. Morton was received with a storm of applause, the audience rising to their feet and cheering for several minutes. He spoke sitting, but through his physical helplessness the power of his mind gleamed more brightly than ever. The place called up the stirring events of the past four years, which he was determined should not perish so soon from the memory of the people of Indiana. He had often spoken from the same platform during the war, calling for volunteers and exhorting the citizens to uphold the general government. After a few brief sentences, referring to these surroundings, he began to read in a low voice, and with evident weakness, a philippic unequaled in modern times for the crushing fierceness of its invective.

''The war is over, the rebellion has been suppressed, the victory has been won, and now the question is presented to us at the coming election, whether the fruits of victory shall be preserved or lost.

''It is beyond doubt that the temper of the Democratic party is not changed or improved since the termination of the war, but, on the contrary, it seems to have been greatly embittered by defeat in the field and at the ballot-box. Its sympathy with those who were lately in arms against the government is more boldly avowed than ever, and it becomes argumentative and enthusiastic in behalf of the right of secession and the righteousness of the rebellion. The true spirit of the Democratic party in Indiana has recently received a remarkable illustration that should command the solemn consideration of the people.

''Some four or five weeks ago a convention was held in the city of Louisville, composed in large part of men who had been engaged in the rebel armies. These men, assembled in convention, proclaimed. themselves members of the national Democratic party, and declared their unfaltering devotion to its time-honored principles. They vindicated the righteousness of the rebellion and declared their stern purpose to maintain at the ballot-box the sacred principles for which they had taken up arms. Prominent Indiana Democrats met with them in convention, mingled their tears with the tears of those who wept over Southern heroes; uttered glowing eulogies upon the memory of Stonewall Jackson and John Morgan, and reiterated the most treasonable doctrines, and to show the complete identity between this assembly of traitors and the Democratic party of Indiana, the Indianapolis *Herald*, the organ of the party, in the broadest and most unqualified manner, earnestly and enthusiastically indorsed these proceedings. . . .

''The leaders, who are now managing the Democratic party in this state, are the men who, at the regular session of the legislature in 1861, declared that if an army went from Indiana to assist in putting down the then approaching rebellion it must first pass over their dead bodies.

"They are the men who, in speeches and resolutions, proclaimed that 'Southern defeats gave them no joy, and Northern disasters no sorrow.' They are the men who exerted their influence to prevent their Democratic friends from going into the army, and who, by their incessant and venomous slanders against the government, checked the spirit of volunteering, and made drafting a necessity. And when the draft had thus been forced upon the country, their wretched subordinates, inspired by their devilish teachings, endeavored in many places by force of arms and the murder of enrolling officers, to prevent its execution.

"They are the men who corresponded with the rebel leaders in the South, giving them full information of our condition, and assuring them that a revolution in public opinion was at hand, and that they had but to persevere a few months longer and the national government would fall to pieces of its own weight.

"They are the men who, in the legislature of 1863, attempted to overturn the state government and establish a legislative revolution by seizing the military power of the state and transferring it to the hands of four state officers, three of whom were members of the treasonable society known as the 'Sons of Liberty.'

"They are the men, who, having failed to overturn the state government by seizing the military power, determined to defeat its operations and bring about anarchy, by locking up the public treasure and thus withholding the money necessary to carry on the government.

"They are the men who, for the purpose of private speculation, and of discrediting the state before the world, conspired to prevent the payment of the interest on the public debt by withholding, through a fraudulent lawsuit, the money re-

ceived from taxes, paid for that very purpose. This lawsuit was
smuggled through the circuit court and lodged in the Supreme
Court before the minutes of the case had been read and signed
by the circuit judge, or he had been made acquainted with its
character, and it was hastily decided by the Supreme Court
against the credit of the state.

"They are the men who introduced and organized in this
state that dangerous and wide-spread conspiracy first known as
the 'Knights of the Golden Circle,' and afterwards as the
'Sons of Liberty,' which had for its purpose the overthrow
of the state and national governments. Not all of them, it
is true, belonged formally to this infamous order, but such
as stood on the outside had knowledge of its existence, purposes and plans, and carefully concealing their knowledge,
were ready to accept its work. To accomplish the hellish
schemes of this conspiracy, military officers were appointed,
military organizations created, arms and ammunition purchased in immense quantities and smuggled into the state,
correspondence opened with rebel commanders and military
combinations agreed upon, rebel officers and agents introduced into the capital and concealed in hotels and boarding-
houses, and it was deliberately planned and agreed that, upon
a day fixed, they would suddenly rise and murder the executive, seize the arsenal with its arms and ammunition, and
releasing nine thousand rebel prisoners in Camp Morton, put
arms into their hands, and with their combined forces effect
a military and bloody revolution in the state. This dreadful
scheme necessarily involved murder, conflagration, robbery,
and the commission of every crime which makes black the
chronicles of civil war, and yet its authors and abettors, with
the proofs of their guilt piled mountain high, are again struggling for power and asking the people to put into their guilty
hands the government and prosperity of the state. Some of
these men who are high in favor and authority in their party,
and are largely intrusted with its management, have hereto-

fore occupied offices of great trust and responsibility in which they proved to be recreant and corrupt.

"They are the men who, in the legislature of Indiana, bitterly opposed and denounced every effort to confer the right of suffrage upon soldiers in the field who could not come home to vote.

"They are the men who labored with devilish zeal to destroy the ability of the government to carry on the war by depreciating its financial credit. They assured the people that 'greenbacks' would die on their hands, and warned them solemnly against government bonds, as a wicked device to rob them of their money.

"They are the men who refused to contribute to the Sanitary Commission for the relief of sick and wounded soldiers, upon the lying and hypocritical pretense that the contributions were consumed by the officers of the army.

"They are the men who excused themselves from contributing for the relief of soldiers' families at home by the infamous slander that they were living better than they had ever done, and by foul imputations on the chastity of soldiers' wives.

"They are the men who declared in speeches and resolutions, and by their votes in Congress, that not another man nor another dollar should be voted to carry on a cruel war against their Southern brethren.

"They are the men who, in the midst of the last great campaign of 1864—at the time when Sherman was fighting his way, step by step, from Chattanooga to Atlanta, and Grant was forcing Lee back into the defenses of Richmond in desperate and bloody battles from day to day; when the fate of the nation hung in the balance, and the world watched with breathless interest the gigantic struggle which was to settle the question of republican government—assembled in convention in Chicago and resolved that the war was a failure; that our cause was unjust, and that we ought to lay down our arms and sue for peace. It was a bold and desperate interference in behalf of the rebellion, at the very crisis of the fight. It was an insult to the loyal armies of the nation, so vast, malignant and deadly that language can convey no adequate idea of its wickedness. And in future times the historian will record the fact with astonishment that the government, at the most critical moment of its life, when a few hours, or a few days at the farthest, must determine whether it should live or die, could permit a large body of its enemies to meet upon its soil in peace and security and publish a flagrant manifesto in behalf of the rebellion.

"Now, I do not mean to say that all the Democratic leaders have done all these things, but what I do say is this: that the men who have done these things are combined together, and constitute the real leaders of the Democratic party. The few moderate men of the party have been stripped of all power and influence, and are carried along merely for numbers and policy, while the living and aggressive element which controls it are the 'Sons of Liberty' and those who acted in sympathy and concert with them.

"They are the men who have perverted the word Democracy from its once honorable meaning to be a shield and cover for rebellion and for every crime that attaches to a causeless and atrocious civil war.

"Every unregenerate rebel lately in arms against his government calls himself a Democrat.

"Every bounty jumper, every deserter, every sneak who ran away from the draft calls himself a Democrat. Bowles, Milligan, Walker, Dodd, Horsey and Humphreys call themselves Democrats. Every 'Son of Liberty' who conspired to murder, burn, rob arsenals and release rebel prisoners calls himself a Democrat. John Morgan, Champ Ferguson, Wirtz, Payne and Booth proclaimed themselves Democrats. Every man who labored for the rebellion in the field, who murdered Union prisoners by cruelty and starvation, who conspired to bring about civil war in the loyal states, who invented dangerous compounds to burn steamboats and Northern cities, who contrived hellish schemes to introduce into Northern cities the wasting pestilence of yellow fever, calls himself a Democrat. Every dishonest contractor who has been convicted of defrauding the government, every dishonest paymaster or disbursing officer who has been convicted of squandering the public money at the gaming table or in gold gambling operations, every officer in the army who was dismissed for cowardice or disloyalty, calls himself a Democrat. Every wolf in sheep's clothing, who pretends to preach the gospel but proclaims the righteousness of man-selling and slavery; every one who shoots down negroes in the streets, burns negro school-houses and meeting-houses, and murders women and children by the light of their own flaming dwellings, calls himself a Democrat; every New York rioter in 1863 who burned up little children in colored asylums, who robbed, ravished and murdered indiscriminately in the midst of a blazing city for three days and nights, called himself a Democrat. In short, the Democratic party may be described as a common sewer and loathsome receptacle, into which is emptied every element of treason North and South, and every element of inhumanity and barbarism which has dishonored the age.

"And this party, composed of the men and elements I have described, in defiance of truth and decency asserts that it is the special champion of the constitution and the Union, which but a short sixteen months ago it was in arms to destroy, and proclaims to an astonished world that the only effect of vanquishing armed rebels in the field is to return them to seats in Congress, and to restore them to political power. Having failed to destroy the constitution by force, they seek to do it by construction, and assume to have made the remarkable discovery that the rebels who fought to destroy the constitution were its true friends, and that the men who shed their blood and gave their substance to preserve it were its only enemies.''

Morton now discussed and justified the clauses of the proposed fourteenth amendment. He insisted that security should be taken against the recurrence of rebellion. He made the following appeal to the young men:

''Beware how you connect your fortunes with a decayed and dishonored party, indelibly stained with treason, upon whose tombstone the historian will write, 'false to liberty, false to its country, and false to the age in which it lived.' The Democratic party has committed a crime for which history has no pardon, and the memories of men no forgetfulness; whose colors grow darker from age to age, and for which the execrations of mankind become more bitter from generation to generation. It committed treason against liberty in behalf of slavery; against civilization in behalf of barbarism, and its chronicles will be written in the volume which records the deeds of the most dangerous and malignant factions that have ever afflicted government and retarded the progress of mankind. . . . .''

During the first few sentences of this speech Morton could scarcely be heard, but as he proceeded in his arraignment of the Democratic party his old-time energy came back, and his voice grew clear and strong. No audience could be insensible to such a speech, least of all, an Indiana audience when Morton was the speaker. Each sentence in his indictment was received with applause. Sometimes this would die away and would be renewed as the force of his powerful attack impressed itself more deeply upon his hearers. After the meeting was over the streets rang with shouts and cheers far into the morning. There had been no such enthusiasm in Indianapolis since the surrender to Grant at Appomatox.

Morton was an intense and bitter partisan, to whom the success of the Democracy meant the loss of all that had been won. He had grouped together every disloyal act, and in a masterly statement, had flung the record, not simply at the guilty men, but at the party which had tolerated their leadership or companionship. It was the speech to win. The Republicans had been divided and lukewarm, the Democrats united and aggressive. Under such conditions the way to success was to awaken old memories, to draw the party lines as closely as possible, to make the fight bitter and irreconcilable, to drive every disaffected Republican back into the ranks by hatred of a common enemy.

The Democrats were filled with rage at the effectiveness of his attack. Shortly after the meeting a number of them met at the office of the *Herald*. It was agreed that Morton's speech was the most damaging blow that the party had received since the close of the war. Unless its effect could be counteracted, there was little hope of success. After some discussion it was decided that the speech could not be answered, and that the best plan was to keep up the attack already commenced upon Morton's personal character. A general chorus of howls and hisses now began. The Louisville *Courier*, the Indianapolis *Herald*, the Cincinnati *Enquirer* and the Chicago *Times* exhausted the resources of billingsgate. Morton was "a fetid excrescence on the body politic," a "cowardly tyrant," a "wretch accursed of God and enjoying a foretaste of hell on earth." His assailants veiled in initials, which were well understood, language so obscene that the men publishing it ought to have been instantly indicted. The attacks were so vile that they produced a re-action. The Louisville *Journal* apologized. Even Perkins refused to co-operate longer in this campaign of calumny. Morton's friends retorted in vigorous English. "Imagination may depict the agonizing shrieks of a culprit suffering the punishment of the 'cat-o-nine-tails' at the whipping post, but the yells of a single malefactor would be oppressive silence in comparison with the roars of agony evoked from Copperhead lungs by the merciless excoriation administered by Governor Morton.''

Meanwhile there was little done to answer Morton's speech. McDonald called his utterances ''the gibberings of the Giant Despair.'' It was characteristic of such criticism that Morton was still regarded as a giant.

The speech was scattered broadcast over the country, and was published in all the leading Republican newspapers. Nearly three million copies were distributed in pamphlet form. It marked the turning of the tide in Indiana. Senator Hendricks said to Holloway long afterwards that he regarded the Masonic hall speech as the most effective political address Morton had ever made; that after it the hopes of the Democratic party in Indiana had withered away

CHAPTER XXXV

CAMPAIGN OF 1868—MORTON ELECTED SENATOR

THE fourth of July, 1866, had been selected as the day for an imposing ceremony. The battle flags of the Indiana regiments were returned to the Governor to be kept among the trophies of the state. General Lew Wallace presented the flags and Morton received them. The speech of General Wallace was full of reminiscences of the great struggle. The response of Governor Morton was given with unusual emotion. So intense were his political feelings that he could not avoid a reference to the issues of the pending campaign. To the soldiers who were gathered before him he said: "You have laid aside your arms, and have assumed the character of peaceable and quiet citizens, but your duties are not all performed. The great question now confronts you and must be answered, whether these precious flags are to be emblems of barren victories, *whether the heroes in war shall become mere children in peace; whether they shall shamefully and blindly surrender at the ballot-box the great prizes which they conquered upon the field, or whether they have now by dread experience learned lessons of wisdom through which they and their posterity may be fortified against the evil passions of the vanquished and protected against the recurrence of like calamities.*"

In spite of his physical infirmities the Governor took an active part in the campaign. He made an important speech in New Albany about the middle of July.

"Some three or four weeks ago," he said, "a Democratic

convention was held in this city, at which a candidate for Congress was nominated. Speeches were made by Messrs. Voorhees and McDonald, and a series of resolutions was adopted. . . .

"The second of these resolutions declares that 'the war was just and necessary to prevent the disruption of the Union and the overthrow of the constitution.'

"Sixteen months after the war was over, the men composing the convention discovered for the first time that it 'was just and necessary,' a truth known to the great body of the people more than five years before. How it happened that this discovery was first made at New Albany, or by what means the truth broke in upon minds so politically benighted, and so far behind the age, does not appear. Nevertheless, New Albany was selected as the place of revelation, and the politicians there assembled were the humble instruments for the dissemination of the new truth. This resolution is a complete and unreserved confession of the disloyal and treasonable course pursued by the so-called Democratic party throughout the war, and a full admission that its principles and practices were hostile to the Union. The country will regard it as a dying repentence forced from a convicted criminal, in view of the scaffold, and springing, not from any change of heart, but from hope of pardon and renewed life. The men making this confession ask the country to take it as evidence that they have from the first been in favor of the war, and they demand that they shall be received as good Union men, who have protected and preserved their country, and not as the friends, aiders and abettors of rebellion. Their request will not be granted. They will be held to the record and can not be relieved from responsibility by the cheap discovery that 'the war was just and necessary' sixteen months after it was ended. It is true, our Savior in his parable described those who came in at the eleventh hour as having received as much pay as those who worked all day, but still it must be remembered that they came in one hour before the work was done and helped to finish it. But these Democratic politicians did not come in until sixteen monhts after the work was over.

"If the war was 'just and necessary,' as these men now say, why did the Democratic party throughout the war denounce it as unnecessary, unholy and unconstitutional and assert that it was forced upon our Southern brethren by a wicked invasion of their rights?

"If the war was 'just and necessary' why did the Democratic members of Congress vote against supplies of men and money, against appropriations and measures necessary to carry it on?

"If the war was 'just and necessary,' why did Democratic politicians throughout Indiana discourage enlistments, labor to keep Democrats from going into the army and exhort the people to resist the draft?

"If the war was 'just and necessary,' why did Democratic politicians argue that the government could not coerce a state, and that each state had a right to judge of an infraction of the constitution as well as the remedy, and to withdraw from the Union according to the determination of its own will?

"If the war was 'just and necessary,' why did the Democracy of Washington county, in a meeting held at Salem in February, 1861, resolve that if a separation took place between the North and the South, the line of separation must run north of Washington county, and that if they were compelled to fight on either side they would be found fighting in the armies of the South?

"If the war was 'just and necessary,' why did the Sons of Liberty conspire to overthrow the state government, release prisoners, seize arsenals, murder the Executive and precipitate Indiana into rebellion?

"If the war was 'just and necessary,' why did not these

31—Mor.

men enter the army themselves, contribute to the Sanitary Commission, help to support soldiers' families, unite in doing those things which should be cheerfully performed by every loyal and patriotic citizen?

"If the war was 'just and necessary,' why did Democratic politicians go to Chicago in the last great campaign of 1864, in the very crisis of the fight, and there resolve that the war was wicked and unconstitutional, that it was a failure, and that we ought to lay down our arms and sue for peace?

"If, in short, the war was 'just and necessary,' why did Democratic politicians fail to proclaim the fact until sixteen months after it was over?

"But when they had done all the harm they could, and when their adherence to the government could do no good, after the rebellion had been suppressed, after the victory had been won, after every enemy in the field had been conquered and every obstacle at home had been overcome, after the Union had been preserved without the aid of the Democratic party, and in spite of it, that portion of the party which inhabits this congressional district came together in convention in the year of our Lord, 1866, and resolved 'that the war was just and necessary to prevent the disruption of the Union and the overthrow of the constitution.' . . . ."

A convention of Johnson Republicans met in the state-house in Indianapolis, on the 19th of July. General Sol. Meredith was chosen president. The convention was a discordant one. Morton came into the hall during the meeting and was referred to in the remarks of some of the members. Judge Gooding read from the Governor's speech, delivered when the Indiana delegation called on the President, just after Lincoln's assassination, and insisted that if Johnson had gone wrong he had done so by following the advice of Morton. The resolutions indorsed Johnson's policy.

A national convention called by the President's friends

met at Philadelphia, on August 14. The delegates from the North entered the convention arm in arm with those from the South; Massachusetts and South Carolina heading the procession. The wigwam was called in derision "Noah's ark," into which there went two and two "of clean beasts, and beasts that were not clean, and of fowls and everything that creepeth upon the earth." The resolutions declared that Congress had no right to deny representation to the states.

This convention was followed a fortnight later in Philadelphia, by another on the opposite side, which had been called by the Union men of the South, who invited Northern co-operation. The object was to promote the adoption of the fourteenth amendment. Morton took part in this convention.

About the first of September President Johnson went to Chicago to lay the corner-stone for the monument to Stephen A. Douglas. He was accompanied by Seward, Grant, Farragut and others. He addressed many turbulent meetings on the way. There were unfriendly demonstrations, with gibes and jeers. Among other places the President visited Indianapolis, and his reception there was quite different from that which had been given to him when he came during the war. A crowd gathered in front of the Bates House and called for various persons in his suite, mostly for Grant and Farragut. Meredith appeared on the balcony and said that the President was fatigued. There were cries from the crowd asking if he was sober. Gooding was next seen, and was invited "to trot out Moses." When the President appeared he was both cheered and hooted, and when he began to speak the tumult was so great that he was unable to proceed.

After "swinging round the circle," as it was called, he returned to Washington politically ruined. The election was a verdict against his administration. In Indiana the Republicans carried the state by twelve thousand majority, and the outcome of the October elections was ratified in November by other Northern states, although in the South the President and the Democratic party were sustained. This result served to emphasize the sectional issue, and Congress became all the more firm in opposing the admission of the Southern states until they had ratified the fourteenth amendment. With the exception of Tennessee these states had rejected this amendment by overwhelming majorities. Thaddeus Stevens now introduced a bill dividing the Confederate states into military districts under officers appointed, not by the President, but by Grant, the general of the army. The bill was passed, vetoed by the President and passed again over the veto.

The President had removed from office many of the men who supported the measures of Congress. Congress determined to deprive him of this power, and passed the Tenure-of-Office Act, providing that persons appointed by consent of the Senate should retain their offices until their successors were in like manner appointed, the President to have merely a power of temporary suspension during recess for certain specified causes which were to be reported to Congress, together with the evidence sustaining them. Members of the cabinet were to hold office *during the term of the President by whom they had been appointed*, and for one month thereafter, subject to removal only by advice and consent of the Senate. The President also vetoed this bill, but it was passed over his veto.

As we have already seen, it was conceded that if the Republicans won the election of 1866, Morton would be the next senator. Democratic papers, it is true, talked about his "ineligibility,[1] and were busy announcing opposition to him in various parts of the state, but Morton had looked carefully to the organization of all doubtful districts, and

---

[1] The constitution provided that the Governor should not be eligible to any other office during the term for which he was elected. The answer to this was that the qualifications of senators were prescribed by the Federal constitution, and that the state could not create other disabilities; hence, the provision in the state constitution was void. Lane had been elected under like circumstances, and Judge Trumbull had recently been chosen senator from Illinois in the face of a similar prohibition in the constitution of that state.

when the Republican caucus met, he was unanimously nominated.

On the 11th of January Morton delivered his message to the General Assembly. The scene was an impressive one. The man, who for so many years, and through so many hardships, had borne the burden of the most onerous duties ever imposed upon any Governor, whose labors and anxieties had paralyzed his strength and broken his health, was about to leave the executive chair, and was really, though not formally, making his last public appearance in office. He discussed with remarkable ability, though with little order or arrangement, a great number of subjects concerning the administration of the state government.

But the principal interest of this message centered in his remarks upon national issues. He discussed the clause in the constitution making it the duty of the United States to guarantee to each state a republican form of government. This guaranty, he said, was to be made by the government of the United States, which was not the President nor Congress, but both together. It must, therefore, be by a legislative act.

"What the extent of this power is," he continued, "has never been settled by any precedent and has not been defined by Kent, Story or any of our writers on constitutional law. It is a vast, undefined power, given to the United States to guard the states against revolution, anarchy or change to a monarchical or aristocratic government. . . .

"Ordinarily when the country is in a normal condition, the subject of suffrage is absolutely within the control of the several states. . . . But if a state government shall fall into anarchy, or be destroyed by rebellion, and it is found clearly and unmistakably that a new one can not be erected and successfully maintained without conferring the right of suffrage upon a race or body of men to whom it has been denied by the laws of the state, it would clearly be within the power of Congress to confer the right for that purpose, upon the principle that it can employ the means necessary to the performance of a required duty.

"Not that Congress could make a constitution for a state in which the right of suffrage should be fixed, but it could call a convention to form a new constitution and establish a new government, and it could prescribe the qualifications of those who should vote for the members of that convention and participate in the organization of the new government.

"The power which I claim for Congress is vast and dangerous, and should be exercised with deliberation, and only in case of clear necessity, as it trenches directly upon the general theory and structure of the government. Yet it unquestionably exists. . . .

"The proposition to introduce at once to the ballot-box half a million of men, who but yesterday were slaves, the great mass of whom are profoundly ignorant, and all impressed with that character which slavery impresses upon its victims, is repugnant to the feelings of a large part of our people, and would be justified only by necessity resulting from inability to maintain loyal republican state governments in any other way.

"But the necessity for *loyal republican state governments that shall protect men of all races, classes and opinions, and shall render allegiance and support to the government of the United States, must override every other consideration of prejudice or policy.*

"If it be found necessary not to accept the present state governments in the South, and to exercise the great power which has hitherto lain dormant in the constitution, the people of the South will have the consolation of knowing that it is their own act and deed. By the unrestrained slaughters of Memphis and New Orleans; by the unpunished murder of loyal men; by the persecution and exile of those who adhered to the Union; by the contemptuous rejection of the generous terms that were offered, they are fast proving that the extraordinary powers of the constitution must be summoned to cure the evils under which the land is laboring."

In this message we have Morton's first public utterance, showing the change of his views in favor of negro suffrage. Since his Richmond speech the conflict between the President and Congress, the conduct of the South and the rejection of the fourteenth amendment had convinced him, as it had convinced the great body of the people, that the only safe basis of reconstruction was universal suffrage.

Of course Morton was criticised for his change of front, but, strange to say, this criticism came mostly from the radical wing of the Republican party, which seemed now to object to his co-operation.

Daniel W. Voorhees was nominated for senator by the Democrats. The two candidates were fit types of their respective parties. Morton had been the embodiment of the war feeling, and was now the embodiment of the feeling which demanded securities for preserving the results of the war. His opponent was the incarnation of the opposite sentiments.[1]

---

[1] Petroleum V. Nasby contrasts them in the following "Lines unto O. P. Morton, the Tirent of Injeanny."

> " Nero* the Sekkund, O, wat horrid fate,
>   Wuz Injeana's in that dredful hour,
>   Thou wust made Guverner, and got the power
> To rool Dimokrasy in that proud stait.

> " Mournin' will not avale, but O, hed Dan-
>   iel Voorhees† only sot where thou hast sot,
>   Dost think that the Gorriller‡ would have got
> The help he hed when fust the war began?

> " Inscribin' 'No coershun' on his banner,
>   Bold Daniel would hev let no man enlist
>   'Cept sech ez wood the Suthren ranks assist
> In rightin' things in constitooshnel manner.

> " The Golden Cirkle wood hev growd in vigger,
>   No sneekin' provo-marshals wood hev vext us,
>   No horrer-spredin' drafts wood e'er hev techt us;
> Wich drag'd us 4th, a fightin' fer the nigger.

---

*Nero wuz a Emperor uv Rome—so ornery that dorgs hev allus bin named after him. His only redeemin' quality wuz his fondnis for music, which wuz so overpowerin' that he fiddled the Arkansaw Traveler wile Rome wuz a-burnin. He persekooted the saints, hentz I likin him 2 Morton.

† Daniel Voorhees is a troo Dimekrat, who resides in Terry Hut. In the knack uv gittin' uther men 2 gallop into what ablishnists call treezen, and keepin' out uv it hisself, he is ekalled by few and serpast by nun.

‡ Gorriller—which is A. Linkin, uv course. To give force to the line I shood hev addid, "Ape and Babboon," hed the measure admitted.

The election was held by the two houses on the 22d of January, and Morton was chosen.

On the following day, he sent to each of the houses his resignation as Governor, and declared that his election to the Senate was more precious to him because it was an indorsement of his administration than on account of the value of the office.

An address to the retiring Governor, expressing personal esteem as well as approval of his administration and followed by some words in eulogy of Governor Baker was passed after much bitter wrangling, and after a motion to strike out all that related to Morton had been supported by the vote of every Democratic member of the legislature. The Democrats were willing to eulogize Baker, but not Morton. Editorials in the *Sentinel* contrasted the two, and the old attacks on Morton were renewed.

"His very name vexes them," said the *Journal*, "his praises drive them frantic. He is like water to a mad dog. . . . He has done them much righteous mischief. . . . He is the embodiment of their defeat, despair and shame, and they ought to hate him."

> "And then Ristine and Athon, and a skore
>   Uv sich-like patriots, wood hev rooled the stait;
>   And Dodd, the grate, wood not now cuss his fate,
> A hopelis exil' on a furrin shoar.
>
> " Teers ain't uv no akkount! but O. P. take my cuss
>   Ez stingin' hot ez helpless hate kin make it;
>   A thirst for venjence with no chance to slake it;
> Hopeless and helpless! kin a fate be wuss?

"(The last stanzy contains the cuss after Moore.)

> " May roses turn 2 ashes 'fore yer eyes—
>   May whisky turn 2 camfene on yer lip—
>   May all yoo hope for frum yer fingers slip,
> Jest ez yoo think yoo've got sekoor the prize."

END OF VOLUME I.